The New Book of
SADDLERY
AND TACK

The New Book of
SADDLERY
AND TACK

Carolyn Henderson

Consulting Editor

Sterling Publishing Co., Inc.
New York

Conceived, designed, and produced by
Quarto Publishing plc
The Old Brewery
6 Blundell Street
London N7 9BH

Consulting editor (1981 edition): Elwyn Hartley Edwards
Consulting editor (1998 edition): Carolyn Henderson
Contributing editors: Jenny Baker, Geoff Clothier, Elwyn Hartley Edwards, Carolyn Henderson, Janet Macdonald, Judy Payne, Diana Tuke, Sallie Walrond

Art editor: Moira Clinch
Art assistant: Helen Kirby
Editor: Patricia Mackinnon
Picture researcher: Marion Eason
Photographer: Ian Howes
Art director: Bob Morley
Editorial director: Jeremy Harwood

Revised (1998) edition: Moira Clinch, Dorothy Frame, John Henderson, Zoë Holtermann, Dave Kemp, Maggi McCormick, Michelle Pickering, Anne Plume, Pippa Rubinstein

Special thanks to: Michael Gidden of W&H Gidden Ltd.; Len Courtice of Western Saddles of America Ltd., Sutton; Mandy Chapman of Westerham Riding School; Jabexz Cliff & Co. Ltd.; Evelyn Slack of York Harness Raceway; Warcop Working Farm Museum; Matthew Harvey and Company; Anthony Parker of George Parkers and Sons Ltd.; Major Phelps of The Royal Mews, London

Library of Congress Cataloging-in-Publications Data is available upon request

10 9 8 7 6 5 4 3 2 1

Published 2002 by Sterling Publishing Co., Inc
387 Park Avenue South
New York
NY 10016-8810

Distributed in Canada by Sterling Publishing
c/o Canadian Manda Group
One Atlantic Avenue, Suite 105
Toronto, Ontario, Canada, M6K 3E7

Copyright © 1981, 1998, 2002 Quarto Inc.

QUART.S&T

All rights reserved. No part of this publication may be reproduced, stored in a retrieval system, or transmitted, in any form or by any means, electronic, mechanical, photocopying, recording, or otherwise, without the permission of the copyright holder.

Typeset in Great Britain by Tradespools Ltd., Frome; Flowery Typesetters, London; and Central Southern Typesetters, Eastbourne
Manufactured in Hong Kong by Graphic Arts; Rodney Howe Ltd., London; and Speedlith Photolitho Ltd., Manchester
Printed in China by Leefung-Asco Printers Ltd

ISBN 0-8069-8893-2 (hardback)
ISBN 0-8069-8895-9 (paperback)

Contents

Robert Dover and Aristocrat competing at West Palm Beach. Their impressive turnout is an encouragement to riders at all levels. Equipment should be well-kept, well-fitting and appropriate for the event in which horse and rider are competing.

FOREWORD · PAGE 6

CHAPTER ONE · PAGE 8
History and Development

CHAPTER TWO · PAGE 42
Making the Modern Saddle

CHAPTER THREE · PAGE 54
The Twentieth-Century Saddle

CHAPTER FOUR · PAGE 90
Specialist Saddles

CHAPTER FIVE · PAGE 114
Bits, Bridles and Additional Aids

CHAPTER SIX · PAGE 146
Driving and Farm Harness

CHAPTER SEVEN · PAGE 186
Training Aids

CHAPTER EIGHT · PAGE 196
The Well-Equipped Stable

CHAPTER NINE · PAGE 222
Ceremonial Trappings

CHAPTER TEN · PAGE 238
Riding Dress

Charles de Kunffy is the top-rated dressage judge of the American Horse Shows Association and a C-rated judge of the Federation Equestrian International. He lectures and conducts courses for riders, judges and instructors worldwide. This photograph was taken at a riders' 'clinic' in England. As well as lecturing, he gives practical demonstrations of how best to ride the participants' own horses.

Foreword

THE NEW BOOK OF SADDLERY AND TACK is remarkable for the breadth and depth with which it treats its subject matter. It discusses all the equipment needed for any man or woman who works with, or handles horses, and its scope goes well beyond that suggested by the title. Indeed, it is the most comprehensive reference book on tack and saddlery of any I have ever seen. It not only discusses contemporary equipment and its uses, but also gives a broad, overall view of its historical development.

This book has already earned great respect from readers since it was first published in 1981, and the new edition has been revised and updated to include the most recent developments that have occurred in every aspect of horse-related equipment. For all those involved with equestrianism, whether as riders, drivers, breeders or handlers of horses, it will prove to be an indispensable source of reference. If we do not have suitable equipment that is correctly adjusted to accommodate the needs of individual horse and horseman, and if we fail to maintain it properly, we cannot succeed or be safe in our relationship with horses. I am a rider who presumes to teach horsemanship; I ride horses to improve them, and I am often asked to judge those who have something to show. I am keenly aware both from personal experience, as well as from observing the work and performance of others, that ill-fitting or unsuitable tack will compromise, or even obviate the chance of doing well.

Consider the top surface of the saddle—the seat—is the negative mould for the rider's physical contact area with the horse, while the underside, the area that contacts the horse, is the inverted mould. The saddle is therefore the intermediary between what are, in truth, two wholly dissimilar physical structures, and in large part is responsible for the rider being able to establish harmony and balance with his horse, a relationship of close communication whereby he can convey the most precise instruction with the very lightest of aids: in short, the fit and comfort of the saddle is crucial to the achievement of this perfect harmony. Were it just slightly ill-fitting, the rider would not be able to maintain his balance easily, or convey the communications that he might wish, to the horse.

Furthermore, were a saddle to offend or bruise the horse's back in any way, it would severely compromise being able to train or compete him successfully, for even small aches induced by badly chosen or poorly adjusted equipment will, with work and time, magnify discomfort and cause the horse to focus on his pain, and not on his rider or on his work.

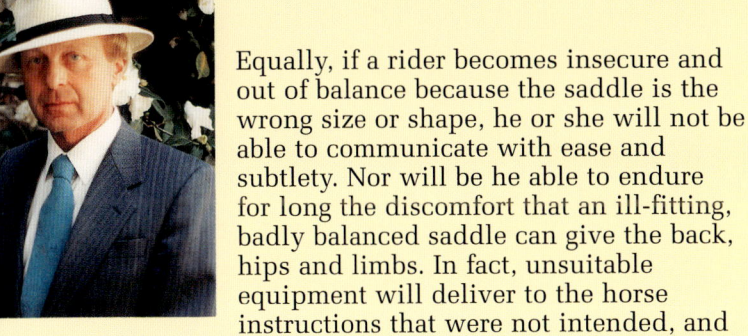

Equally, if a rider becomes insecure and out of balance because the saddle is the wrong size or shape, he or she will not be able to communicate with ease and subtlety. Nor will be he able to endure for long the discomfort that an ill-fitting, badly balanced saddle can give the back, hips and limbs. In fact, unsuitable equipment will deliver to the horse instructions that were not intended, and further, will fail to convey those messages that a rider *does* intend. Thus the finest rider's efforts will be fruitless even on the greatest horse if the equipment via which they are trying to communicate is badly fitting, for one or the other, or both.

The importance of proper equipment goes well beyond success in training and competition: indeed, suitable tack, correctly adjusted, is at the heart of safety. Historically we have had thousands of years' experience with horses and there is no denying that this has taught us the risks inherent in handling them, not because horses are evil and conspiratorial, but because they are big and powerful and because their behaviour may change in a trice from calm docility to agitated alertness and flight. In this circumstance, whatever object or person is in the way of their powerful bulk may be bruised, broken or shattered, and records of much wrecked equipment and many injured equestrians bear witness to this eventuality throughout history. Nevertheless, knowing that driving a car or flying an aircraft may be dangerous does not, and must not, stop us from doing so. However, it will remain eternally wise to inform ourselves as to what equipment is the safest and the most appropriate, and to choose the most suitable and maintain it well for our own safety.

The New Book of Saddlery and Tack provides a broad yet detailed account of what is available; it is also a fascinating story of how these tools developed through the ages. We all need to read it, and to grow wiser from it, and I unreservedly recommend to all horse lovers, and to all those who work with horses in any capacity, that they learn from the pages of this volume.

CHARLES DE KUNFFY

8

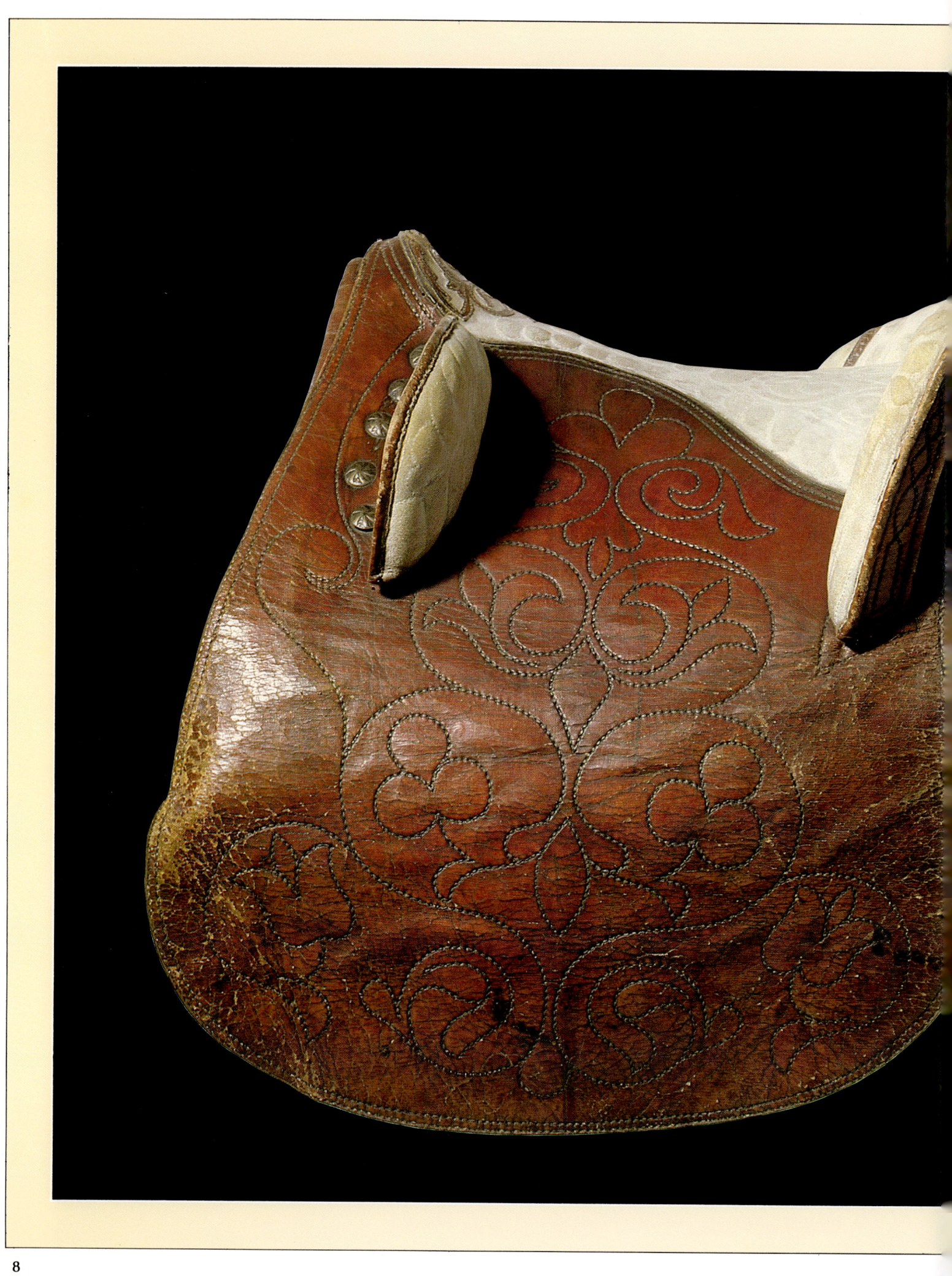

CHAPTER ONE

History and Development

The search for control, from domestication of the horse to present day

A gentleman's saddle of about 1640, with a doeskin seat and the flaps stitched with silver thread. This saddle is part of the Barnsby collection at Walsall, England.

CHAPTER ONE · HISTORY AND DEVELOPMENT

History and Development

The development of harness—the equipment of the driving horse—and saddlery—the equipment of the ridden horse—begins at the point when man began the domestication of the animals which were to help him conquer his environment and to be the cornerstones for future civilizations. The horse, however, was not the first animal to be domesticated for the former purpose. Probably the first domestic animal was the dog, whose association with man began in the Palaeolithic age, around 6750 BC. But, although dogs have been used in draught for centuries—and are still used in Arctic regions and until recently also in western Europe, where they were employed to pull small carts—their influence on equine equipment is scarcely an important factor.

This is not, however, the case as far as cattle, reindeer, donkeys and onagers—the first of these in particular—are concerned. All of these were domesticated and used in draught long before the horse. Additionally, reindeer, donkeys and onagers were used as riding animals well before the horse was employed for that purpose. Archaeological evidence suggests that reindeer, for instance, were pulling sledges in northern Europe as long ago as 5000 BC, whilst cattle, domesticated by Neolithic man prior to 4000 BC, were used in Mesopotamia to draw land sledges before 3500 BC. At about the same time, pack asses are depicted in Egyptian art.

The domestication of the horse took place sometime during the 3rd millennium BC (3000–2000 BC)—probably, as nearly as a date can be fixed, in around 2700 BC. It was effected by a nomadic Aryan people, speaking an Indo-European language, who inhabited the steppes bordering the Black and Caspian Seas. These tough, highly adaptable people kept no records but we know of them through the clay tablets kept by their neighbours to the south, on which mention is made of them.

Initially these people would have used horses in much the same way as cattle, keeping them in herds and relying upon them as a source of food. Mares would have been milked, hides used for making tents and clothing and the dung for supplying fuel for fires. The same lifestyle still exists in these steppe lands today.

The first equipment
Naturally, when the horse began to be used for domestic purposes, the equipment employed was for the most part nearly identical to that which had proved successful with oxen, onagers and so on as far as draught harness was concerned. Saddlery—the equipment of the riding horse—evolved far later and much more slowly. One item of equine equipment—the bit—was a notable exception, however. Oxen, although occasionally guided by a rope fastened to the horns, were, and still are, controlled by either a nose rope threaded through the nasal septum, or by a cord attached to a ring through the nose. The onager, too, was controlled on the same principle. Sumerian art of the 3rd millennium BC shows yokes of four onagers abreast pulling two- and four-wheeled vehicles, being guided by reins attached to rings passed through the nose or upper lip and kept firmly in place by a strap under the jaw. But, though there is evidence to suggest that horses were controlled in this fashion in North Africa—the Greek geographer Strabo mentions the use of such a method—the introduction of a bit seems to have taken place at a fairly early stage in the association between man and the animal.

The very earliest form of control was probably no more than a woven grass halter wound around the nose, from which, it is thought, the idea of a thong tied round the lower jaw developed. This device was used centuries later by the American Indians. North African horsemen, on the other hand, particularly the Numidians, in the century either side of the Christian era, contrived to ride horses without benefit of any form of bridle, 'plying a light switch between their horses' ears', according to Silius Italicus, and evidently obtaining satisfactory results. Today, people in that part of the world ride donkeys in a similar fashion.

Bridles and bits initially made of horn or bone, seem to have been introduced in Mesopotamia in about 2300 BC, when the horse replaced the less amenable onager.

Left: A very early cave painting at Castillo, Puerto Viesgo, in the Altamira region of Spain, dated at 15000 BC. **Below:** An Egyptian tomb model of 2000 BC depicting a plough drawn by yoked oxen. The yoke survived until the time when horses were first used to pull vehicles, although it did not suit the equine conformation. **Right:** Mesopotamian mosaic of about 3000 BC showing a slightly adapted yoke. The horses (very small) are pulling by the strap at the base of the neck, a method of traction almost general until the invention of the collar.

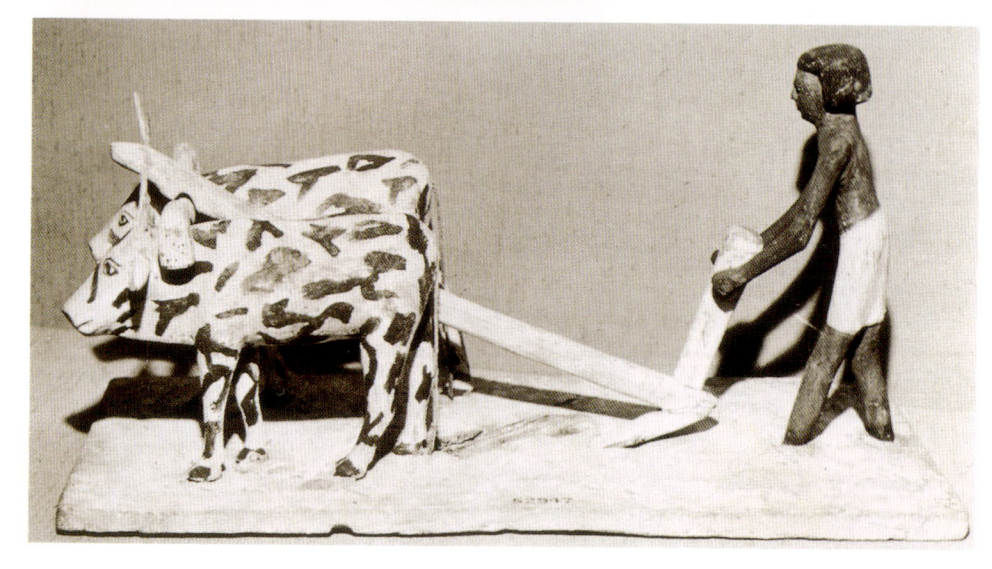

CHAPTER ONE · HISTORY AND DEVELOPMENT

By 1400 BC a jointed metal snaffle bit was in general use throughout the Near East. Although there were numerous variations in the design of the bit rings and in the plain bar and jointed mouthpieces—some of which are remarkably modern in appearance—no important alteration in the shape or action of the bit occurred until possibly the 4th century BC, when the Greek general and writer Xenophon (430–355 BC) mentions a curb bit. Since then, nothing revolutionary in the way of bits has been produced, despite variations on the basic themes of snaffle and curb.

Yokes and harness
It is likely that horses were ridden bareback before they were generally used in harness, but much of the surviving evidence about early usage relates only to draught animals drawing chariots. Possibly the development of wheeled vehicles —largely for the purposes of war but also for travel and transport—took place before riding became widespread. The small size of the horse as it then existed would have prohibited the carrying of an armed man for any distance, while in flat country a wheeled vehicle is a better proposition than a pack animal for transporting goods.

The wheel, an invention which marked a watershed in human progress almost commensurate in importance with the discovery of fire, dates from before 3000 BC. Solid wheels dating from about 3500 BC have been found in Sumerian graves excavated in the Tigris–Euphrates valley. Spoked wheels made their appearance about 1000 years later, when they were used in chariots in Syria and Egypt. Wheeled vehicles drawn by animals were in use in the Indus Valley by 2500 BC, in Continental Europe by 2000 BC, in Egypt by 1600 BC, China by 1300 BC and in Britain by 500 BC.

Whatever the argument, it is an undisputed fact that the horse eventually superseded the onager in the war chariot. When this happened, the harness of the latter, with the exception of the nose rope, was transferred virtually in the same form to the horse, just as the yoke of the oxen had been put to use previously on the onager-drawn vehicle. Basically, a yoke is a baulk of timber attached to a pair of oxen, with a vehicle or a plough then being fastened to this. Anatomically, this simple arrangement is ideally suited to the ox, since the yoke can be placed firmly against the animal's high shoulders. It is not, however, nearly as well suited to the conformation of the horse but, nevertheless, it was adapted satisfactorily enough for chariots to operate effectively over level ground for a period of many centuries.

The ox yoke, lightened and bowed, was secured to a centre pole and fitted with a pad, which rested on the horses' withers just in front of where the pommel of a riding saddle would fit. It was kept in place by a girth and a broad neck strap, so that in fact the horses were pulling their load from their necks. This completely contradicted the accepted principle of equine traction, which is centred on the shoulder.

The yoke system had another disadvantage. The neck strap could rise up in motion and press severely upon the windpipe and jugular vein of the horses. The greater the effort made by the animals, which would result in an extension of the neck, the greater was the pressure exerted on the windpipe by the neck strap. It is the use of this strap which must presumably account for the powerful muscle development on the underside of the neck and the general ewe-necked attitude depicted in the art of the period.

To counteract the throttling action of the neckstrap, an additional strap, the equivalent of the modern harness martingale, was attached to the centre of the neck collar and passed between the forelegs to fasten on the girth. The system was still mechanically inefficient, but the vehicle was light, while the addition of two more horses largely obviated the inefficiency of the pulling power which could be applied. The extra horses were placed on the outside of the two yoke horses, these outriggers being fastened to the chariot by a single trace fitted to a simple neck strap. This was the principle involved in the Roman *quadriga*, in which the basic crew of three manning this forerunner of the modern armoured car (the charioteer, a

11

CHAPTER ONE · HISTORY AND DEVELOPMENT

Right: The 'Desert Hunt' from the casket of Tutankhamun. The detail is remarkable and the relief is a good example of the early use of a central pole to which the two horses were fastened. The fixed rein to the pad appears to involve the use of some form of restraining noseband. The yoke principle is, of course, still evident. **Bottom:** The cylinder seal, probably from Thebes (c. 500 BC) showing King Darius of Persia hunting lions. The very small stature of the chariot ponies is surprising.

bowman and a general help) was sometimes augmented by a fourth soldier riding postillion on the right hand outrigger.

The Roman improvements

Yoke harness which is very similar to the ancient models, still survives today in parts of India—the Bombay 'chariot rig' being a notable example. The Romans, however, adapted the yoke still further to achieve a better fit by curving the ends and adding curved side pieces, which fitted down the neck rather like a modern collar. The Romans, too, must be given credit for the equipment which led ultimately to the modern breast collar. This derives from the arrangement perfected by the Romans to take the place of the early neck collar and trace fitted to the two outriggers in a team of four. The outside horses were given a pad kept in place by a girth to which a breast band was attached. Traces were then fitted to either side of the band and hooked either directly to the vehicle or on to a length of wood at the front of the chassis, which would today be recognized as a swingle tree. In essence the modern breast harness used for every other type of driving activity, is the same as the Roman pattern.

The padded collar resting on the shoulders and made rigid by supporting metal hames was similarly developed from the adaptations made by the Romans to the basic yoke. It is claimed to provide the most efficient method of traction, since it does not impair the horses' breathing or circulation and allows the full weight of the animals to be thrown into the pull. As an instance of this, it has been proved that a team of horses in modern harness is able to pull a load four to five times the weight of the one that could be shifted by an equivalent team in ancient yoke harness.

Asiatic influence

In common with most of the innovations in riding horse equipment, however, modern harness appears to have developed to its fullest extent in Asia. For instance, although the collar existed in its rudimentary shape in the Roman Empire, it reached its most sophisticated form in China during the same period. It was in China, too, that the single horse vehicle drawn from lateral shafts emerged. The frescoes of Kansu, dating from AD 500, show detailed depictions of modern harness, but it was not until the end of the 9th century that such harness was used generally in Europe. Tandem harness also seems to have been perfected in China.

Simultaneous with the invention of shafts came the provision of a padded cart saddle to take the weight off the horse's back and to minimize the risk of chafing. Additionally a simple breeching was introduced to help in braking the load.

Blinkers and bearing reins

Blinkers on harness bridles, however, appear to be a far more modern addition to driving equipment. They also are used for reasons which obviously could not have been matters of concern to the horsemen of ancient times. Though it is worthy of note that North African horsemen ride their Barbs in blinkered bridles, the origin of the practice, as far as driving is concerned, is more probably European and dates from the latter part of the 18th century.

The object of blinkers, leather patches fastened to the bridle cheeks thus preventing lateral vision, is to ensure that the horse can see only to his front. It is held that this will help him to concentrate on the job in hand and ensure that he will not be frightened by objects coming up behind him and will not shy away from objects or happenings on either side. It has never been proved that this is the case, however, and it is more likely that blinkers give the driver a greater (if unjustified) sense of security than they do the horse. Another reason put forward for their use is that the

CHAPTER ONE · HISTORY AND DEVELOPMENT

blinkers prevent the driver's whip from hitting the horse's eye.

Blinkers of a different pattern, but operating on the same principle, are used in modern racing where their employment can be fairly successful—at least initially—on horses which might otherwise run in a half-hearted fashion. In the racing context blinkers are often referred to as the 'rogues' badge' and horses wearing them have the reputation for being un-generous. The circumstances in which blinkers are used on the racetrack are not, however, the same as those applicable to their use with the harness horse.

Bearing, or check reins, on the other hand, are of very early origin; ancient sculptures show bearing reins attached to harness yokes. Their purpose was essentially practical, since their prevention of the extension of the horses' heads and necks not only gave greater control to the driver but prevented the neck strap from riding up on the windpipe, where it could affect the horse's breathing. Judiciously adjusted they could be used additionally as a regulator to keep the performance of the individual members of a team at a common level. The reins, however, had the potential for abuse. Centuries later, men of far more highly developed civilizations misused these reins to impose a high arched-neck head carriage which was as artificial as it was inhumane.

The growth of saddlery
Although the racing of chariots survived in the Roman circus, while horses were used increasingly in transport and agriculture, the accent in the centuries approaching the Christian period shifts decisively towards the mounted warrior. In the centuries which followed the death of Christ, this emphasis becomes ever more evident. From soon after 2300 BC, when recognizable bits and bridles were introduced, the Sumerians were in possession of written manuals on horse-management and kept records of pedigrees, presumably for breeding purposes. It is clear, therefore, that there was an awareness of the need to produce bigger, stronger and faster horses, together with the ability to do so through improved methods of land and animal husbandry. These would have involved the feeding of grain and possibly a degree of selective breeding. From this point in history, the development of saddlery for the riding horse runs parallel with the

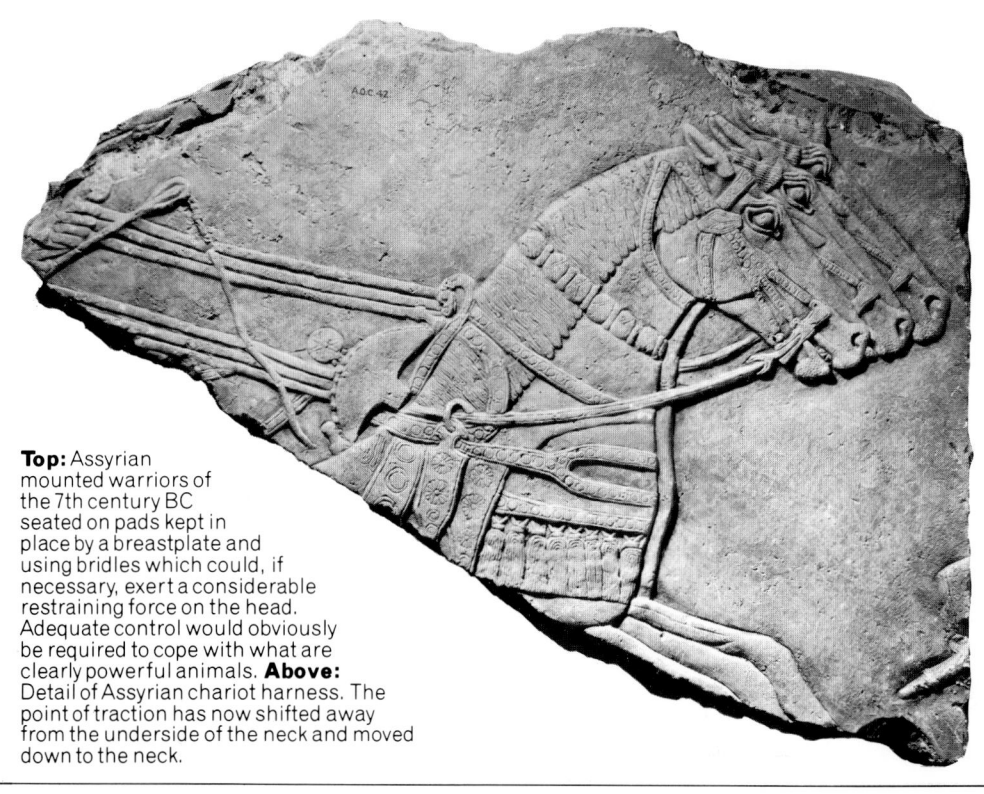

Top: Assyrian mounted warriors of the 7th century BC seated on pads kept in place by a breastplate and using bridles which could, if necessary, exert a considerable restraining force on the head. Adequate control would obviously be required to cope with what are clearly powerful animals. **Above:** Detail of Assyrian chariot harness. The point of traction has now shifted away from the underside of the neck and moved down to the neck.

CHAPTER ONE · HISTORY AND DEVELOPMENT

Left: Elements from the highly-ornamented Assyrian bridles can still be seen in the East and in the cavalry formations of Europe. **Bottom:** This is an Elamite cart captured by the Assyrians. The bridle is simple by comparison with those shown above and the horse pulls from the neck. It is, however, reasonable to suppose that a transport cart would not have the same requirements as a war chariot.

development of the equine species itself and the purposes to which men put horses in their constant struggle to maintain, consolidate and expand their control over their environment.

The Sumerians were not a horse-riding people on the whole and the few plaques surviving from the period which show mounted men are more likely to depict onagers, which as we know were domesticated before the horse. The first pictures of men riding what are beyond doubt spirited horses and controlling them by means of a recognizable bridle are to be found on the tomb of the 14th century BC Egyptian Pharaoh, Horenhab. Thereafter, it is the Assyrians who provide us, for a period, with the bulk of evidence about the ridden horse and its equipment.

The early Assyrians are depicted sitting well back, as men did on the onager and as men do in the east today when riding donkeys. Since, as archers, they needed to be free to handle their weapons, these early equestrians were led by grooms. A century later, however, the cavalry of Tiglath-Pileser III (747–727 BC) presented a very different picture. These were bold horsemen, sitting much further forward on cloths which are secured by a breastplate and girth, whilst they controlled their horses by means of a sophisticated bridle comprising headpiece, throatlatch and browband. The bit is a snaffle, probably jointed, while the cheekpieces of the bridle are divided like an inverted Y to fasten onto the oblong cheek of the bit. The latter is a general feature of the snaffle used in the Ancient World. The horses are stallions, almost certainly corn-fed, and probably requiring some effective means of control if their riders were to use them effectively in either the fields of battle or sport.

Control without the aid of a saddle is a matter of considerable importance. From this point in history, as horses became bigger and were fed increasingly on grain, the trend was constantly towards bits of increased severity, imposing a strong, mechanical control. The idea of the horse being pushed by the legs into accepting

CHAPTER ONE · HISTORY AND DEVELOPMENT

the hand is something that did not enter the horseman's philosophy for almost another two millenniums.

Developments in Persia
Up to the time of the Assyrians, horses are depicted, for the most part, with head and neck extended. The first time that horses are shown overbent is in the sculptures of Persian horses of the 6th century BC. During this period, the Persian Empire was the most important and powerful military force in the world and supported large numbers of cavalry mounted on heavier animals than seems previously to have been the case. Certainly, too, the Persian horses were far more common specimens than most of those of the preceding horse peoples.

It is possible that these horses came about as a result of the Persian connection with the neighbouring Mongolian territories to the east into which they had extended their influence. There, it would seem more than likely that Persian horses could have been crossed with the primitive Przewalskii (Mongolian wild horse), which would account for the coarse appearance and the heavy, Roman-nosed head of the Persian troop horses. Ridden without saddles and corn-fed, such horses, often thick-necked stallions, of this conformation would be difficult to control, quite apart from becoming overbent, unless some form of strong restraint, such as a curb bit, was used. But the curb bit had yet to be invented, so how did the animals become overbent in the way demonstrated by surviving ancient artefacts?

One authority, the British writer Charles Chenevix Trench, suggests that the noseband, which is obviously present in the reliefs of Persian horses, might, in fact, have had a spiked nosepiece, like the present-day Spanish *careta*. This would certainly account for the overbent position of the head and it seems reasonable to suppose that this first appearance of a

Above: An Assyrian relief showing the horseman wearing an armoured suit of sophisticated design. **Opposite left:** Greek warriors of the Leontis tribe (400 BC). No bridles are visible, but the position of the horses' heads, and in particular the muscle development of the underside of the neck, is indicative of an outline obtained by the use of a snaffle bit by a rider sitting bareback.

noseband has a significance beyond mere decoration.

Persian bridles are also of particular interest, because they established a design convention which can be seen repeated continually in the equipment of the horse peoples of following centuries. The points of attachment are made with toggles—the buckle had yet to be invented—in much the same form as the present-day bridles used in South America and parts of Mexico. The cheek of the bridle is divided to fasten to the phallus-shaped cheek of the bit, which is ornamented with a horse's hoof at the lower end. Both are possibly symbolic of the stallion's fertility

Top: An interesting variation on the usual pattern of Assyrian bit. An animal motif was often a feature of early bitting arrangements. **Above:** A bit of a slightly later period from Western Asia, which employs a very 'modern' central link. **Right:** An ornamental terret, also from Western Asia, which employs another animal motif, in this case a horse model which is again remarkably 'modern' in execution.

and the design, suitably modified, persists up to the present day, a very common showing bit for stallions having 'horseshoe' cheeks. There is no way of knowing the exact form of the mouthpiece, but it seems very possible that the shape of the bit cheeks, in combination with the divided cheekpieces of the bridle and the connection to the noseband, would bring the latter into play when the rein was used. Furthermore a degree of pressure would also have been exerted on the poll, via the cheekpieces and the bridle head. This in itself contributes to a lowering of the head and is one of the actions produced by a curb bit.

The use of a noseband by the Persians was not the first time that a device of this sort had been employed. The Egyptian charioteers of nearly a millennium before had used a 'drop' noseband which was brought into action by the use of the rein. The principle of the drop noseband then, as now, was to cause the horse to drop his nose and thus come more easily to the hand. In the Egyptian version, the fitting was so low that a strong pull on the rein would cause a severe restriction of the animal's breathing, imposing an unmistakable check on the most headstrong horse.

The search for greater control

From the very earliest times, horsemen were concerned with the need to devise methods of restraint that would give them greater control over their mounts, which were for the most part stallions. As horses increased in size and strength and the practice of grain feeding became more widely established, the necessity for more effective braking and steering systems became commensurately more urgent.

The first modification to the plain bar bit of the early horsemen was the introduction of the jointed mouthpiece. This produced a squeezing effect across the lower jaw or on either side of the face, depending upon the position of the head at the moment the action was applied by the reins. The severity of the action was fairly quickly increased by modifications to the bit rings or cheeks. The most usual of these was the addition of spikes to the inside of the rings, an innovation which not only increased the stopping power of the bit but also simplified the business of turning to one side or the other.

From the 6th century BC onwards, attention was focussed on the mouthpiece, to which was fitted spiked rollers, sharp discs or spines like those of a hedgehog. These were the bits termed 'rough' by Xenophon, though the Greeks also employed 'smooth' bits once the horse was sufficiently schooled. Xenophon, the first recorder of equestrian theory in a number of technical treatises, also mentions mouthpieces fitted with rollers or short lengths of chain, encouraging the horse to 'mouth' his bit, thus relaxing the lower jaw. Xenophon talks about the horse 'pursuing the bit' with his tongue, which is

CHAPTER ONE · HISTORY AND DEVELOPMENT

exactly what modern horsemen are trying to achieve when they put a mouthing bit, fitted with 'keys' in the centre of its mouthpiece, on a young horse.

The curb bit
The Greeks did not use a curb bit, although Xenophon knew of this important innovation, which was invented by the Celts of Gaul in the 4th century BC. The curb bit, indeed, constitutes something of a landmark in the development of horse equipment, since it was to dominate equestrian thinking in nearly every area up to the present day. It is only in the past three or four decades that the emphasis in riding has been on the snaffle bridle, with or without a drop noseband. Up to the Second World War (and even after) hunting men would have been familiar with the maxim that 'there are three kinds of fool: the fool, the damn fool and the fool that hunts in a snaffle', and in some areas it would have been considered 'incorrect' (the most heinous of hunting crimes) to ride with so rudimentary a bridle as a simple snaffle.

The curb bit achieves control by a simple system of levers, with the curb chain, or its early equivalent, acting as the fulcrum. It causes the mouthpiece to act against the bars of the mouth, encouraging flexion at the poll and in the lower jaw. The severity of the bit and the degree of leverage obtainable depends upon the length of the cheek below the mouthpiece, whilst the length of the cheek above the mouthpiece, to which is attached the cheekpiece of the bridle, governs the degree of pressure which can be applied to the horse at the poll.

From skins to saddles
The development of the saddle in the pre-Christian era is less notable and no specific improvement or discovery comparable to those connected with bitting seems to have occurred. Cloths and skins had been in use since early times. The saddle cloths of the Assyrians, kept in place by a girth and breast strap—sometimes by a 'breeching' passing around the quarters as well—were improved by the addition of cloth rolls in front and behind the rider. On the whole, however, nothing emerged which contributed materially to the security of the rider; indeed, many of the ancients scorned the use of coverings as effete and unmanly, although most, like Xenophon, appreciated the desirability of riding 'round-backed' horses rather than those of an opposite inclination.

Whilst mounted troops were used extensively in the pre-Christian period—it was, after all, the demands of war which made the greatest contribution to both the development of saddlery and harness and to the art of riding itself—their use was limited. Without saddles the distances which could be covered, as well as the speed with which a march could be made, depended, largely, upon the endurance of the riders. Furthermore, no horseshoes were then available—they were not invented until the 1st century AD. Although the Greek military genius Alexander the Great (c. 300 BC) is reported to have used 'boots' or 'sandals' on his horses' feet in rough country, these would have given no more than rudimentary protection and were certainly not in general use.

Nor was it possible for mounted men riding bareback to close with infantry. Their seats were far too insecure for this and therefore they had to confine their

CHAPTER ONE HISTORY AND DEVELOPMENT

action to the throwing of javelins or attacking from a safe distance with bow and arrow. Nonetheless, these early cavalry soldiers must have been considerable horsemen, although it seems reasonable to suppose that many of them would have fought dismounted once they had reached the field of battle.

At the start of the Christian era therefore, horsemen were riding virtually bareback and for the most part controlling

Opposite: Horsemen from the Parthenon frieze. Once more the position of the head and the development of the lower neck is an example of the collection achieved by the use of the snaffle. **Above:** Decoration on a Greek vase of about 500 BC. This is a racing chariot so the vehicle and its harness are as light as possible. The breastplate is prevented from rising up the neck by a martingale or strap passing between the forelegs. **Left:** Early Greco/Roman horse sandal made of iron. The horseshoe, in one form or another, began to come into general use during the first century AD.

CHAPTER ONE · HISTORY AND DEVELOPMENT

Above: A Roman prick-spur discovered during an excavation in the City of London in 1935. **Left:** Celtic horseman of the first or 2nd century BC, from a relief in the Gunderstrup Cauldron found in Denmark. These warriors sit on pads secured firmly both by breastplate and crupper and they wear spurs.

their horses in a variety of snaffles, with and without the addition of nosebands. The Celtic barbarians and their close neighbours, for the moment, were alone amongst the horse peoples in their use of the curb. The security of the rider under these circumstances depended upon the strength of his legs and it must be assumed, in some degree, to how tightly he could hold the reins.

Two styles of riding in this period are also evident. People like the Greeks and Persians of the civilized world sat upright on horses which, because of the rocky terrain, were 'collected' in so far as the quarters were engaged well beneath the body. In nearly all instances with the exception of the Persians, the heads are held high, however, with the nose poked out rather than 'tucked in', as in the Parthenon frieze. This attitude is what would be expected of riders sitting bareback on spirited stallions and using a snaffle, the action of which is predominantly an upward one against the corners of the horse's lips.

An opposite style is evident amongst people, such as the Scythians, living in flatter country with open plain or steppe lands. These horsemen, too, rode in snaffles, but they rode fast with a loose rein, for they were horse-archers, needing two hands to use their weapons. Their horses, with no bit contact to govern the position of their heads, are extended from nose to tail. The riders themselves adopted a more crouched seat in accordance with the outline of their galloping horses and also in accordance with their own conformation, for many are short, squat men, with less length of leg than the more elegant Greek horseman.

Revolutionary improvements

It is from this point, in the first 500 years of the Christian era, that the most significant developments in horse equipment took place. The effect of these was remarkable. The improvements made to the saddle in particular influenced not only the advance of equitational skills but also altered the practice and even the concept of warfare. The horseshoe, invented and brought into general use during the first century of Christianity, played its part as well, since it made it possible for a horse to remain fit for service over extended periods of time and without regard for the nature of the terrain covered.

Initial improvements are most evident in the saddlery of the Scythians, one of the greatest horse peoples of all time. The Scythians were hardly cast in the academic mould and there is therefore no direct information obtainable about these fierce nomadic horsemen. Their delight was in war and feasting rather than in letters. Nonetheless, there are sufficient accounts from people associated with them to appreciate that their saddlery, derived from practical necessity, was in advance of that of their contemporaries. We know of their predilection for the taking of scalps, their grisly trophies being used to adorn their bridle reins or being hung from their saddle bows, and it is these same saddles which mark an important stage in the long story of the development of horse equipment.

Scythian and Sarmatian

Unlike the Greeks, Romans and Persians, who used a simple pad laid on the back secured by girth, breastplate and perhaps a crupper or breeching, the Scythians employed a felt saddlecloth or 'numnah', which, as demonstrated by the examples found intact in the frozen tombs of Pazyryk in the High Altai, was often gorgeously embroidered. Such saddlecloths, however, were by no means for decorative purposes alone. They were given hard usage and doubled as a blanket for the rider at night. On the march they would have been folded under the Scythian saddle and would have constituted an effective protection

The saddle, made of leather and felt, comprised two cushions well-stuffed with deer hair, joined by straps or by a connecting piece of leather from end to end. The cushions, put on over the saddlecloth, lay on either side of the spine, thus ensuring that the rider's weight was carried on the dorsal muscles and ribs. Such an arrangement conforms to the current principle of saddle-fitting, which requires the saddle to clear the backbone both along its length and width. When this principle is observed, the spine itself is not subjected to weight. It is, therefore, unlikely that sores will occur in this sensitive area and, just as importantly, there will be no restriction of the horse's free movement, such as occurs when weight is carried directly on the spine. Horses thus equipped, like those of the Scythians, were therefore less likely to develop sore backs which would limit their effective serviceability, while, because their saddles allowed freedom to the spinal process, they would be physically better able to undertake long marches. That is the measure of importance of the Scythian saddle; it, together with the easy snaffle bridle employed, endowed its inventors with a mobility superior to that of other mounted peoples of the period.

It is interesting to note that the Argentine *gaucho*, perhaps the last in the line of 'horse peoples', uses a saddle today that in its essentials differs little from that of his Scythian predecessor. In the pampas where high grasses obstruct his view, the *gaucho* stands on his saddle, placing a foot on either cushion, so as to be able to see further. The Scythians employed the same tactic, while Mongolian horsemen, themselves the most probable descendants of the Scythians, act in just the same fashion to this day.

Another link with the Scythian saddle, which is not easily explained, concerns the Plains Indians of North America. Since no horses existed on the continent until their re-introduction by the Spanish *conquistadores* in the 16th century, these Indians were pedestrian by necessity until possibly the mid-17th century, when they had acquired horses in sufficient quantity to become riders. Their saddles were almost an exact counterpart of those of the Scythians and, like that war-like people, there were Indian tribes who decorated their saddles and bridles with the scalps of their enemies.

To the east of the Scythians there lived another horse people, the Sarmatians. Unlike the Scythians, the Sarmatians fought as heavy cavalry, using a long, heavy lance which the Greeks called a 'barge-pole', and wearing armour. The Sarmatians, using this heavy lance, were probably the first troops to charge bodies of infantry in the accepted cavalry fashion—previously spears and javelins carried by mounted warriors were hurled at the enemy from a distance. The Sarmatians, too, must be given the credit for the first saddle built on a wooden frame or 'tree'. Such a saddle, built high at the cantle, was essential if horsemen, riding without benefit of stirrups, were to retain their seats at the moment of impact as they

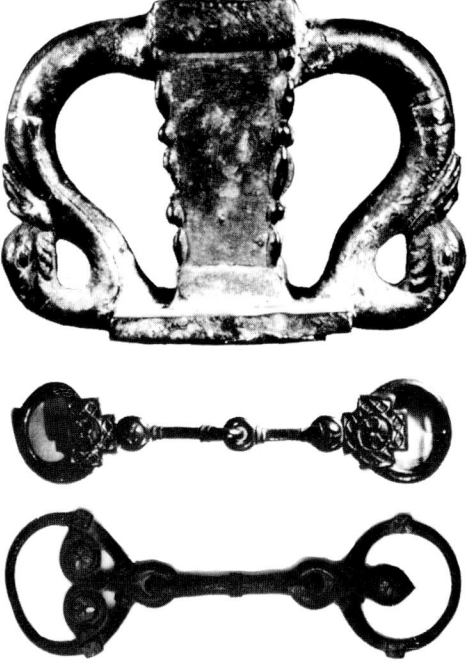

Left: A Gallo-Roman passenger vehicle, forerunner of the stage-coach. The horses are equipped with a recognisable pad and collar and traces are being used. **Above, top:** Greco-Roman rein terret in bronze. **Centre:** A Roman bit found in London. **Bottom:** A chariot bit, found in Yorkshire, with a double-bossed bit ring for fitting to the outside once the horses were in position.

CHAPTER ONE · HISTORY AND DEVELOPMENT

charged into a body of infantry. Without the high cantle, against which the horseman could brace himself, it would have been impossible for him not to have made a rapid exit over his horse's tail.

Thereafter, numerous horse peoples used the shock tactic made possible by the Sarmatian saddle. Having pushed westward from their original homelands between the Black and Caspian Seas, the Sarmatians eventually absorbed the Scythians, who in turn became part of the Goths. All used the couched lance in one form or another but there is no evidence to show that any of them used a stirrup. This was also true of a Negroid race of obscure African origin employed by the Romans as cavalry *foederati*. They are known as the X Group and exactly from where they came is a matter of conjecture.

The X Group used highly sophisticated saddles, which were extravagantly decorated and built high at front and rear, so that the rider was encased between pommel and cantle. Arab saddles of the present day are almost identical to the

Above: Saddle-cloth from the Pazyryk tombs (5th century BC) decorated in felt appliqué with an eagle, griffon and ibex. **Left, top:** Carved wooden facing of a saddle arch from the same source. **Bottom:** Elaborate gold belt buckle of Sarmatian origin (first century BC – first century AD). The noseband fitted below the bit is an early form of drop noseband, used to give the rider greater control. The saddle pad is equipped with thongs to which the rider would have attached his belongings. **Opposite:** This gaily attired horseman appears on a decorated felt wall-hanging found in Barrow 5 at Pazyryk. All the items illustrated on these two pages are in the collection at the Hermitage Museum, Leningrad, which houses the large number of items removed from Pazyryk. Without doubt this collection is one of the most comprehensive and valuable in the world.

CHAPTER ONE · HISTORY AND DEVELOPMENT

CHAPTER ONE HISTORY AND DEVELOPMENT

Left: A Sasanian silver-gilt dish from the collection at Leningrad's Hermitage Museum. The illustration is of King Ardnashir III (628-630 AD) hunting with a bow. The saddle he uses has a clearly defined forearch and is probably kept in place by a girth as well as by the breastplate and breeching. The discs hanging from these items may well be charms to ward off evil, rather like the horse brasses used on heavy harness horses. The tail decoration is unusual and of particular interest. There is no evidence of a stirrup, but this does not seem to inhibit King Ardnashir in his firing of a 'Parthian shot'.

saddles of this mysterious people, whom the Romans called Nobades.

In Africa the lance was customarily used overhand in a stabbing action, but the Nobades couched their weapons like the Sarmatians. Additionally they employed the notorious ring bit, which is often referred to as the Mameluke. This is because the Mamelukes used a similar device much later in time. It would seem reasonable to assume that the ring-type curb bits of the Renaissance masters derived from this source and, indeed, a very similar bit can be found in North Africa today.

Invention of the stirrup

But the greatest advance was yet to come. This was the invention of the stirrup. It seems fairly certain that this came from Mongolia with Attila the Hun, known to the world as 'the scourge of God'. It is impossible to date this momentous happening exactly, but there is written evidence of the stirrup's existence around the middle of the 5th century AD.

The Russian scientist W W Arendt put forward the suggestion that the stirrup could have been incorporated into the girth of Scythian saddles, but it is difficult to substantiate the claim, which was based largely on an illustration on the Chertomlyk vase (4th century BC) and on material discovered in tombs at Novo-Alexandrovska in 1865. If such an item did exist, it seems very unlikely that it took some 700 to 800 years to come into general use. On the other hand, some evidence suggests that Indian horsemen rode with a toe stirrup, a leather loop into which was placed the big toe, perhaps as much as 200 years before Attila. If this were so, it is not unreasonable to suppose that the nomads of Central Asia would, in time, have become acquainted with the practice, adapting the toe thong so as to accommodate the thick felt boots which protected their feet against the cold. In parts of southern India today and in Malaya and Singapore the natives still use a toe stirrup—even when racing.

The advantages bestowed by the stirrup were numerous and far reaching in their effect. Cavalry was able to increase its mobility and range, since the comfort given to the rider by the presence of a pair of stirrups reduced fatigue and allowed longer marches to be made at high speeds. Naturally, it also increased the rider's security a hundred-fold. Heavy cavalry were able to close with bodies of infantry with far less risk of being un-horsed at the moment of impact and, as a result, assumed a far greater importance on the battlefield. However, the clear division between heavy horsemen and the light cavalry of the barbarians like Attila's Huns persisted. The two distinct styles of riding continued to exist alongside each other and continued to do so right through the centuries. Both heavy and light cavalry adopted the stirrup, but the style of riding

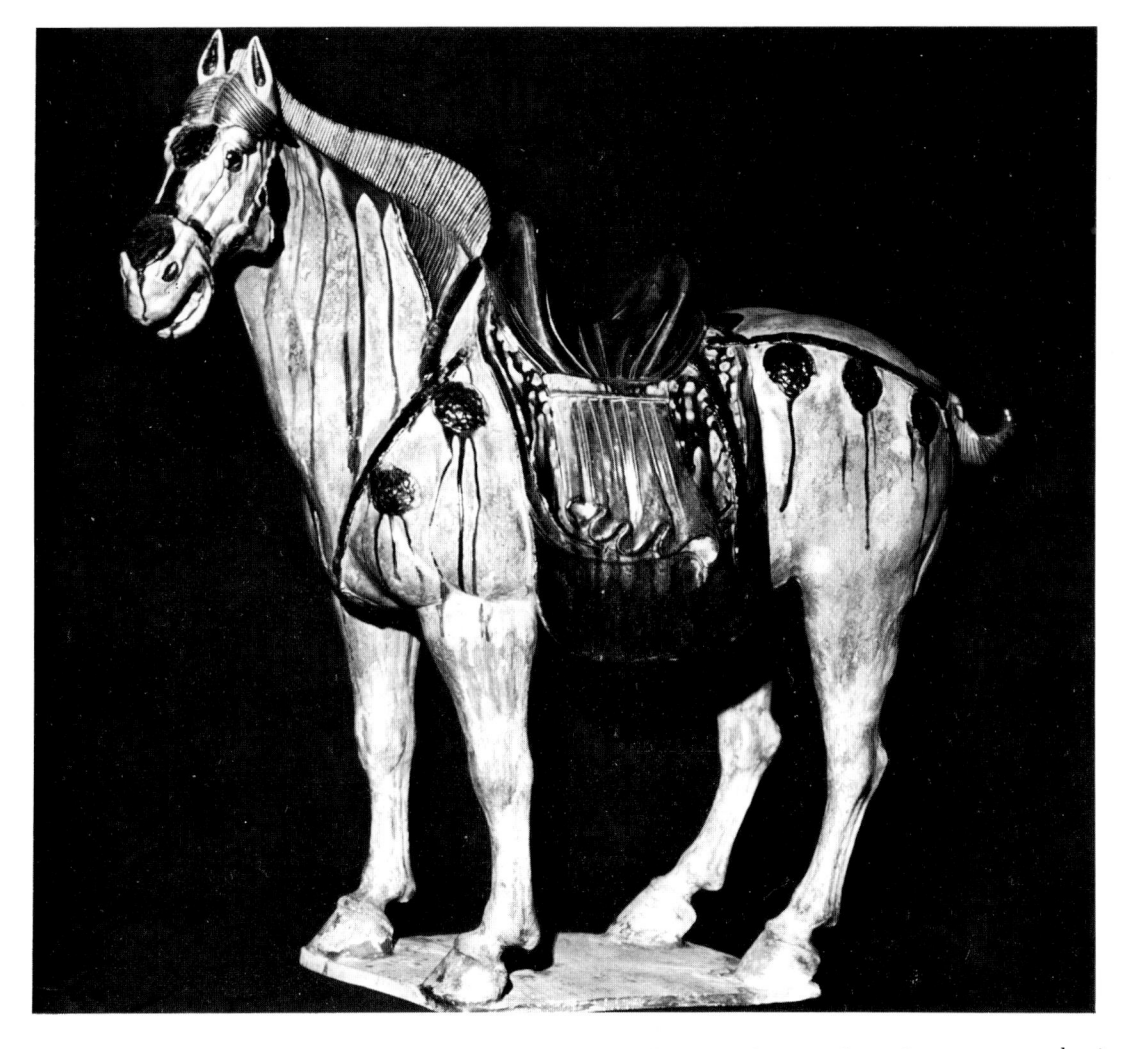

Left: Chinese glazed, earthenware figure from a tomb of the Tang Dynasty (7th-10th century AD). The practice of burying equine representations and equipment, and even the horses themselves, with chieftains and noblemen was widespread throughout Asia. This is a particularly fine example of a tomb figure and the characteristic features of the saddle are clearly defined. The dipped seat persisted until well after the Renaissance period and survives, in a less extreme form, in modern saddles.

and the use made of it was determined by the weapons employed and by the type of horses being ridden.

Heavy cavalry, weighted with armour, had the lance as a principal weapon and used the charge against infantry, or other cavalry, as their tactic. Their horses needed to be strong, robust sorts, but did not need to be excessively swift. This type of mounted soldier used a pretty fierce curb bit to control his horse, achieving a form of mechanical collection by its action, and preserved his equilibrium in the charge by pushing hard on his stirrups and bracing himself against the high cantle of his saddle. He rode, therefore, with seat firmly in the saddle using a fairly long leather and pushing his feet to the front, a position which was enforced by the stirrup attachment being placed well to the front of the saddle.

For the most part the light horsemen originated in the east. They rode smaller horses and relied far more upon speed. They were horse-archers, riding short so as to be able to stand in their stirrups and adopting a remarkably modern-looking seat, with the lower leg drawn back behind the vertical. They rode in snaffles, making no attempt to collect their horses, since their bows required the use of both hands. Their tactic was to gallop across the enemy's front usually from left to right to facilitate the drawing of the bow, then to loose three or four shafts before peeling off and despatching, over the horse's rump, a 'Parthian shot'.

A shift in emphasis

This style of riding persisted long after the bow, fired from horse-back, had given way to other weapons. It was the opposite cavalry school, however, which for centuries dominated the battlefields of the world and was the most significant factor in the development of equitation and of horse equipment.

What was happening was a shift in emphasis from the east to the west. The old horse cultures of Asian origin—the originators of man's association with the horse—were to be overtaken by the practices of Europe. It was the latter which were to exert the greater influence on the future, but not, as will be seen later, exclusively, everywhere or for ever. Hundreds of years later, the two streams of equitation were to merge to produce the modern system of riding.

The first steps in this progress are less well documented than later ones. Man's knowledge of the Dark Ages is sparse in comparison with later periods, from which fairly detailed records survive. Obviously, equipment was adapted and improved in accordance with immediate local needs, but no notable advance in equitational method and theory occurred which was reflected in corresponding improvements in the equipment used.

From about 1066 onwards, however, documentation in words and in pictures

CHAPTER ONE · HISTORY AND DEVELOPMENT

Far right: Paolo Ucello's painting of the battle of San Romano gives a very complete picture of the equipment of the mounted knight and illustrates clearly the need for a saddle which afforded maximum security to the rider and for a bit strong enough to control an excited (and probably heavy) horse with one hand in 'press of battle'. The wide leather reins embossed with heavy brass discs were not entirely decorative – such a rein would have presented a considerable difficulty to a foot soldier attempting to cut it. **Right:** An illustration from the medieval Luttrell Psalter, showing a black St. George killing the dragon using the overhand thrust employed by Eastern horsemen. **Below:** Norman knights preparing to embark for Hastings in 1066, from the Bayeux tapestry. The forward attachment of the stirrup leather, causing the leg to be pushed to the front, is seen clearly on the saddle of the rider leading the group.

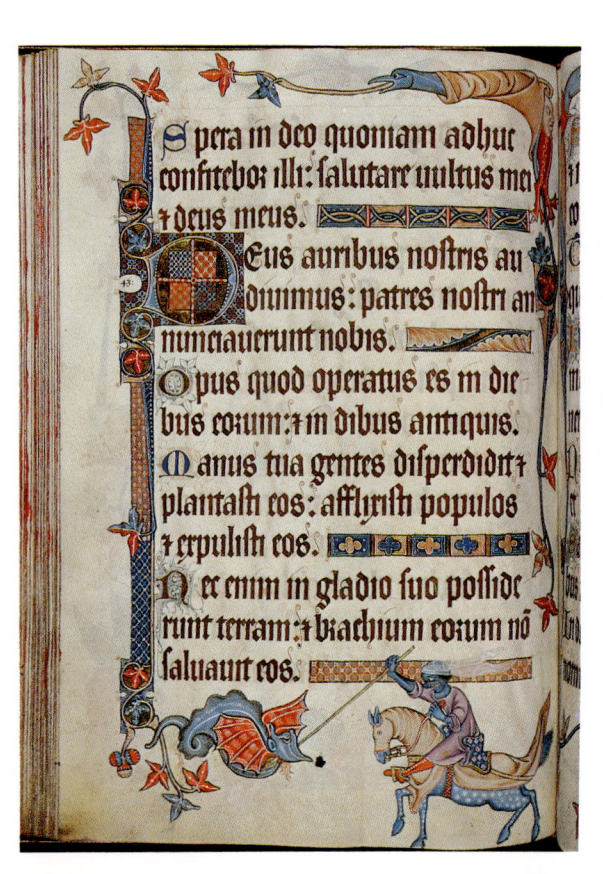

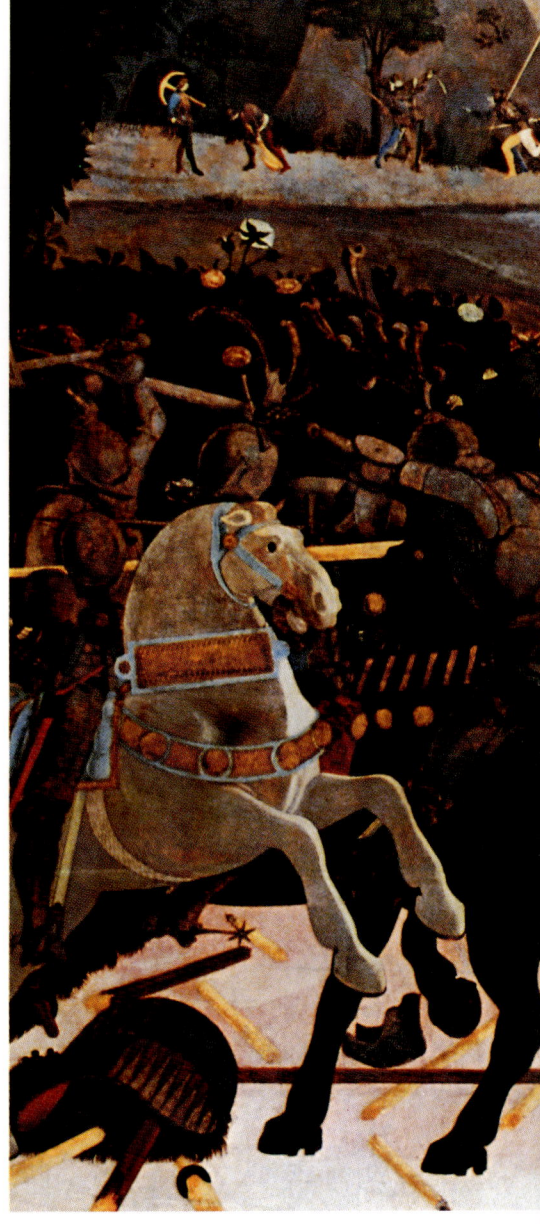

becomes increasingly detailed and, as far as equitation and equipment is concerned, a development is easily discernible. These two facets—the practice of riding and the equipment used by the horseman in improving techniques and advancing his mastery of the horse—of necessity must be considered in parallel, for they are largely interdependent. Sometimes, it is true, the horseman appears to be in advance of his equipment, his physical strength and skills overcoming, if only in part, his lack of the constructions of wood, metal and leather which could have endowed him with greater comfort, security and control in his partnership with the horse. There are also periods, however, when the equipment available seems almost to be a step or two ahead of the rider; there have certainly been occasions when the horseman has been so overwhelmed by a surfeit of saddlery and forceful devices that the art and the empathy he should possess have been reduced to a matter of applied mechanics.

Knights and the Great Horse
In the equestrian context, the tendency is for the Middle Ages to be associated with the Great Horse and the armoured knight. Both became a notable feature on the battlefields and tourney grounds of the time. At the beginning of this period, however, horses were light in build, as can be seen from the Bayeux tapestry, while their riders wore relatively light chain-mail shirts. With all weapons included, plus saddles, the average warrior did not probably weigh more than 16 stone. This was the average burden of a single cavalry troop horse in the First World War.

From the numerous illustrations which have survived, it seems that a snaffle of one sort or another was in more general use than the curb bit. The mouthpieces of these snaffles, however, may very well have been made more severe by the addition of spikes, sharpened edges and so on, while many are obviously connected to a low-fitting noseband. The action of this could also have been strengthened by the addition of a rough metal plate on the inner surface, or by a row of small spikes.

Nonetheless, whilst it is possible that such additional restraints could have been present, the horses are neither overbent nor highly collected, like those of the earlier Persians or those of some 200 to 300 years later. In the former instance, it has to be remembered that, unlike the Norman horsemen depicted on the Bayeux tapestry, the Persians had no stirrups and precious little saddle to give them security of tenure. It is not unreasonable to suppose, therefore, that they would have had some recourse to the reins not only to control their apparently strong horses but also to ensure a safe seat.

As the shattering effect of a co-ordinated charge of cavalry became increasingly appreciated, bigger, heavier horses were bred and employed. They would have required stronger forms of restraint than those afforded by the snaffle; since it was also essential 'in press of knights' that the horses should be responsive and schooled, the more immediate bitting arrangement represented by the curb became a necessity.

Even so the heavier horses used in the 12th and 13th centuries did not approach the Great Horses produced in the following 200 years. The Great Horse evolved as a result of the usual tit-for-tat escalation of the arms' race, which was as much in evidence in the Middle Ages as in today's nuclear era. To counter the effect of charging cavalry, the weapons carried by the foot soldier had to be improved. The most effective of all these weapons was the long-bow, a Welsh product, used with the most devastating effect to cut swathes in the concourse of French chivalry at the decisive moment at Crécy in 1346.

For as long as horses were integral to the battlefield, the developing practices of war

CHAPTER ONE · HISTORY AND DEVELOPMENT

28

CHAPTER ONE · HISTORY AND DEVELOPMENT

Opposite: Knight of the late 15th century in full armour, with his horse armoured and caparisoned with rich cloths. The latter, at least in a form as exaggerated as this, would not have been used other than for full-dress parade occasions. **Left:** Late 15th-century German armour, the horse being equipped with plate and chain mail. The length of the bridle cheeks would allow for tremendous leverage against the jaw: they measure more than 20 inches.

Above left: The immensely powerful ring bit of Moorish origin. This example is of 17th-century Spanish manufacture but similar, if less ornamented, examples can be found throughout North Africa at the present time. **Above right:** A curb bit used by Henry VIII of England. The keys encourage the horse to 'mouth' the bit, and the rollers forming the mouthpiece on either side help to serve the same purpose, also preventing the horse from taking the bit between the teeth! **Right:** A protective chamfron worn over the horse's face. It shows the bear and ragged staff of the Earls of Leicester and is in the collection of the Tower of London.

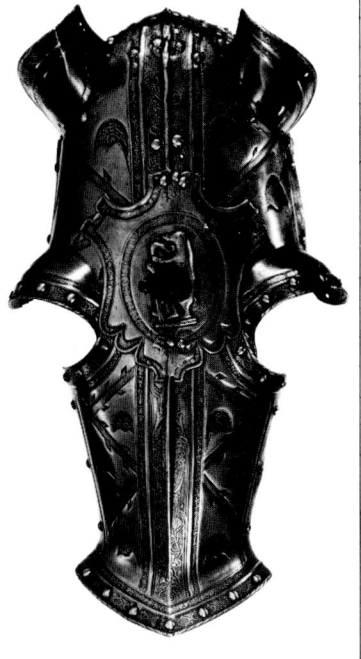

would have their influence upon equitational methods and the complementing equipment used in support of the latter. It was so in this situation.

The cavalry's answer to the long-bow was to equip the knight with body armour. This became increasingly complex and weighty, as the bowmen became more and more skilled with their murderous tool. At Crécy, for instance, the Welsh archers could fire enough arrows to produce a dense, lethal and continuing barrage on the advancing cavalry. To carry the rider's increased weight, a stronger, heavier horse was needed; when it became necessary to provide the horse with protective armour as well, an even more massive—and slower—horse was required for the purpose.

The seat of the knight remained much the same. He positioned himself deep in his dip-seated saddle, its high pommel affording him a little extra protection as well as contributing to his security, whilst bracing himself, with leg straight and thrust forward in the stirrup, against the equally high cantle. As has been seen, this position, encouraged by the forward placement of the stirrup leather attachment, suited the knight's purpose admirably, allowing him to withstand the shock of the charge without becoming unseated. He wore extremely long and very sharp spurs in order to be able to reach his horse and to ensure that so heavy an animal would react to the indications implicit in their use. Without doubt, the ability to control the horse with the legs was now appreciated and understood. The remaining element of control, the bit, was used with one hand only—the left. This held the reins and also the knight's shield and therefore had to be carried high—certainly as high as the chest. The right hand held the sword, lance or mace.

The bit employed was a curb bit of fearsome dimensions. The mouthpiece might be jointed in its centre and made 'sharp' by serrations, spikes or something similar; alternatively it might be fitted with a very high port. This not only allowed the bit to bear directly upon the

CHAPTER ONE · HISTORY AND DEVELOPMENT

Right: A Luttrell Psalter lady hands her caparisoned knight his helm whilst the other lady (a rival out of favour perhaps) is left holding his shield. The saddle encasing the rider is of a type used for jousting before this pastime became so professional that knights, preferring to exit by the back door, had the cantles cut away.

Right: A 15th-century French tournament scene. Although the saddle fixed the rider firmly in position the high cantle was a dangerous feature and could cause serious injury. It was later removed and replaced by a less restrictive support. The fashion of a flower growing out of the top of the head is surely an entirely Gallic conceit!

bars of the mouth by accommodating the tongue, which would otherwise lie over the bars and thus mitigate the pressure imposed by the mouthpiece of the bit, but also bore painfully on the roof of the mouth to provide a horrific degree of leverage. The extent of this can easily be imagined, when it is appreciated that the length of the cheeks could be as much as 15in. The other type of curb bit employed was the fierce, jaw-breaking ring bit of North Africa, similar to that used by the X Group nearly a millennium previously.

Most dressage riders of the present day, more particularly those influenced by German teaching, would break a horse's jaw in five minutes with such a bit if they rode in their customary manner, always supposing that the horse did not rear over backwards first. There is no reason to suppose that the mounted knights would have fared better had they employed our modern 'contact' system, despite the lack of quality in their elephantine mounts.

Instead they rode with one hand on a looped rein, which implies that their horses were schooled to the neck rein for changes of direction and to the raised hand as an indication to decrease the pace or to stop. This is the way the Californian cowboy schools his horse, arriving at the final potentially severe 'spade' (port) bit by a progression of nosebands. In fact, the system of the hackamore (*jaquima*, in Arabic *hakma*) on which the cowboy's method of bitting is based, derives from the practices of the 16th-century Spanish *conquistadores*, who, in turn, had learnt them from the Moors during the latters' 700-year presence on the Iberian peninsula.

The knights of Europe were therefore probably borrowing parts of a system widely used in the Middle East, which had been learnt from contacts made during the long period of the Crusades and from Portuguese and Spanish acquaintances.

As a training ground for war, the knights of the Middle Ages employed the tournament and joust. These sports were directly related to the demands of the battlefield, as, indeed, are many other horse sports. Particularly as the role of the mounted knight became less tenable as a result of the devastating long-bows, tournaments became increasingly artificial and professional—tournament knights 'doing the circuit' much like the modern show jumper. The sport, too, produced specialist equipment. This was often exaggerated in the extreme, particularly as far as the jousting saddle was concerned, but it also advanced the standards of equitation. The horses, heavy or not, had to be schooled to a very high degree if they were to stand any chance in this first of the equestrian 'spectator-sports'.

The saddles for the sport were often built so that the rider was completely encased from the waist to the hips. Eventually the pommel became a vast iron shield, like the windscreen of a motorcycle, while great leg guards were also incorporated. Finally, since fake action with blunted lances had taken the place of conflict to the death, the contenders decided on the sensible option of ejecting via the back door rather than risk being maimed or killed by being imprisoned in the cockpit of the saddle. For this reason,

CHAPTER ONE · HISTORY AND DEVELOPMENT

Opposite: 18th-century prints depicting the High School movements. They are by the Austrian artist Ridinger, who made the subject his speciality. In all the illustrations, except the top right, the upper rein is attached to the cavesson. In the two bottom pictures a draw rein passing through the cavesson ring is in use. **Right:** This elegant rider also employs a rein to the cavesson and displays commendable restraint in the use of the curb. The tail casing has a practical purpose during execution of the 'airs' or leaps above the ground. It is still used at the Spanish School and by the Cadre Noir. The saddle in these pictures is the **Selle Royale**, a streamlined version of the saddle of the medieval knight.

the cantle was removed. This naturally could not have been the case in actual battle.

The riding masters

The tournament had become the medieval equivalent of the jumping arena and the conventional role of the knight in battle had declined by the time that the phenomenon of the Renaissance (literally 'rebirth') of the 16th century, opened a new gateway to rediscovering and developng the old learning in the arts and sciences within the civilized world. Men enthusiastically discovered the classical glories again, amongst them the works òf the great Greek general, Xenophon, the first master of equitation. Young gentlemen began to take an interest in equitation as an art form, regarding it as on a level with an appreciation of music and poetry, an understanding of mathematics and the other varied attributes which now made up the intellectual equipment and social graces of those of gentle birth.

In Italy, at first, and then over Europe baroque riding halls arose and the foundations of 'classical' riding were established. Spain and France were also important centres. In fact, like the tournament this new riding was initially mirrored on war, but without the latter's danger. In the extravagant carousels, the riders performed the same movements which the mounted knight would have executed in battle. The *volte*, *levade*, *pirouette* and *capriole* ensured the handiness of the horse and displayed his ability to over-awe opponents and discourage the attentions of ill-disposed enemy infantry. Then, too, there were the glories of the *passage* and *piaffe*, the elevated trots which showed off the victorious general and his noble horse to best advantage.

Dominating the horse

In the 16th century the horses used in the *manège* (school) were those which would have carried knights into battle; they were coarse, heavy animals and in order to put them back on their haunches so as to perform the highly collected movements required, it was deemed necessary to use strong curb bits and sometimes the *careta*, the studded noseband from which is derived the ringed lunge cavesson and of which the plain cavesson, which does no more than set off a bridle, is a relic, which survives in riding up to the present day.

The accent, indeed, in the early days of classical riding was on 'breaking' the horse. The only reward he received was when the punishment stopped. Grisone, the first of the great riding masters, who wrote his book *Gli Ordine di Cavalcare* in 1550, used some appalling devices, as did his pupil and successor Pignatelli. But in an age when the rack, the thumbscrew and the stake were commonplace, the cruelties practised on animals were no more than relative, while, in spite of their use of some barbarous items of equipment, both Grisone and Pignatelli were swift to condemn any practice that would harden the mouth itself.

The bits were curbs, with or without ports. Some of them had the forerunner of the bradoon—a thin bit which was called a 'flying trench'—attached. The curb was used with a noseband—a cavesson—to which, following loosely the Moorish fashion, the 'false rein' was secured. The cavesson could be studded, like the *careta*, or it might occasionally be of plain leather. Later, the 'false rein' would be fitted to the 'flying trench', or to the top ring of the curb, in the fashion of what has

CHAPTER ONE · HISTORY AND DEVELOPMENT

become known as a Pelham. Finally the curb rein was added to supplement the top rein. What this meant was that the curb, however severe, was never brought into full use. It was, as it were, only the threat of its severe action which was employed to obtain the desired result. The Western horseman of today uses the same system through the *bosal*, a noseband weighted at the rear, and the hackamore, the bosal fitted with heavy *mecate* ropes which are attached to the knot lying behind the curb groove and act as reins. This art, however, is virtually lost to the modern European horseman, who frequently inflicts far more pain upon the mouths of his horses while criticizing the 'barbarity' of the Western bit, or those used by the horsemen of the Iberian peninsular.

Both Grisone and Pignatelli, in common with other riding masters of their era, would attach metal 'keys' to the bit so that the horse should play with the bit and retain a wet mouth. Such 'keys' are frequently seen on modern-day breaking bits.

The saddle, initially, was to all intents the war saddle of the Middle Ages. However, it was gradually adapted to appear more elegant and provide additional comfort and security. It became a padded affair, straight cut in its flap, of course, but as with the saddle of the knight high in front and with a pronounced cantle. For additional security, pads were often fitted into which the riders' thighs could be

Top: A 16th-century Italian saddle presented to Charles V. This is essentially the **Selle Royale** of classical equitation. A very similar saddle is used today in the Spanish Riding School in Vienna and is still made in some numbers in Portugal and Spain where it is in general use.
Right: A horseman of Andalucia riding in a saddle of the same design, but with the heavy Iberian 'slipper' stirrups of that country. He rides with one hand on a cavesson rein and a looping curb rein. Note again the tail casing which differs only slightly from those found in the Pazyryk tombs.

Left: The English master, William Cavendish, Duke of Newcastle (1592-1676), inventor of the running rein but here seen riding with a single curb rein. The heavy horses used for school riding compelled riders to make use of very strong curb bits to obtain the required control.

on that used in the *manège*. Military saddles were often no more than utility versions of the school saddles, but they were practical, as they retained the dip seat, although for the most part the stirrup bar was still placed so far to the front as to prevent the leg from being held other than somewhat in advance of the girth.

The British tradition

In Britain, 'scientific' equitation never really became established. However, riding and the equipment that went with it was to undergo a change following the Stuart Restoration of 1660. Hunting had always been the great sport of the British, but, until that time, it had been confined to the hunting of the stag and hare. Then, as a result of the serious depletion of the deer population in the Civil War, foxes, previously considered as vermin, became the chief quarry. To pursue this swift, straight-running animal, hounds had to be bred lighter and faster. Horses, too, had to be able to gallop and, increasingly, those who rode them had to be prepared to jump if they wished to be in at the kill. In the first place, there was no time to go round obstacles and remain in touch with hounds, while, in the second, the new enclosures of hitherto open pasture and common land were not only changing the face of the countryside but also providing ever more jumping for foxhunters.

By the 18th century foxhunting was a popular sport and the British, either disdainful or unaware of academic riding as carried on outside their island, rode their good horses, largely by the light of nature, over and through whatever came in their way in their devotion to the pursuit of the fox.

The British foxhunter was not an 'educated' horseman in the Continental sense, but followers of the sport were brave, adaptable and willing to let their horses do their full share of the work involved. In a sense they were more in the mould of the ancient horsemen from Asia, although, of course, they rode much longer. Frequently, however, they used a light snaffle bridle, without even the adornment of a

wedged. It survives in only slightly altered form in the *selle royale* of the classical schools of Vienna (the Spanish Riding School) and of Saumur in France, while examples can still be bought throughout Spain and Portugal.

Refinements over the centuries

As far as the classical form of indoor riding was concerned, equipment altered little over the next 200 years, though it perhaps became more streamlined. The 'flying trench' became a bradoon proper and the curb bit became more refined and often also more ingenious in its construction. England's Duke of Newcastle, a notable, though conceited, master of the equestrian art, invented the running or draw rein and placed great reliance on its efficacy. The side-rein attached to a body roller or to a saddle was in general use and was, in fact, the forerunner of Newcastle's running rein. Long-reining, following the use of the lunge rein in the exercise of 'treading the ring', was practised in the early 16th century as, too, was the ploy of fitting weights to a horse's feet to encourage the elevated action in collected paces. The weights were often wooden balls attached to a strap which encircled the fetlock, the ball lying above the heel. A modern version of this instrument can be seen in any stable where American Saddlebreds or Tennessee Walkers are kept.

Nonetheless the accent by the 18th century had shifted decisively from the forceful methods of Grisone to a form of scientific equitation in which the horse was trained with understanding and kindness. This change in emphasis was profoundly influenced by the teachings of François Robichon de la Guérinière (1688–1751). Academic equitation dominated European thinking throughout the century and beyond it—except perhaps in England—and most equipment was based

CHAPTER ONE · HISTORY AND DEVELOPMENT

noseband, which in its drop version—that is, fitted low and below the bit—was virtually a compulsory schooling device on the Continent. Sometimes they might employ a martingale, but all in all their main aim was to encourage their horses to go on freely rather than discourage them from this. Later, however, the snaffle bridle went out of fashion, and in many hunting 'countries' it became 'incorrect' to hunt in anything other than a double bridle—the term used to describe the combination of bit and bradoon.

The necessity of jumping fences meant that foxhunters wisely eschewed the high pommel of the medieval saddle and, to meet their needs, a saddle which by comparison had a flat seat was developed. It was neat, unobtrusive, not exaggerated and extremely durable. Such saddlery was, indeed, to become the envy of every other nation and would in time be avidly sought after by riders everywhere.

The hunting saddle
Although the saddle was fairly straight in its flap, in accordance with the length of stirrup leather in general use, it was wide in the seat and waist, thus distributing the weight of the rider over as large an area as possible. The panel of this saddle (the cushion between the tree and the horse's back) was correspondingly large and followed the shape of the flaps. In later years it was called a 'full panel'. For the most part the panels of these saddles were covered in serge cloth, which might sometimes be overlaid with a covering of linen so as to prevent the serge being dirtied and the panel from absorbing too great a quantity of sweat. The stuffing material used was short, springy wool of various qualities, which could be 'regulated' by the saddler so that the saddle fitted correctly to the horse's back.

This type of saddle, built on a handmade beechwood tree, persisted with no more than minor variations throughout the 19th century and well into the 20th century. In time, saddles of this general outline came to be known by the common title of the 'English hunting saddle'.

In fact, the saddle naturally underwent changes over the course of years as particular makers produced their own specialities, but the pattern remained, nonetheless, the example for saddle manufacturers to follow in many parts of the world. As a saddle it had disadvantages, but it was not entirely ill-suited to its purpose.

In the days before motorized transport, a hunting man spent many hours in the saddle during a day and covered distances which many modern riders would consider unthinkable. Tired riders naturally shift in their saddles to ease their fatigue, but this is hardly the best thing for a horse's back, since the friction which a fidgeting rider produces between panel and back can cause soreness. The shape of these saddles, with their broad bearing surfaces distributing the weight over a wide area of the back, certainly helped to mitigate the possible detrimental effects of long days in the saddle, but whether their durability was an advantage or not is uncertain. It is probable that, because they lasted so long—saddles 50 years old and more were by no means uncommon—they helped to delay the acceptance of the purpose-designed saddles which were so much needed when sport, in terms of show jumping and eventing, became the greatest influence in saddlery design.

Variants and developments
One of the first outside influences was polo, a game played in Persia and in areas of Assam in pre-Christian times and introduced to England in 1869 by army officers who had learnt the game in India. It influenced the construction of saddles in a number of ways. Polo players needed to sit close to their ponies, which the full panels of the traditional hunting saddles did not always allow. To overcome this problem, the bottom part of the panel, which would have come under the lower leg, was removed, the remaining 'half' panel being called, in time, a 'Rugby' panel. Rugby was an early British polo centre. In addition, polo, more than any other equestrian sport, was responsible for the narrowing of the waist or 'twist' of the saddle. The waist is the tapered area between the pommel or head of the saddle and the seat proper. A narrow twist does not spread the rider's thighs and allows him greater contact down the length of the leg. Short-legged riders will appreciate the discomfort which could be caused by a wide-waisted saddle, since the thighs are spread so much that the effective use of the leg becomes difficult.

Increasingly, too, saddle panels began to be lined with leather. This, although it made the job of regulating the panels more difficult, resisted the absorption of sweat more efficiently and was easier to keep clean. A further innovation was the use of felt pads to replace the traditional wool stuffing and felt panelled saddles, their Rugby-type panels lined with leather, became extremely popular. Right up to the time when the modern spring-tree saddles became available, they were made in fairly large quantities, although they never superseded their stuffed wool predecessors.

Other late 19th-century innovations included the use of numerous patented 'safety bars', designed to release the stirrup leather in the event of a fall. They reflected a period when horsemen seemed more than usually concerned with 'devices' of one sort or another, not so much

Left: The picture of Eclipse by George Stubbs. Eclipse, unbeaten in all his races, was arguably the world's greatest racehorse and Stubbs the world's greatest painter of horses. Eclipse is wearing a light racing saddle, which is in fact no more than a cut-down hunting saddle of the period, and a racing bridle, without a noseband and fitted with a simple cheek snaffle. The surcingle is an extra precaution against the saddle slipping.

perhaps so far as their saddles were concerned, but more particularly as far as bits and bitting were concerned.

At the same time, the shape of the saddle tree began to vary. This was a more useful development than the one described above. The head of the tree was shaped back to accommodate high withers. A head might be either half or full cutback, while, in the case of saddles made for American-gaited horses, the head was cut back so far as to earn the name 'cowmouth'.

In the area of bitting, which was dominated again to a considerable degree by Britain, the centre of the bit and the horse furniture industry being the Midlands town of Walsall, the 19th century, in particular, saw bits produced in enormous quantity and in quite astonishing variety. But, for all the ingenuity expended, nothing really new emerged; the designs were no more than variations—sometimes quite complex ones—on the basic forms of bit which had existed for almost 2,000 years.

The principal influence at this time on equestrian developments was the equipment demanded for the carriage horse, an important aspect of the social scene. All manner of bits were devised to impose the high head carriage demanded by the high society of the time. The gag, taken over with enthusiasm by polo players, had its origin in the variety of checks and bearing reins used in the carriage trade, although once more, the device had been known hundreds of years previously. Other riding bits in every shape and size also abounded, most of them designed to produce a high carriage of head and neck.

American saddlery followed the pattern of the British product on the eastern side of the continent and was for the most part imported from Britain. In general terms, this applies today, though imports increasingly came from West Germany, and other Continental countries. But the Americans also had a further requirement in respect of the breeds which they had developed for their own particular purposes. The American gaited horses—the American Saddlebred, the Missouri Foxtrotter and the Tennessee Walker—used paces which are now lost to Europe and required specialist saddlery as a consequence. They needed in particular the flat-

CHAPTER ONE · HISTORY AND DEVELOPMENT

seated, wide-flapped saddle and the various training equipment used to encourage the extravagant gaits. The curb bits used resemble the Western 'spade' bit, but the saddle itself is unique. The native industry naturally produces high quality Western saddles and related equipment in vast quantity, but surprisingly the USA does not have an industry producing European-type saddlery.

The Caprilli watershed

At the start of the present century, however, one of the great watersheds in the evolution of horse tack occurred. This, perhaps the most significant development in the context of modern equitation, came about as a result of the theories expounded by a little known Italian cavalry captain, Federico Caprilli, whose short life spanned the years between 1868 and 1907. In the context of his time, and having regard for the very narrow and conservative field in which he operated, Caprilli's brief and necessarily incomplete *Principi di Equitazione di Campagna*, published in 1901, had much the same impact on the equestrian world as did Darwin's *Origin of the Species* on the more general one.

At the turn of the century, and for many years before, Continental riding was dominated by the cavalry schools, particularly those of Germany. Unlike their British counterparts, the cavalry officers these schools produced did not hunt on horseback and civilians had virtually no influence. The German cavalry schools employed a near-'classical' method of instruction, demanding considerable collection but devoting little time to jumping and cross-country riding. Basically, instruction of recruits was within the confines of the school and the purpose of cavalry was still enshrined in the philosophy of the charge—even though much of their instruction would hardly have fitted the recipients with the necessary skills involved, unless the nature of the terrain had been that of a billiard table.

Caprilli appreciated, somewhat in advance of the generals, that the traditional role of cavalry was no longer valid. A charge against machine-guns was simply not viable—the modern role of cavalry would be increasingly concerned with reconnaissance, which, indeed, had been its original role in the distant past. What

CHAPTER ONE · HISTORY AND DEVELOPMENT

was needed was a cavalry arm that would be able to move swiftly over all types of country, returning, in fact, to the early light horsemen of Asia.

Caprilli saw clearly, however, that existing cavalry instruction would not produce a mounted arm of the sort he thought necessary and it was for that reason that he evolved a new system of training which is now termed the Italian or 'Forward Seat'.

Caprilli abolished the work in the indoor schools. Instead, he trained riders and horses over the kind of terrain in which they might expect to operate. He sought to teach natural balance by natural training. He demanded that the head and neck of the horse be given full freedom, and that his riders do nothing to disturb the horse's balance. By establishing

Top: Lady riders in the 1920s often competed in point-to-point races riding side-saddle. As the sport became more professional and came closer to steeplechasing, equipment and dress changed accordingly. **Above:** Portrait of a park hack by the English artist Herring (c. 1880). The saddle is typical of the period, the seat probably quilted for comfort, with the panel swelling in front of the knee. **Left:** Henry Alken's view of the Belvoir field, all riding with a long leather in plain hunting saddles which were renowned throughout the world for their style and superlative craftsmanship. All the riders use double bridles but there is not a noseband to be seen. **Far left:** To obtain maximum control the polo player has to resort to martingales, side reins and fairly heavy bridles, but he rides in what is virtually an improved version of the conventional hunting saddle.

CHAPTER ONE · HISTORY AND DEVELOPMENT

Far right, top: This photograph clearly shows the need for a forward-cut panel and flap for the higher levels of show jumping.
Bottom: The classical forward position is not always possible or desirable on the cross-country course and for this reason a general purpose rather than a pure jumping saddle is preferred.
Centre: Trail riding in America. The riders are by no means proficient but they manage well enough with the help of the big Western saddle. **Right:** Carriage driving is an increasingly popular—if very expensive—equestrian sport, involving complicated harness for the highly trained horses and great skill on the part of the driver.
Below: An American rider in the classic jumping position of which Federico Caprilli would have approved.

this definite policy of non-intervention, Caprilli was not so much overturning the classical precept as re-affirming it. In essence he was saying that, if it was correct for the rider to sit in balance with his horse at the slower paces, then it was correct for him to do so at the faster ones as well. Therefore, he encouraged his riders to shorten their leathers and to 'perch' in their saddles, the seat at the gallop being raised out of the plate, the hands following the head through the rein and the lower legs being drawn back behind the vertical with the knees pointed. The body weight at the faster paces was then positioned well over the horse's centre of balance and was the least possible burden to the horse, particularly over fences.

Caprilli's theories were expanded after his death by his pupil, Piero Santini. Though they were never accepted in their entirety, they nevertheless form a very large part of modern equestrian thought and practice. Current teaching is possibly a system of half-intervention practised in conjunction with a mixture of Caprilli's forward riding and classical schooling on the flat.

Although Italian teams won show jumping contests in the first decade of the century employing the Caprilli seat, the effect of Caprilli's teaching on saddle design was not immediately apparent. Flaps were cut further forward to accommodate the shorter length of leather used, but the seat of the saddle and in particular the bars remained much the same as ever. In other words, a forward flap was grafted on to what was basically an English hunting saddle. In consequence, whilst riders aimed at sitting or perhaps leaning forward over fences, their actual weight was carried too far back; the result was that they were behind the horse's movement.

The Italian firm of Pariani produced a 'forward seat' saddle between the two world wars, the first in fact with a flexible seat (spring tree), and in Britain Santini produced a similar saddle on what was termed a 'parchment' tree. Both were an improvement on the old hunting saddle, but in neither was it appreciated that the positioning of the bars was critical.

The jumping saddle
It was not until nearly 50 years after Caprilli's death that a correctly designed jumping saddle (which would act as a base for a less exaggerated all-purpose riding saddle) gained acceptance. It came about, surprisingly, in the one country where its acceptance would have been thought most unlikely—Britain. There, hunting folk until well into the 1950s poured scorn on the 'monkey-up-a-stick' style of riding and clung tenaciously to the saddles left to them by their fathers and grandfathers. Even more surprising is not only the fact that the new saddle was produced in Britain but that it was promoted vigorously by a Spanish nobleman, Count Iliàs Toptani. To him, together with his collaborators Colonel F E Gibson and Messrs George Parker of London, should go the credit for the development of saddles which were designed specifically for the precision riding demanded by the equestrian sports of the latter half of the 20th century. Without such saddles, the standards would not be as high today.

Not only was Toptani the first to appreciate the significance of the stirrup bar position, but was also the first to design a saddle in which riders could sit in balance at speed and over fences without undue physical effort. In fact, the Toptani saddle helped the rider to ride and to ride more effectively. It, together with other modern saddles, is discussed in the following chapters. Interestingly enough, these new saddles, the precision instruments of riding, resemble, at least as far as their dipped seats are concerned, the very earliest saddles.

As for the methods of bitting, these have followed the advances in equestrian thinking and have become far more simple. The snaffle and drop noseband has become the accepted bridle, with the double bridle (the bit and bradoon) being used with the horse in a more advanced stage of training.

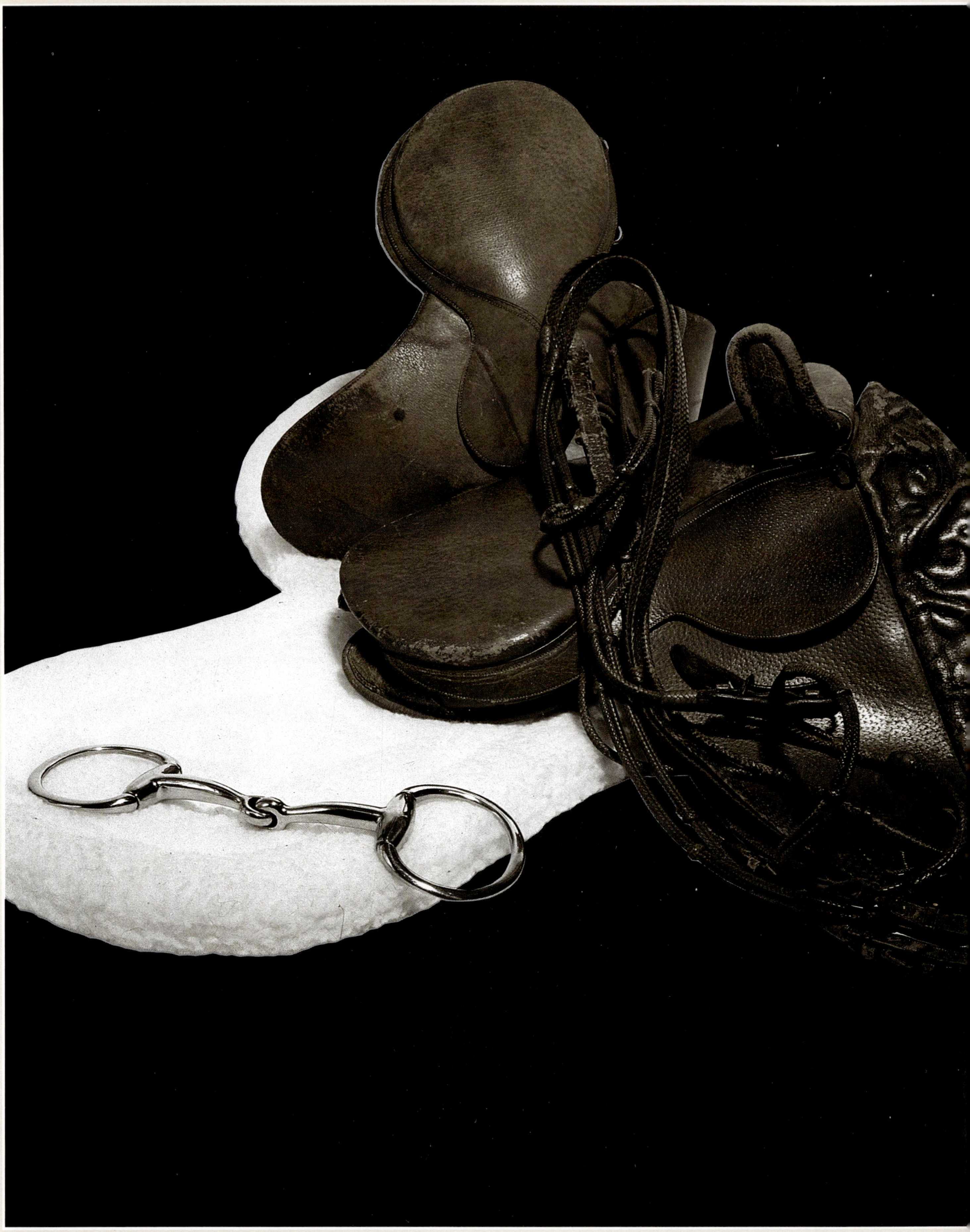

CHAPTER TWO

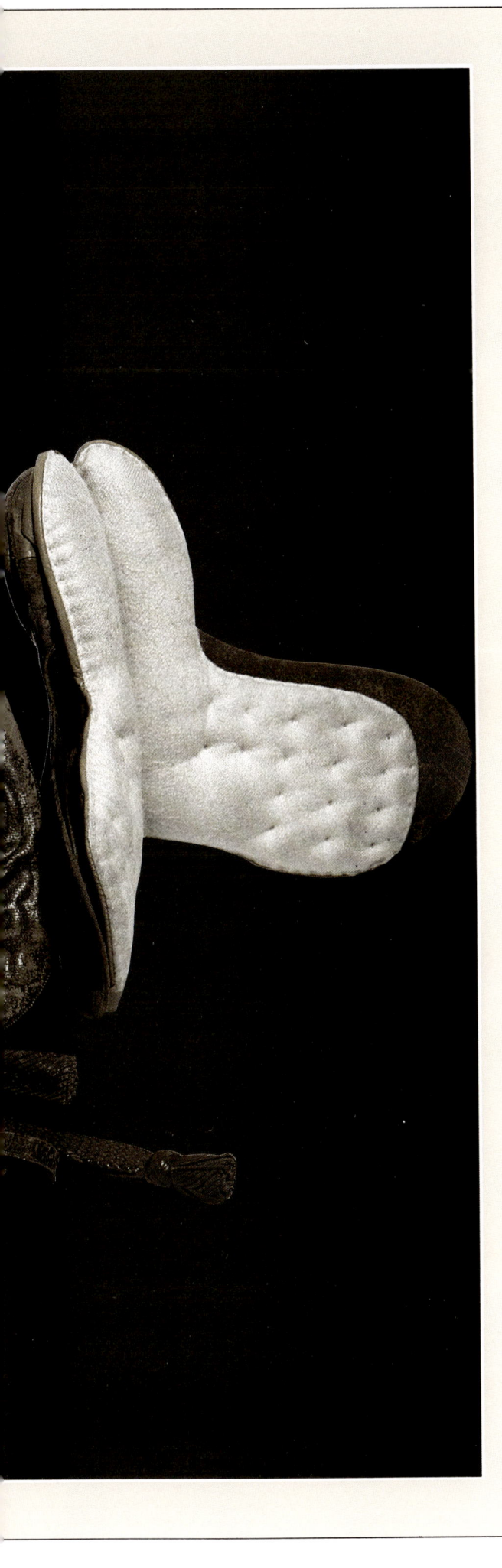

Making the Modern Saddle

Tanning and currying, the leather-making skills

Saddle construction

A group of 19th-century English 'apprentice' saddles made in miniature as an exercise and used as samples by commercial travellers. The snaffle bit gives an idea of their size.

CHAPTER TWO · MAKING THE MODERN SADDLE

Making the Modern Saddle

Traditionally, leather has been the principal material used in the manufacture of saddlery. During the last decade or so, however, other materials have been introduced in order to reduce the heavy costs involved. Nevertheless, leather still remains the first choice for saddles and bridles of the best quality. New saddlery should always be examined carefully. The presence of a greyish overtinge is a good sign, since it indicates the presence of grease in the leather, which should be supple as a consequence.

The quality of leather varies greatly. Good leather will last for years and retain its strength, if cared for correctly. Poor leather, on the other hand, may break as soon as it comes under stress. The latter is naturally less expensive than the former, but, if used for either saddles or bridles, it can be dangerous; a broken stirrup leather, girth strap, bridle rein or headpiece can cause serious accidents, even to the extent of endangering the lives of both horse and rider. This point should govern the selection of all leather for horse equipment, whether it is for straps on rugs or the ends of a leading or lungeing rein. A horse is a very strong animal, capable of exerting tremendous pressure and stress on the straps which are used to control him.

The quality of leather

The finest leather has a distinct 'feel' to it. It is firm but supple, slightly greasy and of good substance—that is, thickness. It is this quality which is commensurate with the material's strength. Dry leather will be brittle and thus likely to break. Leather that is 'pappy' or spongy to handle should never be used, as it is totally unsatisfactory in all respects. The natural reaction of good leather is to wrinkle when bent by hand on both the flesh—the inside—and the grain—the treated outside. On no account, however, should it 'bubble'; when released and straightened out it should return to its normal state.

Leather is made from animal skins. Some 90 per cent of the leather used in the saddlery trade comes from cow hides—the best of this coming from slow-maturing cattle, such as the Aberdeen Angus. The slower the growth, the more the leather's substance has a chance to develop and the greater will be the eventual strength of the hide. The remaining 10 per cent is accounted for by pigskins, which are used primarily for saddle seats and, at one time, for covering saddle flaps; by doeskins, used for seats, covering flaps and knee grips; and sheepskin, known in the saddlery context as basil. The skin has the wool removed; it is used, reversed, for backing saddle panels and lining cheaper saddles.

Possible defects

Imported and home-produced hides are used equally in the major saddle producing countries of the world today. Usually, imported hides have one distinct advantage as far as the temperate countries are concerned. They are less likely to be damaged by warble holes—holes made by the small grubs of the warble fly. These small breathing holes enlarge as the grub ripens. Once the grub has emerged, the hole closes over, but an extremely weak spot is left in the hide as a result.

Wire scars, caused by the extensive use of barbed wire fencing, also cause problems in the selection of sound leather. Such scars, sometimes evident on the panels of less expensive saddles, weaken the leather. They should not be seen on the tops of expensive saddles, nor on bridle leather. Wire marks can not only be a serious weakness; they can cause the

Right: After the raw skins have been cleansed they are placed in lime pits for some ten days. The lime has the effect of loosening the covering hair which is removed during the next tanning process.

CHAPTER TWO · MAKING THE MODERN SADDLE

Modern tanneries are as highly mechanised as is consistent with an industry which still has to depend upon a degree of hand working. **Left:** Rotating drums are used in the cleansing and liming of the hides. **Above:** A machine is also employed for scudding – the removal of surplus matter such as hair roots and fat.

leather to split when it is under stress.

Some wire marks on saddle flaps are erased when the pigskin finish is embossed on ordinary hide to make it match the characteristic grain of pigskin. Only very light racing saddles have real pigskin flaps. Brushed pigskin—the flesh side is brushed and used outwards—gives a suede-like finish—while doeskin is also used when extra gripping properties are required. In this instance, the skin is taken from fallow deer.

Show saddles are often entirely covered in doeskin, whereas it is more usual for show jumping and eventing saddles to have just padded knee-grips of doeskin let in, or sewn, to the flaps.

The making of leather
Hides cannot be used in their raw state; like all animal matter, they soon begin to rot. The manufacture of leather involves the twin processes of tanning and currying so as to render them imperishable. Tanning is an extremely ancient process, dating back to the days of early man. Then, tree bark—this contains tannin or tannic acid—was used to convert raw skins into leather. Mixed with water, the bark produces a liquid in which the hides are soaked. Oak bark was considered the most suitable and is still in use today.

On arrival at the tannery, the raw skins are washed thoroughly to remove dirt, salt and other unwanted contents. They are then placed in pits containing lime. After about ten days, the lime will have loosened the covering hair—the chief object of the process—while the liquid will have swelled the skins' fibres and caused them to separate into their constituent fibrils. This process increases fullness and pliability.

After removal from the lime pits, the hides are thrown back into cold water ready for scudding and rounding. As a result of this the hides take on a recognizable form, the grain side, from which the hair is now removed, becoming relatively smooth. Both operations were once done by hand, but scudding—the removal of loose protein, hair roots, gland tissue, pigment, loose fat and so on—is now done largely by machine. Rounding—the trimming of the hides—is still a hand process. Firstly, the hides are sorted, with the best being set aside for the use of the saddlery trade and other industries requiring top-quality leather. The substance of the hide is one of the chief determining factors in selection. The decision on whether to round them or not depends on whether they are to be tanned whole. In the former case, the hides are rounded—trimmed—by a rounding frame; in the latter, this process takes place before the hides are curried, the stage after tanning.

After the lime has been removed, tanning can begin. Either vegetable tanning, using bark, can be employed; alternatively, mineral tanning, using alum salts or, more recently, chrome salts, can be used. The latter are very resistant to water. Chrome leather (characterized by a blue-grey finish) is extremely strong and is used for girths, the leg straps on New Zealand rugs and sometimes in the making of headcollars. The hides are put into suspenders (deep pits), where they are stacked in the liquor one on top of the other. After several weeks, they are removed so that the tanning liquid can be replaced and are then put back into the pits, this time for a longer period of several months.

45

CHAPTER TWO · MAKING THE MODERN SADDLE

The last stage in the tanning process is termed finishing, an operation which takes time and has to be done very carefully. The hides are oiled, rolled and then dried, the last process being critical, since it is essential that no variations in temperature occur. If a drying hide is exposed to even a slight draught, it will crinkle at the edges and become stained as a result.

Currying and completion

Once tanned, the leather is curried or dressed, but first the uncut hides are rounded. Hides can be cut either as a half-hide or side (split from shoulder to tail down the backbone), or as a back (in the same way as a half-hide, but with the thinner belly portion being removed). If the purchaser requires, the whole hide can be purchased without it being cut; alternatively, it can be cut to separate the belly and the shoulder from the best part of the leather. This area, known as the butts, is on each side of the spine and is used to make the best quality bridles and saddles. The shoulders, which are strong but coarse in texture, are used for headcollars and for the flaps of less expensive saddles.

After rounding, the hides are placed in vats of cold water overnight to swell the leather and remove the scum, which floats to the top of the vats. The swollen hides are then passed through a splitting machine to ensure that the leather is of uniform thickness—no hide is consistent in this respect—and then through the shaving machine to provide the correct substance. This machine is capable of very fine adjustment. After a further few days in the vats, the hides are placed in large revolving drums, fitted with slats on the inside. These drums are first filled with acid, which, in the beating process, both removes bacteria and other foreign matter and cleanses the leather thoroughly. When the acid has done its work, clean water is substituted to wash out the acid.

The next step is the drying process, known as slicking out, which removes the water from the hides. Then most of the natural growth marks are removed by machine. The leather is then at what is termed the russet stage and is hung up to dry on frames, being secured by toggles, a form of clip like a giant clothes peg. When dry, the best leather is put briefly through a buffing machine, before being dyed to the appropriate colour.

In the saddlery trade, dye is applied by

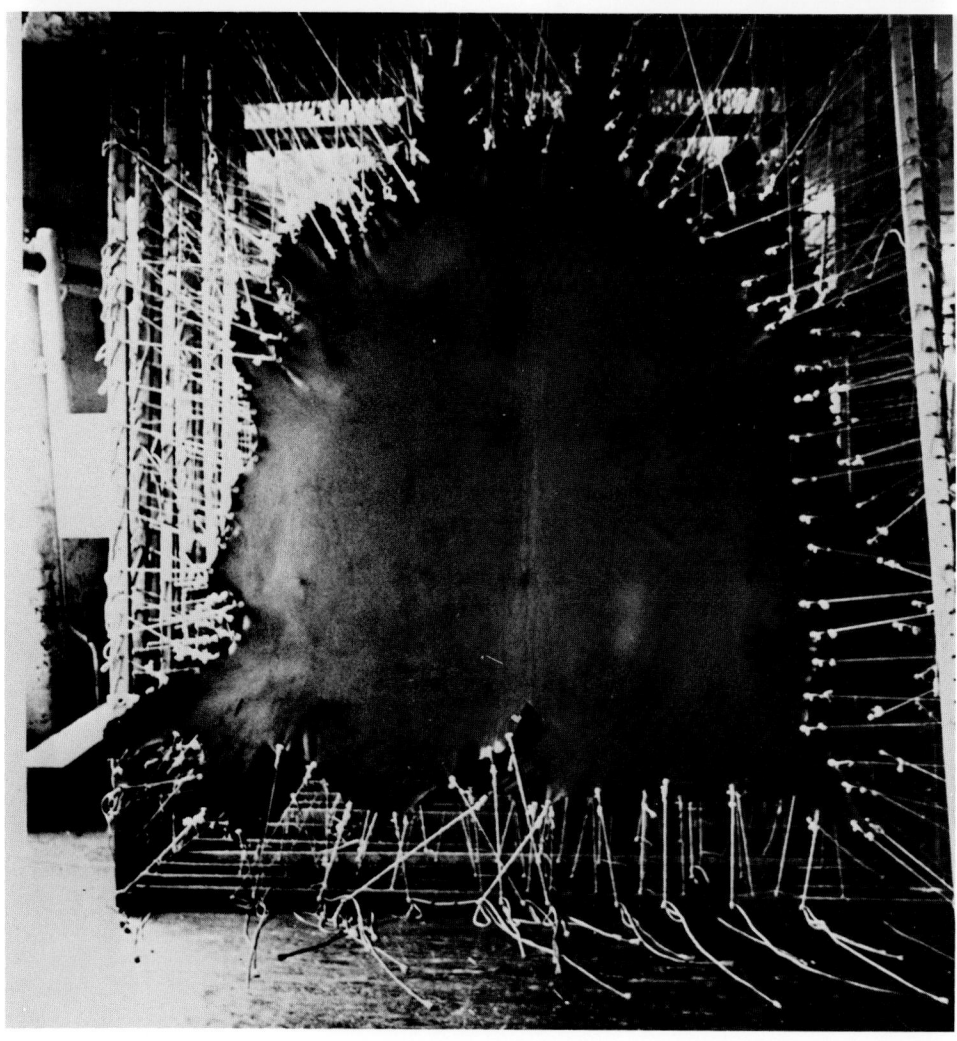

CHAPTER TWO · MAKING THE MODERN SADDLE

Opposite, top: Hides are passed through a splitting machine so as to obtain a consistent thickness. **Bottom:** This hide is pegged out for drying. It is important that the temperature remains constant during this process and that the hide is not subjected to draughts. **Top:** Pegging out the hide on the mesh drying frame. **Right:** Detail of the toggles used. **Left, above:** Although economics dictate the maximum use of machinery, there is no substitute for the skilled hand-polishing of leather. **Below:** Spraying the leather to the required colour.

CHAPTER TWO · MAKING THE MODERN SADDLE

Left: A store-room of top quality leather, which is always kept on racks and laid flat. Leather, like wine and cheese, improves with age, acquiring a greater firmness as it matures. Unfortunately, modern economic conditions do not always allow for long periods of storage.

pad staining (other leather is dyed in vats) or sometimes by spraying. The usual shades are London, a light colour; Havana, a richer brown; and Warwick, which is darker still. Black is also favoured, especially in the USA (this colour is, by convention, required on heavier harness leathers). The plating machine then flattens the leather again, while any embossing—of flap leather, for instance—is also applied. Finally the leather passes through the greasing department to be treated liberally with tallow and cod oil. The more the natural substance of the leather, the greater will be its capacity to absorb the two preservatives.

Saddlery manufacture

For the most part, the saddlery business relies upon individual craftsmen, rather than mass production. Much of the work is still done by hand, although machine stitching is now almost universal practice, except for countries where labour is cheap and plentiful, as in the east. The larger manufacturers employ production-line methods, but, for the most part, the construction of a top-quality saddle is still the work of individual craftsmen. However, the leather specialist's finished product depends on the work of his wood and metal counterparts, since they determine the shape and type of the tree, the foundation upon which the saddle is built. The larger saddle manufacturing companies sometimes have separate departments to produce trees, but most rely on specialist tree-making companies.

The types of tree

The three principal types of tree are the rigid tree, the spring tree and, to a lesser degree, that made of fibreglass. Use of fibreglass means that a somewhat different technique must be applied to the building of the saddle. Rigid trees, so-called to distinguish them from the sprung variety, used to be carved by hand from beechwood. Today they are made from strips of the same wood heat-bonded, or laminated, in a mould with urea *formaldehyde* resin. This technique makes the end product both stronger and considerably lighter than the older type. Spring trees are made in the same way, but achieve the resilience implied by the name by means of two pieces of sprung steel laid from head to cantle of the saddle.

From the foundation upwards

The basic framework is covered in muslin. A waterproof coating is then applied to make the framework and its covering stronger and more resistant to the moisture created by the heat from both horse and rider when the saddle is in hard use. The tree is reinforced with steel or Duralumin plates, the latter being lighter than the former. A gullet plate is fitted on the underside of the pommel, while a head plate is placed on top, the two being riveted together through the tree to form a very strong rigid arch that will be positioned, eventually, over the horse's back behind the withers and straddling the spine. The cantle is also reinforced with steel plates—those in a rigid tree being shorter than those in a spring tree—so as to hold the back of the saddle tree together. With spring trees, the springs—long strips of sprung steel—are riveted in place where the reinforcing plates are fixed underneath at each end to follow the line of the horse's back on either side of the spine. The stirrup bars are also riveted to the tree, usually with two rivets, but sometimes, in inexpensive saddles, with only one. Stirrup bars are either forged, which is the safest method, or cast. They are stamped accordingly.

The bars can be fitted on the outside of the tree, so that, in the finished saddle, they stand a little proud, or they can be shaped so that they are recessed into the flap. In the latter case, they will not cause an uncomfortable bulge under the rider's

CHAPTER TWO · MAKING THE MODERN SADDLE

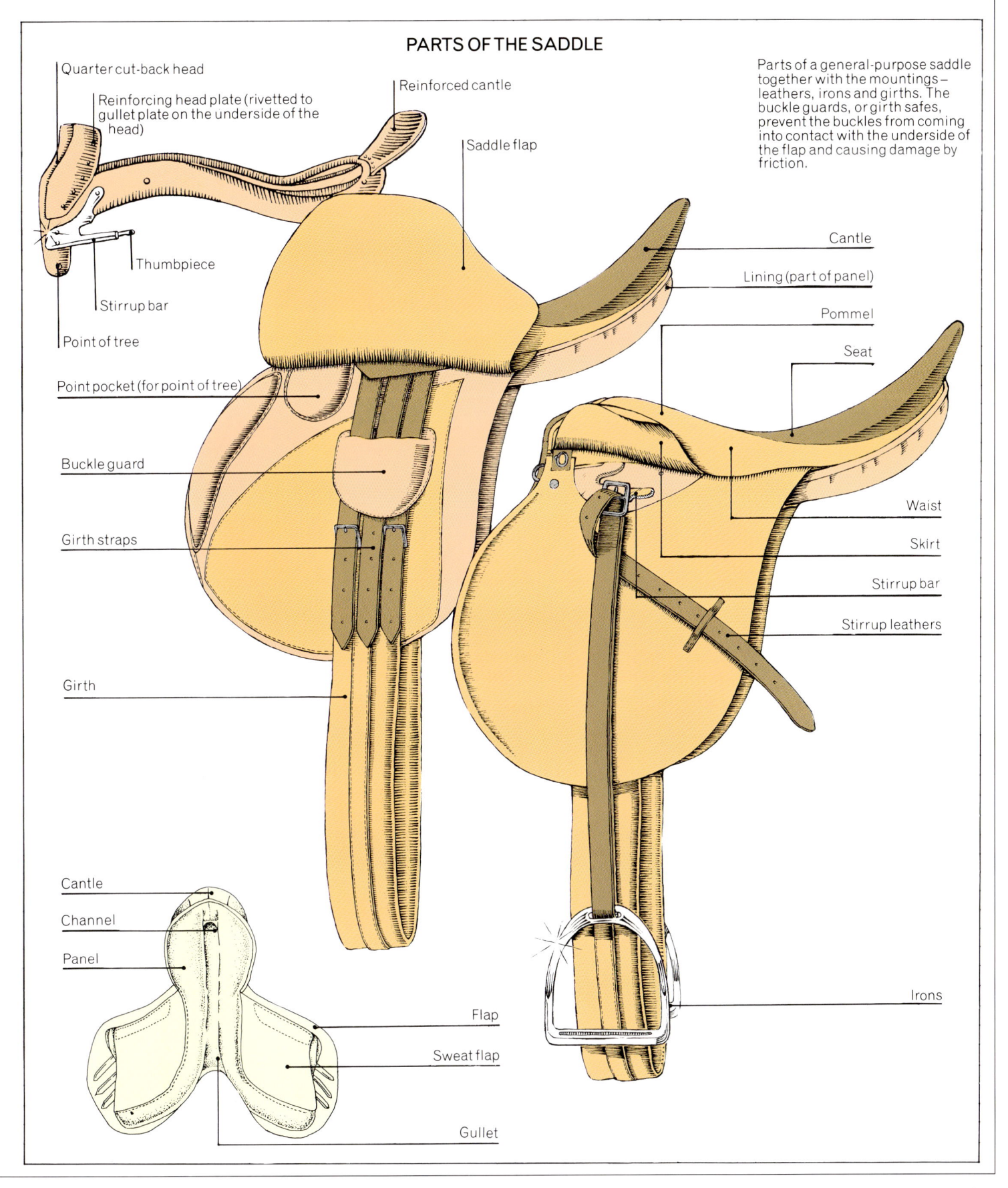

PARTS OF THE SADDLE

Parts of a general-purpose saddle together with the mountings – leathers, irons and girths. The buckle guards, or girth safes, prevent the buckles from coming into contact with the underside of the flap and causing damage by friction.

- Quarter cut-back head
- Reinforcing head plate (rivetted to gullet plate on the underside of the head)
- Reinforced cantle
- Saddle flap
- Thumbpiece
- Stirrup bar
- Point of tree
- Point pocket (for point of tree)
- Buckle guard
- Girth straps
- Girth
- Cantle
- Lining (part of panel)
- Pommel
- Seat
- Waist
- Skirt
- Stirrup bar
- Stirrup leathers
- Irons
- Cantle
- Channel
- Panel
- Flap
- Sweat flap
- Gullet

49

CHAPTER TWO · MAKING THE MODERN SADDLE

Trees of modern saddles are made in sections from strips of beech wood, heat-bonded in a mould. The sections are assembled **(right)** and trimmed with a fret **(below left)**. **Below right, top:** A cut-back spring tree. **Bottom:** A rigid tree without the metal springs set from front to rear.

thigh. The ends of the saddle head, situated behind the shoulder, are called the points and largely determine how well the saddle will fit on the horse. In older saddles, the points were long and therefore the variety of horses the saddle would fit was limited as a result. In modern saddles, the points are cut off short and finished with leather to make what are known as flexible points. These have the advantage of allowing a greater range of fittings, while, as far as the rider is concerned, there is no chance of them projecting to form a lump under the thigh.

Trees are made in a number of sizes—ranging from 12in long up to 18in and sometimes bigger. Each size comes in a wide, medium or narrow fitting to suit the great majority of horses' backs, all of which differ in shape. Variations also occur in the type of head (the front arch of the tree). This depends, in part, on the purposes for which the saddle is intended. Dressage and show saddles, for instance, will employ either a vertical head or one that is cut back, so as to allow a greater range of fitting over the withers. Jumping and cross-country saddles usually have a sloped head, but they, too, may employ the cut-back variety. The technical object of the latter is to allow for high withers, but the present-day trend seems to be to use this type of head whether this is the case or not.

A relatively recent innovation is the fibreglass tree, which, after much initial experiment, seemed to be proving itself satisfactory. However, disadvantages became evident as saddles made with fibreglass trees were subjected to long use. The shape of the tree was liable to change, it was inclined to break and, despite the holes in the seat area—made to allow moisture to flow through—the heat and sweat naturally generated by a horse in work was insufficiently dispersed. In the field of racing, however, where the work load is concentrated, fibreglass trees are used extensively and with great success.

Setting the seat
The first stage in setting the saddle seat on the tree is the laying of pre-stretched

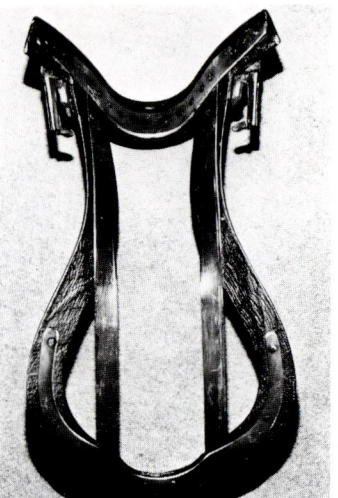

50

CHAPTER TWO · MAKING THE MODERN SADDLE

Left: Finishing the tree by rasping. **Above:** Fitting the metal reinforcement. **Bottom:** A cut-back, almost 'cow-mouth' tree, with laminations clearly visible.

canvas webs from head to cantle. The webs are secured by tingles, tiny, small-headed nails, which are tacked through a small strip of leather laid over the webs and so into the tree itself. The leather strip acts as a washer to prevent the webs from coming away from the tacks. The girth strap webs are then placed across the waist, or twist, of the tree, traversing the longer tree webs and again being tacked to the tree. The rear two girth straps are fastened to these webs, while the third—the forward one—is either stitched to a web going right over the tree, or to one fastened around the tree on either side. Behind the strap webs are placed the back webs and the back straining canvas, a piece of material shaped to cover the whole of the seat behind the waist. This is stretched tightly and then tacked down in position. The combination of tightly-drawn crossing webs—the ones that traverse the long webs force the latter downwards—gives a firm, springy base to the seat. Small crescent-shaped pieces of leather called bellies are nailed to the seat's edges. These save the rider from being forced to sit uncomfortably on the hard edges of the tree.

Covering and padding
The next stage in the preparation of the seat is covering and padding. In older

CHAPTER TWO · MAKING THE MODERN SADDLE

saddles—and in some modern ones, too—wool is the material used for the latter. Present practice, however, is to use rubber or plastic foam rather than wool to provide a resilient seat; this method also entails less labour.

Where wool is used, the seat is covered first with tightly-drawn serge. A small slit is made in this for the wool to be inserted with a seat steel, a thin rod especially designed for this purpose. The wool is spread evenly under the covering by means of an awl, which can be poked through the serge.

When spring trees are used, the two metal strips are covered either in thin leather or linen tape. The covering lessens the risk of the sharp edges of the springs cutting into a panel, if one becomes displaced; it also prevents moisture from rusting the springs.

Traditionally, the final covering of the seat is made of pigskin. As well as being hard-wearing, this has the advantage of being easy to stretch when it is wetted, preparatory to the seat being blocked on the tree. However, many modern saddles—particularly ones of German manufacture—employ calfskin for the seat. Though these are satisfactory, they are more inclined to split and, in general, do not wear as well as the pigskin ones.

The skirts are sewn to the seat, usually by hand but sometimes today by machine, using a hide welt. This is followed by the fitting of the girth straps to the doubled-up ends of the strap webs and then the fitting of the flaps. These can either be plain, blocked (shaped over the knee-roll of the panel), or inset with grips of doeskin or a similar material covering a foam plastic base.

Finally comes the fitting of the panel. Whatever its shape, the panel has the same function of providing a cushion between the tree and the horse's back. Today, it is almost invariably covered in a supple panel hide and is filled either with wool—the advantage of this is that its thickness can be regulated to suit the horse's back—or with pre-cut pieces of plastic foam. There are, however, saddles made with felt panels, like the English show saddles and the ones for the American Walking Horse. When completed, the panel is laced to the saddle top.

The only economy that can be made in the making of saddles is through the use of inferior materials. A seat, for instance, can be set with a covering of hessian, which will probably result in its collapse after a short period of use. The number of girth straps can be reduced to two, panels can be made entirely from the much cheaper, but far less satisfactory, basil, while seats are made from materials other than pig-

CHAPTER TWO · MAKING THE MODERN SADDLE

Opposite, top left: Section of a tree showing the initial web and canvas seat covered by the tightly-drawn, wool-stuffed serge. **Top right:** The pre-stretched webs being tacked across a tree to provide a foundation for the seat. **Below:** Cutting the component parts of the saddle is the work of a highly-skilled craftsman who cuts a hide with the minimum wastage. **Above left:** Using a razor-sharp saddler's knife the craftsman shapes the leather top on the tree. **Above right:** Fitting the girth straps to the tree webs. **Left:** A saddle panel ready for fitting. The slits in the body of the panel through which the stuffing wool is inserted are clearly visible, as are the leather point pockets into which the tree points are fitted.

skin and flaps from the roughest shoulder leather. In days gone by, saddle panels (stuffed with wool) were frequently covered with serge, a material which had some advantages in respect of comfort and ease of panel regulation, but was difficult to keep clean. For this reason, serge panels were frequently overlined with linen.

Bridlework
As with the manufacture of saddles, the pursuit of quality should be the keynote in the making of bridles and other accessories. The best bridles are cut from the butts, the finest leather, and the buckles must be of the same quality.

There are two ways of attaching the bit, or bits, to the bridle. They can be sewn to the bridle, which makes the changing of bits an expensive operation as well as weakening the area of attachment; alternatively, the bits are secured by neat hook studs, the billet passing round the bit ring and being fastened to the stud on the inside of the rein or cheekpiece. The width of a cheekpiece may vary from ½in—for a pony show bridle, for instance—to as much as ⅞in or more for a hunter's bridle.

The use of modern, man-made materials in place of the traditional ones is, of course, evident in the saddlery trade. Headcollars, girths and even bridles can be obtained in nylon, while plastic foam is used for a number of tasks. Nevertheless, **saddlery as a whole relies firmly on the basic natural materials that have been employed almost since the beginning of man's association with the horse.**

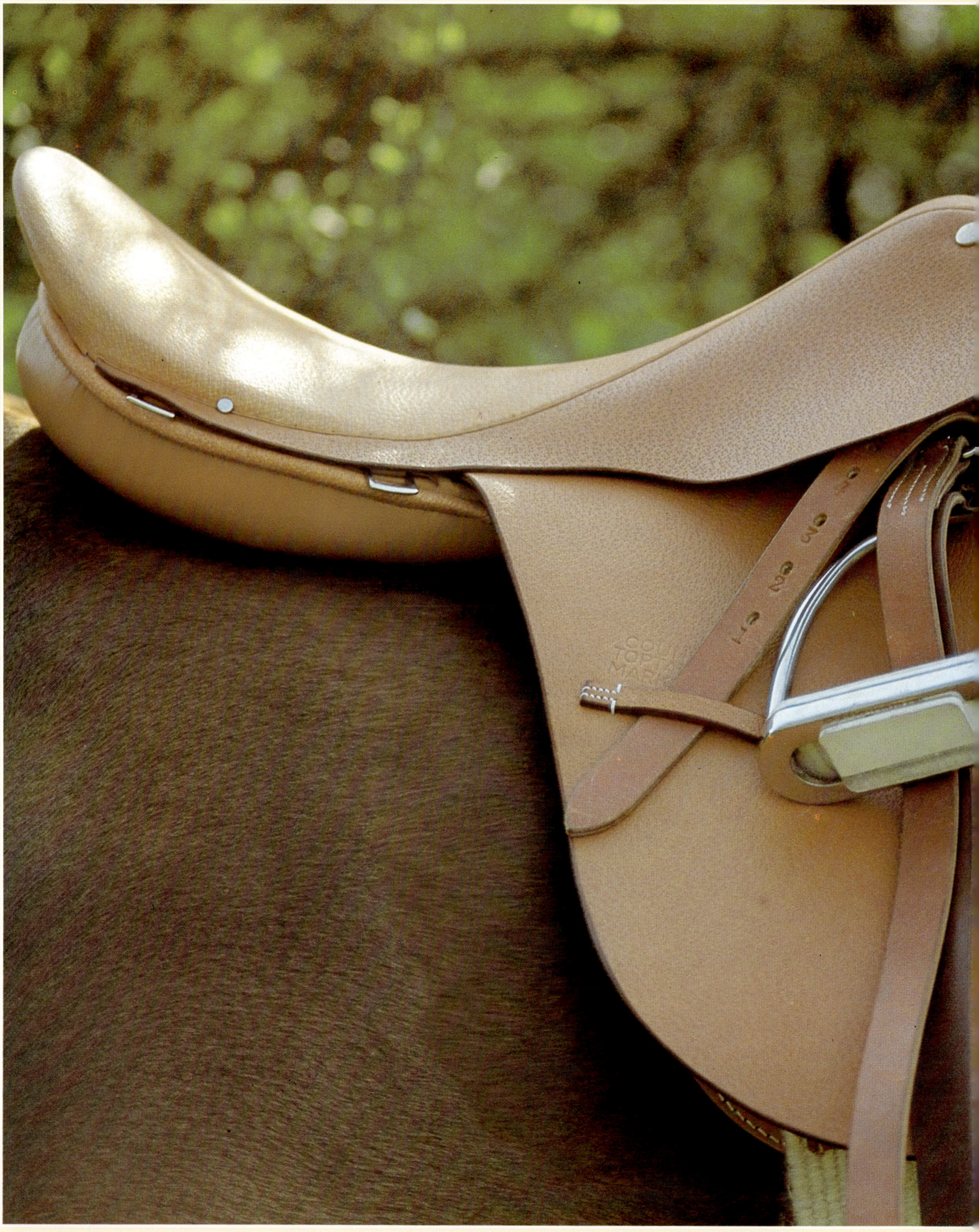

CHAPTER THREE

The Twentieth-Century Saddle

Fitness for Purpose
Some Variations
Mountings
Numnahs
Fitting

The Toptani saddle, developed after the Second World War, has been a most important influence, making it easier for the rider to sit over the horse's centre of balance at all paces, particularly when jumping.

CHAPTER THREE · THE TWENTIETH-CENTURY SADDLE

The Saddle · Fitness for Purpose

The design of modern saddles has been governed by the requirements of the modern equestrian sports in the Olympic disciplines of show jumping, eventing and dressage. Naturally enough, there are variations from country to country, but the basic precept—certainly so far as jumping and cross-country saddles are concerned—is common to them all, with the over-riding influence being that of Count Ilias Toptani (see Chapter One). The saddle that evolved as a result of his work, plus that of others, has played, in its way, as important a part in the history of equipment as that of the Sarmatians or of the X Group people in pre-Christian times.

The first prototypes
As discussed in Chapter One, attempts were soon made to produce a saddle which would conform in its design to the teachings of Caprilli, or to modified versions of his method of riding. Pariani of Milan and Piero Santini, the pupil of Caprilli came nearer than most to producing such saddles, while, in England, there was also the Distas Central Position saddle made by Colonel F E Gibson, just prior to the Second World War, in conjunction with the late Colonel Jack Hance. The latter was one of the greatest instructors of his day.

The story behind the invention of the Distas CP saddle is a curious one. In the days when Hance was teaching at his school in Malvern, he asked Gibson to make a saddle which would place his pupils correctly in its centre. The nearest thing he possessed to a saddle that would achieve this was an old one of foreign manufacture, which had a fairly pronounced dip to the seat. Because it was so comfortable, it was the most popular among his pupils. In fact, as Gibson was quick to see, the dip was unintentional, since it was caused by a broken tree. The result of the two men's work, however, was the Distas CP saddle. Though, at its first appearance at Olympia in London, the new saddle was greeted with derision, the design might well have been developed much further had not the Second World War intervened.

The Toptani revolution
It was after the war that the work of Toptani came to the fore. In those years, he was concerned with the training of South American jumping teams and achieved great success with what were basically Caprillist methods. Not having the benefit of the big, scopy horses of Europe, it was necessary for him to utilize the powers of what were in many respects moderate animals to the full, training them meticulously and making sure that the riders gave their horses every possible assistance.

Toptani's chief problem was with the saddles then in use, as they did not permit the rider to sit in balance with his horse over the fences. Discussions with first the saddler and then the tree-maker were not particularly fruitful; neither had ever sat on a horse, nor did they understand anything about the anatomy and movement of the animal for which they were making equipment. Still less did they know anything about the theory of riding over fences—in other words, jumping.

Toptani, however, made up some prototypes and then came to the London saddlery firm of George Parkers. There he met F E Gibson. Using the old Distas saddle and Toptani's prototypes, the first Toptani saddles were designed, starting with the saddle's formation—the tree. This, which was made in a mould with

EARLY EXAMPLES
Below, left: An American saddle which was described as a 'Tourist' saddle and is an obvious adaptation of the Military Universal. **Centre:** This early 19th-century saddle makes an attempt to provide a knee support in the panel. **Right:** This hunting saddle of the same period has a pronounced cut-back head which was popular in the US. All three were made in Walsall, England. **Bottom:** A conventional English pattern hunting saddle in common use at the turn of the century. In this example a knee swell is incorporated into the flap.

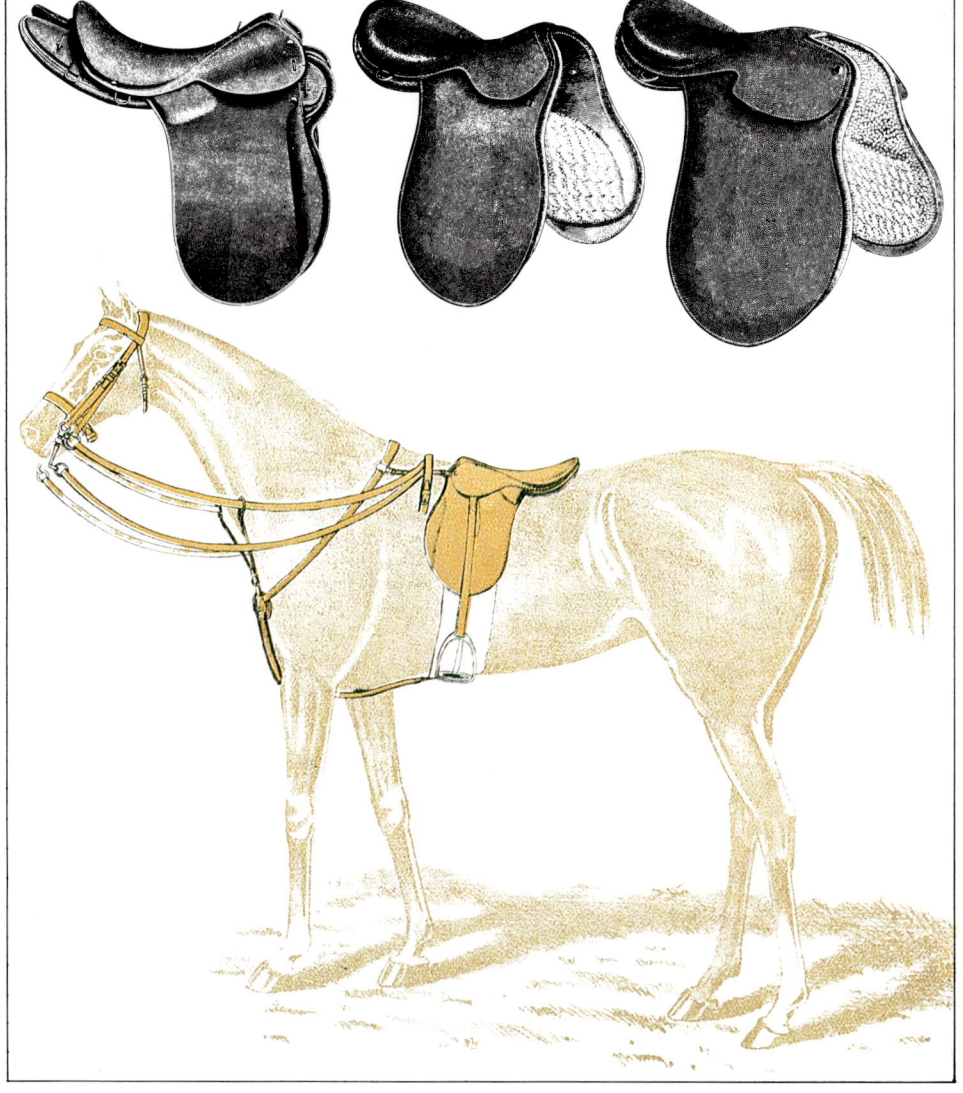

FITNESS FOR PURPOSE

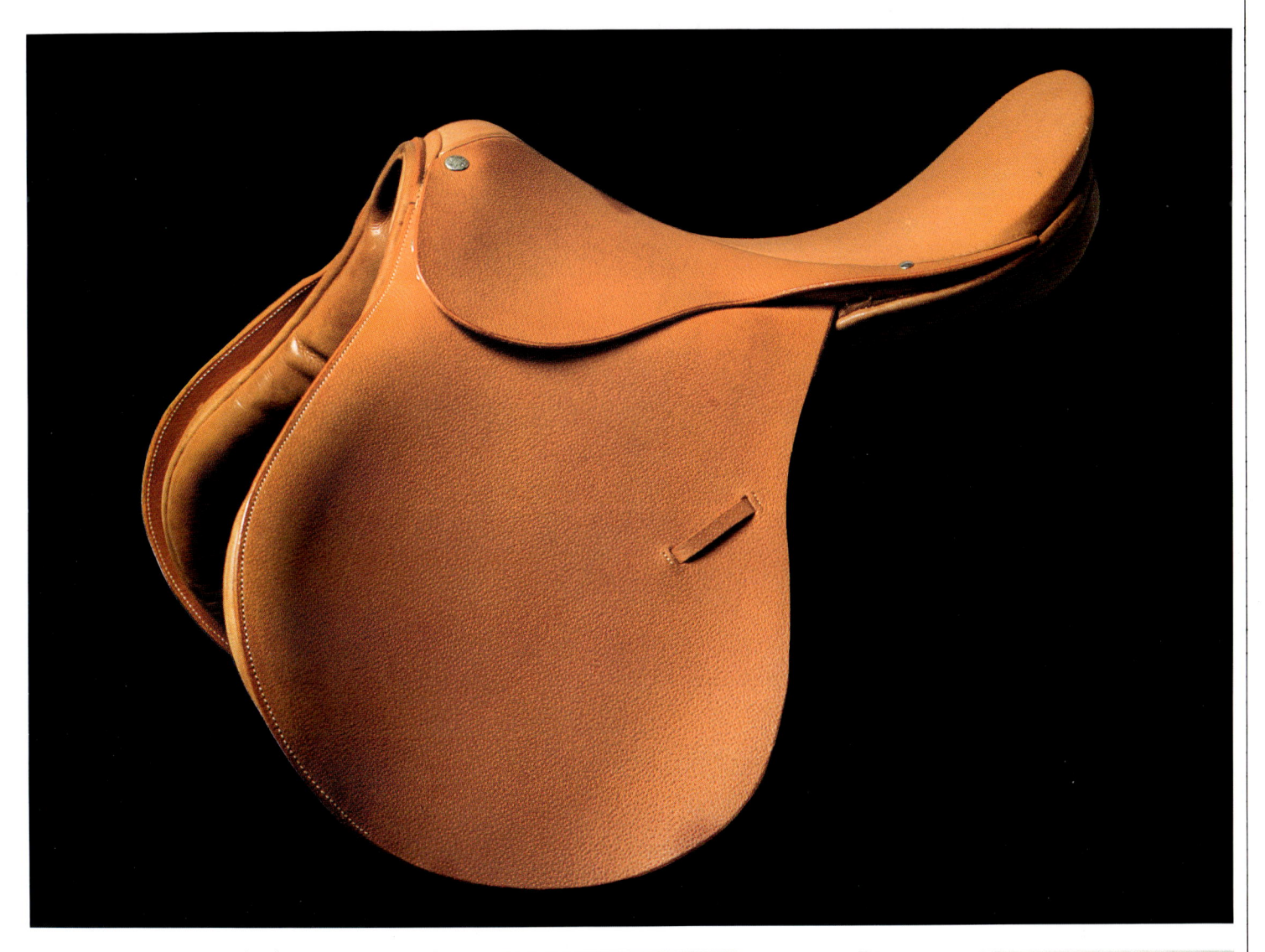

Above: A jumping saddle by the Italian firm of Pariani, the first to produce saddles which attempted to conform to the Caprilli theory and also responsible for the early 'spring' trees. **Right:** Detail of the Pariani panel, showing the knee and thigh rolls. The girth straps are placed so that the girth will lie in the sternum curve and so that the buckles, as long as the girth is of the correct length, will be clear of the riders leg. **Far right, top:** The panel of the Pariani, showing the narrow waist which was intended to place the rider close to his horse but which resulted in too small a bearing surface on the back. This could contribute to excessive weight-bearing on a relatively small area, causing back injuries. Today, good saddles aim to provide the horse with as large a weight-bearing area as possible. **Bottom:** Inset stirrup bar, laid on the underside of the tree so that no bulk is formed under the thigh.

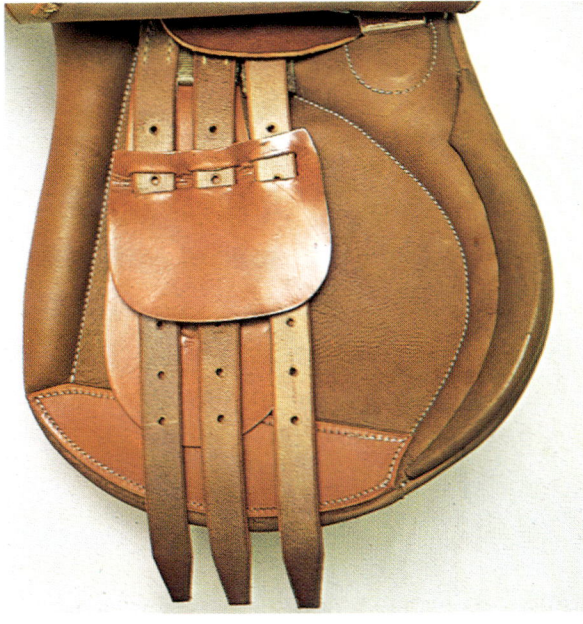

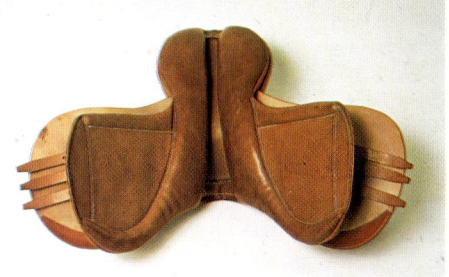

CHAPTER THREE · THE TWENTIETH-CENTURY SADDLE

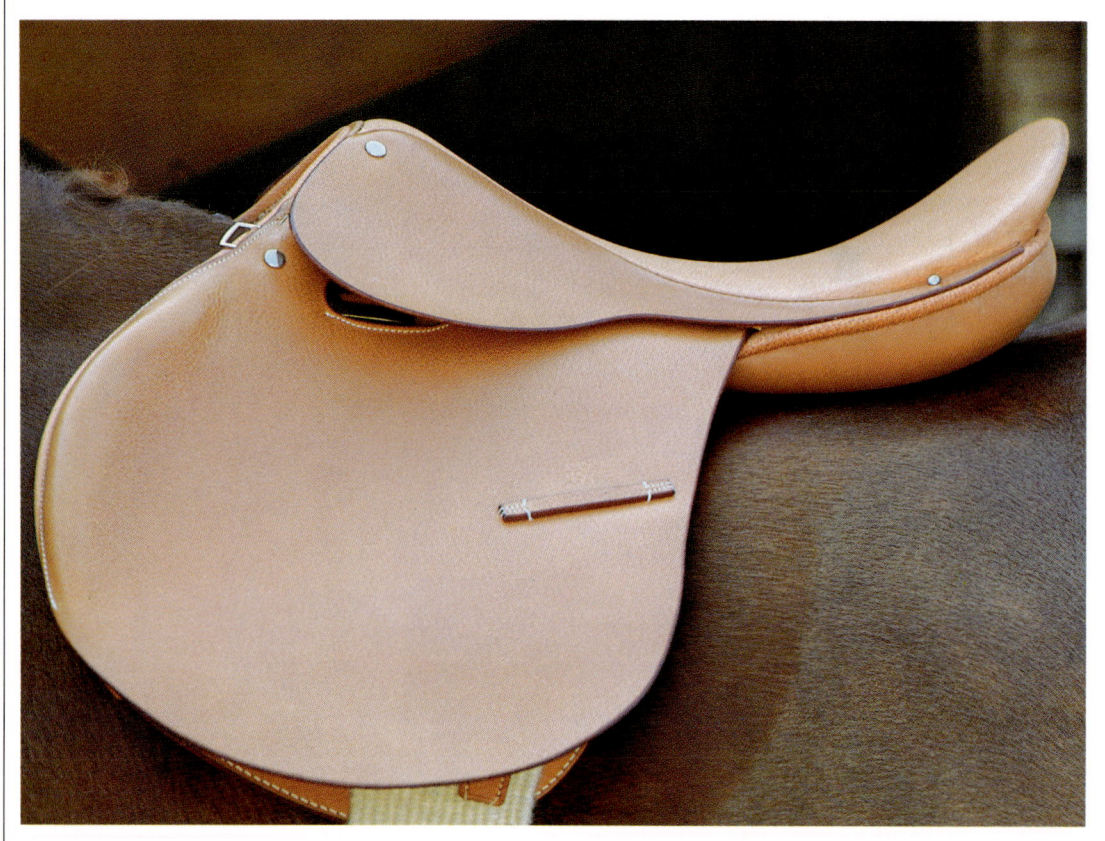

Left: The accentuated slope of the head which positions the bars further to the front is a feature of the Toptani jumping saddle, which must be regarded as a turning point both in design and in equestrian practice. This photograph shows the correct fitting and positioning on the horse's back. **Opposite, left:** The Toptani panel, showing the girth straps placed well to the rear out of the way of the rider's thigh. The swab on the rear rolls keeps the girth straps in place. **Centre:** The characteristic waistline of the panel is an early design feature of the panel saddle and follows the line of the tree. **Right:** The inset bar which was first introduced by Toptani. The George Parker trademark, unchanged for nearly a century, appears on every Toptani saddle.

treated wood so that each was identical, incorporated seven noteworthy design features. The tree was given a pronounced dip in the seat. It incorporated 'a spring seat'—two strips of light, tempered steel being laid along its length from the saddle's head, or pommel, to the cantle.

The waist, or 'twist', was shaped to lie parallel with the back on each side and was curved very considerably. The stirrup bar, which previously had been fastened always to the outside of the tree in two places—on the arm of the tree just to the rear of the head and on the point of the tree—was now set on the inside, so that the bar became recessed. The points, which, in previous designs, had extended for as much as 4in below the point of attachment of the bar, were now cut off short. The head of the saddle, instead of being vertical in relation to the body of the tree, was sloped *forward from the points*, so that the stirrup bar was positioned some inches *in front* of the conventional patterns. The metal reinforcements at the head and cantle were of alloy, which combined with the laminated construction to make the tree extremely light.

The completed saddle inevitably followed the lines of this tree. The flaps, in line with the points, were cut well forward; in addition, the leather used was thin in substance and very supple. The panel was of the so-called Continental type, which had been used in the early Pariani and Santini saddles. This one was narrow at the twist, to conform with the shape of the tree, and continued forward to provide the rider with a substantial knee roll. The so-called thigh roll, at the rear of the panel flap, was not to give support to the rider's thigh, but to prevent the girth straps from shifting backward and off the panel at the rear.

Thus, the advantages of the Toptani saddle were substantial. It was extremely light in comparison with the older types. The dipped seat positioned the rider centrally and encouraged him to sit deep in the saddle. The narrow waist did not spread the rider's thighs. The recessed bars allowed the stirrup leather to lie flat under the rider's thigh, eliminating the very painful protrusion which was often a characteristic of the older saddles. The shortened points could not dig into the rider's thigh, while they also facilitated the correct fitting of the saddle to the horse's back. The forward position of the stirrup bars had the effect of placing the rider's weight further forward. It therefore made it easier for the rider to sit over the horse's centre of balance at all paces and when jumping. The spring tree gave resilience to the saddle seat, making the ride more comfortable. It also allowed the influence of the rider's seat to be transmitted more directly to the horse. In a rigid tree saddle—that is, a saddle with no springs and therefore no resilience in the seat—much of the driving force of the seat bones, assuming they were used, was not immediately evident to the horse. Additionally, when the rider sat in the saddle, the spring in the tree 'gave' to the movement of the horse's back underneath it. The thin flap and panel, in conjunction with the narrow twist and deep seat, placed the rider as close as possible to the horse. This ensured that the aids of legs, seat and weight could be applied in the most effective manner. The forward roll of the panel combined with the other design features to assist materially the rider's security, helping him to maintain his leg position and virtually anchoring the lower half of the body in position.

In summary, like the theory of Caprilli, the Toptani saddle conformed to the basic principle of equitation. This is that the rider should be *in balance* with the horse by positioning his weight over the latter's centre of balance at all times.

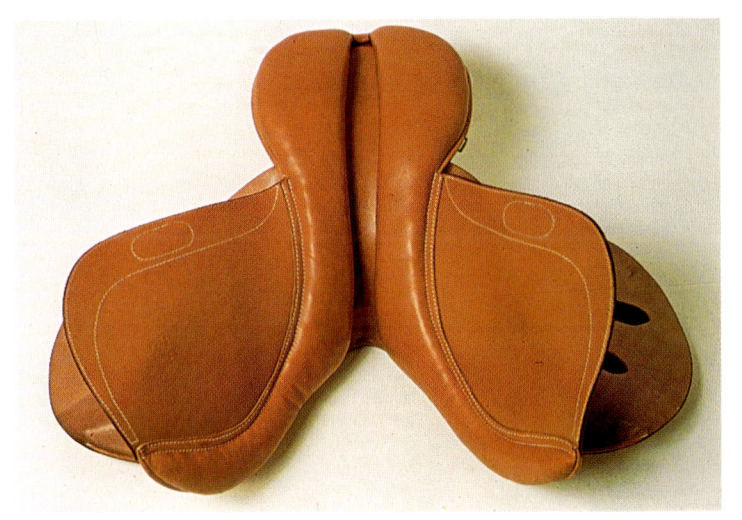

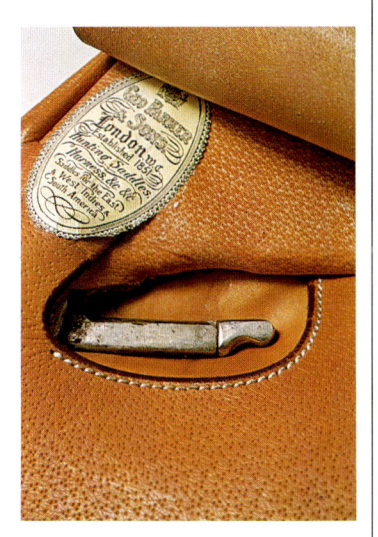

The nature of balance

By experiment, the centre of balance of the horse both at the halt and when carrying the head and neck naturally has been shown to be in the centre of the body at the junction of two imaginary lines. One is drawn from a point about 8in behind the highest point of the withers vertically to the ground; the second is a horizontal line drawn parallel to the ground from the point of the shoulder to the rear. In effect, the point of balance is in the centre of the animal's body.

The point of balance alters as the horse moves and in relation to the gestures the animal makes with the head and neck, which are the balancing agents of the body mass. Thus, as the horse increases his pace, while at the same time stretching forward and lowering the head and neck, the point of balance advances. In order to position his body over that point, so as to be the least possible encumbrance to the horse, the rider must incline the trunk of his body forward. If the bars of the saddle, as in the case of the Toptani, are placed well forward in any case, it is easier for the rider (whose weight is carried over the bar) to position his body more in line with the horse's advancing centre of balance.

The most extreme instance of this is in jumping. Here, it is easy to understand how the point of balance is thrust forward very swiftly by the violence of the movement. Equally, it can be seen how easy it is for the rider to be left behind the movement, unless the position he takes when approaching the fence is such that he can, without great physical effort, follow the point of balance with the weight of the body. The Toptani saddle assisted the rider to do just this and, very importantly, without loss of security.

Another example shows not only how important this principle is, but also how simple it is to follow. Anyone who has ever given a child a piggyback ride will appreciate the importance of the weight being carried over the centre of balance. If the child sits still and upright there is no difficulty in carrying him, since his weight accords with the point of balance of the person carrying him. If, however, the child leans back or throws himself too far forward, the difficulty of the task is increased immediately. Should he, instead of sitting still, shift his weight back and forth as the carrier attempts to run, it becomes almost impossible to carry him.

Conversely the position changes in the collected movements. There, the outline of the horse is shortened, the head and neck being held high and the croup slightly lowered as the hindlegs become engaged under the body. The point of balance moves slightly to the rear as a result, but this, naturally enough, does not concern the jumping rider, for whom the Toptani saddle was designed.

Advantages and disadvantages

In what ways did the conventional hunting saddle fail to assist the rider in these respects? It did have certain advantages—notably because it distributed weight over the largest possible area. But it was by no means ideally suited for the precision required in competitive riding.

The chief deficiencies of the conventional saddle in competition were as follows. The saddle was heavy. The seat was relatively flat, and the head of the saddle, when it was in position on the horse's back, was often higher than the cantle. The twist was often so wide as to spread the thighs. The bars were placed on the outside of the tree, so forming, with the accompanying stirrup leather, a hard lump under the rider's leg. The points of the tree were long and similarly pressed uncomfortably into the leg. The head of the saddle was vertical in relation to the body of the tree. As a result, the bars were placed further to the rear and the flap, unless deliberately cut forward, was too straight for a rider riding with relatively short stirrup leathers. The tree was rigid in construction. There was no forward roll to the panel to give support to the thigh above the knee and to contribute to the rider's security. The flap leather was so thick and stiff that it might take years before it softened. The length of the panel could often prevent the rider from being in close contact with his horse.

It may well have been as a result of these deficiencies that the now notorious 'hunting seat'—leg thrust forward and seat to the rear of the saddle—developed. In all probability, it was more the result of badly designed saddles than of any conscious effort by the rider to emulate the armoured knights of the Middle Ages. The shape of the tree and the position of the bars, which were well behind the centre of balance, contributed to this behind-the-movement seat, while the uncomfortable lumps under the leg must have encouraged the rider to sit toward the rear in order to escape the discomfort. In fact, in many saddles it was difficult to sit other than at the cantle end.

CHAPTER THREE · THE TWENTIETH-CENTURY SADDLE

The Toptani saddle, however, also has disadvantages. Though it was and is supreme for the purpose for which it was intended—show jumping and schooling for show jumping—it is not so satisfactory when used as a general purpose or cross-country saddle. Not surprisingly, it is of no use at all for competitive dressage. The Toptani's disadvantages in these fields are, firstly, that the waist is so narrow that the weight tends to be concentrated over a small area rather than spread over the bearing surface provided by the back. This does not matter if the rider is in the saddle only for short periods, as would be the case when jumping in competition. However, the continual concentrated pressure could cause the horse back troubles if the saddle were used for many hours at a stretch. Secondly, if the rider rides with relatively short leathers at jumping length and uses the saddle for any length of time, a 'rock' can develop in the saddle leading to its moving forward, with the resulting friction causing the horse soreness.

General purpose and dressage
Largely because of these disadvantages as far as general use was concerned, a general purpose saddle evolved. This was, in fact, a less exaggerated version of the jumping saddle. The slope of the head was reduced, so that the bars were not carried quite so far forward and so that a less forward-cut flap and panel could be fitted. This allowed a rider to use the somewhat longer leathers favoured for cross-country riding and hunting. The twist was made a little less narrow, so that the weight could

Left: The Toptani jumping saddle perfected by Count Ilias Toptani and marketed by George Parker and Sons of London. **Right:** Danloux pattern jumping saddle by the German firm, Stübben, based on the original design of Colonel Danloux. The panel, particularly the forward roll, is considerably heavier than in the majority of jumping saddles. The inclusion of padded suede inserts on the flap is thought to provide a better grip for the knee.

be spread through the panel more evenly. These design changes considerably reduced the danger of sore backs.

The general purpose saddle, however, failed to cope with one particular area. Though it is quite possible to use a general purpose saddle for dressage up to the level of event dressage, thereafter a properly designed dressage saddle is necessary.

The dressage saddle has nothing in common with the jumping or cross-country saddles, except that it seeks to position the rider in balance with the horse. In the case of dressage, where movements are slow and the outline of the horse is shortened, the balance remains central and the saddle is therefore designed to that end. There is therefore no need for the head of the saddle to be slanted forward, since that would position the stirrup bars unnecessarily far to the front. As a result, the head is vertical, with the flap following that line to accommodate the longer leg position. Essentially, the stirrup bar should be an extended one, that is a bar longer than the normal fitting and 'extending' further to the rear. This means that the stirrup leather lies down the centre of the flap and thus positions the rider's weight directly above the point of attachment in accordance with the required balance. Such an arrangement will also allow adequate flap in front of the rider's lower thigh and knee. This nicety, however, is not always appreciated or practised.

The seat of the saddle is certainly dipped, but not excessively. Nor must it be so short that it does not allow movement of the rider's seat. Whether the tree is sprung or rigid is a matter of preference; there are arguments for both types. It is, however, absolutely essential that the saddle should sit dead level on the horse's back. To this end, the panels of the dressage saddles—these are of Continental type with knee supports—nearly always have a gusset at the rear, which permits more stuffing to be inserted than would otherwise be the case.

The German influence

In recent years, Germany has had a wide influence on modern saddle design, as it has on riding practice, particularly in dressage. Opinion is divided for the most part on the value of the influence. The majority of these saddles are made with cut-back heads, but there seems to be no obvious reason or advantage in this, particularly in the case of jumping saddles. The theoretical usefulness of a cut-back head is to accommodate very high withers, but, in fact, the modern sloped head is, in all but exceptional cases, perfectly able to accommodate this. In addition, a cut-back head weakens the structure of the tree and, by placing the bars farther to the rear, makes it more difficult for the rider to sit in balance with his mount.

CHAPTER THREE · THE TWENTIETH-CENTURY SADDLE

The Saddle · **Some Variations**

A number of saddles have been designed with a specific purpose in view. They are either artificial or intensely practical.

The show saddle
This is a peculiarly English product. It is designed for use in the ring, to show off the horse's conformation to best advantage. In general use, it is not a practical item of equipment either for horse or rider, though it holds a firm place in the show ring. Many competitors, however, use a more conventionally shaped saddle.

Essentially the show saddle is a cut-down, streamlined version of the old hunting saddle, and is fashioned to allow both horse and rider to present themselves to their best ability. For instance, a particularly desirable feature in the show horse is the possession of a 'good front'—that is, a long, powerful and sloping shoulder in front of the saddle—combined (as such a shoulder must be) with a good 'length of rein'. (The 'length of rein' is the distance from the poll, down the crest of the neck to the withers.) The show rider seeks to display this second point by riding with as long a rein as he can while still maintaining perfect control, but even this aspect can be helped by the saddle. The 'front' of the horse, on the other hand, can definitely be emphasized and even exaggerated by the right saddle.

The classic show saddle is constructed on a plain, fairly flat-seated tree with either the usual vertical head or one of the cut-back variety. To be correct, as well as practical, the tree should be fitted with an extended stirrup bar. This fitting is particularly important, because the flap of the show saddle is cut absolutely straight in order to display as much as possible of the horse's shoulder, and in some cases it is even cut to the rear of the vertical. The extended bar puts the stirrup leather further to the rear, so that it lies down the centre of the flap, and thus allows room for the rider's leg. With a normal bar, set further to the front, it would be impossible for the rider's knee not to be off the flap and lying in front of it. Such a knee position would reveal the saddle as being a stratagem to deceive the eye.

The panel of the true show saddle is made of relatively thin felt, covered with leather, and is nearly always a half panel.

Below: An Owen-type tree is ideal for use in building a show saddle. **Right:** An English show hunter at the Royal Windsor Horse Show some years ago, wearing an original Owen saddle which although cut slightly forward in the flap, sits well behind the shoulder. **Opposite:** A classic, straight-cut show saddle with a half ('skeleton') panel made of felt covered with leather.

62

SOME VARIATIONS

This arrangement allows the saddle, with its relatively flat seat, to fit close to the horse's back and so not to interfere with the 'line'. Possibly the most important feature is the provision of a girth strap, which is laid under the point of the tree and is called a point strap for that reason. When this strap is used with the first of the two normally placed girth straps, the aim is to hold the saddle further to the rear than would otherwise be possible and so, once more, give emphasis to the 'front'. In other words, the saddle can be positioned inches further back than would be either usual or normally advisable.

The same thing can be achieved with the three girth straps on any saddle. These can be used to move the saddle either forward or back according to the conformation of the horse. A girth attached to the first two puts the saddle a little more to the rear, while the use of the centre and third strap will move it forward.

A particularly good saddle, which was extremely suitable for the show ring, was the pattern made by Hermès of Paris. Known as the English saddle, it was a model of quiet restraint. The seat was just sufficiently dipped for comfort, the flap was not too straight, and it was fitted with a light panel which included a flat, unobtrusive knee roll to give some support to the rider. A much older saddle, also extremely popular among show riders, was made by the old London firm of Owen. With its quarter cut-back head, rounded cantle—show saddles, as such, usually have a shaped, square cantle—and flaps of exactly correct proportions. It was a most elegant design and showed off a horse very well.

CHAPTER THREE · THE TWENTIETH-CENTURY SADDLE

Many traditional show saddles are still in use in British and Irish show rings, and there is no doubt that they do favour the old-type seat where the rider rides with the feet thrust somewhat forward, a position which affects his whole balance and the horse's way of going. However, many top-level showing professionals do now use dressage saddles as they make it easier to attain a seat in balance with the horse's natural centre of mass or gravity, an advantage which in turn does—or should—improve the horse's way of going and make him better able to give his best and be more comfortable, too.

Dressage saddles are cut fairly straight in the flap, so they still show off the horse's front, and if they are used with a normal, long girth, rather than the short belly or dressage girth—which so often produces an ugly and, to the horse, uncomfortable buckle attachment panel right behind his elbow or thereabouts—they are fine for showing. They offer a more comfortable feel to the rider and, therefore, the judge in classes in which the horse is ridden and marks are given for the ride. Dressage saddles which are not cut exaggeratedly straight in the flap and underlying panel can also be quite suitable for hunter and even working hunter classes, in which faster gaits and jumping take place.

The gaited horse saddle

In the USA, the American gaited horse saddle derives from the English show saddle, differing only in its extreme cut-back head ('cow-mouth') and the width of the flaps. In the American saddle, these extend to within two or three inches of the cantle and appear to be out of proportion as a result. There is, however, a practical purpose in so wide a flap. The attitude of the horse—very high in front and almost

Left: The ultra flat-seated Walking Horse saddle made on a 'cow-mouth' Lane-Fox tree and fitted with an extra-wide flap to prevent the rider's leg from coming into direct contact with the horse. **Below:** The tree together with a direct side-view of the saddle. Saddles for the American gaited horses (the American Saddlebred, the Tennessee Walker and the Missouri Foxtrotter) are supplied almost entirely by the Walsall-based British saddle companies. In most instances these specialist saddles are fitted with a forward girth strap, as in the saddle on the left, which is laid under the point of the tree (point strap), allowing them to be fitted well behind the horse's shoulder. **Right:** The attitude of the American Saddlebred in movement, very high in front and almost squatting over the hindlegs.

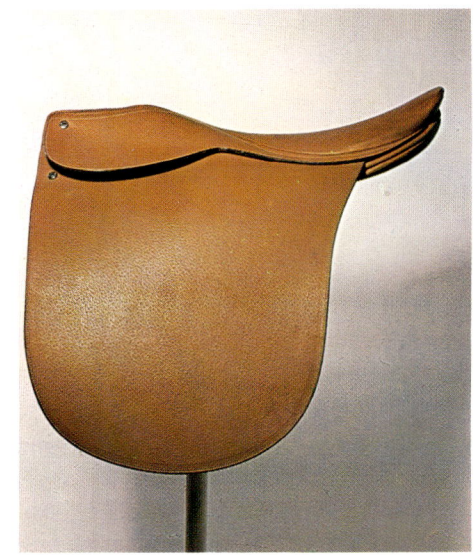

squatting over the hindlegs—together with the saddle's flat seat forces the rider to sit well back. In this position the rider's thigh would rest on the horse if a conventional saddle were used and, as a result, would be subjected to the inevitable sweat and dirt from the coat. The extra wide flap prevents this unpleasant happening.

The American saddle seat is a form of equitation now very specifically American, although there are some exponents of it in Britain and Australia where American breeds such as the Morgan, American Saddlebred and Walking Horse are popular. In its original, less exaggerated form, it came to North America with European settlers in the 16th, 17th and 18th centuries, but has been further developed for the American show ring today.

Because the rider sits well behind what is widely considered to be the horse's centre of mass or gravity, many claim that the American saddle seat is not a balanced seat as far as riding in harmony with the horse's balance is concerned. The rider's weight, they point out, encroaches on the horse's loins, which are generally regarded as a 'no-go' area as far as being weight-bearing is concerned, not least because of possible injury to the kidneys. Despite this, the seat continues in popularity, and the saddles used for it continue to be widely made and available.

The stockman's saddle

The saddle used by the Australian stockmen must be considered, with the Western saddle, as one of the most practical and utilitarian saddles in the world. Built to withstand the toughest treatment that can be imposed upon it, the Australian stock saddle is purpose planned to give comfort to both man and horse during droving trips that may last for as

CHAPTER THREE · THE TWENTIETH-CENTURY SADDLE

long as six months. It is made so that the stockman can make his own repairs with the minimum of tools and trouble, and it is designed to keep the rider firmly in place.

Although the American cowboy and the stockman do similar work, their saddles are entirely different. The American one owes its origins to the Spanish saddlery of the *conquistadores*, while the Australian saddle derives from the English hunting saddle, which was introduced to Australia by early European settlers.

The saddle's characteristic shape is evident even in very early models; by 1911, the stock saddle had developed a narrow twist to the tree and a good dip to the seat. Obviously, security was a much appreciated commodity, so the Australian saddles of the turn of the century were fitted with very substantial knee rolls—some of wing-like proportions—set not as part of the panel but on the flaps themselves. Such rolls, though not as large, are to be found on some English saddles of the period and it is extremely likely that they inspired the Australian variety. Fairly quickly, too, an additional roll, smaller and placed high on the back edge of the flap, was also incorporated. The effect was to lock the thigh in position in an exactly identical manner to the medieval knight and his war saddle.

Later models, dating from about 1919, were made with shorter pads fitted high on the saddle to support the thigh but leaving the knee free. The back pad, however, remained to support the rear of the thigh and the design gave no less security to the rider. At least one maker put a horn on his saddles—the Humphreys Breaking-in Saddle is an example—similar to, but smaller than, that found on American saddles. The purpose of the Australian horn

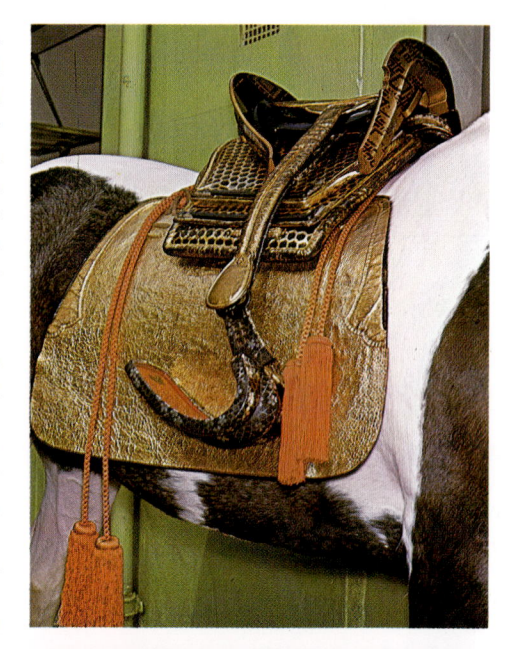

Above right: An ornate and highly decorated saddle of the Iberian Peninsula, richly quilted and infinitely redolent of its Moorish ancestry. Despite its extravagance, it is nonetheless an essentially practical piece of equipment, giving security to the horseman and comfort to his mount. **Right:** One of the most utilitarian saddles in the world is the Australian stock saddle. Built to stand up to the hardest use, it still incorporates design features which give the rider a very high degree of comfort and security on what may on occasions be very rough horses. The seat is dipped and narrow in the 'twist', and the 'wings' set in front of the rider's upper thigh are a powerful support in times of emergency. The solid, well-stuffed panel of the Australian saddle, although adding to the weight, distributes it admirably over the whole bearing surface. **Opposite, left:** A 19th-century donkey two-seater for the larger Victorian family. **Opposite, right:** The very practical modern felt pad has no fitting problems, whatever the size of the pony or young rider.

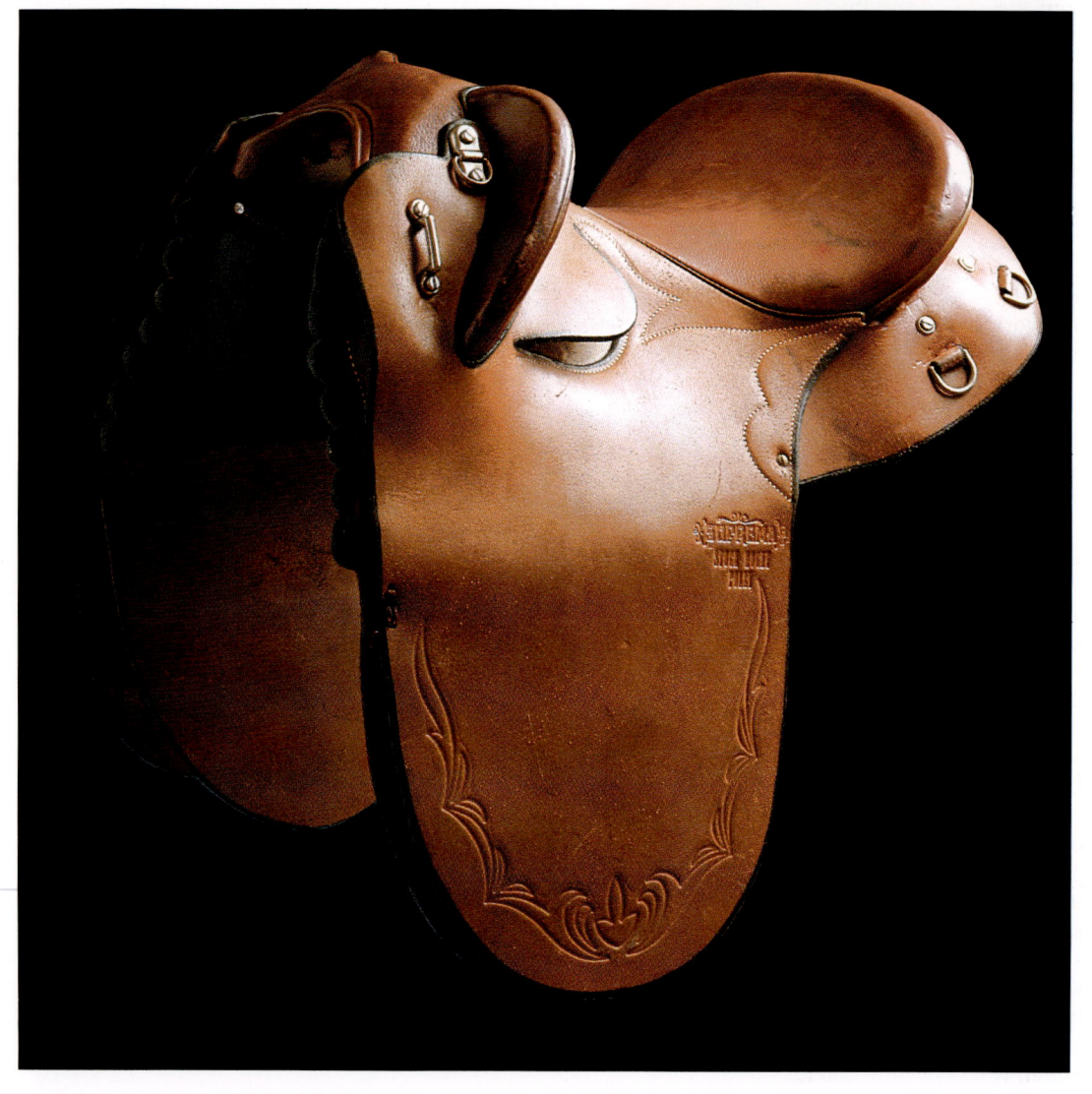

66

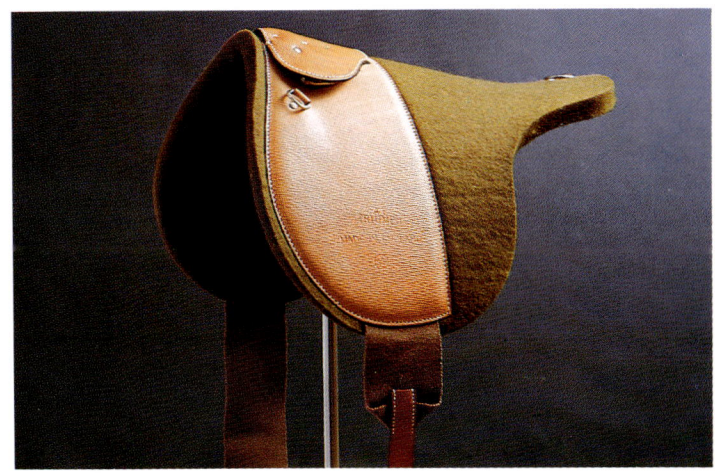

was also different. It was intended as a 'grab-hold' in emergencies; it was not used for roping, as in the American variety, since the Australian stockman does not use a lariat to the same extent or in the same fashion. From this time, too, the flap lengthened to give the rider's legs greater purchase—stockmen riding for the most part in cotton trousers.

The panels of the Australian saddle are admirable. They are very well stuffed, serge-covered panels fitted with gussets at the rear to ensure that the saddle lies level on the back. As a practical, working saddle the Australian product is extremely hard to beat, and it is interesting to note how the work involved produced a saddle that was ideally suited to its purpose. It is of equal interest to appreciate how close the design features are to those employed in the saddles of a thousand years ago—which goes to show, perhaps, how very practical those features were.

Trekking saddles

In view of the popularity of trekking as a holiday activity—particularly in Europe—it seems the more surprising that very few saddles suitable for this purpose have developed. The problem in this instance is the safeguarding of the horses' backs against inexperienced riders whose riding is of a very low standard. Many trekking operators rely very widely on the military troopers' saddle, which is pretty well proof against the inexperience of the rider. It is, however, expensive to manufacture and in increasingly short supply as a sound secondhand article, but a utility saddle is being made following similar lines. In particular, it retains the traditional extended 'fans' bearing the panel, which ensure the horse's comfort.

This must certainly be the chief aim of any trekking saddle; the fact that the rider is carried high above the horse's back, generally a great disadvantage, and not in close contact with his mount is irrelevant in this instance. The burgeoning in popularity of endurance riding has produced saddles suitable for this sport, and these may be used for trekking.

Facsimile saddles

Harking back to the medieval saddle and, more particularly, to that of the Renaissance, it seems remarkable, at first thought, that modern facsimiles should still exist and, indeed, be widely used. This is so, however. The saddles of the Iberian Peninsula, particularly of Andalusia, do not differ at all from those which originated with the Moorish invaders and were in use four centuries ago. Built high in front and behind to encase the rider, and often quilted for comfort, they are used for all forms of general riding—for displays at the *feria*, for herding the black bulls, and as the saddle of the *rejoneadore*, when horse and man face a fighting bull in the ring.

The inflatable saddle

The one saddle which stands out on its own as being entirely original and modern is an inflatable saddle, made of nylon fabric coated with neoprene synthetic rubber. The saddle was sold with a special pump adaptor and could be blown up to whatever degree of firmness was required with an ordinary bicycle pump. When not in use, the saddle was deflated and could be rolled up rather like a plastic raincoat. No instructions were given as to what to do in the case of a sudden puncture, but obviously it was a wise precaution for users of the saddle to equip themselves with a repair kit. Surprisingly, for so modern a concept, the shape of the inflatable was distinctly medieval in appearance, as historical comparison shows.

Children's saddles

For the most part, children's saddles follow those of their elders in design, but there are saddles produced specifically for children which have been in use in one form or another for a century or more.

The cheapest saddle of all is a pad of felt to which is attached a girth, a leather handle across the front for the small rider to hold, fittings for stirrup leathers and leather reinforcements to prevent stirrups from wearing a hole through the felt. This is, in fact, a most satisfactory arrangement for the very young, whose diminutive ponies rarely have the conformation to carry a conventional saddle. There are no fitting problems to consider, and it is far more comfortable for the rider's short legs.

The felt pad, however, should not be confused with the Cobbar felt saddle. This, too, was a very practical saddle, which was comfortable for horse and rider and was neither too heavy nor too expensive. It was made of heavy quality felt fitted to an attenuated tree. In fact, the tree was no more than the fore arch, with arms just sufficiently extended to allow the fitting of a stirrup bar. Unlike the simple felt pad, the Cobbar had a panel, built conventionally with a channel between the two halves and extended to provide a knee roll. Its principal use was as a race-exercise saddle, but there were occasions when it was used by point-to-point riders and by some show jumpers of perhaps two decades ago. In Australia, the country of its origin, it was used in bush racing.

CHAPTER THREE · THE TWENTIETH-CENTURY SADDLE

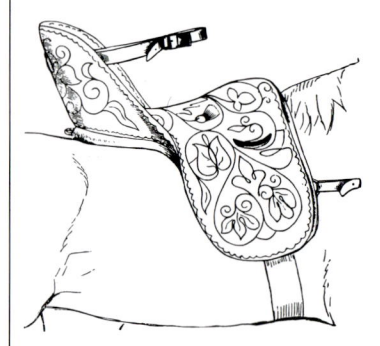

Above: An elaborate quilted child's saddle of the 19th century.
Right: A refinement on the felt saddle is the flexible leather pad made up on a half-tree, which is little more than a front arch and a pair of stirrup bars. It is, of course, a relatively cheap solution to the young rider's saddle requirement, but rarely seen today.

The other type of child's saddle was the 'basket' saddle, which resembled a miniature howdah. The basket was made with conveniently sited holes, through which the rider's legs protruded, or was sometimes fitted with a small seat. It was, of course, impossible for a child to fall out, but, naturally, the pony had to be led.

Turning full circle—almost
The swing during the late 1950s and 1960s toward saddles with narrow waists or twists combined with recessed stirrup bars certainly resulted in increased comfort for the rider in that the thighs were not forced apart to such a degree, and there was less bulk under the thigh from stirrup leather buckles. Unfortunately, however, when promoting and perpetuating this trend, saddlers, trainers and riders did not seem to realize the effect on the horse's back of narrower twists: with the new saddle design, horses ended up carrying the same amount of weight but with a significantly reduced weight-bearing surface, and obviously, with the same amount of weight being carried on a smaller area of the back, this meant increased pressure on the skin, muscles and other soft tissues and, ultimately, more bruised, painful backs.

At about the same time, horse sports of all kinds were experiencing a burgeoning popularity, and horses were used and bred more specifically for competition as opposed to leisure riding such as hacking and hunting. They were worked harder and put under more stress—yet at the same time, the newer generations of horse enthusiasts came increasingly from families with no equestrian tradition. Old knowledge, understanding and empathy were very often not part of their equestrian upbringing, and scientific research into such topics as exercise physiology and equine physiotherapy had not seriously begun. This resulted in a certain blissful ignorance of what horses were really experiencing in terms of stresses and strains, and in connection with saddlery, the real effects of the tack being used on them.

Now, toward the very end of the 20th century, the recurring back problems suffered by so many horses are better understood—as is the role of the saddle in causing or preventing much of the stress and injury they experienced. (Of course, bad riding is always a serious stress factor which no saddle, however marvellous, can alleviate entirely.)

So-called classical riding—the principles of which can be applied when working over fences as well as on the flat—is being 're-discovered', and this has resulted in the production of saddles of improved design. The best incorporate wider under-seat panels and, therefore, a larger bearing surface, thus distributing the weight over a wider area of the back, yet avoiding the old problem of forcing the rider's thighs uncomfortably apart.

It is now more widely accepted that the positioning of the stirrup bars will also affect the rider's seat, and this point, too, is being taken in, with the provision of different placements according to the equestrian sport or discipline involved, and extended stirrup bars. Interchangeable panels have also been developed to allow for the different 'cuts' and knee rolls. Perhaps most significantly, scientific methods using sensors can now measure the pressure inflicted by the saddle on a horse's back.

Another factor is the now-widespread popularity in show jumping and dressage of the continental European warmblood horse. Until quite recently, most high-level competition horses, other than dressage mounts, had been Thoroughbred, or

Left: A Lauriche classical dressage saddle. This saddle was specifically designed along the lines of the saddles used by the famous European masters of equitatino but with modern features such as relatively low pommel and cantel to give support without restriction, an 'old-fashioned' wide bearing surface which, providedd the saddle fits the horse in the first place, gives greater comfort to the horse, lessening back pressure, with saddle stability, and a girthing system which increases the latter effect.

largely so, and typically had a fairly oval-shaped rib cage; the warmblood, on the other hand, with its cold-blood or old-type Iberian ancestry, has a more rounded barrel, and this calls for a tree of different shape. This factor, too, is being addressed.

All this must gradually make life better for horses and riders alike. Some of the newer designs of saddles which are widely available at the end of the 20th century are detailed here.

The Lauriche classical dressage saddle

The makers of this popular saddle, A J Foster, declare that it incorporates the same designs and principles as those used by the great European masters of classical equitation. The saddle's seat is broad with a lower pommel and cantle than is often found even on dressage saddles; this means it gives adequate support yet without the restriction sometimes experienced with a higher pommel and cantle.

The panels have a wide bearing surface and are designed to fit the horse's back from front to back as well as from side to side (provided the correct saddle is chosen for the individual horse, of course). It is claimed that this makes the saddle very stable, obviating the rocking experienced with some saddles, and it also allows the rider's weight to be distributed over a much larger area of the horse's back than with some conventional saddles. The gullet between the panels is also wide enough to avoid pressure from the edges of the panels. The girthing system of the Lauriche assists in achieving stability, balance and even pressure: in addition to a girth tab or strap at the point of the tree, an angled girth tab comes from the swell of the tree toward the back of the saddle.

The exact fit and the positioning of the girth tabs depend on the individual horse's conformation, as does the shape of the panel and other features, so each saddle is fitted specifically to the horse for which it is intended.

The position of the stirrup bars is farther back than in many dressage saddles, thus helping to prevent the rider's legs from coming too far forward and facilitating a correctly balanced, central position in the saddle.

The company also makes appropriately designed show-jumping and cross-country saddles, always using top-quality materials and with superb craftsmanship.

The Heather Moffett posture saddle

As a remedial teacher of riding specializing in the correction of positional faults and in resolving incorrect interaction with the horse's movement, Heather Moffett soon became aware that saddle design was very often the major cause of many a rider's problems. She felt that in many saddles the seat was not central enough in relation to the position of the flaps, and also—and perhaps most important—the stirrup bars were invariably too far to the front, causing the rider to have to fight constantly the backward swing of the stirrup leather in order to maintain the optimum position of balance in which the ear, shoulder, hip and heel are in vertical alignment.

Having developed bursal enlargements of her seatbones in her pursuit of the classical seat, she set about designing a saddle that would actually help the rider to sit correctly and also offer great comfort. The average saddle has a layer of plastizote, a firm, resilient foam which, when topped by a drum-tight leather seat, makes it very difficult for the rider to sit to the horse's movement, particularly a horse with big, scopy gaits. The posture saddle has a seat made from

CHAPTER THREE · THE TWENTIETH-CENTURY SADDLE

a foam originally invented and used to absorb shock in Air Force pilots' ejector seats. This material is not like normal plastic or latex foams in that it does not spring back but moulds to the rider's shape, taking a few seconds to recover and so 'damping down' some of the upward movement of the horse's stride without reducing rider 'feel'. The stirrup bars are positioned so that the stirrup leathers hang perpendicularly under the rider's leg, allowing a correct position to be attained far more easily. This is further enhanced on the dressage model by the addition of large rolls on the front of the flaps which stop the knees from gripping upward, keeping the thigh deep and preventing the rider from sliding too far toward the cantle and adopting a 'chair' seat.

The saddle is made in Walsall, England, by Barry Swain, and is notable for its attention to detail regarding the individual fit of each horse plus quality of craftsmanship and materials.

The Reactorpanel saddle
This is probably the most revolutionary saddle on the market today, but in fact it is not dissimilar to the 19th- and early 20th-century military saddles, which had broad, weight-spreading bars or fans under a leather seat, usually slung almost hammock-fashion. Not only was it supremely comfortable for the rider, but apparently it was also very acceptable to the horse, judging by the reputation of the saddle (when fitted properly) for not causing back injuries.

The Reactorpanel saddle is so named because the panels react and adjust to the movements of the horse's back and shoulder blades. They are attached by means of aviation velcro to the upper, seat part of the saddle—which is a normal seat, not 'slung'—by adjustable Sorbothane 'shock-blockers' or mounts which absorb the force coming down from the rider and up from the horse. The gap between the panels and the underside of the saddle seat allows the panel to change its angle constantly according to the horse's movement, so permitting one tree width to suit a wide range of horses.

As mentioned elsewhere in this book, any pain or discomfort caused by any item of tack will cause distress to the horse, uncooperativeness, schooling/work problems, apparent disobedience and even dangerous behaviour. Although riders, trainers and good horse managers should look automatically to their tack and equipment under such circumstances, it is surprising how many do not do so, and even punish the horse for bad behaviour when, in fact, he is reacting to pain in the only way he can. However, it has been shown many times that a properly fitted saddle will greatly reduce or even eliminate such problems, because the horse, once comfortable, soon realizes he can move freely and will perform his true gaits. The Reactorpanel saddle does seem to permit relatively free movement and many users report improved behaviour and performance in their horses.

The saddle never needs restuffing, although the mounts may need readjustment occasionally, usually after several months' use. The panels are made of layered leather, foams and plastics, and clients are provided with spare mounts and shown clearly how to adjust them, if necessary. In practice, few if any adjustments are needed if the saddle is used only on one horse, even allowing for changes in its condition. When the saddle is used regularly on several horses, however, the mounts may be subject to more movement and may need more attention. Also, horses which have been subjected to continual abuse to their back due to badly fitting saddles, usually affecting the muscles just below and behind the withers, may have a pronounced dip in that site, and initially the panels may need more frequent adjustment as the muscles 'regenerate' (being able to move in a comparatively unhindered way and with a much improved blood supply).

Computerized sensor tests of the Reactorpanel saddle and other conventional saddles, both good and bad, show the Reactorpanel to have the widest and most even weight-bearing surface, resulting in less pressure than any other saddle tested. The weight-bearing surface area of a good, well-fitting conventional saddle is 140sq in, whereas a Reactorpanel provides around 400sq in. Sensor tests also show that even when a conventional saddle seems to touch the horse's back evenly, pressure can be uneven (and not noticed by the rider/owner), particularly on the muscles just behind and below the withers, to a level of 4 pounds per square inch. This involves considerable flattening and closure of the capillaries, resulting in decreased blood circulation and possible damage to tissue from lack of blood supply, and the exacerbated effects of a badly fitting conventional saddle can easily be imagined. By comparison, the pressure from a Reactorpanel saddle is about 1½ to 2 pounds of pressure. The above figures were achieved in tests with riders sitting in the saddle normally.

It is traditionally believed that riders can take the weight off their horses' backs

Left: The Heather Moffet posture saddle concentrates on comfort for both horse and rider. The seat ins central in relation to the position of the flaps and the stirrup bars are far enough back to enable the rider to sit correctly. The seat is padded with moulding rather than springy foam which provides rider comfort and absorbs upward movement from the horse.

Top left: The three girth tabs on a Reactorpanel saddle, showing the normally recommended method of fastening using the first tab near the front of the saddle and the third, angled tab toward the cantle, which helps stabilize the saddle. It is used here with an Aerborn humane girth. **Bottom left:** The underneath of a Reactorpanel saddle, showing the unique panels. **Above:** One of the shock-absorbing mounts on the rear of a Reactorpanel saddle, between the underside of the seat and the panel. Each saddle has four mounts—two each at pommel and cantle.

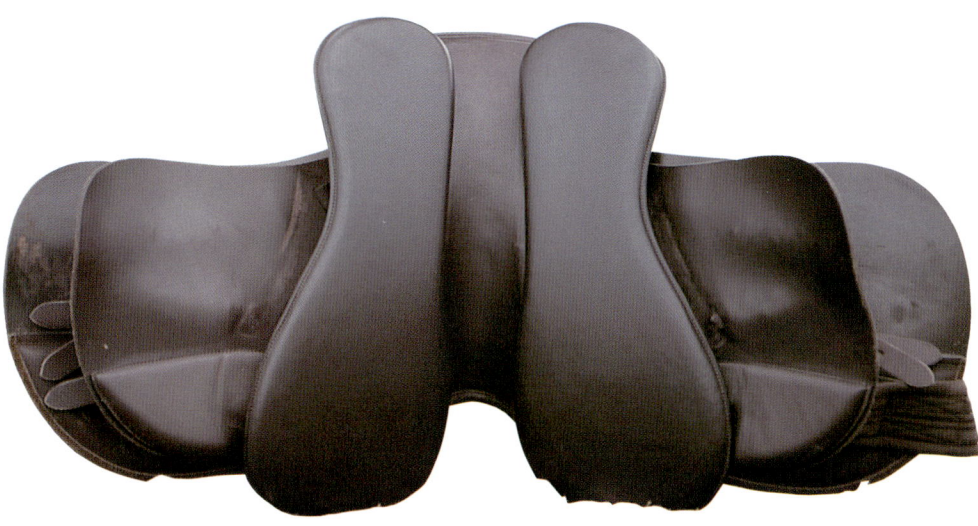

by standing in the stirrups, but in fact it takes only a little intelligent thought and common sense to show that not only can this not be true (since the rider's weight has to go somewhere unless he or she is either flying or walking on the ground!) but also that the practice must, in fact, make matters even worse because all the weight is then concentrated on just two small areas: those directly underneath the stirrup bars/points of the tree. In practice, standing in the stirrups can therefore cause significant damage to the skin and muscles under that area. As a matter of interest, any pressure over 4 pounds per square inch indicates total closure of the capillaries under the relevant area, with a significant impairment of the blood circulation to those tissues. Quite a thought.

The Reactorpanel saddle is available through Roe Richardson Ltd in England, and the company's policy is to fit and make each saddle for the individual horse and rider: the seat is made to fit the rider, and the panels are adjusted to suit the horse. In addition, there are models for all equestrian disciplines and personal requirements can often be taken into consideration. The saddle can be used without a numnah, or saddle pad, but the company can supply two-part numnahs, each panel needing its own special numnah which fits onto it and secures with velcro to the top of the panel beneath the saddle seat; these are available in various materials. An added benefit is that the company can also often convert existing saddles, providing them with the Reactorpanel underparts while retaining the existing top or seat part of the saddle.

Albion saddles

Many of the most brilliant ideas are very simple—and obvious, with the benefit of hindsight after their invention—and this is undoubtedly the case with the Selecta saddle made by Albion Saddlemakers in Walsall, England. As equestrian sport becomes increasingly popular and the multitalented, often family animal becomes more in demand at the lower and intermediate levels of the various competitive disciplines, so the problem

CHAPTER THREE · THE TWENTIETH-CENTURY SADDLE

arises of acquiring a different saddle not only for each animal owned but also for the disciplines in which those animals take part. Potentially, the number of saddles required soon becomes out of the question.

The Selecta saddle addresses this question by using interchangeable front panel sections which can be removed and changed around as desired, so that one saddle can be used for several different disciplines. They can also be used on other Selecta saddles of different tree widths for use on different animals, thus making saddles versatile and reducing the inconvenience and expense of buying, maintaining and storing several saddles. The Selecta is available in pony as well as horse styles and sizes.

Another interesting Albion saddle is the ladies' Narrow Comfort: it is deep seated and primarily designed to assist rider comfort and also to provide weight dispersement appropriate to the female anatomy without the disadvantage to the horse of concentrated (excessive) back pressure.

The company is also currently researching extensively, with the aid of the veterinary and physiotherapy professions, into back injuries in horses, particularly the deep muscle bruising which can occur so easily in equestrian sport but especially, claim the company, in the lower levels of dressage. The sitting trot is a gait some people find particularly difficult to master, and the twice-a-second pressure inflicted on the horse's back by less-than-good riders is felt to cause more bruising than the weight taken by the back under the stirrup bars and points of the tree when a rider lands from even a high jump. The deep muscle tissue immediately above the bones on the horse's back suffers the most pressure because it contacts hard bone.

Albion has developed what it calls its 5,000 tree system to the point where it is being used in its saddles even while more research continues into improving and perfecting it. Basically, the system aims effectively to redistribute the pressure by means of tree shape and panel stuffing, normally concentrated on areas which tend to restrict the muscular function, to a maximum effective dispersement across the rib cage, thus minimizing pressure from the tree points; this also takes advantage of the cushioning effect provided by the muscles which envelop this area.

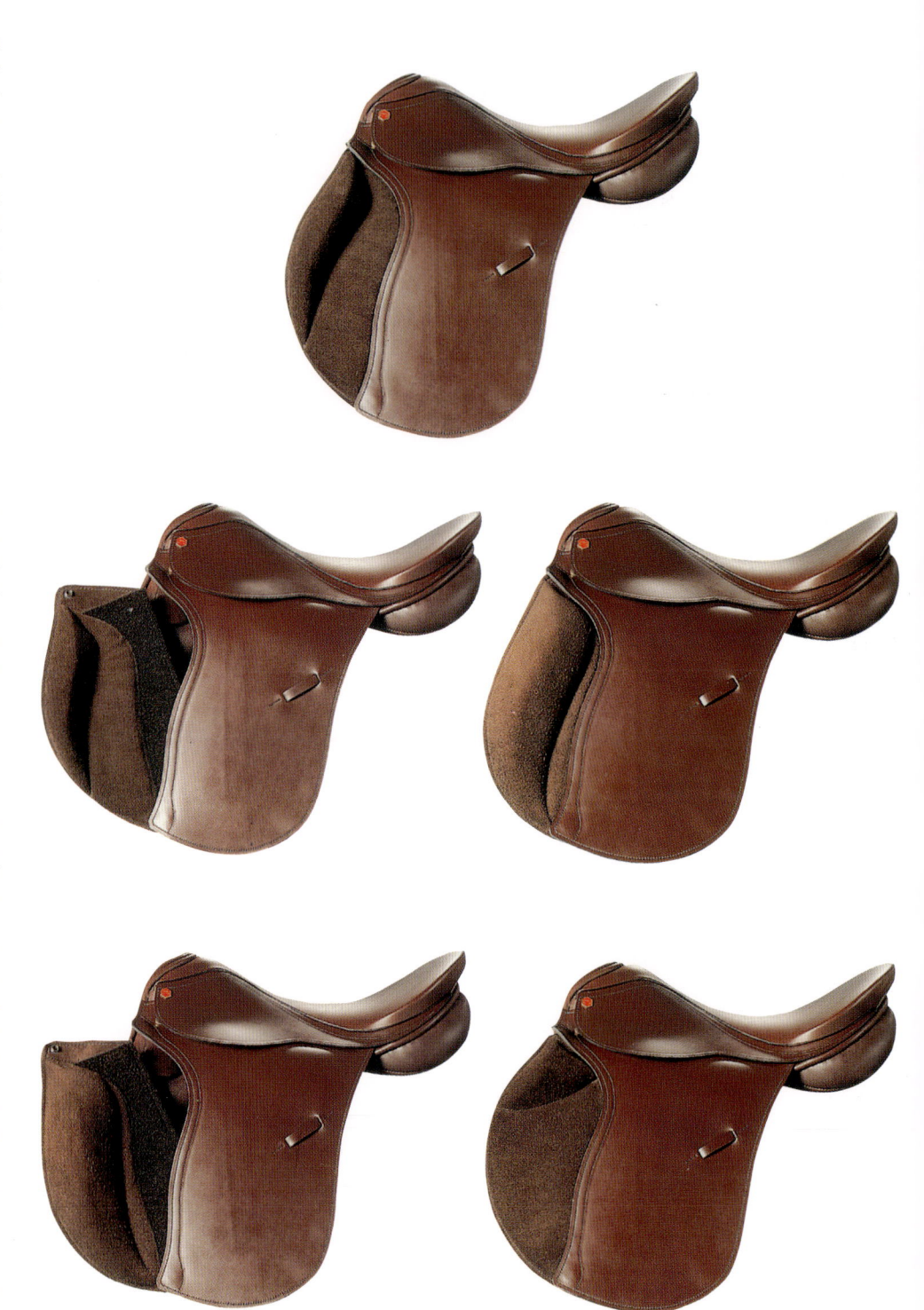

The Albion Selecta saddle is an excellent idea which showed up very well in electronic sensor tests for back pressure. The idea of being able to interchange the panels/knee rolls obviates the need for several saddles. **Top:** The Selecta saddle as an all-purpose saddle. **Centre left:** A stud mechanism and heavy-duty Velcro ensure that the panels remain safely and securely in place when in use but can also be removed easily. **Centre right:** The Selecta saddle as a dressage saddle. **Above left and right:** The dressage panel is removed and replaced with one that is suitable for show jumping.

Again, much emphasis is put on individual fitting for saddles, and Albion has developed a system of saddle fitting which involves using charts, profiles and a questionnaire, together with step-by-step instructions and tools allowing the client to note all the horse's details, which are needed for the company to supply the most appropriate saddle.

Gidden saddles

One of the most famous names in traditional saddlemaking is W&H Gidden Ltd, still thriving after nearly 200 years.

The Gidden general purpose saddle is a consistently popular saddle. As with nearly all comparable saddles today, all Gidden saddles are made by hand on spring trees and from laminated wood, using top-quality materials. With a slightly cut-back pommel, large knee and thigh rolls and a soft flap insert to allow the rider's leg to sit immediately behind the knee roll, the Gidden general purpose saddle offers excellent support, comfort and security. It has a gussetted panel with a wide bearing surface for stability on the back, and is traditionally stuffed with wool flock to allow for individual adjustment.

Left: The Albion show-jumping saddle is increasingly popular, being well designed and balanced for the rider and providing good levels of comfort for the horse. **Above:** The Albion dressage saddle. By means of redistributing the pressure on a horse's back through tree shape and panel stuffing, pressure under the tree points—a common problem area— is minimized. This is particularly important in dressage in which sport the sitting trot is used extensively, often causing very significant bruising to the horse's back should the rider be less than competent.

CHAPTER THREE · THE TWENTIETH-CENTURY SADDLE

Right: The Gidden polo saddle, with a close-contact, wool-stuffed panel and reinforced, cut-back head. **Below, left:** The Gidden international show jumper saddle, made for the serious competitor. The seat is wide and has a felt panel to provide close contact. The bearing surface of the panel is also wide, providing good weight distribution for the horse's comfort. It is available in medium and wide trees. **Below, right:** One of the new breed of side saddle made by Gidden, with an adherent rather than doeskin seat.

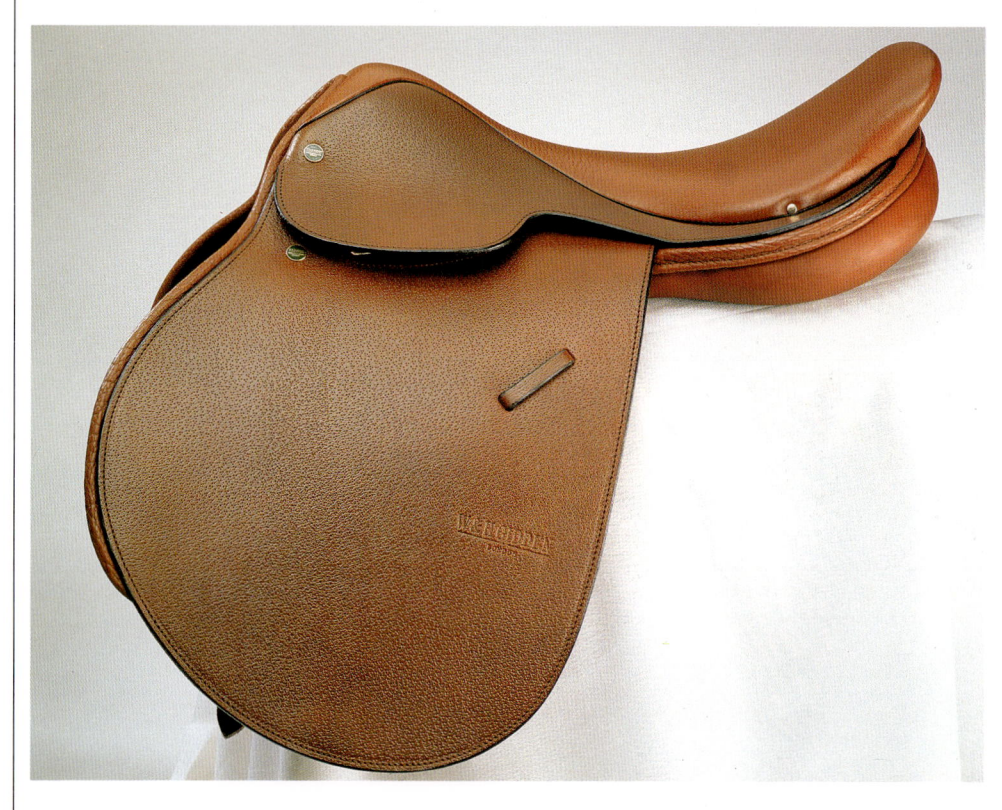

74

Left: Gidden's all-purpose saddle with knee and thigh rolls under the flap, close-contact seat and a good balance for most unspecialized riding. **Below:** A sheepskin seat-saver adds considerably to the rider's comfort and so, indirectly, may also help the horse. It is shown here on a Gidden saddle.

The Gidden International Show Jumper saddle is more forward cut and has a felt panel, unusual today, providing close contact between the rider and horse with a wide bearing surface on the horse's back. The company's dressage saddle is also widely used. It is designed with a deep, central seat which still permits the rider movement without restriction while positioning him or her correctly in the saddle.

Giddens also market other brand names, probably the most famous being the German Stübben saddles which are traditionally produced in all sizes of tree to accommodate almost any horse. A saddle the company describes as 'one of the world's most popular saddles' is the Stübben Siegfried 1994 VSS, a general purpose saddle cut, they say, 'with a tendency for jumping' and often used for cross-country riding.

Crosby saddles
Crosby is a name synonymous with American excellence, and their Excel (XL) line features several impressive saddles.

CHAPTER THREE · THE TWENTIETH-CENTURY SADDLE

Right: The Crosby Excel M is specially designed for top-level, modern show jumping with its slightly longer stirrup and consequently less forward-cut flap. **Below:** The Crosby Excel E is a comfortable all-purpose saddle for the everyday, general rider, with the shallower seat some riders prefer because of its lack of restriction.

The Excel M is specially designed—and used—by US Olympic medallist, Michael Matz, for show jumping with its high cantle. It continues the late 20th century trend of using the ergonomic approach to design first used in the Excel range. This saddle is made of synthetic materials, being light, durable and easy to clean. The saddle has a medium-deep seat, level panels for comfort, and is generally more forward-cut than average. It is moderately forward cut for show jumping, and has padded flaps with a shock-absorbing material for grip; it has a medium deep seat.

The Excel E is designed for riders who hunt and enjoy general equitation, having a shallower seat, yet being comfortable and soft, the design offering a smooth divide between seat and flap for increased comfort under the thigh.

The Klimke-Miller dressage saddle
The top-level dressage competitor Dr Reiner Klimke recommends the famous American Miller company's dressage saddle for all levels of dressage. The Klimke-Miller dressage saddle has a close-contact late 20th century comfortable and soft seat with a design that is supportive but not constricting. It echoes many deep-seat dressage saddles, and provides close contact, thus enhancing rider 'feel', and is stable on the horse's back, and the design of the flap, plus the larger knee rolls, helps the rider to position the leg correctly.

Synthetic saddles
A major development in the 20th century horse world is that of synthetic saddles. Plastics, polymers, acrylics and other synthetic materials are used in the production of even the tree and panel stuffings, as well as for the visible parts of the saddle. It is perhaps surprising, however, that these have not been quite as popular as it was first imagined they would be, despite their advantages of lightness, ease of maintenance and economy. Certainly there were early problems of weak trees which 'spread' with use, but several firms now produce synthetic saddles and have largely overcome these difficulties. Moreover, these saddles are much cheaper than traditional leather ones; some people even conclude that 'at that price, you can just chuck one away and get another', a sensible attitude towards late 20th century equipment. This attitude may be coming full cycle as saddles are becoming more and more expensive. Synthetic saddles do not need the traditional washing, soaping and oiling of traditional leather tack—you simply brush and/or rinse off, a dunking in water or a shower on a rainy day is not a disaster, and you do not have to wait for days for the panel stuffing to dry out. They are much lighter than traditional saddles, and are made in designs and styles for all competitive disciplines.

Initially used for everyday riding while leather tack was kept for competition or special occasions, synthetic saddles are now used in serious competition, particularly in endurance riding where their lightness and ease of care make them the saddle of choice with so many competitors. It has to be said, however, that because of their traditional appearance, their feel and even their smell, leather saddles are still extremely popular and will probably continue to be so for the foreseeable future.

Top: The Klimke-Miller dressage saddle, designed in association with the renowned Dr Reiner Klimke, has a high cantle and a deep, central and soft seat, providing close contact and stability. **Above:** Synthetic saddles are increasingly popular and light, needing minimal care and much cheaper than leather saddles. The Wintec endurance saddle offers a wide bearing surface on the back (note the bars or 'fans' extending the seat below the cantle) particularly beneficial for endurance riding.

CHAPTER THREE · THE TWENTIETH-CENTURY SADDLE

The Saddle · **Mountings**

The term 'mountings' is used to describe girths, stirrup leathers, stirrups, breastplates and cruppers, which are attached to saddles to help keep them in place or to help the rider stay on.

Girths
It is in the area of girth manufacture that synthetic fabrics have really come to the fore, although girths of traditional materials are still available and in use. The old favourite, all-purpose (other than racing) girth was always the straight, three-fold leather girth with a layer of oiled cloth, usually serge or flannel, laid inside the folds; this became softened by the heat from the horse's body and so kept the leather (usually baghide) soft and supple. Although these are not on general view in many saddlers' shops these days, they are available from the more traditional firms, and any competent saddler can make one for you. The rounded, folded edge must be placed to the front, behind the horse's elbow, to prevent the cut edge from injuring the skin, which is very sensitive in that area.

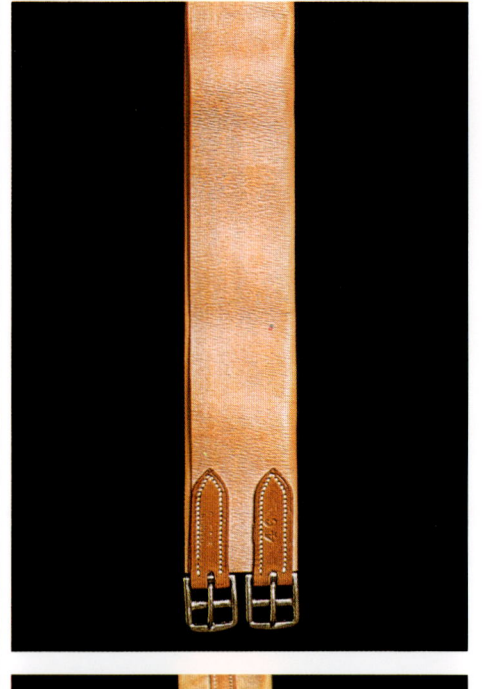

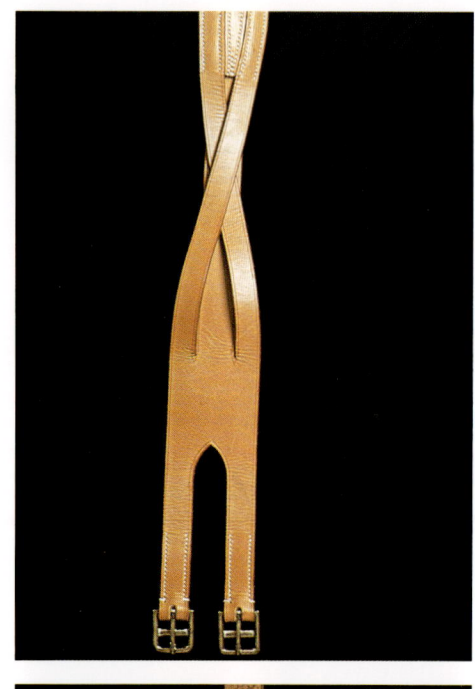

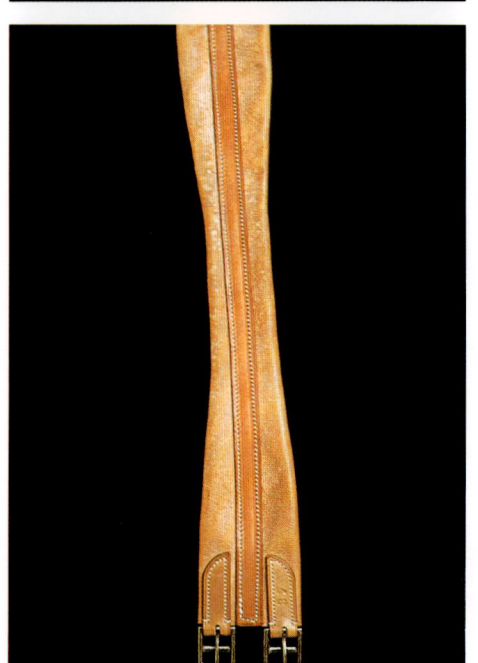

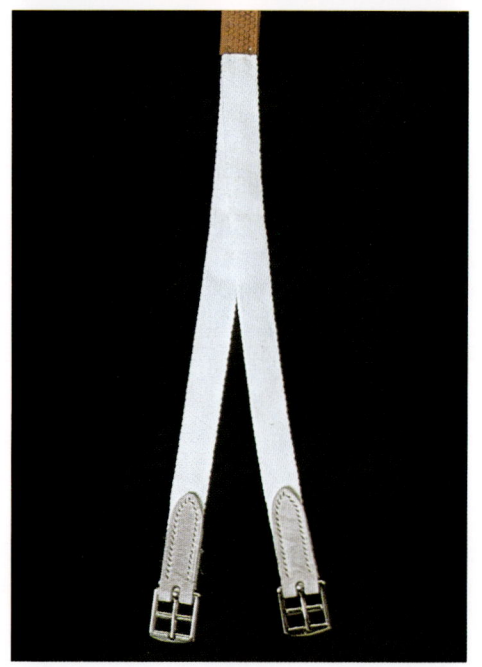

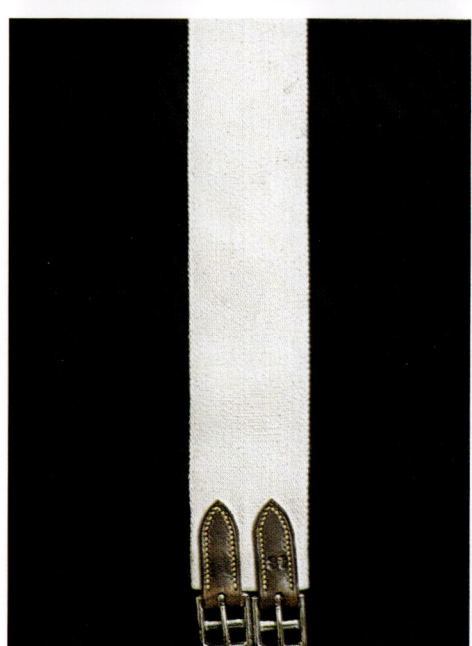

Top: The three-fold baghide girth, usually made with an oiled flannel inlay. **Bottom:** The Atherstone pattern girth, shaped to avoid galling at the elbow.

Top: Balding girth, originally designed for polo and again shaped to obviate chafing. **Bottom:** Tubular web, twin pony show girth fitted with rubber centre to prevent slipping.

Top: A wide woven horsehair girth of a pattern frequently seen in the US. **Bottom:** The soft lampwick girth which is ideal for use on horses who are fat or susceptible to galling.

MOUNTINGS

Two other designs of girth still used and traditionally made of leather are the Balding and the Atherstone. Both styles are shaped to leave room for the movement of the horse's elbow (see photographs), the Balding being constructed of crossed leather sections, and the Atherstone being cut and sewn to shape with a centre reinforcement. This shape of girth has always been favoured by riders of active horses—competition horses and hunters—because of the freedom of contact around the elbow.

Other traditional natural materials regularly used were cotton, wool, horsehair (more used in North America than Europe) and lampwick (a mixture of cotton and wool). Just because a fabric is natural does not mean it is faultless, of course; for example girths made of cotton web, now rarely seen, could become very hard and sharp and were also dangerously weak. Wool web was better, and surcingles which go over the saddle and all around the horse's body to support the ordinary girth in keeping the saddle on, are still seen in eventing, racing and team

Above left: A humane girth. The girth straps can slide for a couple of inches on the strong dee fixed to the girth, so moving with the horse and increasing his comfort. **Above:** A standard Aerborn girth in their now-famous material Cushion-Web, which is said to provide more even, widespread pressure for the horse with a small amount of natural stretch. The fabric also encourages moisture to pass through it and evaporate, helping to keep the horse drier under his girth.

Above: Elastic inserts on top of the fabric in a short dressage girth. This makes such a girth more comfortable for the horse.
Below: A wither pad of specially shock-absorbing, resilient material, to use as a temporary measure where a saddle needs lifting at the pommel.

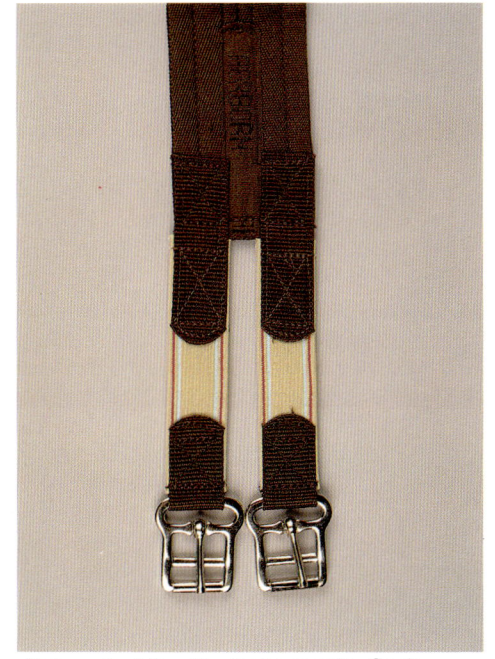

Above: A girth with elastic inserts. Such inserts increase the horse's comfort by 'giving' with his movements. Inserts should be put on both ends of the girth, not merely on one end.

CHAPTER THREE · THE TWENTIETH-CENTURY SADDLE

Right: Right and wrong. The buckles on the left are good, well-made ones with a groove for the tongue. Such buckles will not cut up the flap, nor will the tongue slide out of its central position. On the right is a cheap, poor-quality buckle, which is nearly always unsatisfactory.

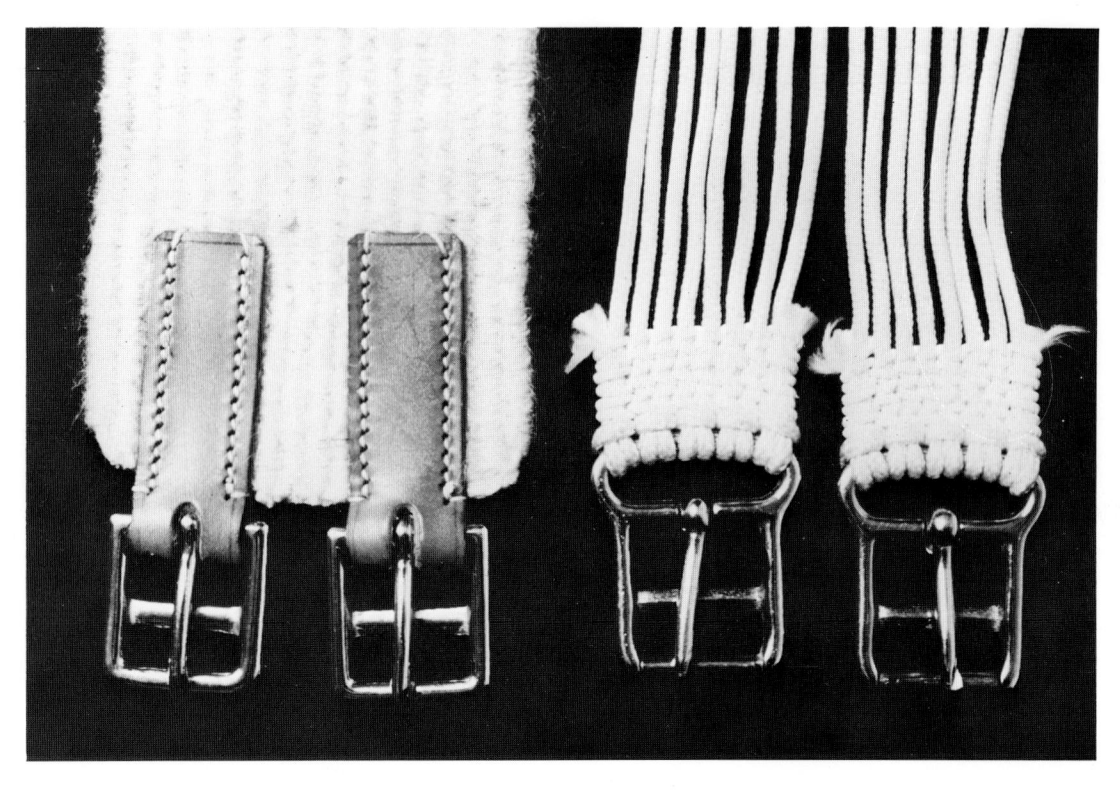

chasing. Cotton, string or cord girths are still sometimes seen, and if kept clean, have the reputation of being cool in summer and easy to care for. Thin, tubular web twin girths are still popular for use in some children's show pony classes; they are usually joined in the centre with a length of dimpled rubber to keep them and the saddle in place.

Probably the most satisfactory girth of natural materials was of tubular lampwick. This is a very soft material; it's absorbent, and if kept clean, most suitable for sensitive, thin-skinned or soft, unfit horses. It is still obtainable by special order.

People thought nothing of it at the time, but the first synthetic girth was the ubiquitous nylon string girth which must in fact have tortured far more horses and ponies than its users ever imagined. Nylon is a hard, abrasive material which, even when clean, can easily rub and cut the skin, particularly in the elbow area which is thin and constantly moving. String girths of any fabric tend to coalesce until they become almost a rope, despite the reinforcing patches woven into them; this obviously lessens the pressure-bearing area, making significant discomfort, galls and bruising even more likely. However, today's synthetic girths, and girth design in general, are improving all the time.

Girth fabrics and designs

Following the lead from the clothing sector of the equestrian industry, textiles and fabrics have been developed for girths which allow the easier evaporation of moisture away from the horse, and which also have a slight degree of integral stretch, a feature negligible in natural materials unless elastic inserts are incorporated. The word 'wick' is widely used to indicate the former quality, meaning that the material is able actively to draw moisture away from the skin and hair of the horse and carry it to the outside atmosphere where it evaporates. In fact, at the time of writing no material can actually do this, although some do permit the easier passage of moisture through them so that the horse's hair and skin does, in effect, stay drier.

Leather girths absorb very small amounts of moisture, particularly if well cared for and dressed or oiled, but natural fabrics such as cotton and lampwick are absorbent and much better than the old-fashioned nylon and early acrylic and polyester girths.

Any fabric for girths should obviously be non-abrasive and have no hard or worn areas, raised stitching, or sharp or hard edges; and care should be taken to see that the plastic tags which currently attach price tickets and packaging are fully removed from the fabric before use.

In the area of improved design, again things are progressing continually, with more thought being given to providing a wider area of pressure bearing, movement and 'give', as well as shaping to accommodate the horse's movements and individual physique. It is worth mentioning here that some modern girths have a central reinforcing strip down the middle, and although they appear to be wide enough for comfort, in practice they evidently concentrate pressure on that narrow strip and feel, to the horse, like a tight, narrow belt around his rib cage. Better designs mean the pressure is borne across and along the whole width and length of the girth.

A common way of providing more comfort in action while still ensuring security is to use an elastic insert on the girth, though unfortunately this is almost always inserted only at one end of the girth, giving an uneven, awkward pressure. Inserts at both ends or, even better, in the centre give a more even and comfortable feel. A potential problem is the area where the elastic joins the other fabric, which is often bulky, unyielding and uncomfortable. Roe Richardson Ltd, makers of the Reactorpanel saddle, have designed a leather girth which is shaped to allow for the elbows, provides even pressure, and has a wider central area to spread pressure

Far right: Leather hunting breastplate used to keep the saddle in place and prevent it from sliding backward. **Right and below:** Two types of Aintree pattern racing breastplates, one made from leather and the other from webbing.

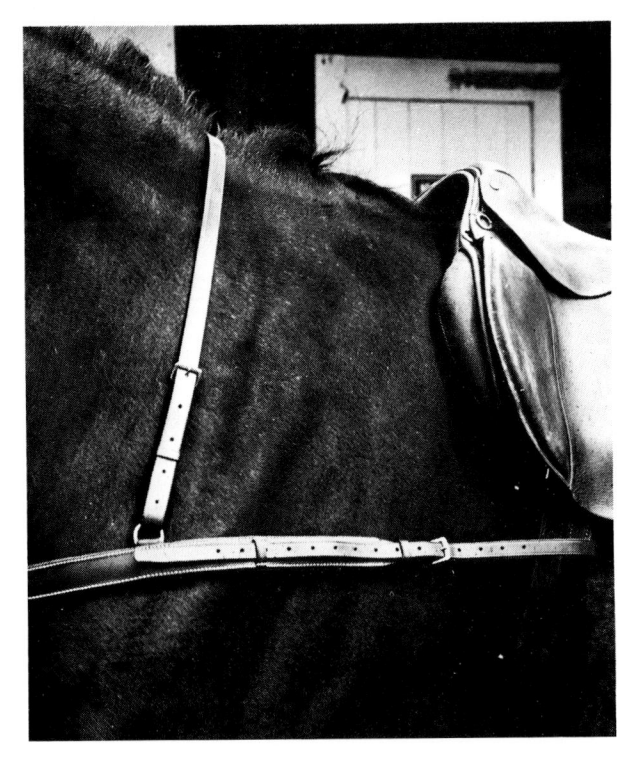

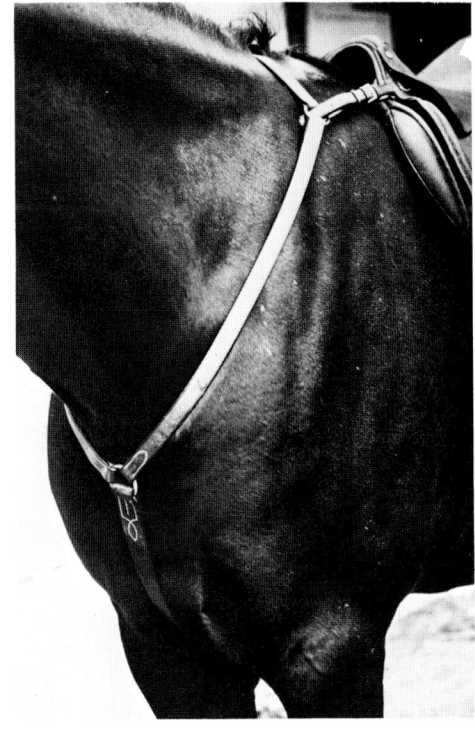

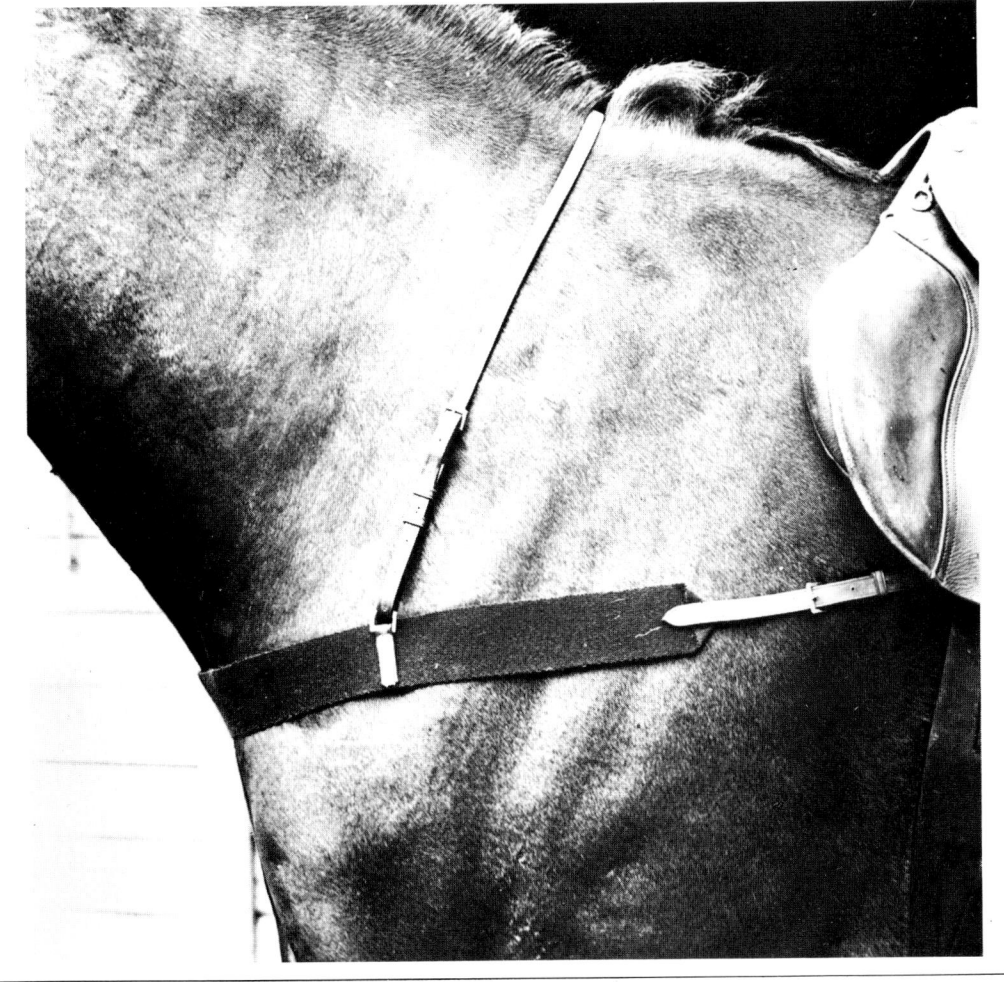

more on the breastbone; its ultimate design feature is a wide length of elastic running over the top of the leather part which touches the horse and to which the girth tabs of the saddle are fastened, thus providing an evenly disseminated pressure with comfortable shaping which is in constant accord with the horse's movements and breathing.

The short 'belly' or Lonsdale girths commonly used with dressage saddles constructed with long girth tabs are intended to remove the potentially uncomfortable girth attachment from under the rider's leg; however, these are used less now as they were often found to create their own problems of bulk, usually immediately behind the horse's elbow, so interfering with his comfort and all-important movement. Many dressage saddles now have shorter girth tabs and normal-length girths which, if carefully measured, can usually be devised to have their buckles behind the crook of the rider's knee, out of everyone's way.

Use of a breastplate

There are two reasons for using a breastplate, a device which stops the saddle from slipping back toward the horse's tail. The first is if conformation demands it; the second is when riding in hilly country.

CHAPTER THREE · THE TWENTIETH-CENTURY SADDLE

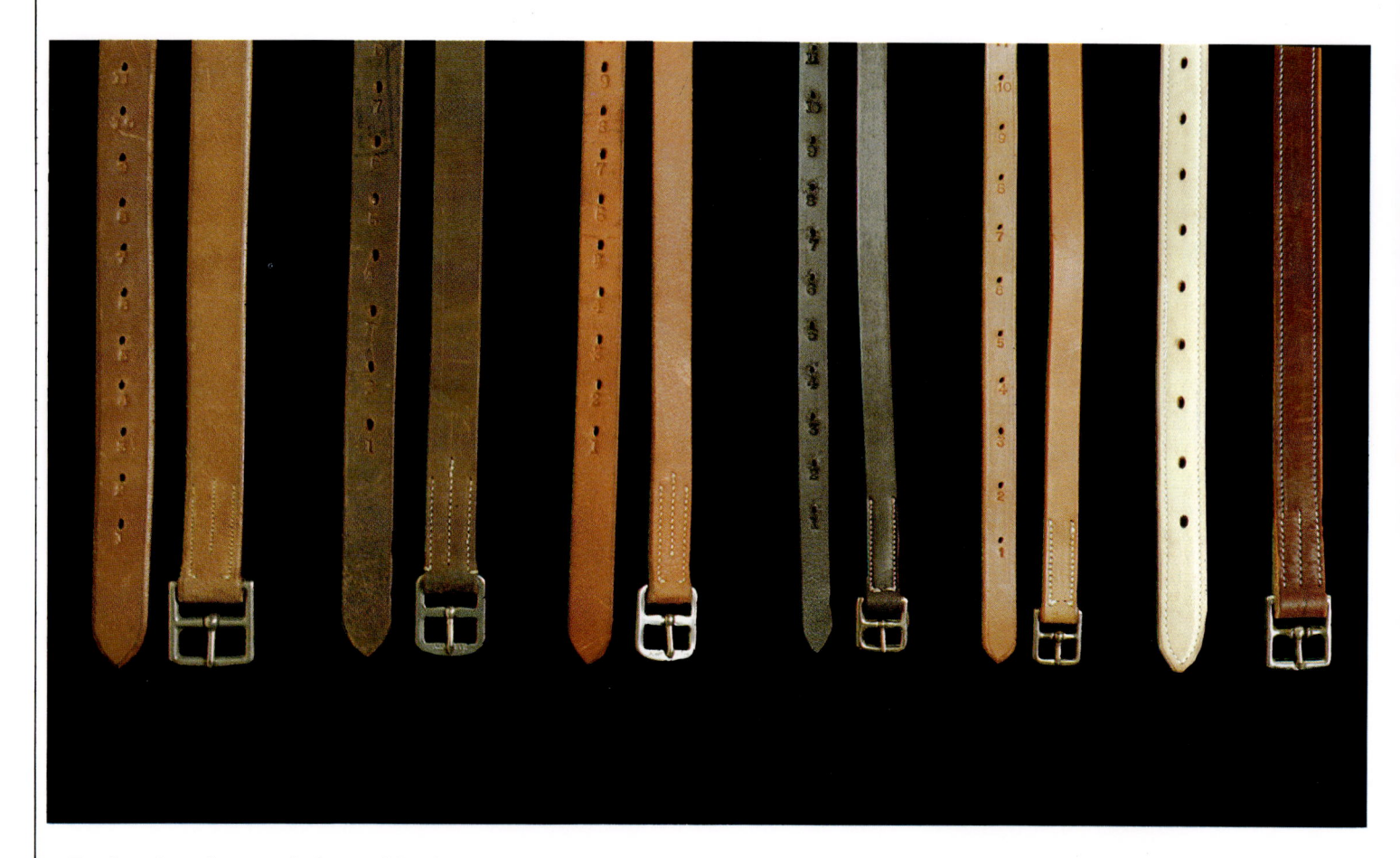

For hunting, the straightforward leather breastplate is the most suitable. This is fastened by adjustable straps to the front dees of the saddle and, after encircling the base of the neck, is secured to the girth between the forelegs. The same type—though much narrower in width and thus considerably lighter—can be used for racing, too. For the most part, however, racing breastplates are made of web, or sometimes elastic, and are of what is termed the Aintree pattern. These breastplates encircle the chest and need to be adjusted carefully, since it is possible for a badly fitting one to ride up to the neck. A similar type, made more substantially in leather, is used for polo and has a loop on the inside of the chest strap through which a martingale can be passed. When martingales are used with a hunting breastplate, they are shortened affairs, which are attached to the ring in the centre of the horse's chest.

Stirrup leathers
Stirrup leathers are made from either cowhide, rawhide or buffalo hide. In the case of the first two, the leathers are made so that the flesh side faces outward. The reason for this reversal of usual practice is so that the grain side, which is the harder wearing of the two, will receive the friction caused by contact with the 'eye' (slot) of the stirrup iron. When buffalo hide is used, this precaution is not necessary since the leather is virtually unbreakable. Buffalo hide, which is characteristically red in colour, has only one drawback, which is its propensity to stretch. All stirrup leathers stretch in use but the 'red leathers' stretch more than most. They are nonetheless extremely long-lasting.

A pair of leathers will not necessarily stretch equally; indeed, they are most unlikely to prove so obliging. For this reason, plus the fact that all but the most skilled riders tend to put more weight upon one iron than on the other, it is advisable to change new leathers from side to side daily. For convenience the holes punched in the leathers are usually numbered. It is best to insist on the holes being punched fairly close ('half holes'), to allow for a greater range of adjustment.

Racing leathers are necessarily very narrow, perhaps no greater than ½in in

Above: Stirrup leathers in a variety of widths and leathers. It is preferable for the holes to be punched fairly close, to give greater adjustment, and for them to be numbered. Stirrup leathers are made from cowhide, rawhide or buffalo hide. **Below:** The 'hook-up' or extending stirrup leather—a useful item for short-legged owners of tall horses.

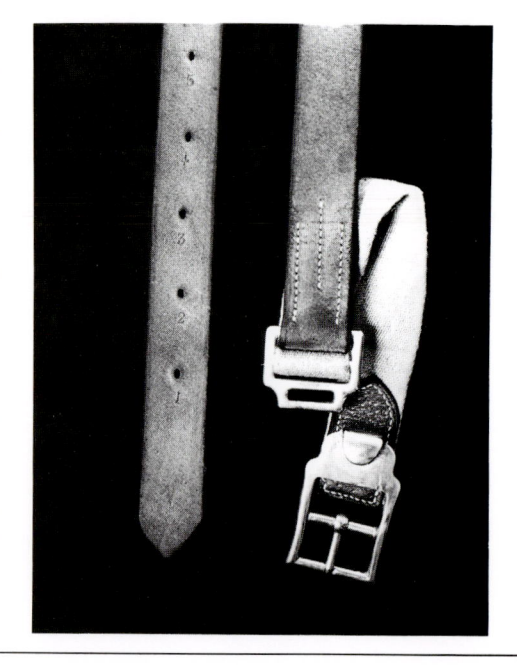

MOUNTINGS

Top: A stockroom of stirrups at a Walsall foundry. **Far left:** The 'Tally-Ho', one of the many safety irons which proliferated in the 19th century. **Left:** Stirrup irons and, in the foreground, castings. **Above:** Example of finely-ornamented stirrups which were made by craftsmen in Europe well into the 17th and 18th centuries.

83

CHAPTER THREE · THE TWENTIETH-CENTURY SADDLE

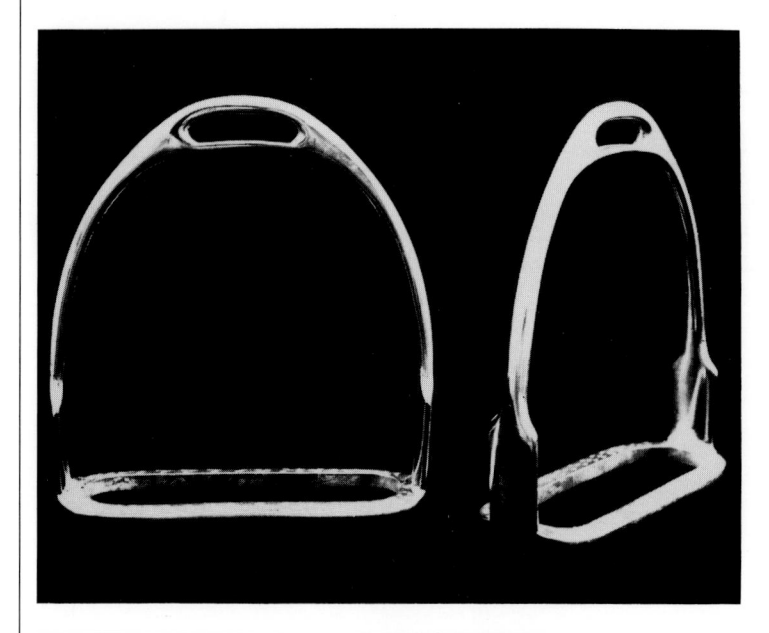

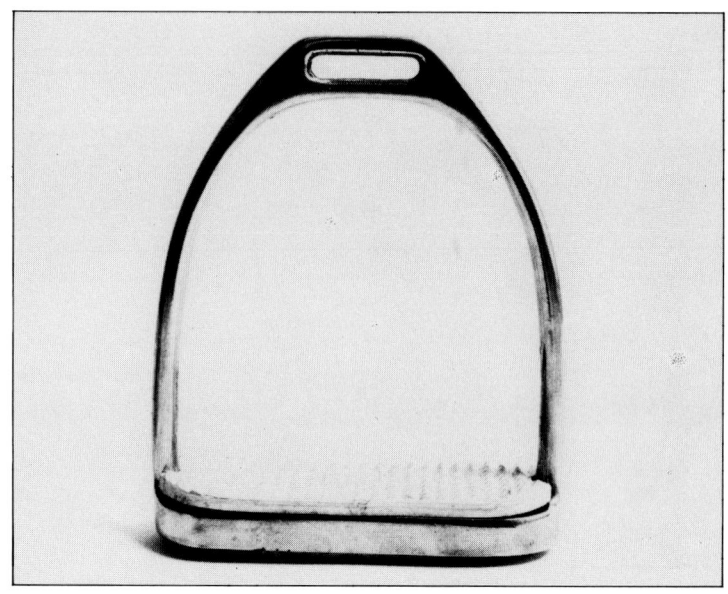

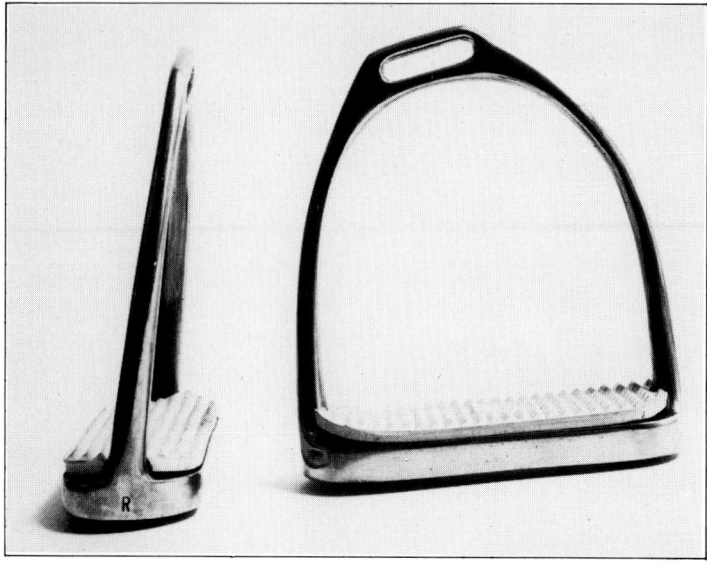

Above left: Plain, Prussian-side, open tread irons. **Above:** Knife-edge irons with heavy tread fitted in addition with anti-slip rubber treads which help the rider maintain the foot position. **Left:** Kournakoff pattern iron with shaped side and tread and cock-eye. The iron was developed for jumping and was designed to fix the rider's foot in what was thought to be the most secure position.

width. Often the material used is not leather at all, but lengths of tubular web, which are naturally very much lighter.

An annoying characteristic of the stirrup leather is the bulge it makes under the rider's thigh, a protrusion which will be more prominent if the stirrup bars are not recessed in the manner described elsewhere. To overcome this problem, as well as to allow the rider's thigh to lie flat against the saddle, it is possible to obtain a stirrup leather which is adjustable at a point about 8in above the stirrup iron, after the military fashion. This type of adjusting leather is found frequently in Europe but rarely seen in the US or Britain.

For those who experience difficulty in mounting, it is still possible to obtain a 'hook-up' or extending leather. This device consists of a hook and slot attachment connected by a length of approximately 8in of stout web. It allows the leather to be extended when mounting, and it can then be easily hooked into place when the rider has gained the saddle. The disadvantage of the arrangement is its bulk when in position, but it is a help when short-legged persons are confronted with long-legged horses.

Stirrup irons
A notable feature in the saddlers' catalogues of the 19th century was the large number of safety stirrup irons—all designed so that in the event of a fall they would release the foot and thus prevent the rider from being dragged. There were many ingenious devices, some of which, however, acquired a reputation for anticipating a fall and thus leaving the rider in place but without the benefit of stirrups.

With two exceptions—the Peacock safety iron, which is still used by children, and the Australian Simplex—modern irons are straightforward in design. Most, however, are used with a stirrup tread, a piece of equipment which seems to have become an essential part of the modern tack room. It assists the rider in keeping the foot position, and it helps to keep the extremities warm by insulating them against the cold metal. Before the introduction of the stirrup tread (a relatively recent innovation), riders relied on the tread of the iron being roughed to give a better grip to the sole of the boot.

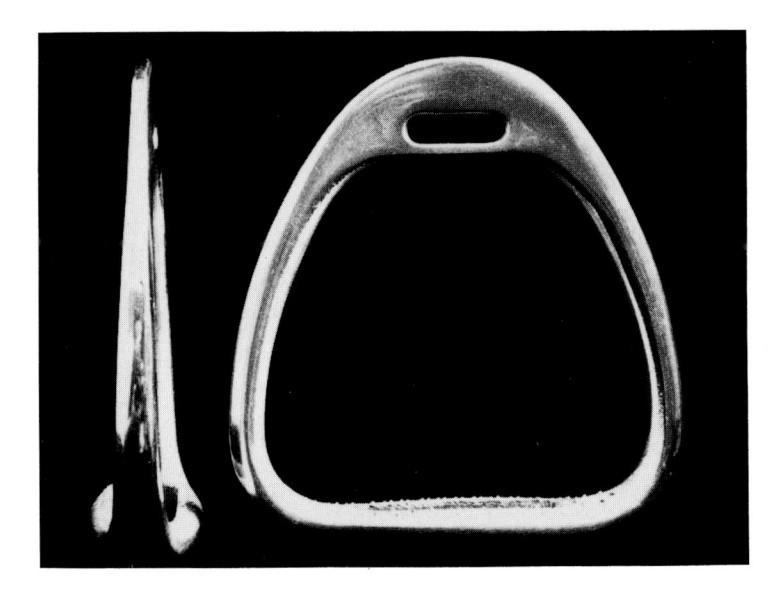

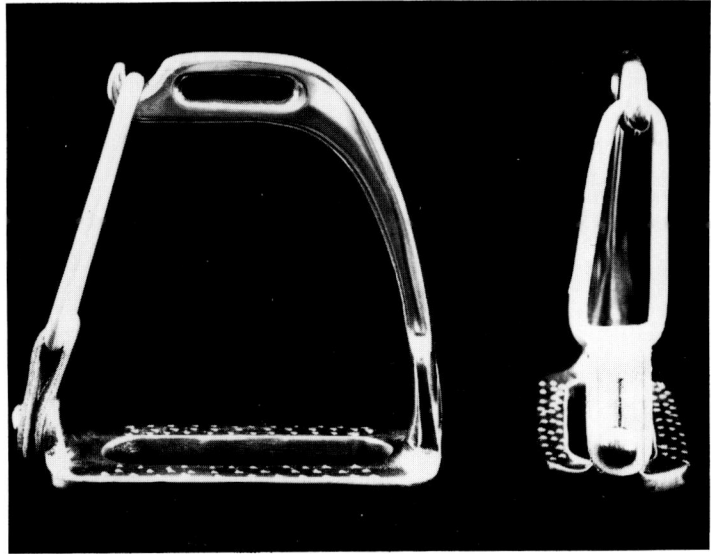

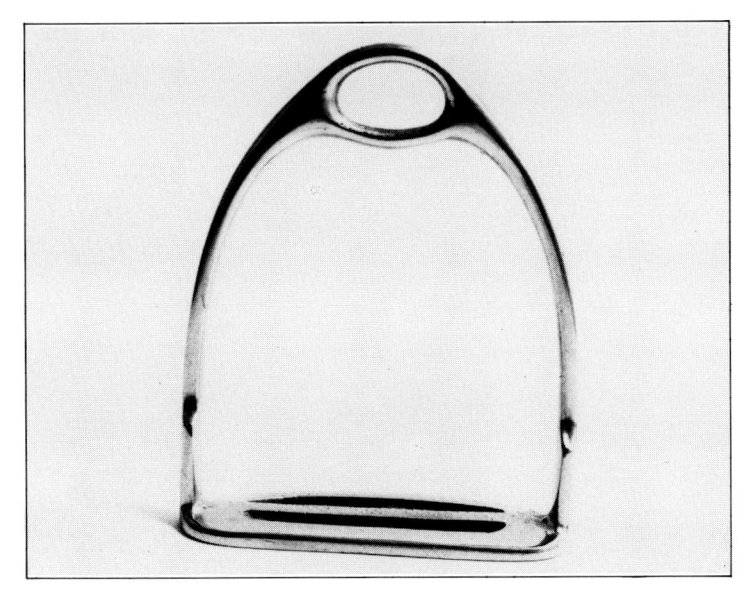

Above left: Aluminium 'cradle' pattern race irons, stronger for racing over fences. **Above:** The Peacock children's safety iron is fitted with the rubber on the outside of the rider's foot so that it will be pulled off its hook should the foot press against it in a fall. Replacing worn or perished rubbers with binder twine or any other non-stretch material is a recipe for disaster, especially the extremely strong synthetic twine used nowadays. Always keep a spare pair of rubbers in the tack room—or don't use the stirrups! **Left:** Round eye side-saddle iron.

The disadvantages of the Peacock iron are considerable, and in the light of these, it is probable that the provision of a fair-sized, heavy conventional iron, through which a child's foot could not slip, as well as insistence upon the wearing of proper footwear would contribute just as effectively to the child's safety. Since, in effect, the Peacock has three sides instead of four, the outside of the iron being the rubber ring, its strength is correspondingly reduced. As a result, the tread can become bent by the action of mounting and will thus affect the child's foot and leg position. Furthermore, the rubber rings decay and are easily lost, frequently being replaced by binder twine or some similar substitute. Finally, it is quite surprising how many people fit the irons the wrong way round with the rubber ring on the inside. Another pattern of stirrup iron with a built-in safety feature is the Australian Simplex, with the forward bulge of the outside arm of the iron permitting the foot to slip out easily in emergencies. A simple and very sensible variation to the basic pattern can be made by bending the top of the iron away from the instep. This will save the boot from being worn in that area if the foot is placed fully home in the iron and is, of course, more comfortable for the rider.

A once popular jumping iron was that invented by a Russian cavalry officer and takes his name—Kournakoff. This iron was designed to position the foot in accordance with Caprilli's system of forward riding. The eye is offset to the inside, the sides are sloped forward and the tread sloped up from the rear. In consequence, the rider's foot is held with toe up and heel down and with the outside of the sole higher than the inside. This position in combination with that of the rest of the leg, is held to give very great security since the knee and thigh are pulled inward onto the saddle. The Kournakoff pattern is not suitable for dressage riding, however, and it is disastrous in the event that the left iron is fitted to the right-hand side of the saddle by mistake and vice-versa.

Racing irons are usually made in a cradle pattern, which is more comfortable when wearing thin boots, and are as light as possible. Sometimes aluminium is used as an alternative metal.

CHAPTER THREE · THE TWENTIETH-CENTURY SADDLE

The Saddle · **Numnahs**

Numnahs, or saddle pads, are items of equipment placed under the saddle to give greater comfort to the horse's back and to remove any risk of the animal becoming galled. In effect, anything of any substance placed between the saddle and the back may be regarded as a numnah, whatever material it is made from.

Traditional numnahs
The traditional numnah is made of sheepskin. The skin can be used in its natural state or the numnah can be covered with linen. Not surprisingly, in recent times, sheepskin has been largely replaced by man-made material. The advantage of sheepskin is that the wool is resilient and is less likely to become flattened in use. On the other hand, it is difficult to wash and even harder to dry, whereas man-made fabrics can be put in a washing machine without coming to any harm. However, they become flat with use, while some types of fibre can prove to be abrasive. Foam plastic is another man-made product used in the making of numnahs and is usually covered in cotton or linen cloth. Although soft and resilient, it can absorb sweat and is then something of a problem for horse and rider.

Another traditional type of numnah is made from thick felt. It is shaped to the horse's back and is a very durable article, although again it will absorb sweat. A numnah of this type was often used in cases of sore backs, with a 'chamber' cut in the felt in the area of the sore place so that no pressure could be put on the wound.

Advantages and disadvantages
To what extent the use of numnahs is practical is a matter of doubt. It is certain that some horses appreciate the comfort they afford, and it is probably a wise precaution to put one on a young horse whose back has not hardened, or on one brought up from grass in soft condition. However, there are drawbacks. A numnah does not permit the free passage of air down the channel of the saddle; it can cause backs to become overheated and therefore more likely to be made sore, while, if it is used in dirty condition, it may cause galls on the horse's back. From the viewpoint of the rider, the presence of a numnah places him that much farther away from his horse, therefore preventing the close contact that is desirable. Finally, there is the temptation to employ a numnah to counter the effect of an ill-fitting saddle, when the real answer is to have the saddle regulated to the back.

There is, of course, another form of numnah which is designed purely for the benefit of the rider. It usually goes under the name of 'seat cover' and is made of sheepskin to fit over the top of the saddle. It is very comfortable but can become unpleasantly warm in hot weather.

Wither pads and saddlecloths
A wither pad can be used as a temporary measure should a saddle have become too low in front, when there is a danger of the front arch bearing on the withers. It is therefore a useful tack-room item. A wither pad may be made of foam plastic, an oval piece of sheepskin, or of a similar substitute. The best ones, however, are knitted from wool; these are exceptionally soft and resilient. Wither pads are nearly always used with very light race saddles which would otherwise, because of their construction, bear down on the wither. The purpose of a saddlecloth, other

Below: Made from hard-wearing cotton velour and padded generously with polyester, these saddle pads afford significant padding and comfort for the horse.

than for pure decoration, is to keep the panel of the saddle clean and free from the sweat deposits which would otherwise occur during use.

Modern practices
Some numnahs of man-made fabrics are very poor in design and performance, probably the worst being the nylon-covered plastic foam type which are harsh to the back, non-absorbent, hot and which flatten completely under pressure. Modern foams such as Sorbothane compress but conform to the horse's back without springing back immediately, so providing 'shaped cushioning' to the back and, when used in saddle seats, to the rider's seat.

'Wicking' fabrics which allow sweat to pass through them from the horse's coat relatively easily are readily available, as are soft (as opposed to abrasive) synthetic fleeces; these can, however, be rather hot in use. Polyester fillings which are soft and resilient and which do not ball or mat into injurious lumps are also commonly in use.

Gel pads, which again conform to the horse's back, are now widely used, too, particularly in the endurance world, although some kinds appear to create too much movement when used with a saddle, and so are not, perhaps, as comfortable as they are intended to be.

Cotton-covered numnahs with an interior padding of cotton or synthetic material are very popular, although some physiotherapists maintain that the constant slight movement of the diamond-shaped rows of stitching creates friction on the backs of fine-skinned horses and consequently sore skin. Physiotherapists now often recommend using no numnah at all or at least one of a material giving an even feel (no stitching) to the back, such as sheared fleece or even a leather version. At least one British saddler is currently reverting to the old practice of lining his saddle panels with wool serge, so this is a development worth watching.

With any numnah, it should fulfil its objective of providing increased comfort to the horse, possibly absorbing sweat, and perhaps temporarily helping to adjust the fit of a saddle without causing further problems, such as rucking up, friction, pressure, overheating and so on.

A common problem with numnahs is that they can restrict the free passage of air down the saddle gullet, and can also be pressed down hard onto the spine by the saddle, especially onto the vulnerable wither area; of course, this actually negates the value of a clear channel down the spine. They should always be pulled well up into the saddle arches (pommel and cantle) and gullet to avoid this.

Left and inset: A selection of numnahs in various materials, from **left to right:** felt; quilted cotton; foam-filled cotton; synthetic fur; real sheep wool. Numnahs are shaped to fit the saddle and are worn between the horse's back and the saddle for greater comfort. **Above:** Brightly coloured Western blankets, always worn with a Western saddle.

CHAPTER THREE · THE TWENTIETH-CENTURY SADDLE

The Saddle · **Fitting**

The saddle lies on the horse's back behind the big muscle of the shoulder, the panel bearing on the blocks of muscle on each side of the spine. In order that the horse should be entirely comfortable and able to move and to jump without any restriction being imposed by the saddle, it is vital that the various key points concerning fitting are observed.

The importance of fitting the saddle correctly cannot be over-stressed. A badly fitting saddle, which pinches the horse or interferes with the movement of the back by pressing on the spine, detracts from the free movement of the limbs and can even cause the horse to move so unevenly as to appear lame. It will also prevent the horse from using himself fully over fences and, in extreme cases, may result in the animal refusing to jump at all. A saddle that distributes the weight of the rider unevenly, concentrating the pressure over one particular area, acts to unbalance the horse in movement. To compensate for this, the animal will become very stiff on one side of the body, and the regularity and smoothness of the gaits will be affected. In all cases the horse is likely to sustain injury to the back which will incapacitate him for normal working purposes.

The rules of fitting
The general rules of saddle fitting are as follows. In the first instance, the tree must fit the horse's back. It follows from this that, when the saddle is made and as long as the panel is properly fitted, the completed article will be a correspondingly good fit. Too narrow a tree will cause the points to pinch the horse below and on each side of the withers. This cannot be changed by alteration, for it is rarely satisfactory to attempt widening the tree. Too broad a tree will mean that the fore arch will bear directly on the withers. To put more stuffing in the panel in an attempt to rectify this puts the saddle out of balance and is more than likely to cause soreness.

The completed saddle must sit on the back so that, when the rider is in position, there is adequate clearance of the withers at the fore arch (it should be possible to insert three fingers); the saddle should at no point touch the backbone along the whole of its length; the channel dividing the panel must be wide enough to ensure that the weight is borne on each side of the spine and no pinching of the latter is possible. If the channel is too narrow or becomes closed, pinching of the spinal vertebrae will occur. When viewed directly from behind with the rider in position, it should be possible to see daylight at the fore arch end of the channel.

The saddle must sit level on the back so that the weight of the rider is distributed evenly over the entire bearing surface of the panel. If the saddle is stuffed too high at the cantle, it will throw the rider forward, concentrating the pressure over the forepart of the saddle and thus creating the risk of a sore back developing. Similarly, a saddle that is too high at the front throws the rider's weight to the rear. An unevenly stuffed panel will put the weight more on one side than the other; this will also occur should the tree of the saddle be slightly twisted.

In all these instances, the concentration of weight over one part of the back is likely to cause soreness, and all will affect the free movement of the horse. When viewed from behind, it is very easy to see whether or not the saddle is sitting level and true.

The saddle must not be cut so far forward as to interfere with the action of the shoulder, while the panel must be clean, resilient and free of all irregularities. A lump on the panel creates a pressure point on the back which will cause soreness.

While conforming to all these points the saddle should fit as closely as possible so that there is no chance of it rocking and causing soreness by friction. An over-stuffed panel holding the saddle too high will cause this type of problem.

It is also important that the length of the saddle relates to the length of the horse's back and the size of the rider. Short-backed horses and the back structures of many Arabians will prohibit the use of

Left: A modern saddle sitting level on the back but allowing clearance along the length of the backbone.

It is necessary for the saddle to lie level on the back so that the weight of the rider is distributed evenly over the whole bearing surface and points of pressure are avoided.

It is just as important for the cantle to be well clear of the back as it is for the head to have adequate clearance of the withers.

It should be possible to insert three fingers between the withers and the top of the front arch.

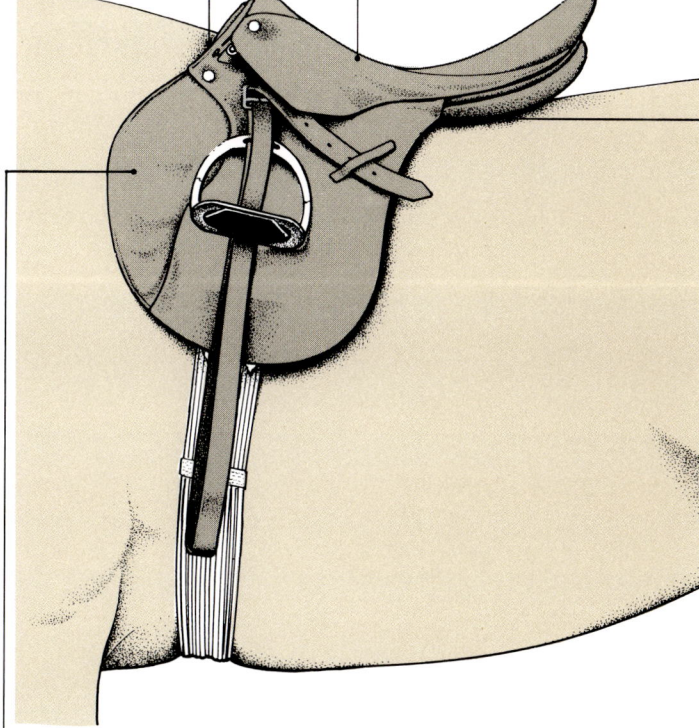

Panels must be level, clean and free from irregularities which might cause points of pressure and result in galling.

The forward inclination of the panel and the flap should not be such as to obscure the shoulder or interfere with its free movement. The saddle should at all times lie behind the shoulder, whatever the shape of the latter.

saddles that are, say, 17½in or 18in long. As far as the rider is concerned, it is a matter of the plate being big enough for the joint. Too small a saddle, coupled with an overlarge and overlapping posterior, will result in too great a concentration of weight over too small an area.

The problem of fatness

It is never advisable to fit a saddle to a fat horse, for what fits him when he is in gross condition will gall him when he is fit. Fat ponies will hold a saddle in place better if a point strap is fitted, as in a show saddle, plus a girth with a centre of dimple rubber, which lies in the sternum curve (or where, in the case of ponies, the curve should be). The problem can often be overcome by keeping the pony in a body roller. This, like a corset, is to encourage a better configuration.

New saddles with stuffed panels need to be regulated about three months after purchase if the use has been normal, and thereafter should be serviced once a year.

Modern fitting systems

These basic rules of saddle fitting always apply, and even synthetic saddles, with synthetic panels and stuffing, need to be checked regularly to make sure that they still fit, if only because of a horse's changing body weight and shape. Now, though, at the end of the 20th century, we and our saddlers have, if we wish to take advantage of it, computerized and electronic sensor equipment of various designs which can really improve our knowledge of just what happens to a horse's back under a saddle, where most of the pressure is, plus how to improve saddle design and fit. Some companies are developing their own technology-assisted measuring and fitting systems, and new designs incorporating up-to-date knowledge will improve not only saddle fit and effect but also design. These are all developments worth watching.

90

CHAPTER FOUR

Specialist Saddles

Western Saddles
Racing Equipment
Side-Saddles

The Western saddle presented by Buffalo Bill Cody to King Edward VII when he was Prince of Wales. The horn is decorated with a silver relief of Buffalo Bill riding a bucking steer.

CHAPTER FOUR · SPECIALIST SADDLES

Specialist Saddles · **Western**

Just as the Spanish horses brought to the Americas by the 16th century *conquistadores* form the base of North American horse culture, so the Spaniards' saddle and bridle form the basis of Western riding equipment. The saddles used by the *conquistadores* were an amalgam of European and Moorish styles and had been evolved to suit the needs of the horseman in battle. Most important of those was the rider's security, both when wielding his own weapons and receiving blows from those of his adversaries. It was to provide maximum security that the saddle of that period was equipped with a very high pommel and cantle which, together with the metal armour which encased his legs, obliged the soldier to ride with a long stirrup and with his legs straight. The saddle sat high on the horse's back and the seat sloped steeply downwards from pommel to cantle so that the rider's weight was forced to the rear of the saddle.

This was the saddle inherited by the Mexicans, who became the west's first cattle ranchers in the southern states of North America. When cattle ranching became big business, it was natural enough that the saddlery already in use should form the basis of the cowboy's equipment. He needed a saddle which would fit any shape and size of horse—the cowpuncher worked on the *remuda* system, keeping a number of horses which he worked in rotation—and in this respect the high Mexican saddle served him well enough.

The cowboy saddle

The cattle ranching industry of the brief 'cattle kingdom' period that followed the US Civil War was of a different type from that practised by the Mexican *vaqueros*. Cattle were herded hundreds of miles from the southern plains where they were raised to the rail terminals which served the fast-growing towns of the northern states. Cowboys spent such long periods of time in the saddle that comfort also became a very important prerequisite and

This diagram shows the parts of the Western saddle

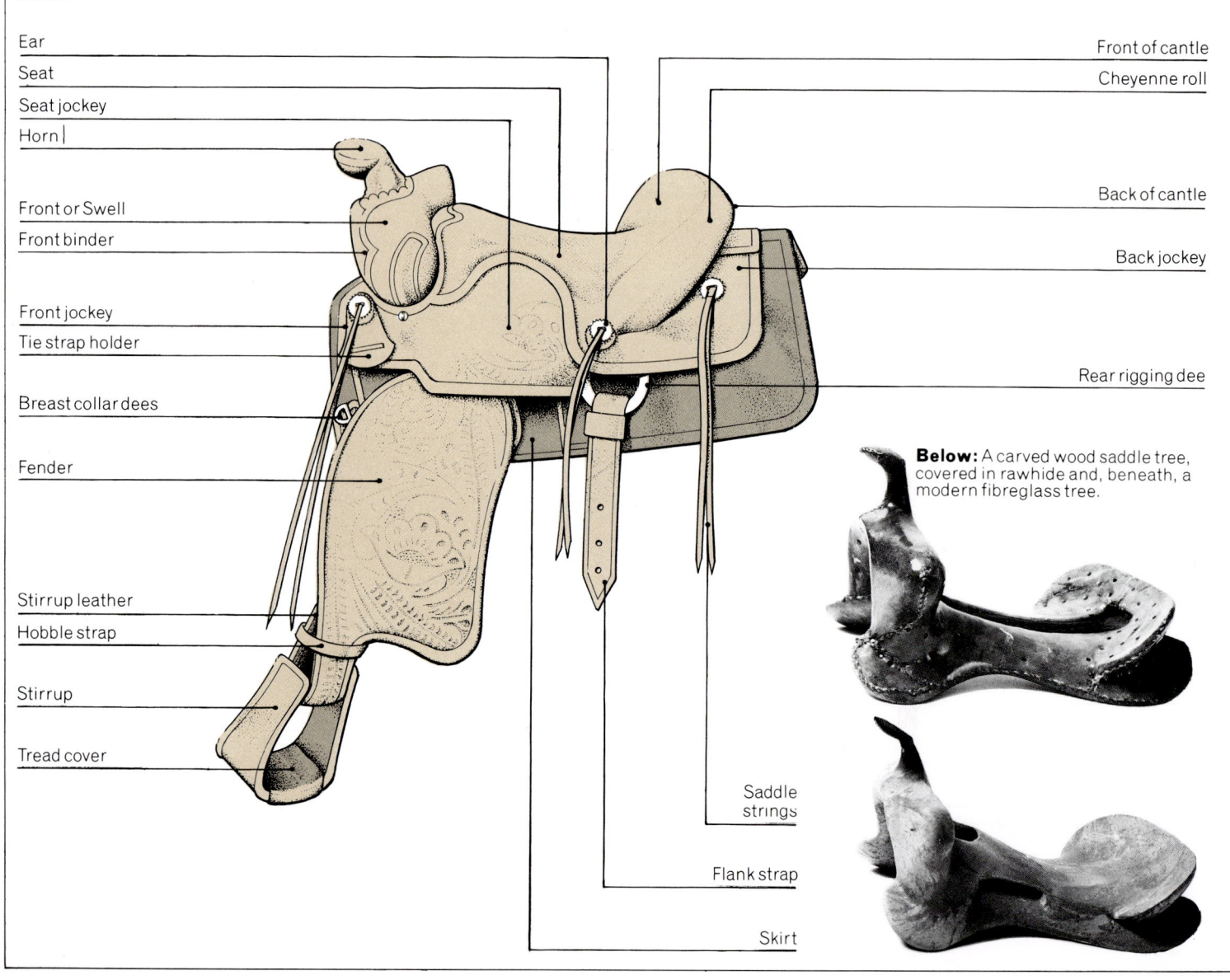

- Ear
- Seat
- Seat jockey
- Horn
- Front or Swell
- Front binder
- Front jockey
- Tie strap holder
- Breast collar dees
- Fender
- Stirrup leather
- Hobble strap
- Stirrup
- Tread cover

- Front of cantle
- Cheyenne roll
- Back of cantle
- Back jockey
- Rear rigging dee
- Saddle strings
- Flank strap
- Skirt

Below: A carved wood saddle tree, covered in rawhide and, beneath, a modern fibreglass tree.

92

WESTERN SADDLES

Left: A working cowboy of a century ago. His clothes are as practical as his saddlery: the broad-brimmed hat gives shade from the sun; the kerchief can be pulled up over the face in dusty conditions; the gloves protect his hands from rope burns; the chaps protect the legs from cactus cuts and keep out bad weather and the spurs, worn on strong, high-heeled boots, jangle as the horse moves and warn the cattle of the rider's approach. The saddle accommodates all his necessary possessions and affords a comfortable seat during long working hours. **Below, left:** A Great Plains saddle of the late 1800s. Saddle patterns varied from one territory to another and it was possible to tell a man's origin from his 'rig'. **Centre:** A similar saddle of the same period but with regional differences, for example the cinch fastening and connecting strap. **Right:** A skillfully-designed side-saddle, probably made in the early 1900s and certainly of Mexican origin.

CHAPTER FOUR · SPECIALIST SADDLES

various improvements were made to the Mexican-style saddle to prevent chafing and soreness of the seat and legs. The horse, too, had to be considered in this context, for he was the cowboy's lifeline. The saddle developed specifically for ranch work was a heavy item, weighing as much as 40 to 50lb. It was, however, so designed that this weight was spread over a large area of the horse's back, thus reducing the likelihood of saddle sores developing. To help achieve this, the skirts of the saddle were considerably enlarged. Further protection was afforded to the horse by the use of a thick blanket which was folded several times and placed under the saddle. This blanket had the added advantage of doubling as a bed roll for the cowboy, who often had to sleep rough in the open air and in all weathers for nights on end.

As well as enlarging the skirts, the pioneers of Western riding introduced fenders, which are, in effect, a much enlarged version of the narrow stirrup leathers used on the old Mexican saddles. The fender is a wide piece of stout leather which affords the rider's leg considerable protection, preventing sweat from the horse's sides from soaking into his clothes and also minimizing the risk of chafing. Stirrups were attached to the bottom of the fenders; the stiffness of the latter ensured that the stirrups themselves moved very little, a great advantage to the cowboy who often needed to mount in a hurry.

The cowboy's stirrups were made of wood, covered with rawhide. This was a much more satisfactory arrangement than metal, since the latter could be extremely cold on the feet in winter while becoming unbearably hot under the blazing summer sun. Stirrups were made with varying widths of sole supports and were heavy items of equipment. To protect his feet when riding in rough scrub country, the cowboy adopted the stirrup covers used by the Mexicans and known as *tapaderos*. These looked like boxes and were made of tough leather. The cowboy called them 'taps'. In cold weather they could be lined with fleece to give extra protection to the feet. Californian cowboys developed their own distinctive design.

The other major modifications which the Mexican saddle underwent were directly influenced by one particular aspect of the cowboy's work—roping. When he wanted to separate a steer from the herd, he did so by lassooing it. The cowboy secured his end of the lasso to the front of the saddle which had to take the strain when the roped animal struggled against the restricting rope. For this purpose the cowboy added a horn, shaped like an inverted Y, to the high pommelled Mexican saddle. The front arch of the saddle was strengthened with steel and widened to ensure complete clearance of the withers. The heavy shoulders, known as 'swells', thus created at the front of the saddle added to the rider's security by supporting the thighs.

The horn itself served the desired purpose satisfactorily. However, the enormous strain put on the saddle when the rope linking a calf to the horn was suddenly pulled taut caused the saddle to be

Left: A very rare example of an early Mexican-style saddle built before the advent of the dish horn. This saddle is a collector's piece and the inset shows the high quality embossed decoration. **Right:** A relatively lightweight saddle made on a carved wooden tree with laced-on seat covering.

WESTERN SADDLES

CHAPTER FOUR · SPECIALIST SADDLES

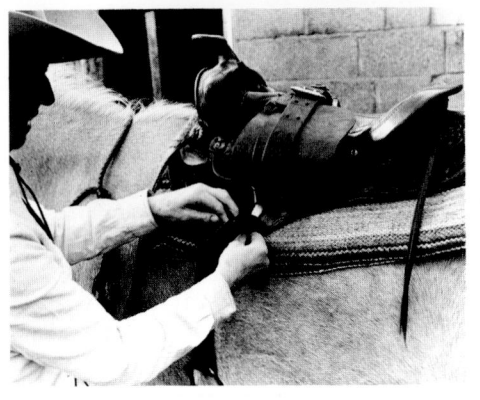

Far left: Putting the Western saddle over a carefully folded blanket and attaching the cinch. **Left:** Detail of the way in which the cinch is buckled or, in this case, tied. **Above:** Having secured the cinch it is necessary to pull each leg forward in turn in order to ensure that there are no wrinkles of skin below the elbow.

dragged forward, often causing painful cuts to the horse's shoulders and elbows. Indeed, it was not uncommon for the rider to be unseated, or for the tree of a saddle actually to break, when subjected to such rough usage.

Strengthening the cinches
The solution to the problem lay in the positioning of the cinches, the Western term for girths. Mexican saddles were single-rigged—that is, they were secured by one girth placed around the horse's belly, not far behind the elbows. Since the roping process caused the cantle to be pulled upwards and then the whole saddle to shift forwards, the obvious solution was to employ a second cinch, fitted behind the rider's leg.

Under normal riding conditions, it was the front or forward cinch which continued to hold the saddle in position, the rear or flank cinch being fastened fairly slackly. The latter came into play when pressure was exerted on the horn, preventing the saddle being pulled upwards and forwards. It is a system which was soon in common use throughout most of the ranching country of the west and is known as double-rigging or full-double rigging.

The forward cinch of a cowboy's saddle was usually made of mohair, horsehair or cord, the ends of which were woven on to large rings. Leather straps were used to secure these rings to the rigging rings attached to the saddle itself. The nearside strap, called the latigo strap, was wrapped several times around the cinch ring and finished with a knot. The flank cinch was made of leather and had a buckle stitched to each end. These buckles were fastened to straps attached to another pair of rigging rings fitted on each side of the rear of the saddle.

The one disadvantage that arose from the provision of a loosely fastened flank cinch was its tendency to swing backwards and forwards. This could cause galling, while, in the case of geldings or stallions, the cinch could hit and damage the horse's sheath. To prevent this, a connecting strap was fitted, linking the two cinches under the horse's body.

These, then, were the major modifications made to the original Spanish-based Mexican saddle by the cowboy of the west. In addition he added sets of strings, which he fitted to the near and offside saddle skirts. To these strings, the cowboy, who was virtually a nomad, attached his personal possessions. There was usually another set of strings fitted to the front of the saddle at the base of the pommel and also a latigo carrier.

The Californian variant
Although the pattern of saddle described above spread throughout the main cattle ranching areas of Texas, Arizona and New Mexico, there was one regional variation, which was directly related to a difference in terrain. In the far western cattle rearing areas of California the countryside was much more open than elsewhere and this led to the development of a type of roping somewhat different in nature.

The Texan cowboy's method of roping was to wrap the end of the rope round the horn several times and to hold it firm when it was tautened by the weight of the steer, thus jerking the latter to a sudden, violent stop. In California, on the other hand, the cowboy had more room to manoeuvre and would play with the steer in much the same way as an angler plays with a fish. He, too, wound his lasso around the saddle horn, but, when the steer began to tauten the rope, the cowboy would pay out a few feet or so by allowing some of the coils to unwind from the horn. By repeating this process he brought the calf to a gradual halt. As a result the saddle did not have to withstand such a strain

WESTERN SADDLES

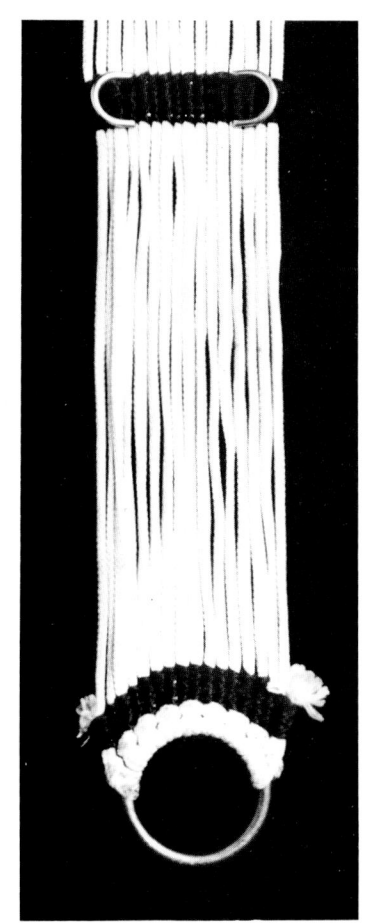

Left, top and bottom: Examples of woven hair and cord cinches, the former, in particular, giving a very firm, non-slip purchase. **Top:** A decorative Mexican saddle blanket which is as practical as it is colourful. **Above:** Two patterns of leather breastplate which again combine practicality with decorative effect. **Right:** The Western stirrup is made of willow wood shaped over wood and, in this instance, covered with leather.

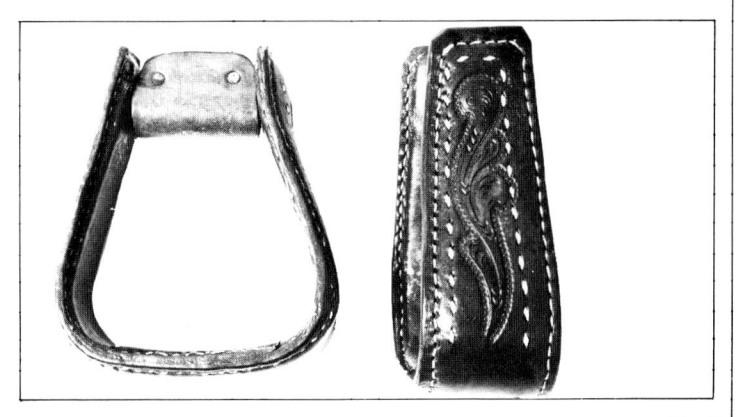

CHAPTER FOUR · SPECIALIST SADDLES

and thus did not require the addition of a flank cinch. For many years, therefore, the Californian cowboy retained the single-rigging system of the Mexican saddle.

This type of roping became known as 'dallying', from the Spanish *de la vuelta* (to give a turn), and the cowboys who employed it were called dallymen. A disadvantage of their roping technique was its tendency to injure the hands—many dallymen apparently had the odd finger severed by means of a fast-moving rope.

One final item of equipment which was in general use, particularly in mountainous regions, was the breastplate, made of leather or cord and fastened to the rigging D rings situated at the front of the saddle. A strap, passed over the horse's withers, kept the breastplate in place; sometimes another strap was attached to the centre, passed between the forelegs and fastened to a D on the front of the forward cinch.

The McClellan saddle

While this modified version of the old Mexican saddle served the cowboy well for the duration of the ranching boom, another and quite different type of saddle was adopted by the US army. It hailed from Hungary and was taken to North America by an officer called McClellan, whose name it subsequently bore. Despite much criticism on account of its lack of comfort, it was used by the US cavalry until as late as 1940.

The earliest McClellan saddles did not have panels, so the rider's thighs were not protected from the risk of chafing against the horse's sweaty body. Soldiers are said

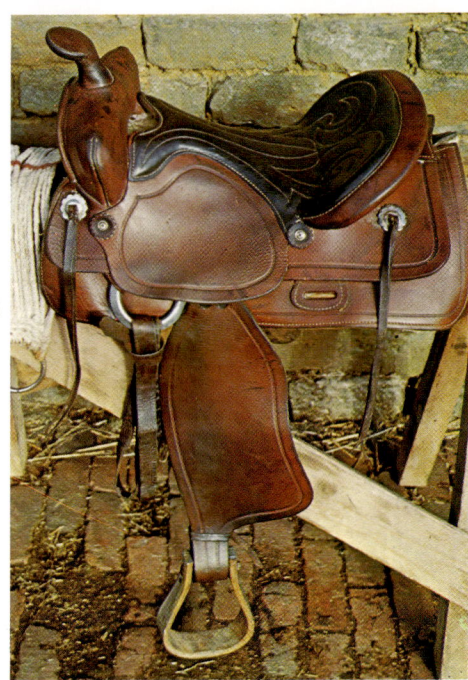

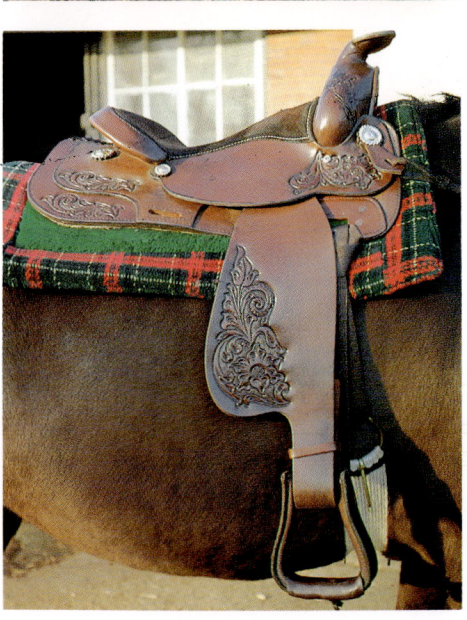

Above: Three-quarter size pleasure saddle with seven-eighth rigging and with the leather parts deeply engraved. It would be suitable for a teenager or a lightweight adult. **Top right:** Another teenager's saddle but with a cutting-type fork and plain wooden stirrups. **Right:** A lightweight pleasure saddle in position over a folded blanket.

Left: A lightweight barrel racing-type saddle with hand-tooled leatherwork and a padded seat. The wooden stirrups are sheathed in steel.

CHAPTER FOUR · SPECIALIST SADDLES

Left: An extravagantly-constructed Grand Parade saddle in black leather decorated with stainless steel studs. Elaborate saddles such as this are used in carnival and rodeo parades.
Above: Matching, similarly elaborate **tapaderos** or stirrup covers.

to have suffered a good deal from saddle sores before the advantage of panels was appreciated, although even then many saddles of the old type continued to be made. But, despite its drawbacks, the McClellan saddle had one advantage. It would fit any animal and did not, apparently, cause undue back troubles.

Modern changes
Some 20 years before the McClellan saddle finally sank into disuse, the cowboy's saddle began to undergo further modifications. As elsewhere in the world, the emphasis in riding had switched from work to pleasure. In the USA, trail riding, known in Europe as trekking, became popular, together with Western equitation show classes. While the existing saddle

Below: A very well-constructed exercise or training saddle of the early 1900s. **Far right:** Its modern counterparts, pads made from fibreglass with the trees covered in fur fabric. **Right:** The strongest equipment is needed for the rough, tough sport of saddleback broncho riding.

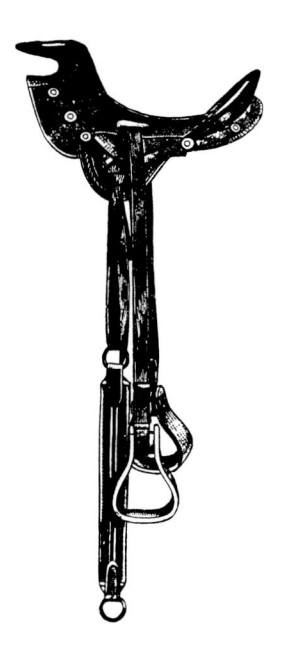

was ideal in many respects for these sports—certainly its basic concept was what was required—it proved unnecessarily cumbersome for pleasure riding.

As a result the Western saddle as it exists today has a much smaller horn. In addition, this is sloped forwards, so as to eliminate any possibility of injury to the rider's midriff should he be pitched forward against it. Both cantle and pommel have been made lower and, while the excellent weight-distributing properties of the saddle have been retained, the saddle itself is now somewhat lighter. One of the reasons for this is that, unless the saddle is to be used for competitive calf roping, there is no necessity for it to be fitted with a heavily reinforced front arch. Such saddles, complete with a proper roping horn, are of course still made, but they are not necessary for the average pleasure rider.

Nor is the rear cinch absolutely essential and modern saddles have reverted to the old single-rigging system. This, however, has also undergone some modification, for a saddle secured solely with a cinch positioned so far forward that it is directly below the front arch (as was the Spanish system) lies on the horse's back in such a way as to force the rider to sit well back towards the cantle and to adopt a position not altogether suited to modern equitation. In addition, the conformation of some horses is such that the cinch can cause chafing to their elbows.

Consequently, saddles are made with a variety of cinch positions. The opposite extreme to the Spanish style of single-rigging is when the cinch is placed absolutely centrally between pommel and cantle. This is called centre-fire rigging (a term which derives from a gun cartridge in which the firing pin strikes the centre of the primer). Between Spanish and centre-fire rigging, there are alternative positions known as ⅞, ¾, or ⅝ rigging. Which system is favoured depends very much on the conformation of the individual horse and the purpose for which the saddle is to be used.

Unless they are to be used for roping contests, most modern double-rigged saddles are fitted with 'in-skirt' rigging for the back cinch. In other words, the rear rigging rings have been replaced by leather straps attached directly to the saddle. This arrangement, while not strong enough to withstand the strain of cattle roping, is adequate for other types of Western riding. It has the advantage of being less bulky and therefore more comfortable for the rider's leg, which also has closer contact with the horse's sides as a result. In some saddles the front rigging rings have also been eliminated to reduce the bulk still further.

The concept of the forward seat has also had a certain amount of influence on the Western saddle. Today the seat of the latter does not slope as steeply backwards as it did in the past, while the stirrup is placed further back, nearer to the centre of

CHAPTER FOUR · SPECIALIST SADDLES

Left: A typical Californian-type saddle of modern design. The deep seat, prominent horn and distinctive **tapaderos** are typical features.
Right: A deep-seat cutting saddle, silver-laced on the skirt and with Cheyenne roll and swell. The horn is covered with a laced raw-hide strip.

the saddle, than formerly. As a result the rider does not sit so far back. The leg is not as straight, nor is the foot pushed forward so exaggeratedly, as was the case with the old-time cowboys.

The lighter tree, lighter leathers and elimination of rigging rings for the back cinch mean that the modern Western saddle weighs around 30lb, a considerable improvement on its predecessor. Many modern saddles are elaborately tooled, stamped or engraved and decorated.

Broncho busting
A final variation on the Western saddle is the model developed for broncho busting, which derives from the cowboy's method of breaking in wild horses. Nowadays it is a popular sport, not a necessity, and the bucking horses are as professional as the competing riders with their eyes on the prize money. Saddles must conform to the rules laid down by the governing body of the sport, the Rodeo Cowboys' Association, and come in two types, the bronc saddle and the bareback rig.

The former is much like a normal Western saddle, but the exact dimensions such as the size of the tree and the height of the cantle, must be adhered to by all competitors. The bareback rig is little more than a piece of sturdy leather, with no seat or cantle, secured to the horse's back by means of centre-fire rigging. The rider is provided with stirrups and a leather hand-hold at the front, but otherwise the rig provides little security.

WESTERN SADDLES

CHAPTER FOUR · SPECIALIST SADDLES

Specialist Saddles · Racing Equipment

The making of racing equipment—in particular race saddles—is usually confined to specialist firms operating in the main racing areas. Apart from exercising tack for race purposes, it is not usually the province of wholesale saddlers.

Racing saddles for flat racing can be as light as 12oz when they are made and will weigh only a little over 1lb when mounted with girths, leathers and irons. Steeplechasing saddles are naturally bigger and heavier, but a 4lb or 5lb saddle is not unusual.

The lightest racing saddles are, indeed, little more than a convenient point of attachment for the stirrup leathers and irons. In common with conventional saddles, they can be made on a wooden tree or—a practice which is now increasingly

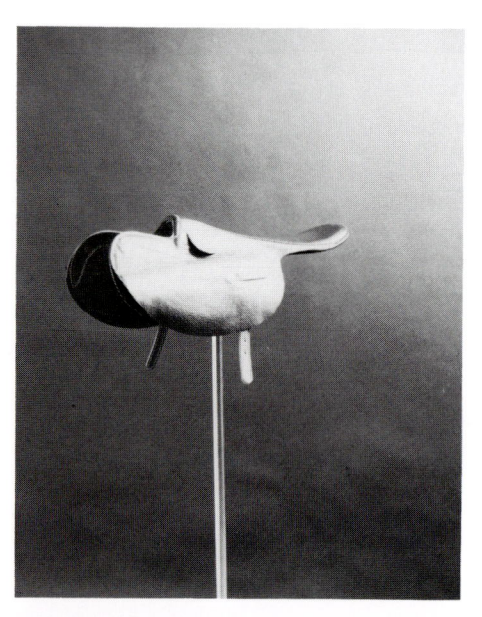

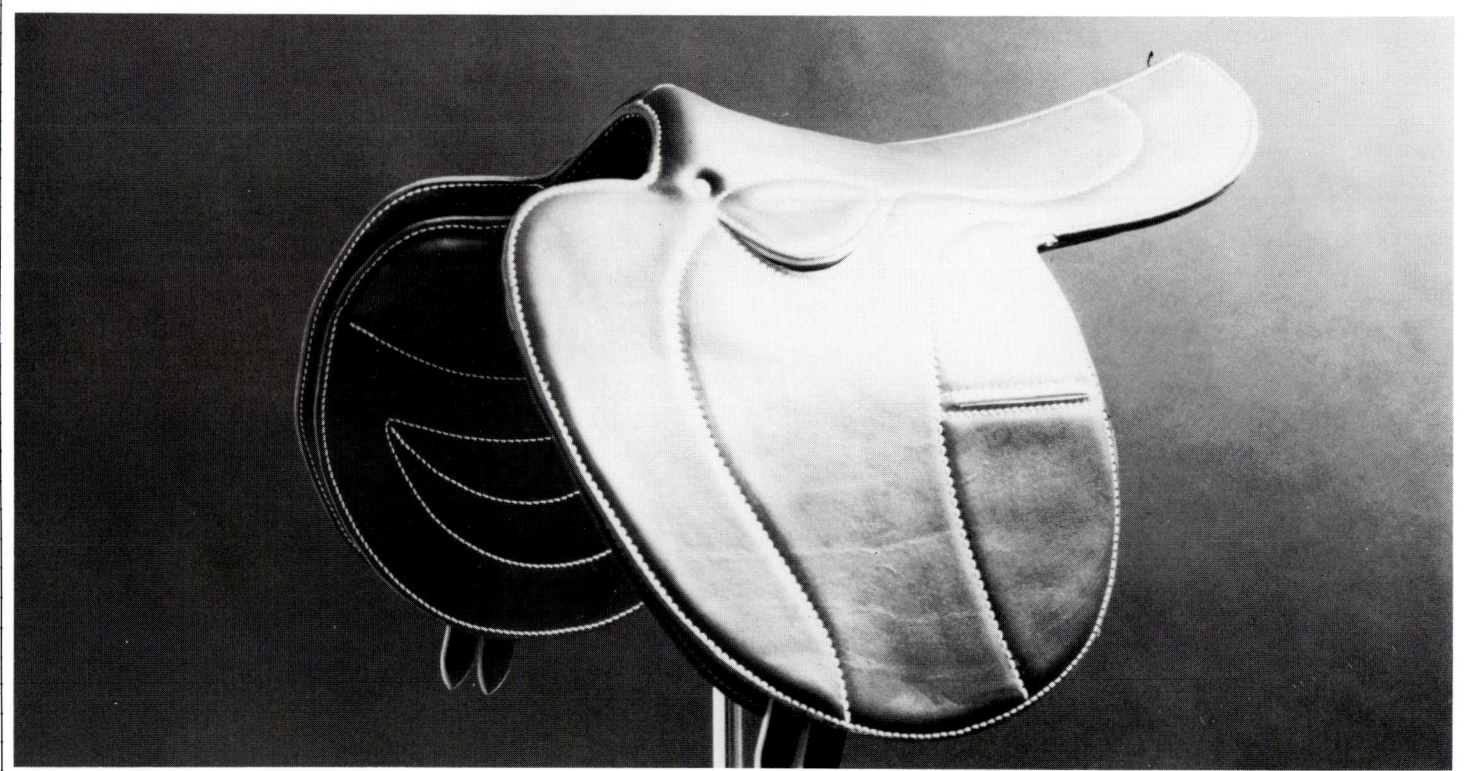

Top left: A race exercise saddle popular in America which could also be used for racing itself where weight requirements permitted.
Top right: The half tree on which the race exercise pads are built and, underneath, a conventional racing tree without, of course, stirrup bars. **Above:** A flexible exercise pad, built on a half tree. **Right:** A heavier pattern race exercise saddle used extensively in Europe. **Far right:** A weight cloth, which might also be used for show jumping or eventing as well as for racing.

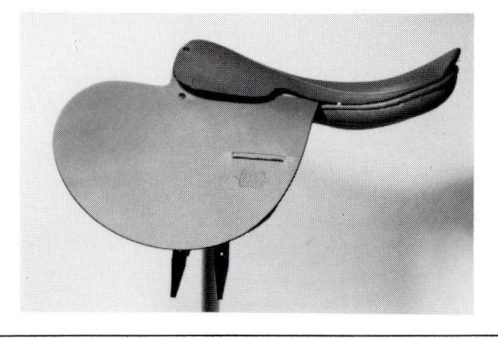

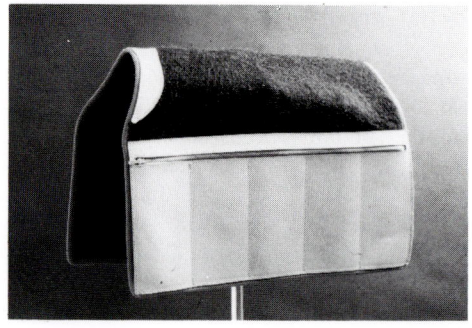

104

A contrast in styles. **Right:** A Vanity Fair cartoon of the American jockey Tod Sloan (1874-1933) who introduced the short-leather, crouching style into Europe in 1897. **Above:** The classic long-leg style favoured by jockeys before the adoption of the short leather. This picture is of Fred Archer, for many years English champion jockey, riding Iroquois, winner of the 1881 Derby.

frequent—on one made from fibreglass. Fibreglass has been used for riding saddles, as well as other forms of plastic, but it is only in the racing saddle that this material has been completely successful. Very light leathers, either pigskin or calfskin, are used, while the panels are no more than a thin layer of fine wool covered in silk. There are no stirrup bars; not only would these increase the weight but in view of the size of the tree, they would be impractical in any case. In fact, the stirrup leathers are passed round the tree on either side, a practice also frequently followed with the heavier saddles.

Design and fitting
Racing saddles are not made for sitting in and the seat is therefore almost flat. The flaps, however, are cut well forward to allow for the very short stirrup leather used, although in flat racing jockeys frequently ride so short that the knees are above the saddle and not in contact with it at all.

Steeplechasing saddles follow the same pattern, but are obviously more robust. It is important that they, too, are fairly flat in the seat. A conventional cantle is a very uncomfortable thing to land on should the jockey get even slightly 'left behind' at a fence. Probably the best 'chasing saddles were the Australian Boscas, made of kangaroo hide, and they still are much sought after.

The fitting of racing saddles, other than the heavier ones, differs completely from normal practice and principles. Most are used with a wither pad under the front arch and, since the weight is carried only for a very short time and then for the most part on the stirrup leathers, fitting in the conventional sense is of no consequence.

Saddles used in racing stables for exercising must naturally be much stronger in order to withstand the hard usage involved. These exercise saddles are made, therefore, on a stout, rigid tree, which has a little more of the conventional dip to the seat. The flaps are cut forward, so that the rider may ride with short leathers, and the panel is a 'full' one, following the shape of the flaps, and often, but not always, lined with serge. The American pattern race exercise saddle is a rather neater affair; it is nearly always leather lined.

Another form of race exercise saddle, sometimes used also for 'chasing, is that which is built on a 'half' tree. The tree is just the front arch, plus a sufficient length of arm on which the bars can be fitted. The seat and flaps are then made as one, as a sort of pad, with the leather panel built in beneath. This is a practical type of saddle, the absence of a tree being a definite advantage in a racing yard, where saddles are frequently treated with insufficient care and where, as a result, saddle trees are frequently broken.

Changing styles
Up to the early 1900s, racing saddles were made with very much straighter flaps. The reason for this was that jockeys up to that time rode with a long leg, much as they would have done in the hunting field, and sat in the saddle when riding a finish. The forward cut saddle, together with the practice of riding short, came about largely through the crouching style adopted by the American jockey Tod Sloan (1874–1933). He introduced the practice to England in 1897 and may have had some influence upon the theories expounded by Caprilli. The race saddle, as it exists today, conforms very closely to the Caprilli requirements in that it positions the jockey's body weight well forward and over the centre of balance of the horse.

For the most part the aim of all racing equipment is to achieve the maximum lightness possible, but there are exceptions to this general principle. These occur particularly in point-to-point racing where the stipulated weights the horses must carry may well be above the riding weight of the jockeys.

In order to make up the weight required a jockey can either use a heavy, and sometimes deliberately weighted, saddle, or the extra weight can be carried in the form of lead pieces inserted into the pockets of a weight cloth.

The guiding principle about carrying dead weight is to see that it is placed as far forward, and as near therefore to the centre of balance, as is possible. Weighted saddles are made by inserting lead into the tree itself. Every effort is made to keep the weight toward the front, although, in the case of a saddle weighing as much as 32lb, the lead would have to be introduced throughout the length of the tree and round the cantle as well.

CHAPTER FOUR · SPECIALIST SADDLES

Specialist Saddles · **Side-Saddles**

The origin of the side-saddle goes back 600 years, to the European courts of the 14th century. Anne of Bohemia, wife of Richard II, brought the fashion to England, for example, and soon ladies who had previously only ridden pillion behind a man—or, in some cases, astride in a split skirt—began to adopt the new fashion. The saddles at that time were little more than stuffed platforms, the rider sitting at a complete right angle to her horse's spine, with her feet resting on a platform called a *planchette*.

The rider would have had very little control over her horse in this position, and so the saddles soon acquired a pommel in front, over which the rider could hook one knee, which enabled her to face the way she was going. It is difficult to date the development of the pommel accurately, but it is known that Catherine de Medici invented a second pommel in about 1580. Both were still positioned on top of the saddle, the rider wedging her knee between them to gain a little more security.

Examples of these early saddles still survive in the Hermes collection in Paris. Another interesting feature is that the seats were level from back to front, with no sign of the dipped seat which was prevalent in the middle of the last century.

Improvements of the 1800s

A manual on riding for ladies published in 1826 shows a level-seated saddle, little changed from those used over 200 years previously, but by 1860 the dipped seat had been introduced. This may have been in an attempt to get the rider a little closer to her horse, for at that time the 'cut-back' head, which allows the horse's withers to rise through the front of the saddle had not been invented. If the seat was to be level, the whole saddle had to be much higher on the horse's back, and would, therefore, be more prone to slipping. A design of this sort was likely to give the horse a sore back, because of the friction arising from the lateral movement of the saddle and there was, additionally, a very real danger

Below: An elaborate and very beautifully worked saddle of the 19th century which has the characteristic deep seat of the period. **Bottom:** Detail of the tapestry used to cover the seat. **Right:** Up to the 14th century ladies either rode pillion behind a man or astride in a long split skirt in the manner of the equestrienne on the left of the pair.

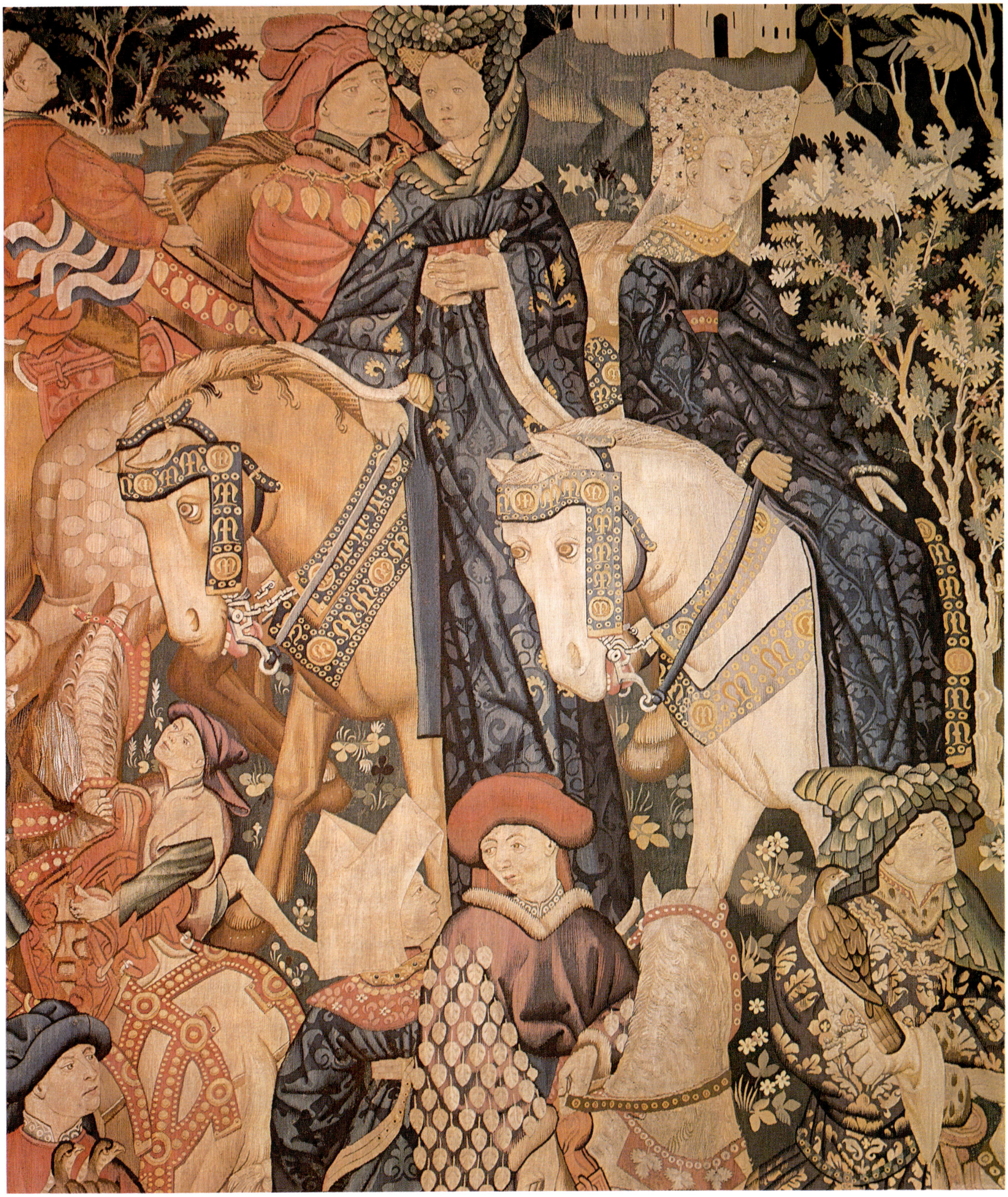

CHAPTER FOUR · SPECIALIST SADDLES

of the rider being deposited on the ground. As a counter to the poor fit of the saddle grooms would often girth up so tightly that the horse had trouble breathing, or would even try to roll to get rid of its burden. Then some anonymous genius invented the balance strap. This first appears in drawings in the 1820s, when it was connected to the stirrup leather. In its modern form, however, it goes from the nearside front of the saddle to the offside rear, a balance being effected by pressures on opposite corners of the saddle. Some riders prefer a short balance strap sewn to the girth instead of buckling independently to the saddle—but this is a matter of taste since both types are effective.

The most important invention in the history of the side-saddle came in 1830, when a French riding master, Jules Pellier, invented the 'leaping head'—a pommel screwed into the saddle and curving over the rider's left thigh. It was this invention which gave the side-saddle its reputation for safety and security. Without a leaping head only the most intrepid rider would dare to jump, for if the horse chose to play up she had little chance of staying mounted. With it, any of the movements which might pitch the astride rider over the horse's shoulder, serve merely to strengthen the side-saddle rider's seat, as her thigh slides firmly into its support. It must have a left-handed thread to its screw, or it will loosen when the rider jams her leg against it when employing the emergency grip to retain her seat.

Changes dictated by fashion
By the 1860s, most saddles had three pommels—the two either side of the right knee, plus the leaping head—but the pommel on the extreme right was already becoming smaller. By the mid1870s it had almost disappeared and the side-saddle rider was equipped to enter the hunting field. Before then, while ladies might ride to the meet to see their menfolk off, it was not considered respectable actually to follow hounds. Then, in 1876, the Empress Elizabeth of Austria came to England to hunt and fashionable ladies followed her lead, taking to the hunting field with great enthusiasm. They soon began to give

108

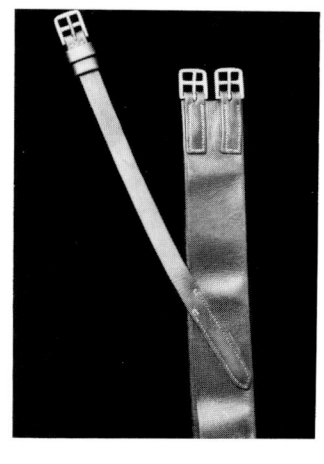

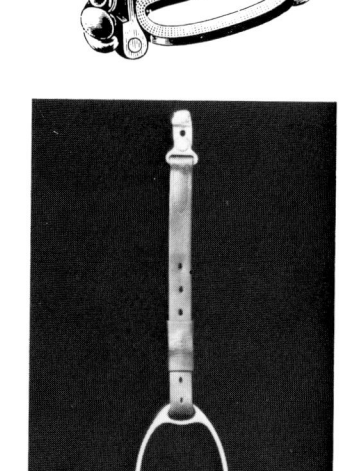

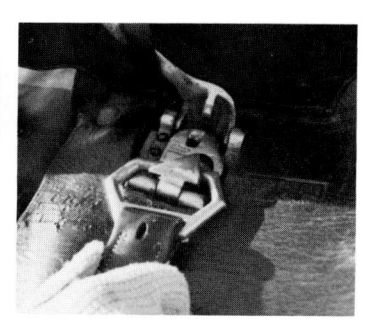

Opposite: J.F. Herring's picture of a pair of Queen Victoria's hacks. The saddles are fitted with two pommels but have no leaping heads. **Above left:** The balance strap, which obviates the danger of the saddle slipping round, was invented in the 1800s. **Left:** The ultimate safety device was the quick release which allowed both stirrup and leather to come away. **Top:** 'Safety' stirrups previously in general use. **Above, left:** The short balance strap sewn to the girth. **Right:** A modern leather with a hook for adjusting the length.

more thought to their saddles, for what was tolerably comfortable during a gentle ride was not necessarily suitable for a hard day in the hunting field.

The first casualty was the dipped seat. With this the rider had to sit facing over the horse's shoulder and had to twist at the waist in order to face forwards. A posture of this sort quickly becomes tiring, if not actually painful; at one time it was thought necessary to ride on different sides on alternate days in order to avoid a curvature of the spine. With the introduction of the cut-back head, however, saddles reverted to the level seat, so the rider was again able to ride on her right thigh, instead of her bottom, and face forward. She could then see where she was going, control her horse with both hands and jump safely.

The only problem remaining was what happened if the rider was to fall. Provided the skirt did not become entangled round the pommel (this problem was soon solved by the development of the apron skirt), the main worry was to ensure that the foot came free of the stirrup so that the rider was not dragged. A whole series of patent 'safety' stirrups were invented. These were mostly irons that broke open in various ways to release the foot, but they depended on the foot being placed in them the right way round, and they were not totally successful. The problem was finally solved by quick-release devices at the top of the stirrup leather, which allowed the stirrup *plus* the leather to come off the saddle.

The heyday of the side-saddle

The great heyday of side-saddle riding was between 1890 and 1930 and during this time the level seat became almost universal. Additionally, the doeskin seat, which gave greater purchase to the rider, became increasingly popular. The pommels were made wider and were better padded, while the leaping head altered its position and angle of rake as riders realized the advantages of a more forward seat for jumping.

The great side-saddle *marques*, like Owen, Mayhew, Whippy and Champion and Wilton became established and these are the makes still sought by connoisseurs.

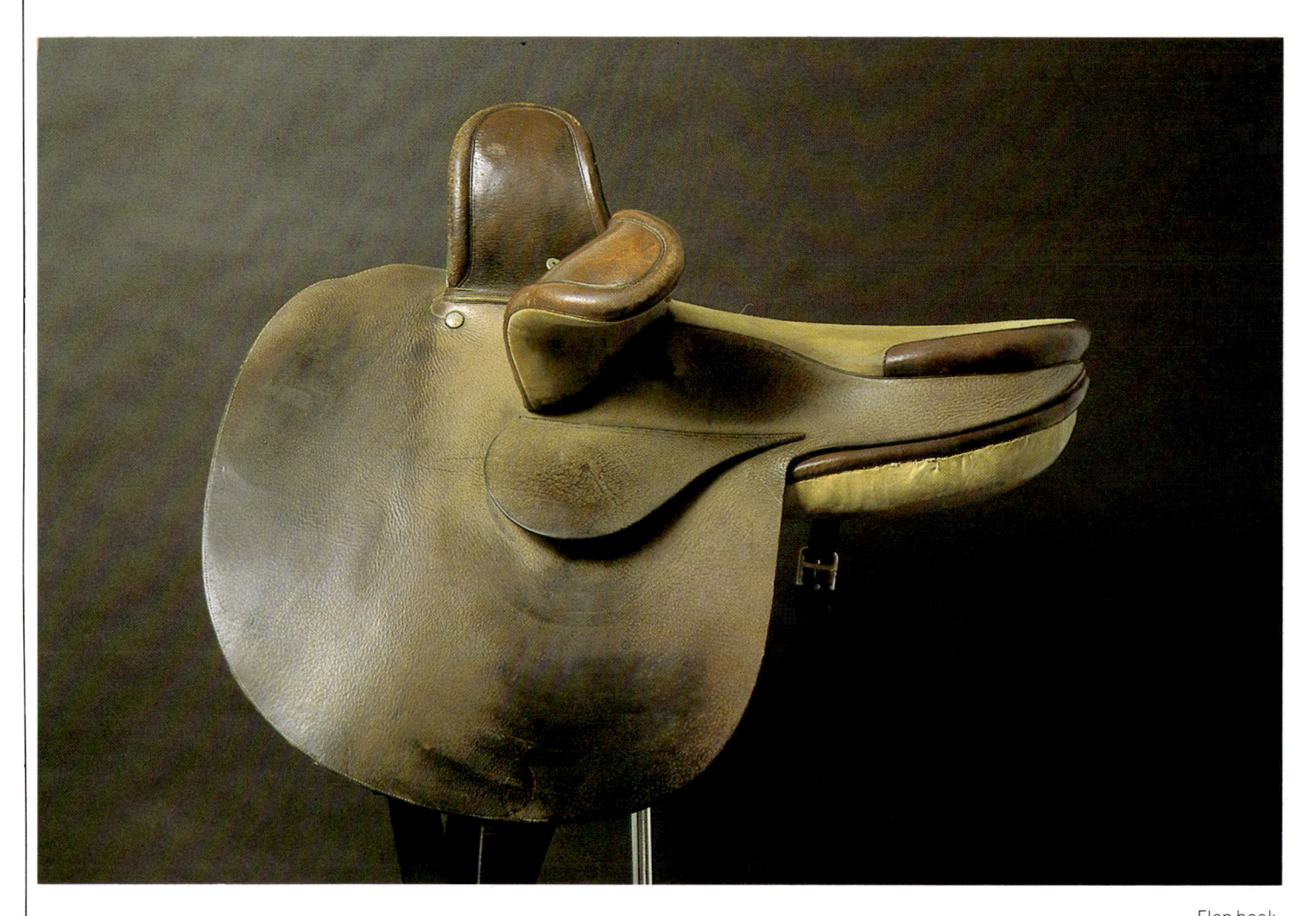

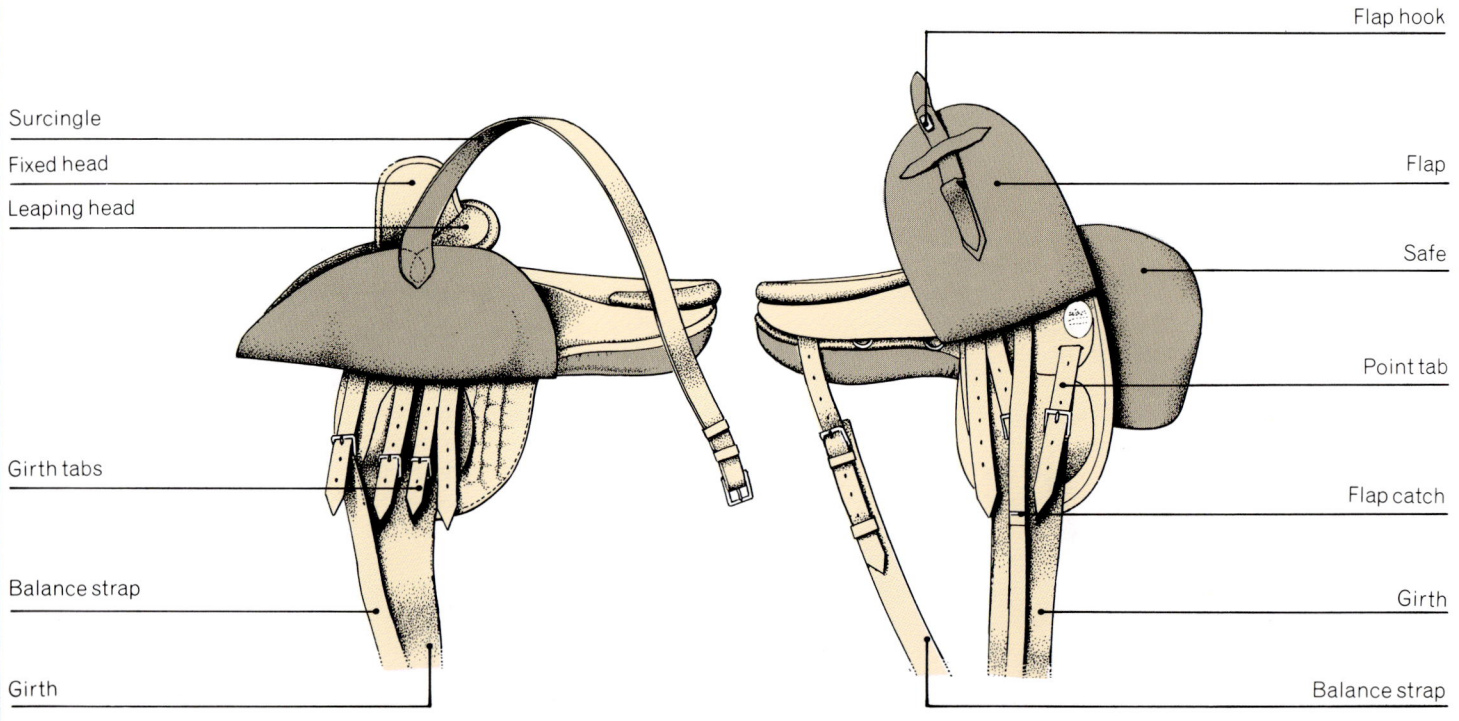

CHAPTER FOUR · SPECIALIST SADDLES

Surcingle
Fixed head
Leaping head

Girth tabs

Balance strap

Girth

Flap hook
Flap
Safe
Point tab
Flap catch
Girth
Balance strap

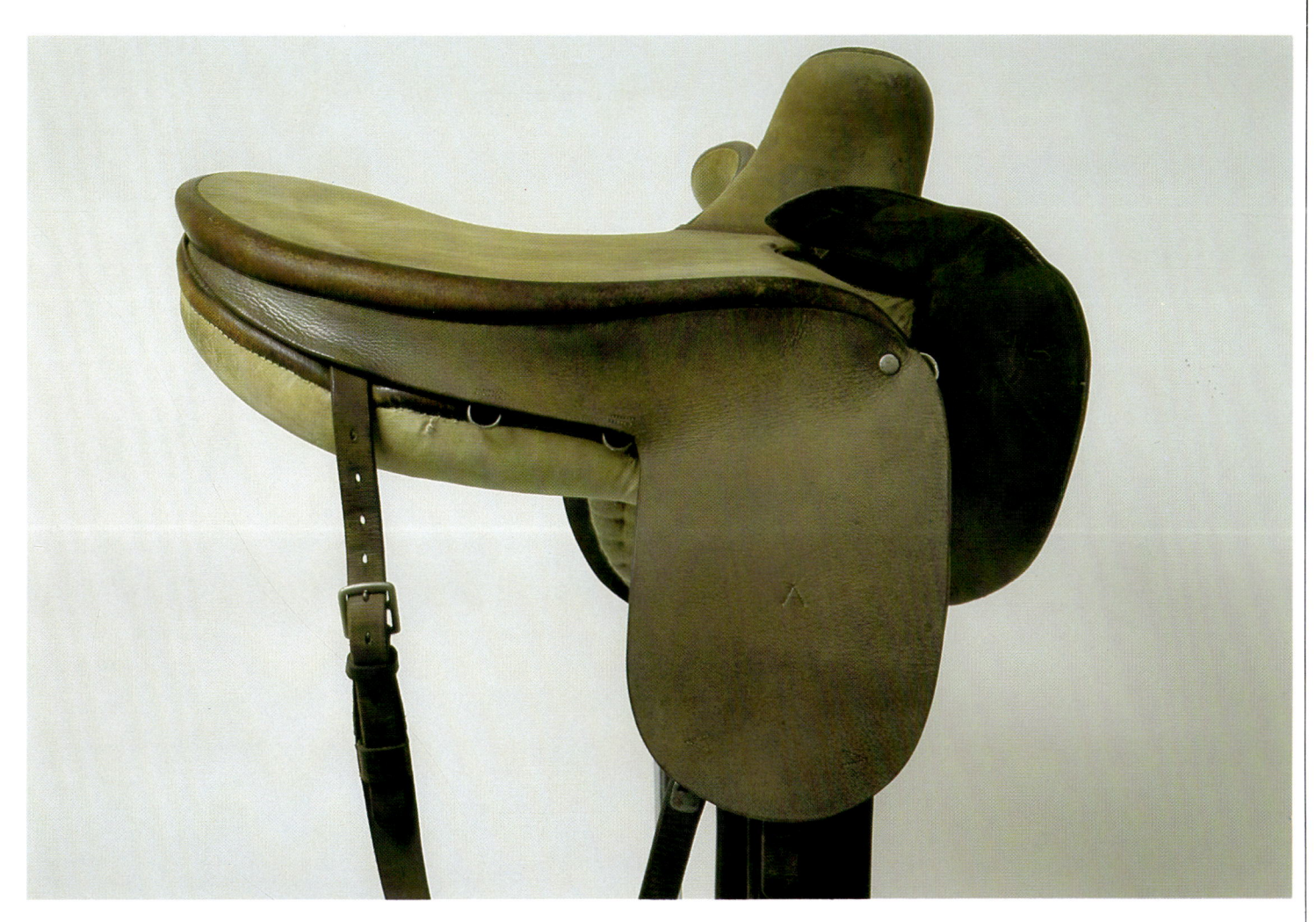

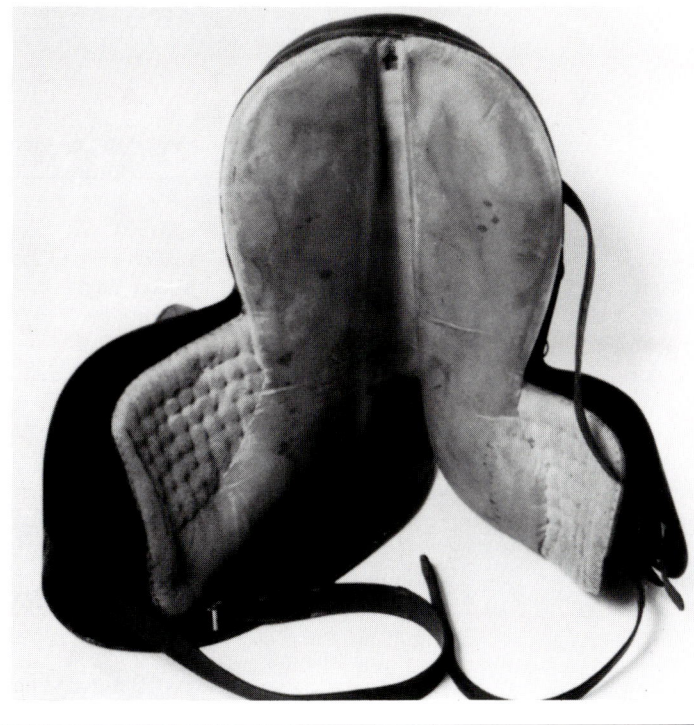

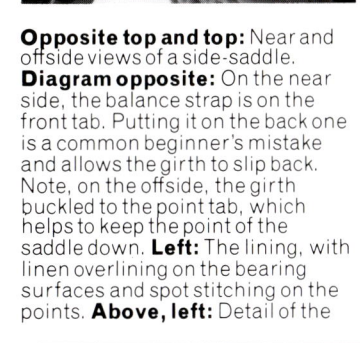

Opposite top and top: Near and offside views of a side-saddle. **Diagram opposite:** On the near side, the balance strap is on the front tab. Putting it on the back one is a common beginner's mistake and allows the girth to slip back. Note, on the offside, the girth buckled to the point tab, which helps to keep the point of the saddle down. **Left:** The lining, with linen overlining on the bearing surfaces and spot stitching on the points. **Above, left:** Detail of the doeskin and cut-back head. **Right:** Underside of flap, showing the hook for holding down the flap strap.

CHAPTER FOUR · SPECIALIST SADDLES

Left: A saddle made in about 1900. The large offside flap is characteristic of the period as are thin pommels and the notably dipped leather seat. It would not be suitable for a modern side-saddle rider. **Right:** A saddle made in Walsall between the wars. Although the quality was good, Walsall never really mastered the art of side-saddle manufacture, which remains the prerogative of the London houses. **Below left:** A saddle made by Owen of London in about 1920. The pommels are much narrower than in later models. **Below:** A very good model of a modern Owen, with the larger pommels shaped to accommodate the active rider and to position her securely and in balance.

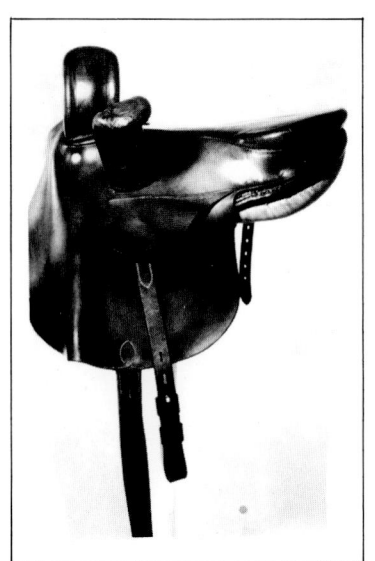

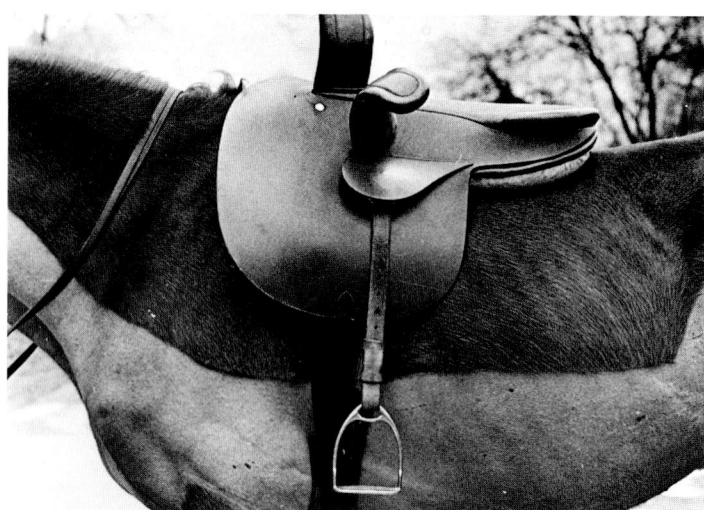

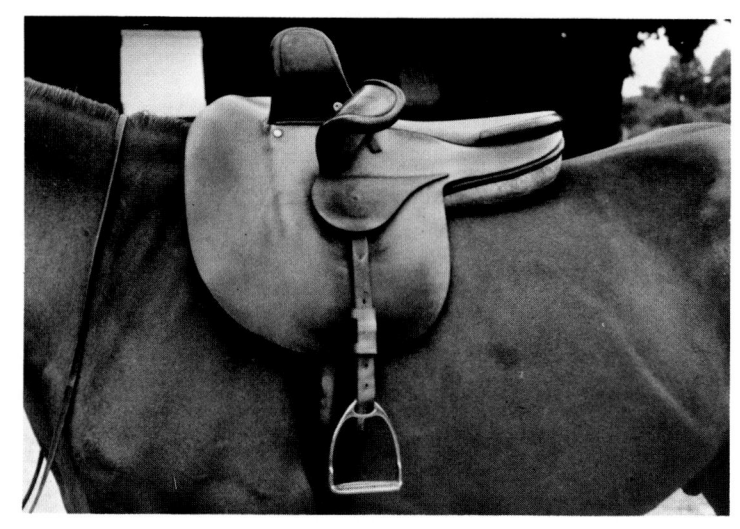

As well as excellent workmanship and good design in respect of the position and shaping of the pommel, they have the essential virtue of balance. It is noticeable that the seats of these saddles, if looked at from the rear, are deeper on the left side than the right. This is particularly evident in the case of the Owen saddles. The important point is that this extra depth is built into the top of the saddle, and is not achieved by putting extra stuffing in the panel. Added to this, the seat at the back is shaped to tilt the rider on her right seat bone, thus counteracting the effect of her having both legs on one side, and balancing her weight evenly on both sides of the horse's back.

Made to measure

It is, of course, essential that the saddle should fit the rider, or she will never be able to ride correctly. The main considerations here are length and pommel position. Side-saddles are measured from the extreme rear of the cut-back head straight across the seat to the centre of the cantle; the desired length corresponds to that of the rider's thigh from behind the knee to the back of the buttock as she sits. As a rough guide, a rider of 5ft 6in will probably need a 16in saddle. It is, however, always better to ride in a saddle that is too long than too short, as in the last instance the rider's weight will push the rear of the saddle down on the horse's spine.

Pommel position is even more important than length. When ladies had saddles made to measure, the saddler took the size of the thighs into account and positioned the pommels accordingly. Thus, a saddle made for a full-legged lady has the fixed head well to the left of centre to allow for the extra thickness on the inside of the thigh. A slimmer-legged rider would never be able to sit in the centre of a saddle made in this fashion with her right thigh parallel to the horse's spine; she would also find that the leaping head had too wide a curve to hold her left thigh in an emergency. Conversely, a saddle made for a slim lady will have too tight a curve for a larger thigh, while the fixed head will be positioned too far to the right and probably too low for safety also. Fixed heads cannot be altered without making radical changes to the saddle; for this reason beginners are advised against buying side-saddles without advice from an experienced instructor.

Having ensured that the saddle fits the rider, it is also necessary for it to fit the horse. Providing the saddle has a medium-fitting tree and the horse has a good back, withers and shoulders, this is comparatively easy. Problems arise if the horse's shoulders are asymmetrical, or square with a low wither development. This sometimes occurs with the Arabian type of horse and with the stuffy, cobby types. For this reason it may not be possible to fit a side-saddle to such an animal with any guarantee of its remaining in place.

A properly-made saddle should be fitted to the horse who is going to wear it, and this cannot be done entirely in a workshop. The correct method is for the saddler to put the saddle on the horse and do up the girth and balance strap; he must then study it from the rear and from both sides to assess what needs to be done in the way of regulation. Having decided, the saddle is removed and wool stuffing inserted into the front through slits in the top of the panel near the tree points should this be necessary. Stuffing is introduced to the rear of the panel by slitting a few of the stitches that hold the lining material to the leather backing and inserting as much wool as may be required. The position of the saddle can then be checked again on the horse and with the rider up, further adjustments being made if they are required.

To check the correctness of the fit, the saddle should be viewed from behind, without a rider. It should sit with its seat sloping markedly from left to right, with the gullet sitting to the right of the horse's spine. Once the rider is on the saddle, it should settle with the seat level and the gullet should fall exactly over the spine. Viewed from the side, the seat should be level from front to back. The weight should be borne by the inside two-thirds of the offside of the panel and the outside two-thirds of the nearside.

Only when all these criteria are satisfied can the rider be sure that the saddle will not throw her off balance, or slip and cause damage to the horse's back.

The usual lining material for side saddles is serge, with a linen overlining. Leather linings are rare and the old school of saddlers do not like them, as they consider them difficult to stuff correctly. Some older saddles have a panel of felt covered with red 'sorbo' rubber, but, once this has dried up and perished, it cannot be replaced. Other saddles have a detachable felt panel, called a 'Wykeham' pad. The idea of this was that the rider owned one saddle together with a selection of pads made for different horses, so that the saddle could be put on another horse when the rider changed to a second horse during a day's hunting. Unfortunately it is not possible to add stuffing to these pads once the felt has compressed, or if the pad is wanted for a horse of a different back conformation.

FITTING A SIDE-SADDLE

Right: A badly fitting saddle which is already sitting to the left instead of centrally. In use, with a rider on board, this tendency will be exaggerated. **Below:** The rider's weight pulling the saddle over to the left. A saddle fitting as badly as this one is almost certain to cause a sore back.

Right: The same saddle after regulation by an expert saddler. It is now somewhat to the right of the horse's spine but will sit centrally once the rider is in position. **Below:** The saddle fitting correctly and sitting level on the horse's back. Compare this picture with the one on the left.

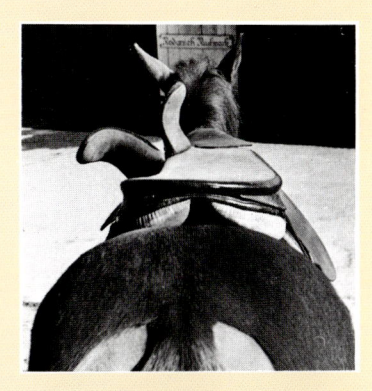

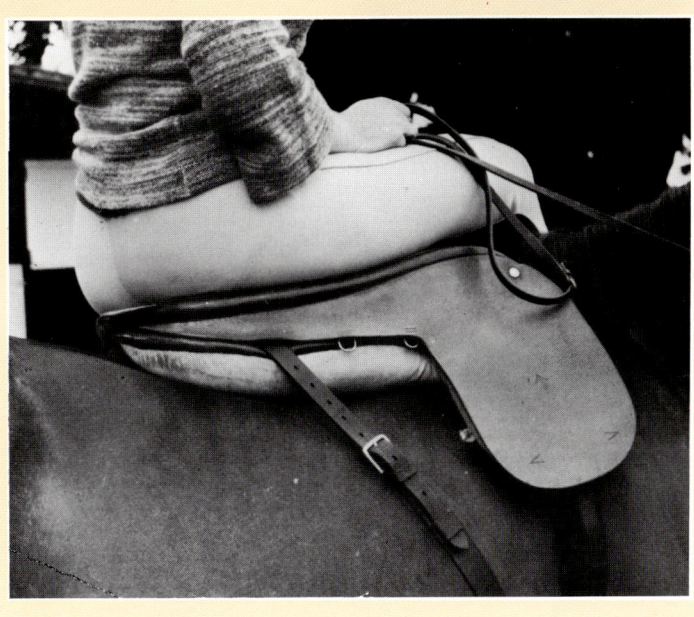

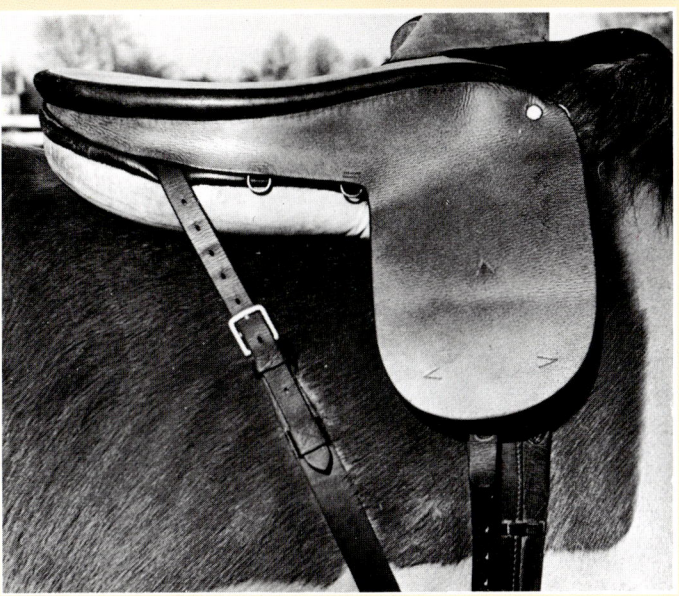

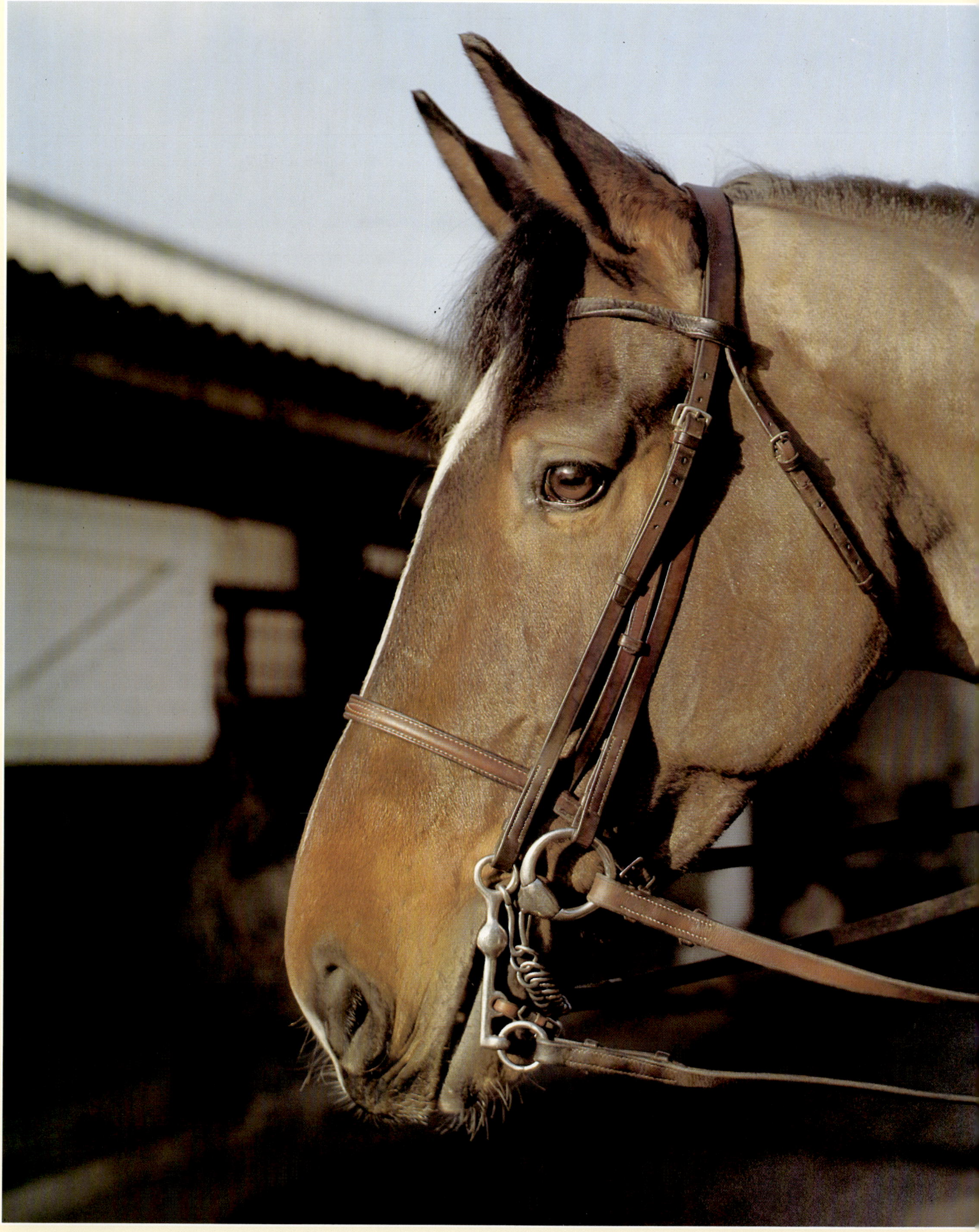

CHAPTER FIVE

Bits, Bridles and Additional Aids

Bits and Bitting
Martingales
Nosebands
Bridles – Types and Fitting
The Western Hackamore System

The plain double bridle is the hallmark of the schooled horse, and perhaps also of the educated rider. It is the universal bridle for ridden classes in the show ring and for all but the elementary dressage competitions.

CHAPTER FIVE · BITS, BRIDLES AND ADDITIONAL AIDS

Bridling Aids · **Bits and Bitting**

It is now 6000 years since it was first realized that putting a bit in a horse's mouth gave enough control to ride him. The first bits were probably pieces of hide fastened to cheekpieces made from pierced antlers, but although they were crude, they revolutionized our relationship with the horse by changing him from a prey animal to a means of transportation. Today there are hundreds of bit designs, and no sign that riders or manufacturers have run out of ideas. To anyone who does not ride, the idea of putting a piece of metal in a horse's mouth may seem strange or even distasteful. But as long as the bit fits correctly, and provided it is used by a competent rider, the horse will be comfortable. The design of a bit affects its action and potential severity, but it is the rider's skill (or lack of it) that determines how mild or severe an effect it has.

Philosophies on the relationship between horse and rider have changed over the centuries, sometimes going around in circles. Xenophon, a cavalry officer of ancient Greece (430BC) recommended persuasion rather than force and believed that bit design should follow the same principles. In the 16th century, horsemen used formidable-looking bits which exerted great leverage, although the idea was that the horse was taught to respect the potential power of the bit so that he could be ridden with the lightest touch.

In 1832, Don Juan Segundo invented a system of bitting with interchangeable mouthpieces, cheekpieces and curb chains so that riders could devise the perfect combination for each individual horse. The flaw in his system was the assumption that every rider had sufficient knowledge of the way horses' mouths can differ in shape and how to select designs accordingly. Having said that, the same applies today, and many riders use bits without really understanding how they work.

Riders have always required horses to work in a round outline with their necks arched to some degree. While potentially severe bits such as those of the 16th century made the horse back off from the rider's hand, the 21st-century horseman (a term which is also meant to include women) realizes that the horse's 'engine' and source of power is in his hindquarters and hindlegs. He can only carry himself proudly and be a light, responsive ride if the engine is engaged, so the bit is merely a part of the rider's communications system rather than at the centre of it.

The bit families

Although there are more types of bit than ever before, we can divide them into five main groups: the snaffle, the double bridle, the pelham, the gag snaffle and the bitless bridle. The last might sound a contradiction in terms, but it works by putting pressure on the nose rather than the mouth. Within the bit groups are numerous variations provided by different mouthpieces, cheekpieces and materials.

Bitting is a controversial subject and one in which there are few hard and fast rules —although you will often hear them quoted. For instance, it is often said that a thick mouthpiece is milder than a thin one, because pressure is spread over a wider area. In theory this is true, but if the shape of the horse's mouth means that a thick bit is literally too much of a

Below: Diagram showing parts of the horse's head affected by bit and bridle.

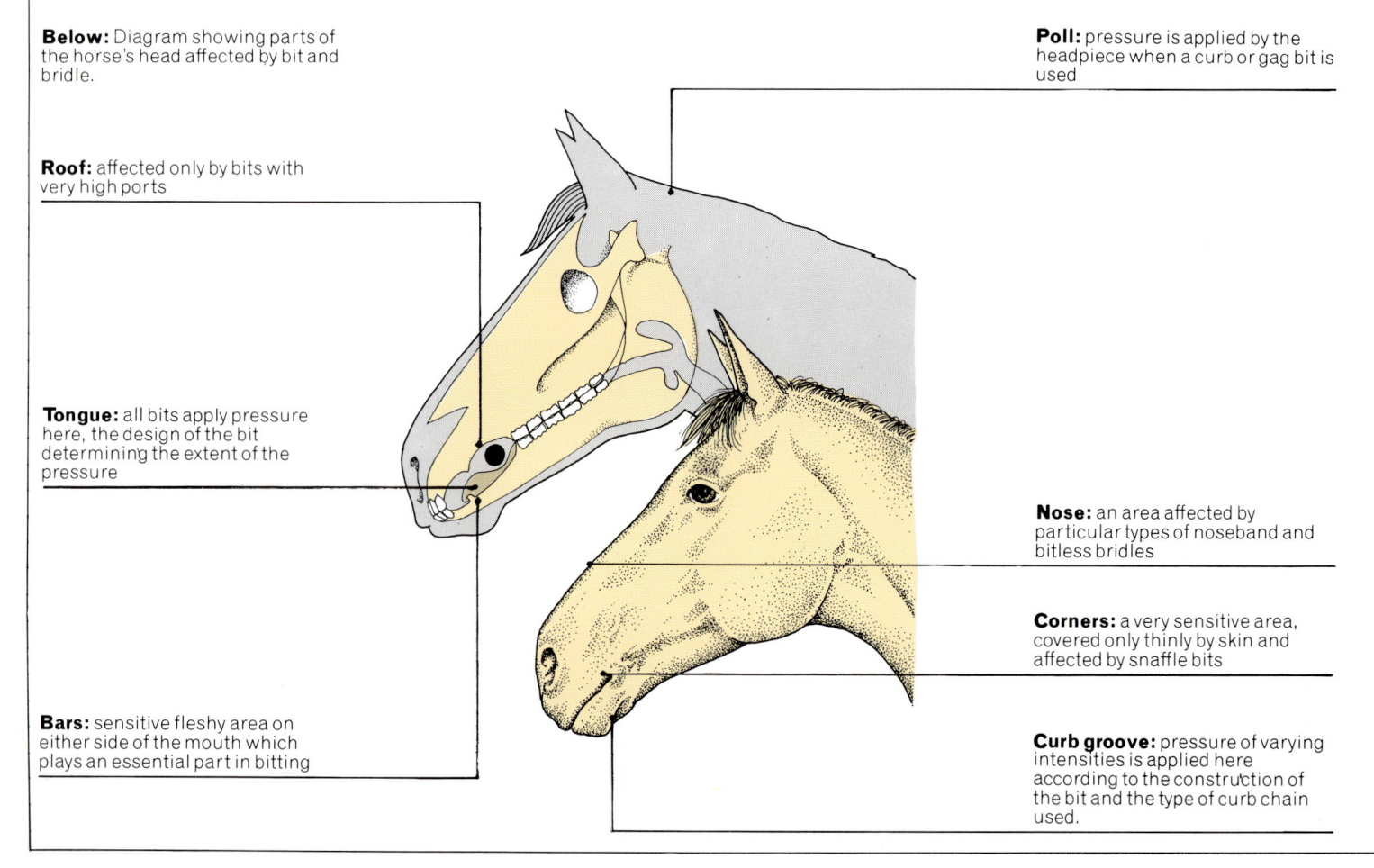

Roof: affected only by bits with very high ports

Tongue: all bits apply pressure here, the design of the bit determining the extent of the pressure

Bars: sensitive fleshy area on either side of the mouth which plays an essential part in bitting

Poll: pressure is applied by the headpiece when a curb or gag bit is used

Nose: an area affected by particular types of noseband and bitless bridles

Corners: a very sensitive area, covered only thinly by skin and affected by snaffle bits

Curb groove: pressure of varying intensities is applied here according to the construction of the bit and the type of curb chain used.

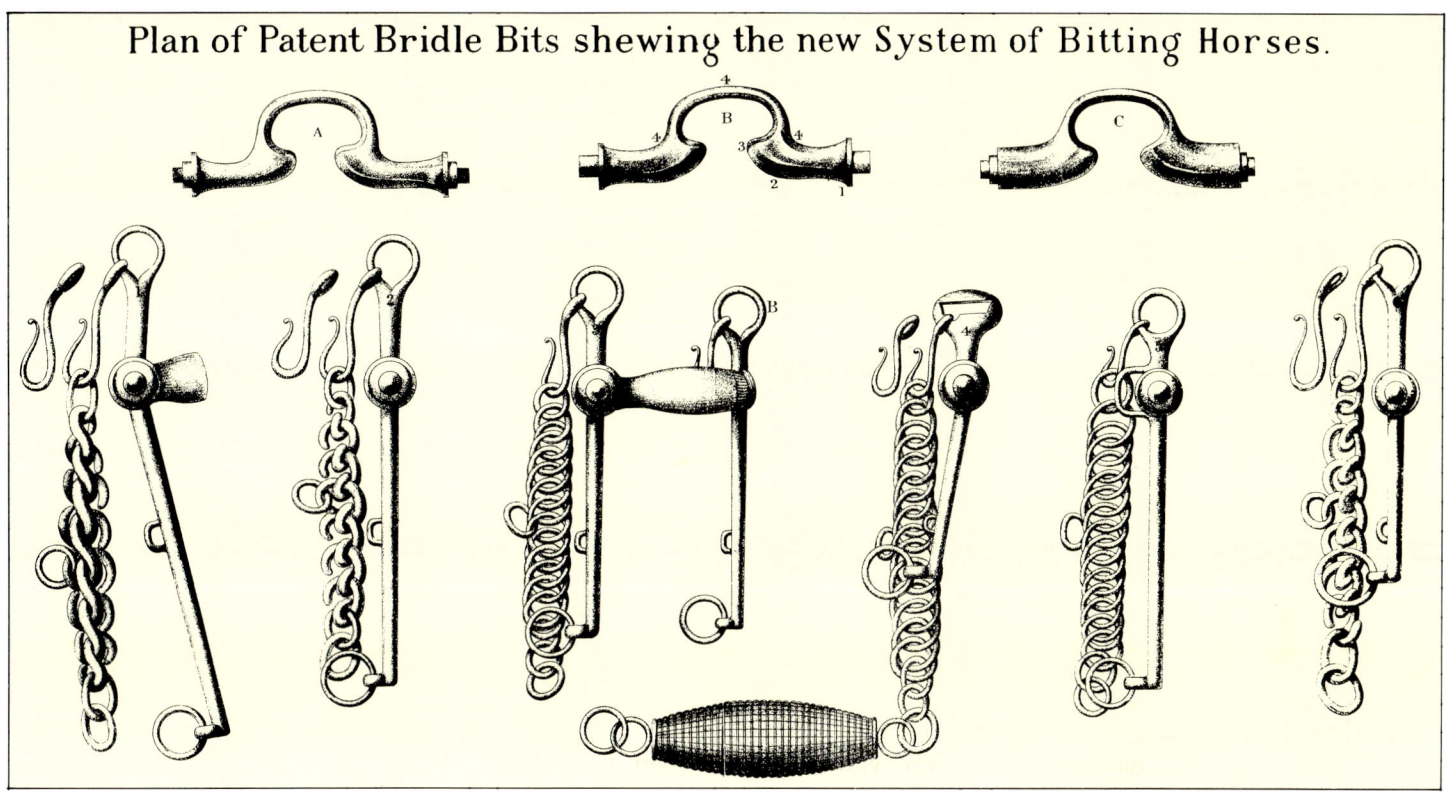

Plan of Patent Bridle Bits shewing the new System of Bitting Horses.

Above: The bits involved in the system of bitting devised by Juan Segundo. Mouthpieces, cheeks and curb chains were interchangeable according to the conformation of the horse's mouth and the way in which the head was carried in relation to the hand. Segundo's treatise was printed in *The Loriner*, published by Benjamin Latchford in 1883.

mouthful, he will often be more comfortable when ridden in a thinner one.

Another debatable maxim is that it is always best to ride a horse in a snaffle, which is the simplest in design and is used with a single pair of reins. Many horses go very well in snaffles, and competitors in the lower levels of dressage are restricted to certain designs within this group, but there are also many animals that are more comfortable and easier to ride in a bit with a curb action, such as a pelham.

Materials

Bits have been made from metal since about 1200BC, but the oldest complete ones date to about 1500BC. They were made from bronze and came from the Ukraine, north of the Black Sea. Bronze continued to be a favourite material even during the Iron Age (about 500–51BC), although iron itself was also used. Nickel, an alloy of brass and silver, was a favourite material until 1940, when it was replaced by the 'miracle metal' stainless steel. Although nickel is soft, which meant that bits could eventually bend or break, it had a warmth that steel lacks. Although many horses accept steel perfectly well, many more are happier with a warmer material and perhaps with a different taste. Horses are very much individuals, however, and for every one that likes a rubber-covered mouthpiece or one containing copper, there is another that becomes too fussy.

Rubber-covered and vulcanite mouthpieces are necessarily bulky, so while some horses are comfortable with them, others dislike them. Modern alloys containing copper have become increasingly popular, as have sweet-iron mouthpieces, said to have a sweet taste; this is due at least in part to the fact that their use is recommended by the legendary American trainer Monty Roberts. Plastic mouthpieces are often acceptable to young and sensitive horses—one company even makes bits it claims are apple-flavoured! Any bits made from a material that could be chewed through must have a central metal core, for safety's sake; otherwise, the mouthpiece could break, leaving the rider with no brakes or steering.

The snaffle

There are four basic designs of snaffle, which give varying degrees of pressure on the tongue and the corners of the mouth: the straight-bar snaffle, the mullen mouthpiece, and the single-jointed and double-jointed snaffles. There are also snaffles with rollers set around or in the mouthpiece.

The unjointed straight bar snaffle and mullen mouthpiece act mainly on the tongue; the latter, which has a slight arch, is probably more comfortable for the ridden horse. The single-jointed snaffle is the one most commonly used, and although it is often described as having a nutcracker action, it should not be uncomfortable. Double-jointed snaffles have a central link which removes the nutcracker action, and a lot of horses prefer them because of this. It is important not to confuse the French link snaffle, which has a kidney-shaped central plate that does not press on the tongue, with the Dr Bristol: this has a flat-sided central plate designed to apply tongue pressure and give extra control.

Rollers are often said to make a bit's action more severe, but this is not necessarily true. Their constant movement dissuades a horse from leaning on or grabbing the bit, and may thus make him more controllable. Bits with rollers set around the mouthpiece, such as the cherry roller snaffle, have a softer action than the Magenis snaffle, which has rollers set inside a squared-off mouthpiece.

Lorinery, the making of such items as bits and spurs, was for centuries a hand craft, the best bits being carefully hand-forged in steel. Today, of necessity, mass-production methods have been adopted. **Above:** A selection of bits ready for the first finishing stage. **Right:** Patterns for bits.

BITS AND BITTING

Top, above and left: One of the basic materials of bit-making is steel, which is poured in its molten state into the moulds. Modern steel is stainless, but steel used in the 19th century had to be kept clean by the laborious use of materials such as sand and oil.

CHAPTER FIVE · BITS, BRIDLES AND ADDITIONAL AIDS

BITS AND BITTING

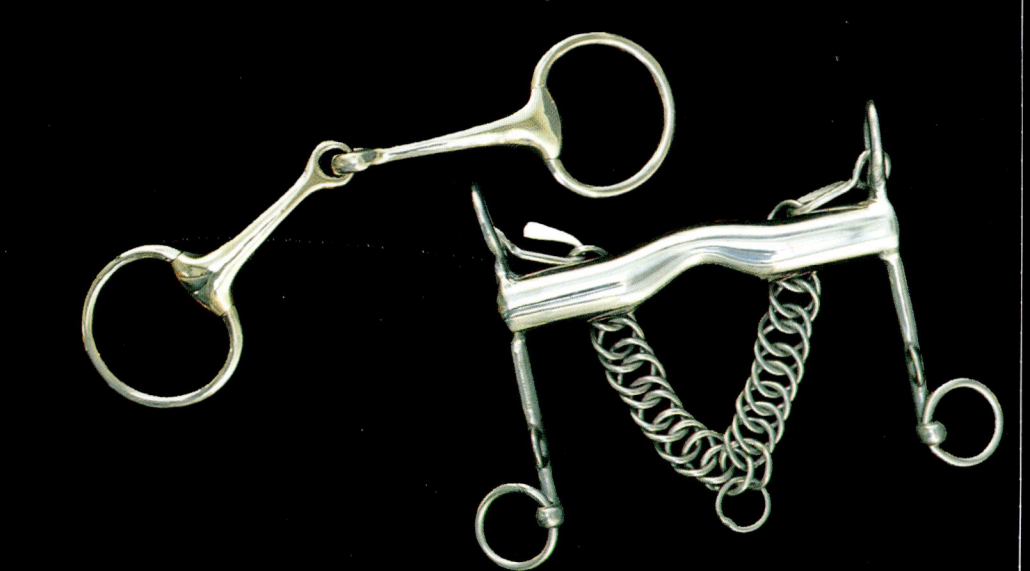

Above: The mouthpiece joints in a batch of eggbutt snaffles being closed by welding. **Far left:** Cleaning out the bit rings and eyes on Pelham and curb bits is a job still done by hand. **Left:** Making curb chains in a Midland foundry. **Top right:** Finishing continues to be a process of hand work at the polishing stage. **Above right:** Bits ready for electro-submersion in an electro-plating tank. **Right:** The finished product, smooth and lightly polished, in stainless steel.

CHAPTER FIVE · BITS, BRIDLES AND ADDITIONAL AIDS

Cheekpiece design also plays a part in defining a bit's action. A fixed cheek such as an eggbutt keeps the bit fairly still in the horse's mouth, while a loose ring allows for constant slight movement. The former is more suitable for a horse which tends to come behind the bit or is reluctant to accept contact, while the latter is more effective on a horse which sets himself above the bit or tries to lean on it. Full-cheek and Fulmer snaffles often help with steering in the case of young or unschooled horses, although a few use the cheekpieces to lean on, which rather defeats the object. D-rings also help with steering and have a slight lifting action, which can again make them useful for the horse which leans on the rider's hands.

The snaffle in action
The action of the snaffle is usually assumed to be an upward one against the corners of the lips, thus encouraging the horse to raise his head. In fact, this is the case only if the head is held low, as is usual with a young horse, and it would then be wrong to attempt to raise the head forcibly with the hands. The head is raised by the rider's legs encouraging a greater engagement of the horse's hindlegs underneath the body; the hands do no more than assist, or give greater emphasis to, the action of the legs.

The action of the snaffle varies in accordance with the position of the head and in the light of such auxiliaries—a martingale or noseband, for instance—which may be employed to alter or emphasize certain actions of the bit. In the case of a horse with a relatively high neck carriage, whose head is held a little in advance of the vertical, the action of the snaffle is across the bars of the lower jaw, the action being intensified if the mouthpiece is jointed.

There are a number of potentially strong snaffles, the strength being provided by the construction of the mouthpiece. Examples of these are the Magenis, which has rollers set within and across the mouthpiece; scorriers, which have two sets of rings and a single mouthpiece; 'Y' or 'W' mouth snaffles, with two mouthpieces; and the somewhat barbaric twisted mouth snaffles.

The double bridle
The double bridle, comprising curb bit and bradoon (a light snaffle bit), goes generally under the name Weymouth, although a century ago there were many combinations called by a variety of names. Today the difference is between a slide-cheek and a fixed-cheek Weymouth. The combination of curb and bradoon is the most sophisticated of bridles, and is probably the most effective one.

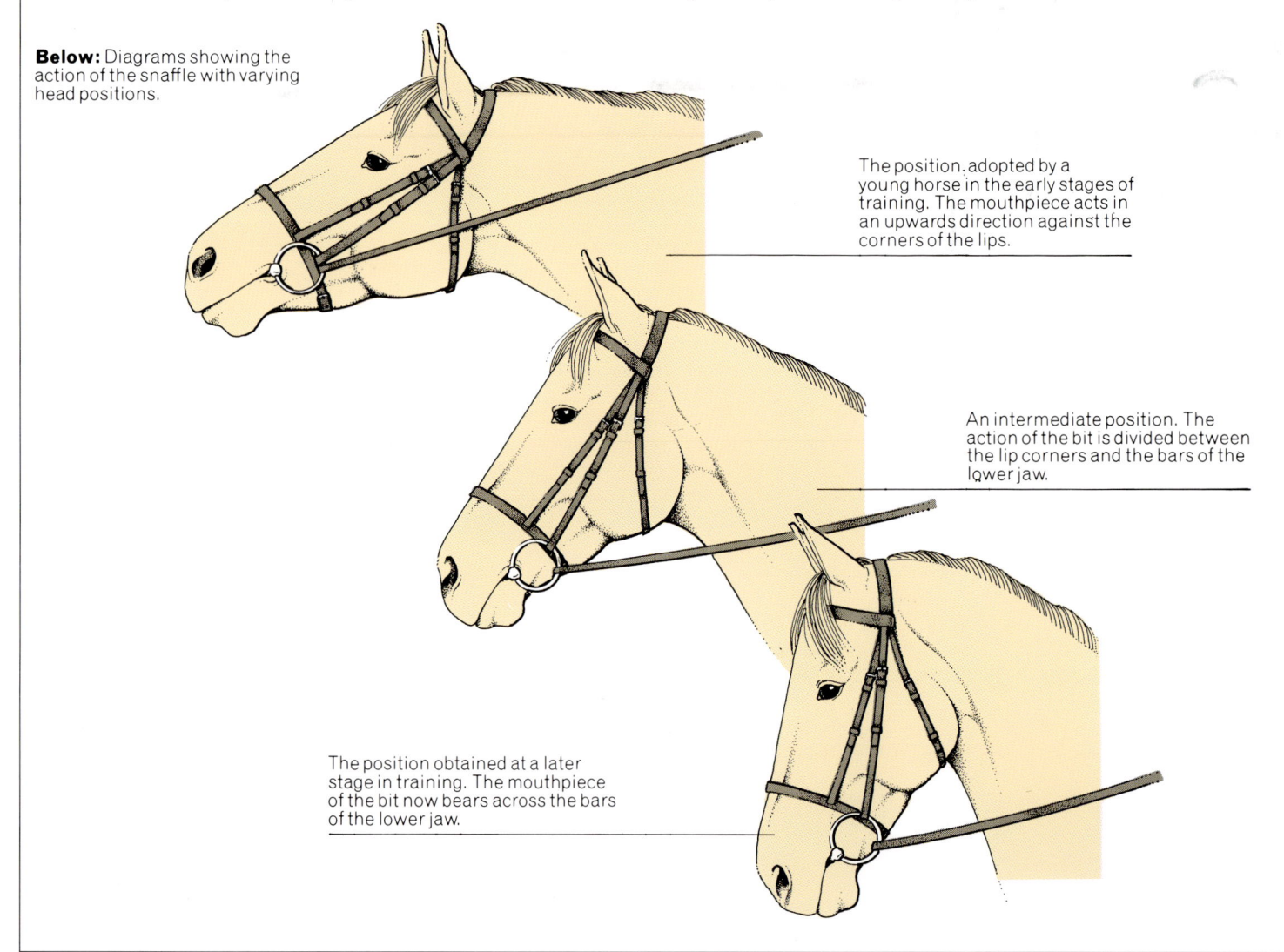

Below: Diagrams showing the action of the snaffle with varying head positions.

The position adopted by a young horse in the early stages of training. The mouthpiece acts in an upwards direction against the corners of the lips.

An intermediate position. The action of the bit is divided between the lip corners and the bars of the lower jaw.

The position obtained at a later stage in training. The mouthpiece of the bit now bears across the bars of the lower jaw.

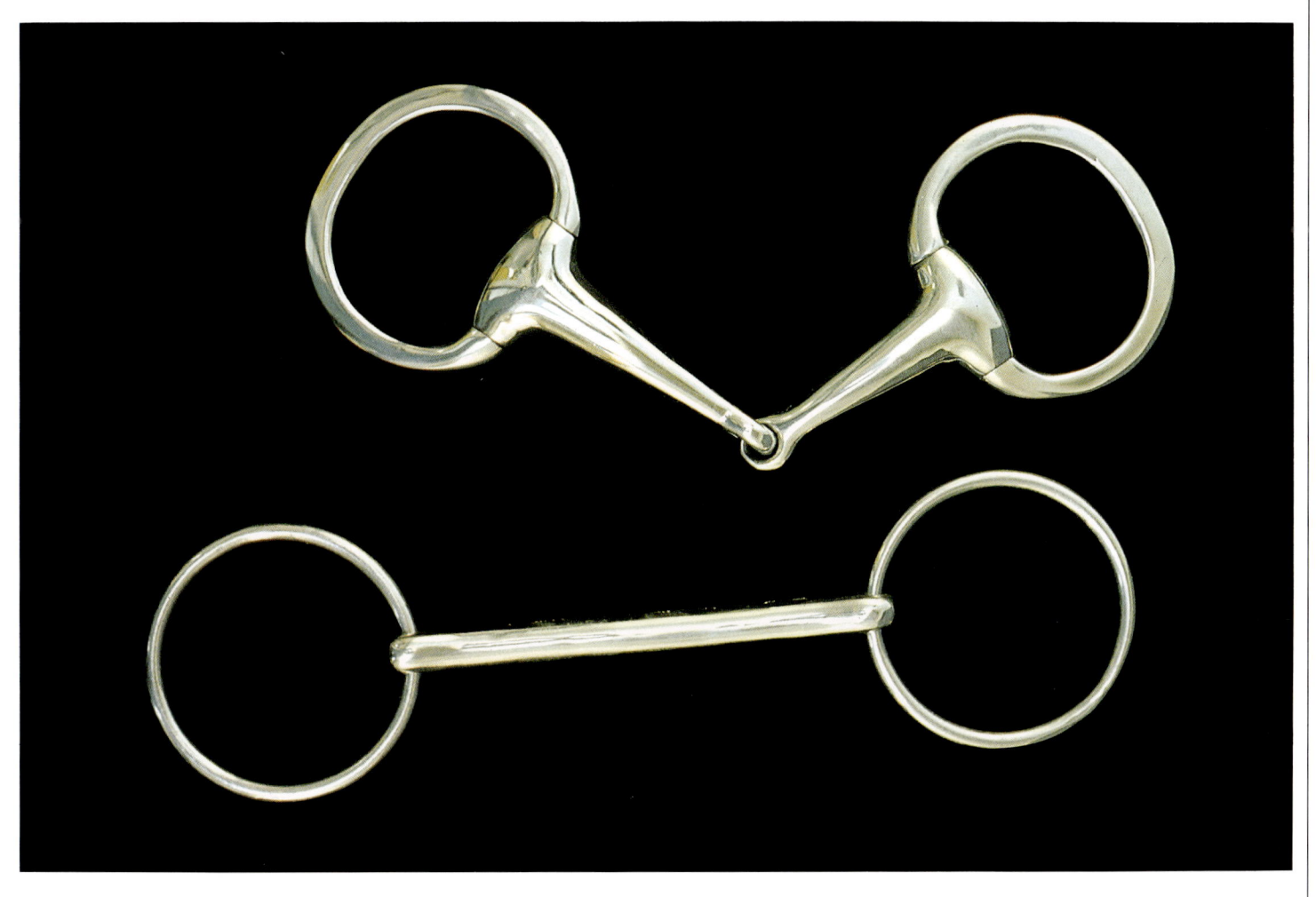

Above: The popular eggbutt snaffle, which obviates pinching of the corners of the lips, and a straight-bar bit, used for stallion or in-hand bridles.

The bradoon, fitted in the mouth above the curb bit, does, in this instance, act to raise the head by exerting pressure on the corners of the lips. The curb bit acts upon a number of points in the mouth and on the head to lower the latter and retract the nose, the degree of pressure imposed being governed by the length of the cheek both above and below the mouthpiece. The longer the overall cheek, the greater will be the possible leverage. The length of the cheek above the mouthpiece is important, since upon it depends the extent to which pressure is put on the poll. The longer the cheek above the mouthpiece, the greater will be the poll pressure that can be applied. Poll pressure, which induces a downward action, is transmitted by the forward movement of the eye of the curb bit, through the bridle cheek and thus to the headpiece. This occurs when the bit assumes an angle of about 45° in the mouth and thus causes the eye of the bit to move forward and down. This action also brings into play the curb chain which lies in the curb groove. The tightening of the curb chain produces a downward and backward pressure on the horse's lower jaw.

The pressures on the mouth depend on the shape of the mouthpiece of the curb bit. In most instances, the mouthpiece is a straight bar, with a port—a raised section—in its centre. The port accommodates the central portion of the tongue, the latter appearing to rise up naturally into this curve. This action stops the tongue from lying over the bars of the mouth (the area of gum between the molar and incisor teeth) and thus prevents the bearing surface of the bit from coming into direct contact with the bars. The action on the bars is a downward one with the direction of the pressure being toward the rear.

The shape of the port governs the degree of pressure which can be exerted on the bars. A deep, wide port, allowing more room for the tongue, puts more direct pressure on the bars through the bearing surfaces of the mouthpiece. On the other hand, a mullen-mouth bit, which makes no provision for the tongue, puts little pressure directly on the bars.

CHAPTER FIVE · BITS, BRIDLES AND ADDITIONAL AIDS

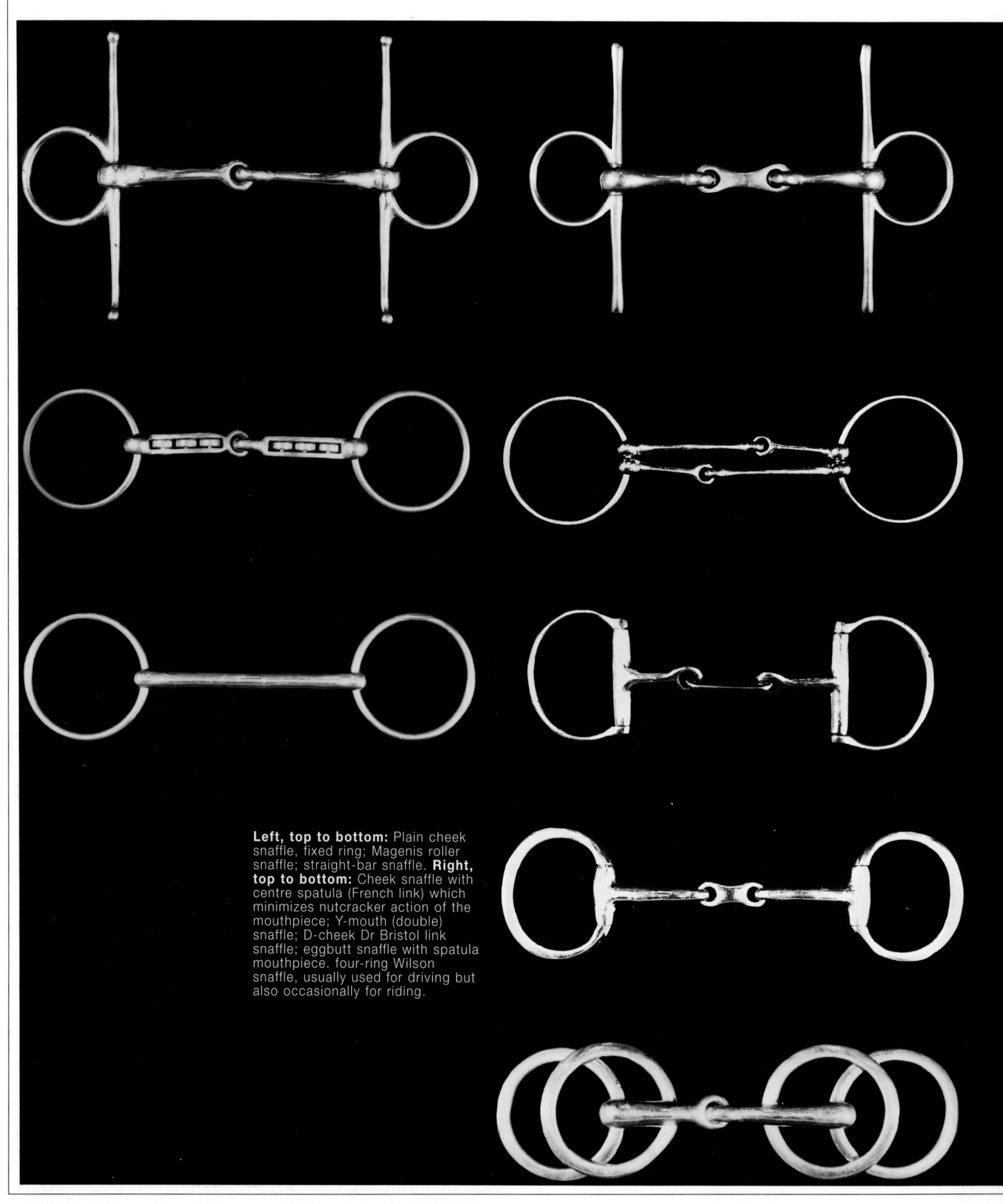

Left, top to bottom: Plain cheek snaffle, fixed ring; Magenis roller snaffle; straight-bar snaffle. **Right, top to bottom:** Cheek snaffle with centre spatula (French link) which minimizes nutcracker action of the mouthpiece; Y-mouth (double) snaffle; D-cheek Dr Bristol link snaffle; eggbutt snaffle with spatula mouthpiece. four-ring Wilson snaffle, usually used for driving but also occasionally for riding.

BITS AND BITTING

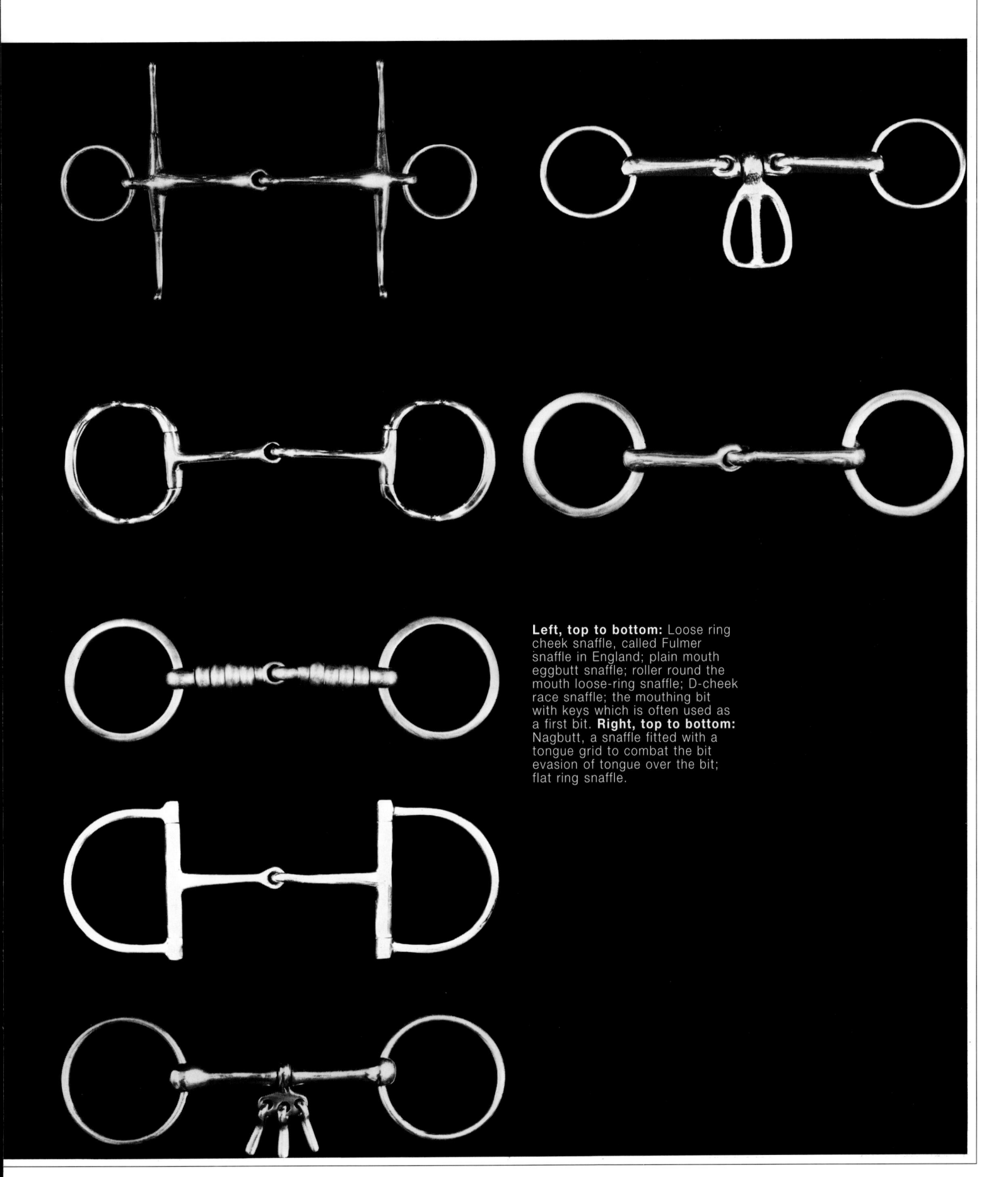

Left, top to bottom: Loose ring cheek snaffle, called Fulmer snaffle in England; plain mouth eggbutt snaffle; roller round the mouth loose-ring snaffle; D-cheek race snaffle; the mouthing bit with keys which is often used as a first bit. **Right, top to bottom:** Nagbutt, a snaffle fitted with a tongue grid to combat the bit evasion of tongue over the bit; flat ring snaffle.

125

CHAPTER FIVE · BITS, BRIDLES AND ADDITIONAL AIDS

Below: Diagram showing the action of the double bridle, the ultimate aid in assisting the rider to suggest a positioning of the head.

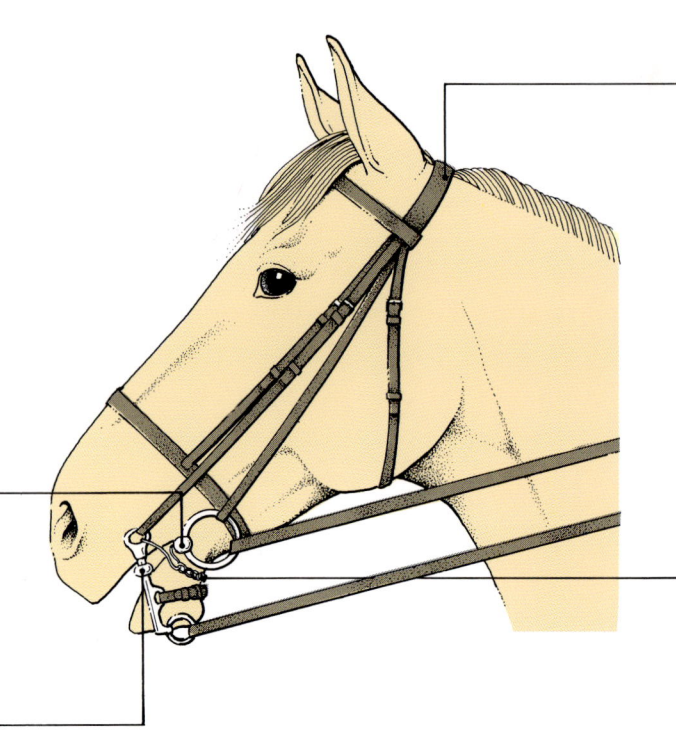

Poll pressure, exerting a downward action, varies according to the length of the cheek above the mouthpiece and is transmitted by the forward movement of the eye of the curb bit.

The bradoon acts to raise the head by a slight upward pressure on the horse's mouth.

The curb chain is also brought into play by movement of the curb bit, causing downward and backward pressure on the horse's jaw.

The curb bit exerts pressure on the bars of the mouth as well as on the curb groove and poll to cause a lowering of the head, retraction of the nose and flexion at poll and lower jaw.

The action of the two mouthpieces, the bit and the bradoon, together with the pressures exerted on the poll and curb groove, make this bridle an extremely sensitive instrument. When employed on a schooled horse, it can 'place' the head with greater finesse than is possible with any other bridle in current use.

The slide-cheek curb bit which allows movement of the mouthpiece in the mouth itself, is perhaps potentially more severe than the fixed mouthpiece, which permits no such movement. The reason for this is that the slide-cheek gives something like an extra ½in of leverage when the bit is brought into play.

The pelham
The pelham is often looked on as the poor relation of the double bridle, though it has plenty of value in its own right. It is an attempt to combine the actions of the bradoon and the curb in one mouthpiece, and while the theory might be slightly shaky, in practice it is a bit with which many horses and riders find great success; for instance, many cobs, native ponies and Arabs find the two bits of a double bridle too bulky, but take kindly to being ridden in a pelham. Pelhams act on the poll and the curb groove as well as the bars and corners of the mouth, and when used correctly will often persuade the horse to flex via subtle aids from the rider; many classical teachers use them to great effect. Unfortunately, they are not allowed in dressage competitions.

Ideally, the pelham should be used with two reins, the top one corresponding to the bradoon rein of the double bridle and the bottom one to the curb. They should be used independently, not together, and the bottom rein obviously gives more leverage. Some riders prefer to use a single rein, fastened to leather couplings or 'roundings' linking the top and bottom rings, although this gives a less definite action.

There are many different forms of pelham mouthpiece. The most common is the mullen, which curves slightly to allow room for the tongue. Many horses go even better in a Cambridge mouthpiece, which has a small port, or arch, in the centre. Some riders are doubtful about using bits with ported mouthpieces because they are worried that the port will dig into the roof of the horse's mouth, but for this to happen the port would have to be very high and the rider's hands very rough. A small port takes pressure off the centre of the tongue, and this, together with the way the bit is suspended in the horse's mouth, means that many find it comfortable.

The Rugby pelham has a ported mouthpiece and loose rings set outside the mouthpiece at the top. This theoretically gives more play, though the effect will only be slight. It is a popular bit in the showing world because if an extra sliphead is fastened to the loose rings, it gives a more finished appearance to the horse's head, like a double bridle.

The SM and Hanoverian pelhams also have many showing devotees. The former is named after Sam Marsh, a horseman who first made its use popular; it has a broad flat mouthpiece with a small port, and the big difference between the SM and other pelhams is that it has cheeks which move independently, and the mouthpiece remains in the correct position no matter how the horse holds his head. It requires tactful hands but can be particularly effective. Sam Marsh also invented the Scamperdale pelham, which has cheeks bent slightly back from the mouthpiece to eliminate the risk of chafing. The Hanoverian pelham has a port with rollers set around the mouthpiece, intended to encourage the horse to relax its jaw and play with the bit.

BITS AND BITTING

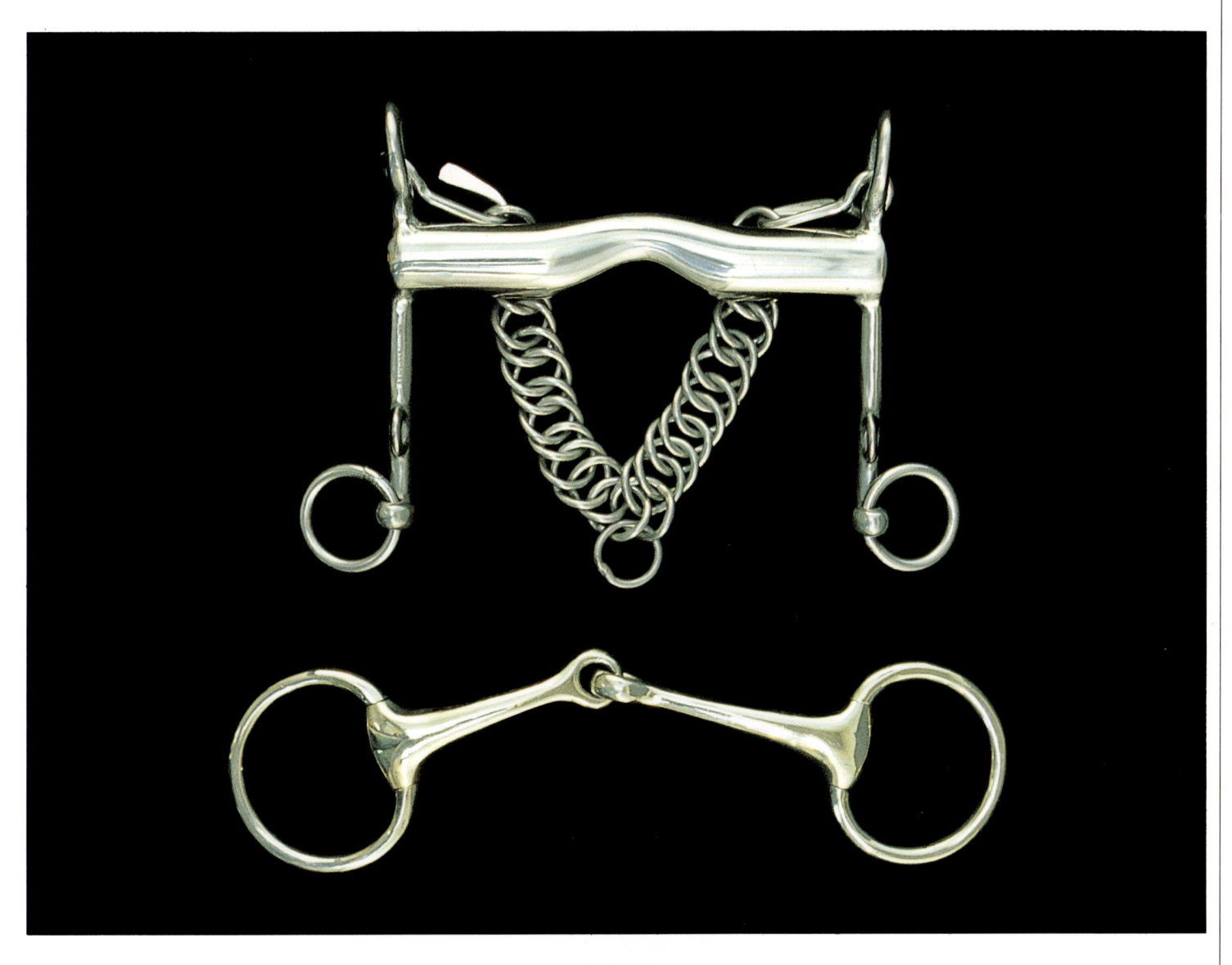

Above: Fixed-cheek Weymouth curb bit with broad mouthpiece and eggbutt bradoon. This type is much favoured for dressage.
Right: The slide-cheek Weymouth bit.

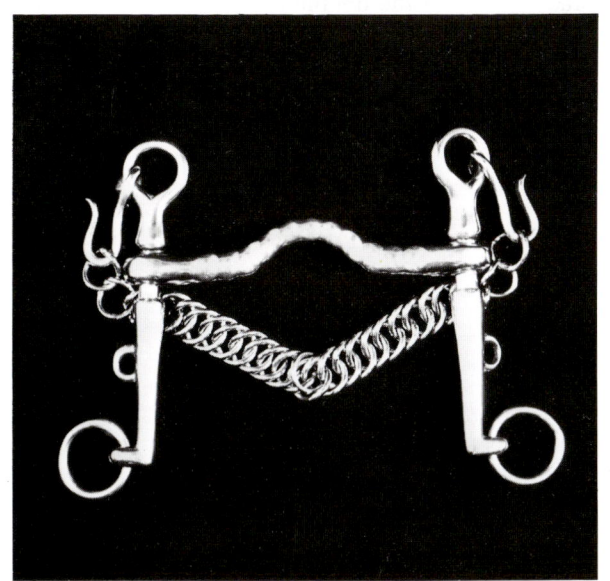

Below, top to bottom: A selection of curb chains: elastic curb; flat link chain; single link chain; double link chain. Curb chains are integral to the functioning of the curb bit, acting on the curb groove as a restraint and also assisting in the relaxation of the lower jaw.

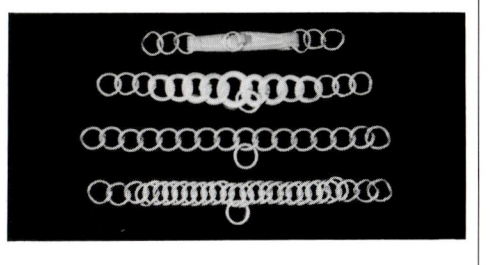

127

CHAPTER FIVE · BITS, BRIDLES AND ADDITIONAL AIDS

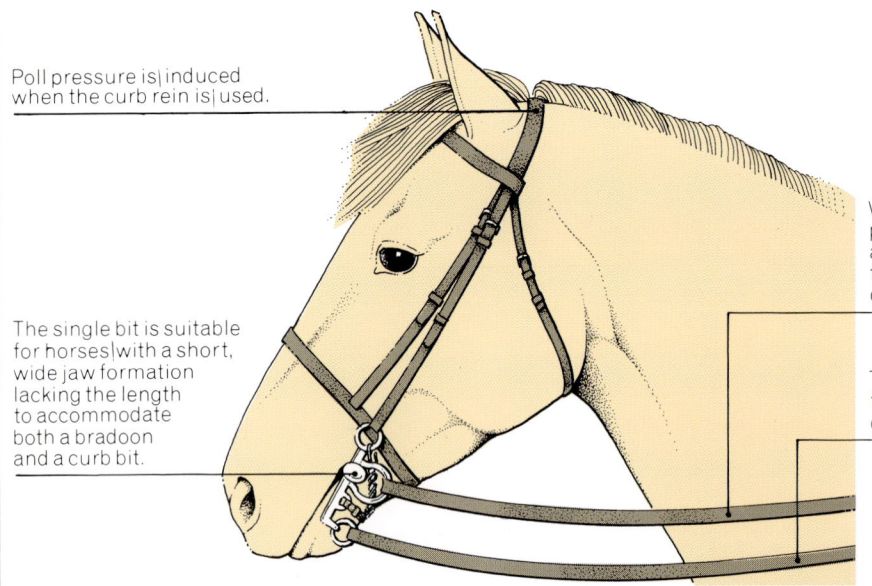

Poll pressure is induced when the curb rein is used.

The single bit is suitable for horses with a short, wide jaw formation lacking the length to accommodate both a bradoon and a curb bit.

When the bradoon rein predominates, the action imitates that of the bradoon bit of the double bridle.

The curb rein imitates the action of the double's curb bit.

Left: The pelham bridle in position. In essence it seeks to obtain the same result as the double bridle while employing a single mouthpiece. **Below left:** The SM pelham is of American origin. The mouthpiece is broad and flat and the cheeks move in a restricted area. **Centre:** The rubber mullen-mouth pelham. **Right:** The kimblewick, sometimes known as the Spanish jumping bit, although employing only a single rein, is still a member of the pelham group. **Bottom:** The Scamperdale has the mouthpiece turned back so that the cheek cannot chafe the lip area, a fault with most pelhams. This bit was the invention of an English horseman, the late Sam Marsh.

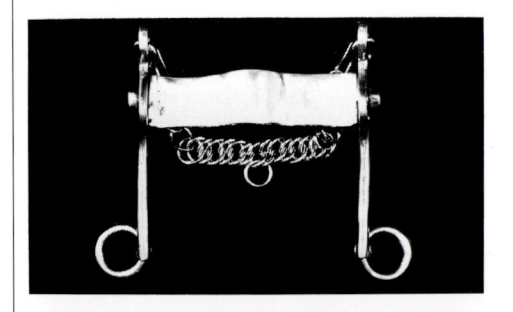

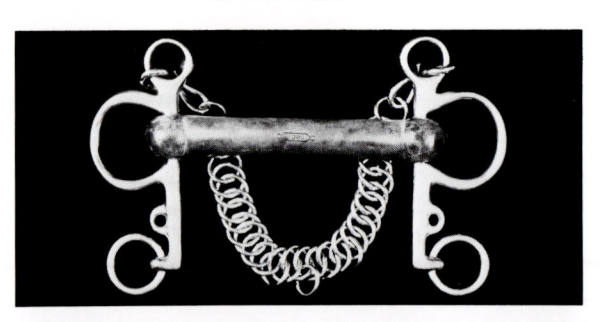

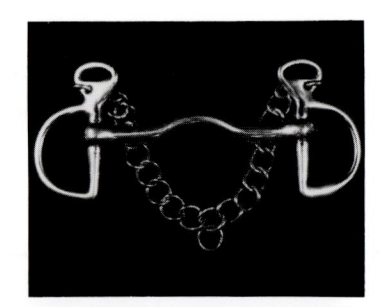

The jointed pelham is rarely as effective as unjointed designs, mainly because its design means that the curb chain tends to ride up the horse's jaw. However, there are some horses who ignore all the theories and prefer this—or variations such as the French link pelham—to any other.

The kimblewick
In the US the name has become corrupted to kimberwick. Originally known as the Spanish jumping bit, it was taken to Britain in the 1960s. In some respects it is a pelham with the bottom rings sliced off. It is often said that if a kimblewick is used with the rider's hands kept fairly high it has a snaffle action, while lowered hands produce the action of a curb; but the amount of leverage possible is so slight that there really cannot be that much difference. The original design had a ported mouthpiece, though mullen ones are also available, and some kimblewicks have slotted cheeks to give slightly higher or lower rein positions.

Mouthpiece materials
There are as many variations in mouthpiece materials for pelhams and kimblewicks as there are for snaffles. They range from stainless steel, hardened rubber and copper alloys to plastics such as those used in Nathe and Happy Mouth bits.

Curb chains
Curb chains are the final part of the equation when considering double bridles, pelhams and kimblewicks. The single link curb chain has been generally superseded by the double link one, which has greater flexibility; if necessary, it can be passed through a rubber or leather sleeve to give a milder action. Mildest of all are leather and elastic curb chains, which are still effective on sensitive horses. In theory a lipstrap should always be used to help keep a curb chain in place, though many riders now tend not to bother with one.

The gag snaffle and lever snaffles
The gag snaffle, often used to provide extra brakes, is used with sliding bridle cheekpieces made from rolled leather or cord which pass through slots in the top and bottom of the bit rings. The headpiece buckles to one end and the reins to the other, although for safety's sake, a second pair of reins should be used on the bit rings, as with an ordinary snaffle. This means that the rider can use the ordinary rein most of the time and needs only to bring the gag rein, which raises the bit in the horse's mouth, into play when really necessary.

Snaffles which exert poll pressure, and often leverage, have become increasingly popular over the last few years. The most subtle is the hanging cheek snaffle, a mild bit which is suspended in the horse's mouth, thus reducing pressure on the tongue, and designed to encourage flexion by applying slight poll pressure. It is permitted in dressage tests.

Three-ring snaffles—also known as Continental snaffles, or Belgian or Dutch gags—are effective on many onward-bound horses and are particularly popular with show-jumping and event riders. Three rings offer a variety of rein positions, and obviously the lower the rein, the greater the leverage that can be exerted. The American gag, a variation on the Tennessee Walking Horse bit, has sliding cheekpieces and therefore offers a limited raising action on the mouthpiece.

It should be remembered that using a potentially more severe bit does not necessarily mean better brakes. Horses pull against pain and against riders who set their hands ... so look to your riding technique for help as well as your saddle shop or mail-order catalogue!

Below: Diagram showing the action of the balding gag with a top rein fitted to the bit ring.

The top rein acts as an ordinary snaffle.

The bridle cheeks pass through two holes in the bit ring, giving accentuated upward action.

CHAPTER FIVE · BITS, BRIDLES AND ADDITIONAL AIDS

Bridling aids · **Martingales**

Martingales are designed not to hold the horse's head down, but to prevent him from raising it above the angle of control. Some are more sophisticated in their action than others, and like all items of tack, they come into and fall out of fashion. All must be fitted with care, and it is essential that a rubber 'stop' is used at the junction of the neckstrap and the part which runs to the girth to prevent the martingale from dangling between the horse's front legs, when he could possibly put a foot through it when jumping.

The standing martingale
The standing martingale is the most basic, because it is the only one to have no effect on the bit and therefore the horse's mouth. It starts at the girth and runs between the front legs, then attaches to a cavesson noseband or to the cavesson part of a Flash noseband. It should never be fastened to a drop noseband, or to the drop part of a Flash noseband, nor to a Grakle, or figure 8, as it would restrict the horse's breathing. The textbook adjustment is for it to reach into the horse's gullet when pushed up, although it may be necessary to adjust it a hole shorter.

At one time, the standing martingale was standard equipment in the hunting field and on young horses, as it gave extra control through putting pressure on the nose rather than the mouth. Nowadays it is used less frequently; moreover, some trainers believe that a horse can set himself against it and thus build up muscles on the underside of the neck, exactly where you do not want them. Critics also maintain that it can restrict a horse over a fence, although as a horse's head and neck should move forward and down rather than up as he jumps, this argument is probably not sustainable. Many American riders like to use a standing martingale on green hunters and jumpers, whose arc over a fence is not affected unless the martingale is too tight.

The running martingale
The running martingale is more popular and is often used as a standard piece of tack for show jumpers and for eventers

during the jumping phases (no martingale at all is allowed in dressage or in the dressage phase of horse trials). It starts at the girth and passes between the front legs, where it divides into two straps, each with a ring at the end. The reins pass through the rings, so when the horse raises his head too high, there is direct pressure on the bars of the mouth.

The traditional method of fitting a running martingale, so that the rings can be stretched back nearly to the withers, does not take into account different types of shoulder conformation. A more accurate fitting is obtained by adjusting the martingale so that the rings reach into the horse's gullet when the straps are stretched along the underside of his neck. Running martingales limit the extent to which the rider can open a rein to the side, although there should still be enough leeway in most situations. When used with a bit which stays relatively still in the mouth, such as an eggbutt snaffle, it can lessen the slight jerking effect on the reins that novice and/or unbalanced riders are often unable to prevent.

A running martingale should always be used with rubber stops on the reins, as well as one at the neckstrap junction, to prevent the rings from sliding too far down. Some riders like to use two stops on each rein to limit the backward as well as the forward movement.

The bib martingale

The bib martingale is used mainly in the racing world, although it also finds favour with other riders of young horses. It is basically a running martingale where the straps have been joined with a triangular piece of leather. It is a much safer version to use on horses which like to grab hold of running martingale straps, but it limits severely the extent to which you can open a rein to the side. Again, it should be used with rein stops. Ideally, both running and bib martingales should be used with snaffles, although they are sometimes seen with pelhams and even double bridles. As a curb bit already has a lowering effect, using one with a double bridle seems excessive.

The Irish martingale

The Irish martingale is rarely seen outside racing, and strictly speaking is not a martingale at all as it has no effect on the horse's head carriage. It comprises a short piece of leather with a ring at each end through which the reins pass, the idea being that if a racehorse pulls the reins out of his jockey's hands in a fall, they will not be jerked over the horse's head.

The Market Harborough

The Market Harborough is usually classed as a martingale, although strictly speaking it is really a cross between a martingale and draw reins. Named after a British town in Leicestershire, it is very effective on a strong horse which puts his head in the air to pull—although its action is in fact more sympathetic than many people realize.

Its design follows that of a running martingale, but there are clips rather than rings at the end of the straps. These pass through the bit rings and clip onto small D-rings sewn onto the reins; if adjusted correctly, the Market Harborough only comes into play when the horse puts his head too high, the straps then exerting a downward pressure on the mouth which yields as soon as the horse 'gives' to its action. It is therefore operated by the horse rather than the rider, and he is rewarded as soon as he reverts to an acceptable head carriage. As always, a rubber stop should be used to prevent it from hanging between the horse's forelegs.

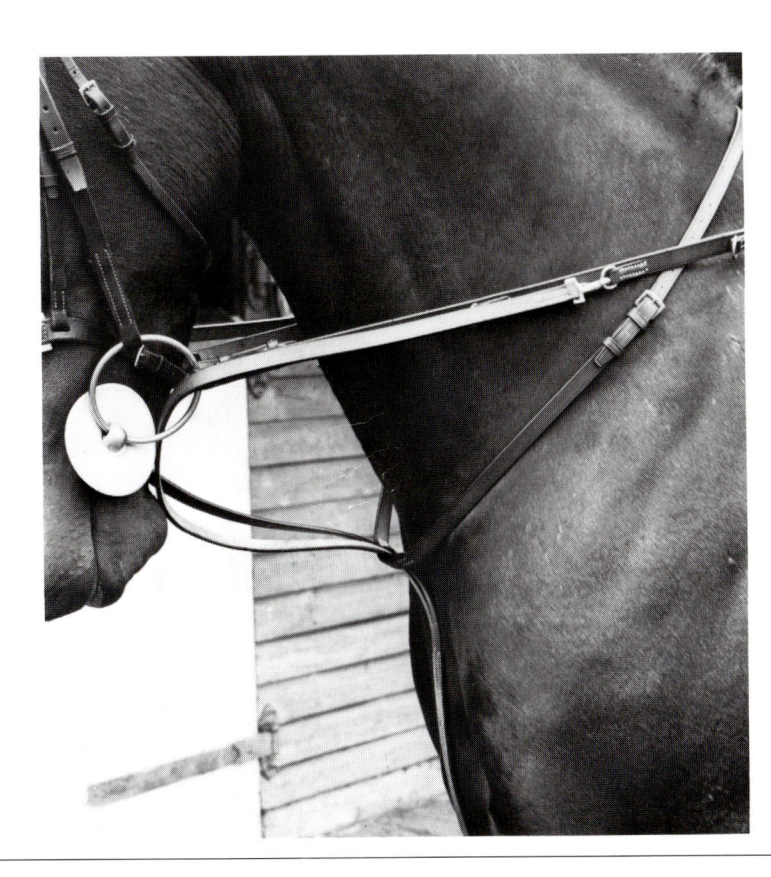

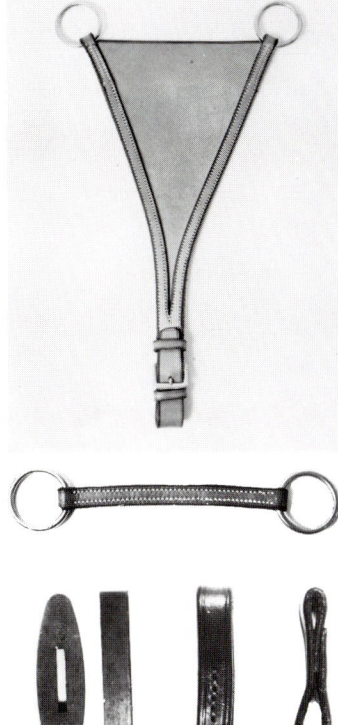

Left to right: Standing martingale, showing the rubber 'stop' at the junction of the neckstrap and the part of the martingale which runs to the girth. The stop is essential on all martingales to prevent them from hanging between the horse's front legs; Running martingale, imposing control by pressure on the mouth. The 'stops' in advance of the ring prevent the latter from sliding forward and becoming caught on the bridle or over the tooth; The Market Harborough acts when the horse evades by throwing his head above an acceptable level; Bib martingale and (**below**) Irish martingale, and rein stops made from rubber and leather.

CHAPTER FIVE · BITS, BRIDLES AND ADDITIONAL AIDS

Bridling Aids · **Nosebands**

Most horses are ridden with nosebands, often to give the rider extra control, but also because it looks more stylish. Racehorses, especially those which run on the Flat, are the exception: more often than not they are ridden without them, unless some form of restraint is needed.

The cavesson noseband is the simplest of all: it is a strap which fastens around the nose, far enough below the bottom of the cheekbones not to cause rubbing. If you want to use a standing martingale, the horse must be wearing either a cavesson or a Flash. Although the cavesson's use is primarily cosmetic, a broad, flat one fastened slightly tighter than normal may help to dissuade the horse from crossing his jaw.

The drop noseband, used in the Spanish Riding School of Vienna, went out of favour for some time but is currently enjoying a revival among riders who appreciate its action. It should be fitted at least 3in above the nostrils so that it does not restrict the horse's breathing, and it fastens below the bit, in the curb groove. If the horse opens his mouth too wide, the front strap presses on his nose, and then hopefully he will lower his head and accept the bit.

The Flash noseband is a much later design and has a less definite action. It was originally developed for a show jumper of the same name so that his owner could also use a standing martingale. There are undoubtedly horses which resent a drop but are happy in a Flash—but there are also those which have little respect for a Flash but respond to a drop! Both styles help to keep the bit central in the horse's mouth. To be effective, a Flash noseband must have a fairly substantial top half; if the cavesson is too lightweight, it will be pulled down the horse's face, whereas a broader design will stay in place.

The Grakle, or figure 8, noseband, first designed for the 1931 winner of the English Grand National, forms a figure-eight, the straps passing through a central point halfway up the horse's face. It is

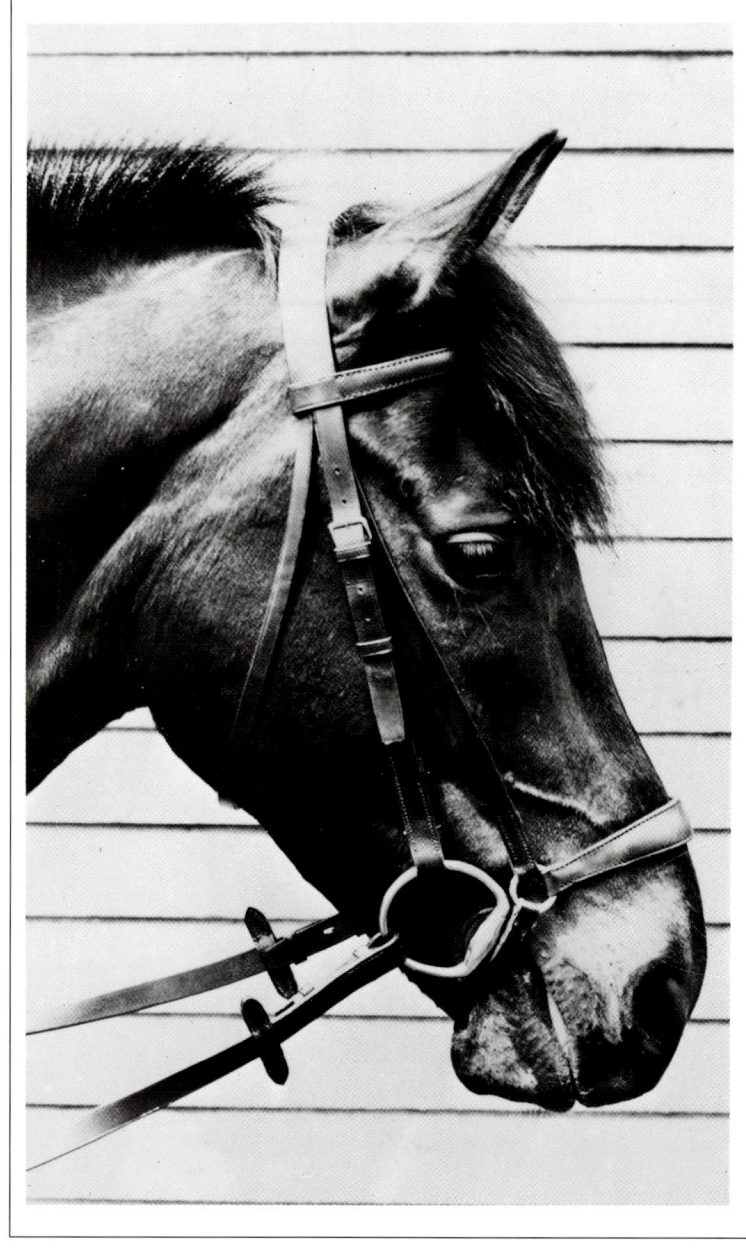

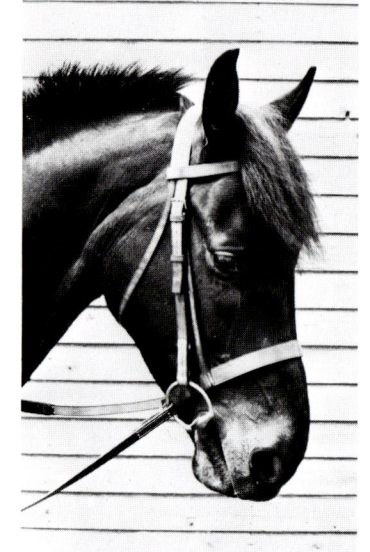

Left: Drop noseband, fastening below the bit. **Above:** Plain cavesson noseband. **Above right:** Flash noseband. **Right:** A raised, show-type noseband with a snaffle bridle.

132

designed to give extra control over horses that cross their jaws to pull, and it is particularly popular with event riders. The top straps of the standard Grakle fasten just below the cheekbones—although those of the American Grakle, which is rapidly gaining popularity in other parts of the world, fasten even higher. Many riders believe that the American Grakle is more comfortable for the horse.

Nosebands that have some form of fastening below the bit should theoretically only be used with snaffles, as the bottom strap could muffle the effect of a curb chain. However, many top riders use Flash and Grakle nosebands successfully with pelhams or kimblewicks, and it has become much more generally acceptable to do this.

As a double bridle should be used to provide subtler communication with a schooled horse, and not extra brakes, it should not be teamed with any noseband that fastens below the bit. In the past few years, some riders have adopted cinch or doubleback cavessons, which can be fastened slightly tighter than ordinary ones without pinching the horse.

Not all nosebands rely on preventing the horse from opening his mouth too wide to give extra control: the kineton, or puckle noseband has metal loops which fit around the bit and transfer rein pressure to the nose, while the American cheeker is said to have a psychological effect: two rubber discs fit around the bit and are joined by a central strap running down the horse's face, and many racehorse trainers believe that the horse can see the centre strap and back off it. The American cheeker also keeps the bit quite high in the horse's mouth and so may dissuade those which try to put their tongues over the bit.

Another idea which has spread from racing to show jumping and eventing is the sheepskin noseband—a sheepskin sleeve which slots over a cavesson or the cavesson part of a Flash. It is supposed to encourage the horse to lower his head, which he must do in order to see over the top of it.

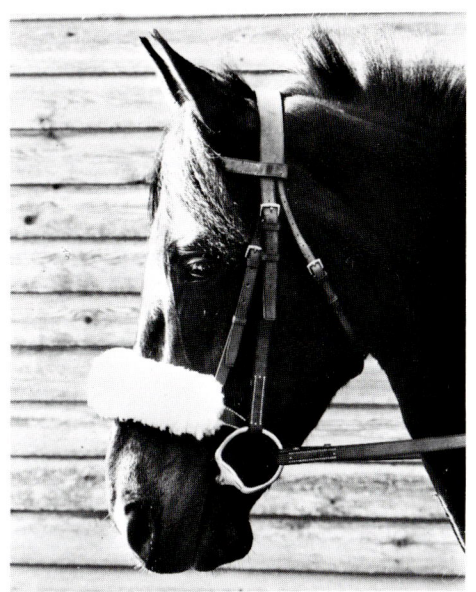

Top, far left: Grakle, or figure 8, noseband. **Left:** Sheepskin noseband. **Bottom, far left:** Kineton, or Puckle, noseband. **Bottom right:** Australian cheeker.

CHAPTER FIVE · BITS, BRIDLES AND ADDITIONAL AIDS

Bridling Aids · **Bridles—Types and Fitting**

The various parts of the bridle are virtually common to all types, although they may not look the same or employ the same method of fastening. The headpiece, passing over the horse's poll, has attached to it the cheeks to which the bit is secured. The throatlatch (pronounced throatlash) is usually incorporated in the headpiece, though in some instances, it is a completely separate strap attached to the head by a loop fixed between the horse's ears, as in some American patterns.

Certain types of bridle omit the throatlatch completely. There are, for instance, no throatlatches on the bridles used in the Spanish Riding School in Vienna. The reason is that a throatlatch, if it is too tight, can discourage a horse from flexing at the poll, because of the discomfort it would cause. The Spanish School Lipizzaners are, in any case, naturally thick through the jowl, and since they are unlikely to get

Right: Parts of a double bridle. The extra pair of reins is also a requirement of the Pelham and Gag bridles.

- Browband
- Cheeks
- Noseband
- Lipstrap
- Headpiece
- Throatlatch
- Bradoon sliphead
- Bradoon rein
- Curb chain
- Curb rein

Right: Fine leather, lightweight show bridle with raised and swelled noseband. **Above:** Weymouth bridle in a more general purpose weight. Bridles can be attached to bits by hook studs, or very occasionally, buckles.

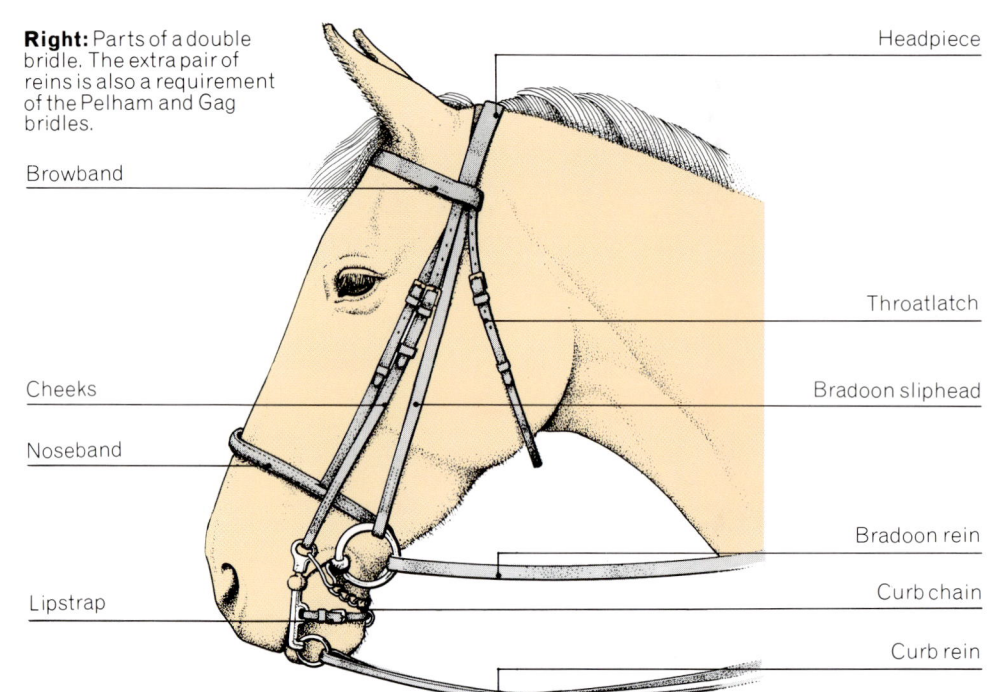

134

BRIDLES—TYPES AND FITTING

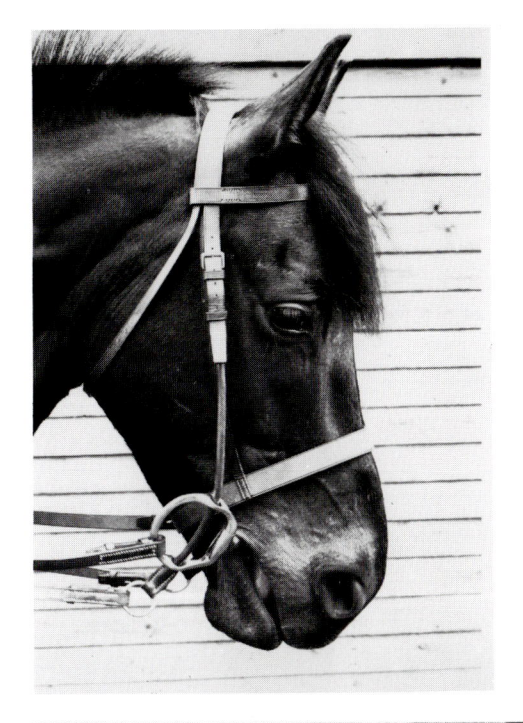

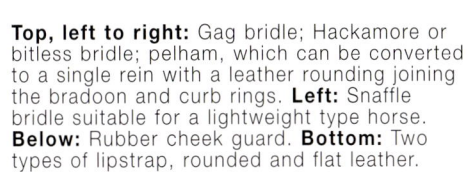

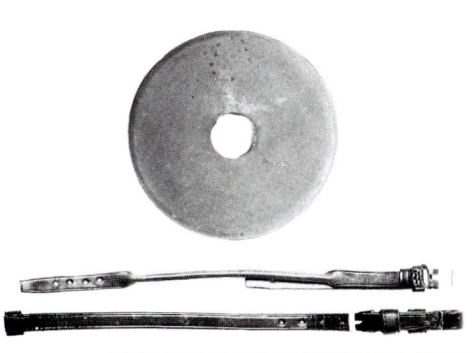

Top, left to right: Gag bridle; Hackamore or bitless bridle; pelham, which can be converted to a single rein with a leather rounding joining the bradoon and curb rings. **Left:** Snaffle bridle suitable for a lightweight type horse. **Below:** Rubber cheek guard. **Bottom:** Two types of lipstrap, rounded and flat leather.

135

CHAPTER FIVE · BITS, BRIDLES AND ADDITIONAL AIDS

Reins are made in a variety of patterns and materials, usually with a view to giving the rider a better grip, particularly in wet weather or if the rein becomes wet with sweat. **Left to right:** Plaited rein; laced rein; plain leather rein; rein with rubber grip; dressage reins with rubber grip on one side only.

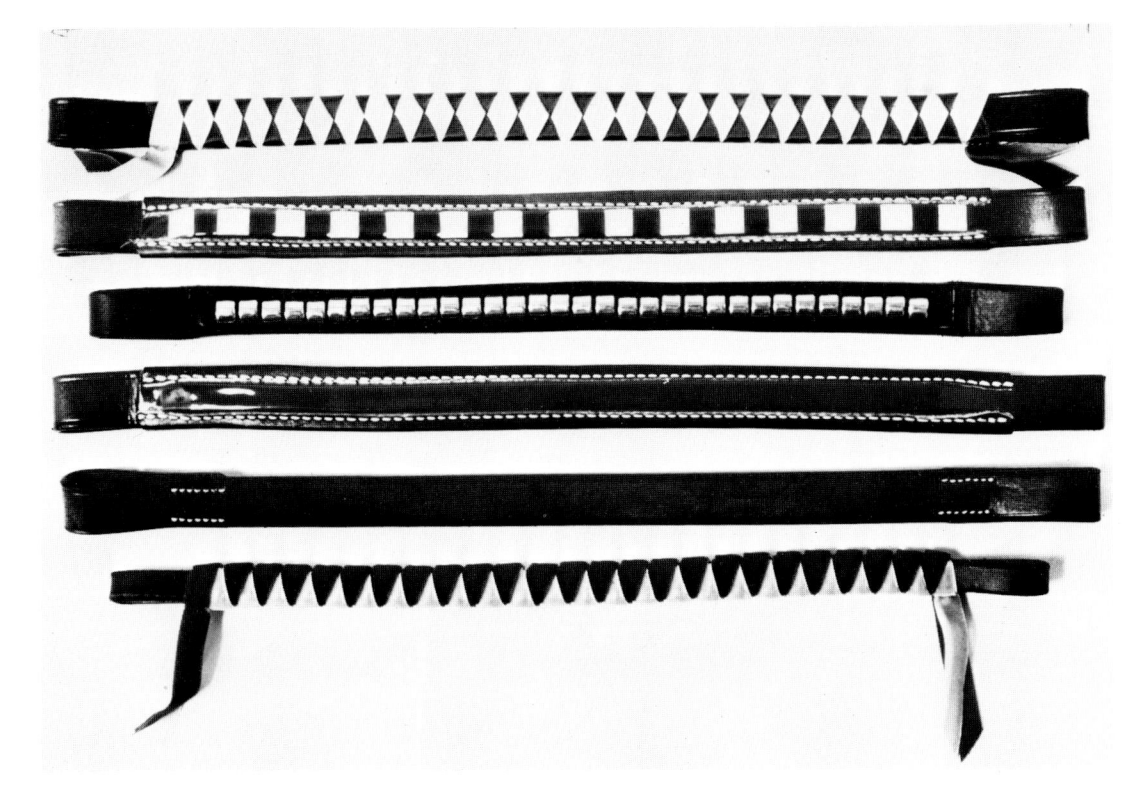

Left: Browbands are available in numerous patterns. Those covered in coloured silk or plastic are usually reserved for show bridles. Brass-mounted 'clinker' browbands are sometimes used with in-hand bridles. **Below:** American browbands are considerably more elaborate than the European variety.

into situations in which the bridle may be pulled off, there is no need to use a throatlatch. Its other purpose is to keep the bridle from coming off in the event of a fall. A number of Western bridles also dispense with the throatlatch, preferring to keep the bridle in place by a slit passed over either both ears or a single ear.

The browband, or 'front' as it is sometimes known, is fastened by loops to the headpiece and acts to keep the latter from sliding backward. There is then, in most bridles, but not in all, a noseband and then finally a pair of reins.

Double bridles and pelhams

The above describes the composition of a snaffle bridle, but in the case of double bridles and pelhams, additions are needed. On a double bridle, for instance, there has to be a sliphead from which the bradoon is suspended. A sliphead is a strap and one cheekpiece passed through the loops of the browband under the headpiece. The cheek of the sliphead is placed on the off-side so that its buckle matches that of the noseband on the nearside.

In both the double and pelham bridles, a pair of extra reins is necessary, the curb rein always being the narrower of the two. There is also the addition of a lipstrap, which is attached to the Ds halfway down the cheeks of the bit and through the 'fly' (flying link in the centre of the curb chain). Its purpose is to keep the curb chain in place.

Leather, buckles and reins

Bridles are made in different weights of leather to suit different types of horse. For safety's sake, any bridle should be workmanlike enough to stand up to strain and should therefore be made from good-quality leather. The lightest bridles of all are ornate designs made for Arabs, but these have a metal core running through the thin, rolled leather straps.

The more substantial the horse, the more substantial should be the bridle. Hunters and cobs traditionally have bridles with broad, flat nosebands and flat browbands, while lightweight animals such as show hacks and Thoroughbred types are suited to more lightweight bridles, perhaps with padded nosebands and browbands. Coloured browbands, usually bound in two or three colours of velvet ribbon, are popular for show ponies and show hacks; ones with brass mountings are traditionally meant for driving horses, although some owners like to see them on riding animals.

Cheekpieces and reins are attached to the bit in two ways: either with buckles, or with hook stud (billet) fastenings. Buckles are safer, especially for rein fastenings, but hook studs look neater. Buckles fasten on the outside and hook studs on the inside. They are usually made from strong stainless steel, but some stallion and showing bridles have brass buckles. At one time bits would be sewn in, but this is rarely done nowadays as most people like to be able to interchange bridles and bits.

Reins can be plain leather, or made in a variety of ways and materials to give better grip. Plain leather becomes slippery when wet; laced leather is better. Plaited leather looks smart, but is difficult to clean and sometimes stretches in use. Rubber grip reins, where the handpart has been covered with rubber, are the favourite for most event riders, and are standard on racing bridles. Continental reins are generally made from webbing with leather grips sewn along them; they are lightweight and particularly popular with show jumpers. If you are using a double bridle or pelham with two reins, the bradoon rein should be wider than the curb rein so that the rider can differentiate between them by feel.

Fitting the bridle

A bridle must be correctly fitted for the horse to work comfortably. A bit that is too

CHAPTER FIVE · BITS, BRIDLES AND ADDITIONAL AIDS

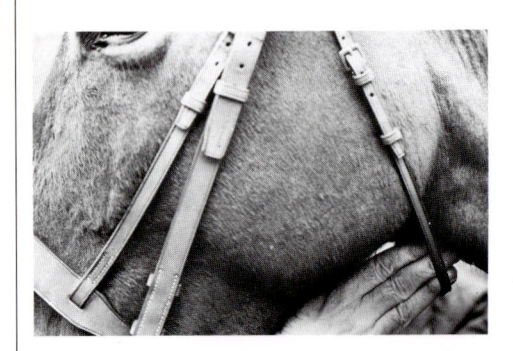

Fitting: The throatlatch must be loose enough to allow flexion of the poll without restriction of the gullet.

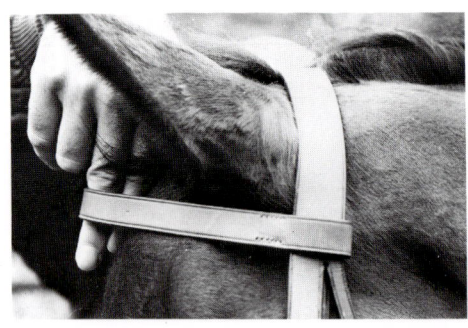

The browband needs to be sufficiently large so that the headpiece is not pulled up against the back of the ears.

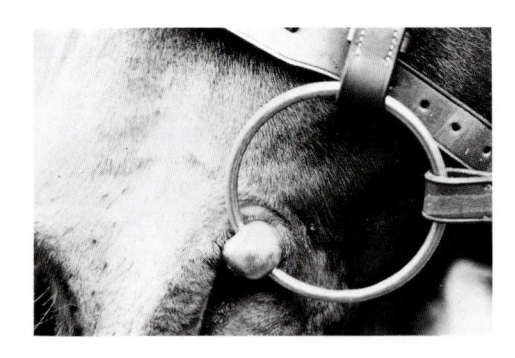

The bit should fit high enough in the mouth to prevent the horse from trying to put his tongue over it and should project no more than ½in each side.

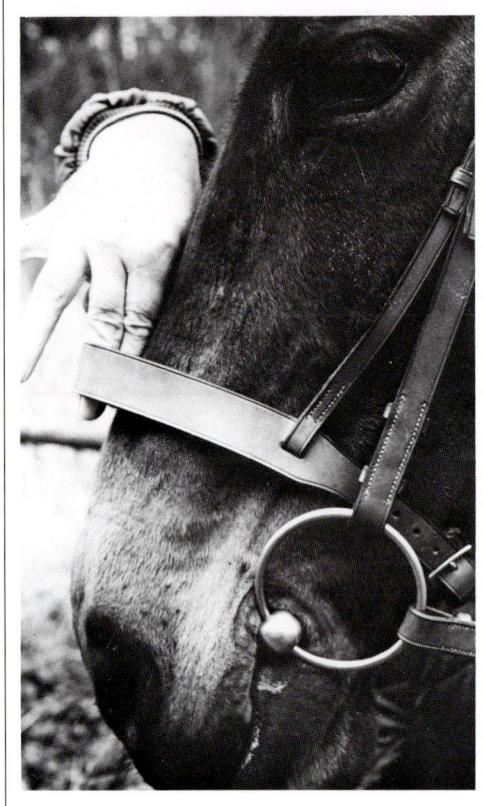

Above: Cavesson nosebands should permit the insertion of two fingers. A tighter fitting noseband is permissible if a partial closure of the mouth is required. **Right:** A Flash noseband with a snaffle bridle. The top part should be sited just below the facial bones and the bottom strap should be tight enough to prevent the horse from opening his mouth too wide, but not so tight that he cannot flex his jaw.

BRIDLES—TYPES AND FITTING

small or too large, or a bridle that pinches or rubs can cause discomfort and/or evasions—for instance, a browband that is too short will pinch the ears.

Many people use bits that are too large and often compound the problem by adjusting them too low in the mouth. As a general guide, there should be no more than ½in between the cheekpieces or rings and the horse's mouth; full cheeks, D-rings and eggbutts can usually be fitted slightly more snugly. To judge the fit of a jointed bit, straighten it in the horse's mouth. Make sure the horse's lips cannot be pinched between loose rings and the holes they slot through, and if necessary, use rubber bitguards.

Bits should be high enough in the mouth so that the horse is not encouraged to put his tongue over the mouthpiece. If the horse has fleshy lips, the corners should be wrinkled; if not, the bit should be snug in the corners of his mouth. Jointed bits need to be slightly higher than unjointed ones. With a double bridle, the bradoon should be adjusted in the same way as a snaffle, with the curb below it.

Browbands should be long enough not to pull the headpiece onto the base of the ears, and there should be a hand's width between the throatlatch and the side of the horse's face. There should be at least a finger's width, and preferably two, between a cavesson noseband or the top of a Flash and the horse's face. Drop, Flash and Grakle, or figure 8, nosebands should be tight enough to prevent the horse from opening his mouth too wide, but not so tight that he cannot open it at all. A horse whose mouth is strapped shut will not be able to flex his jaw and accept the bit.

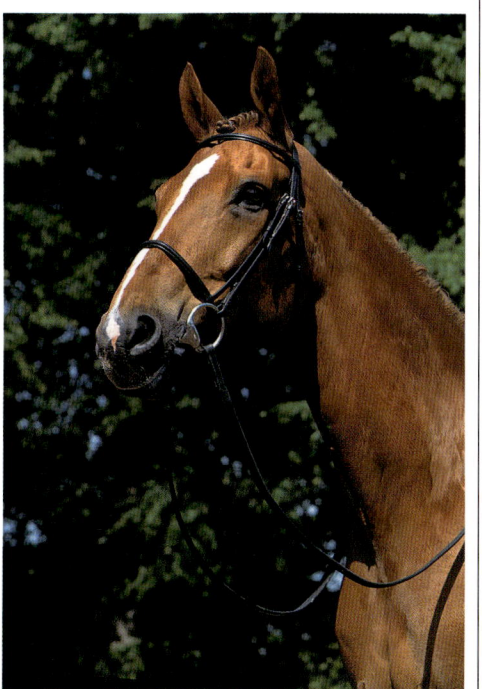

Left: The correct fitting of the double bridle.
Above: A correctly fitted snaffle bridle with cavesson noseband. This is 'made-to-measure' quality; note how the buckles of the noseband and cheekpieces are in line with the horse's eye.

CHAPTER FIVE · BITS, BRIDLES AND ADDITIONAL AIDS

Bridling Aids · The Western Hackamore System

The ultimate bitting development in the horsemanship of Europe was the curb bit. The curb dominated European equestrian thinking for centuries, but in the Middle East there survived a different riding tradition which placed a greater emphasis on control and submission being achieved through pressures concentrated on the nose, rather than the mouth. This tradition extended into the Mediterranean countries, where its influence is still to be seen, as well as in areas farther to the east. In countries of the Middle East today, horses are ridden by means of a thick wool rope attached behind the lower jaw to light chains encircling the nose.

A more sophisticated variation on this basic simplicity can be seen in the painting by Henry Bernard Chalon of *George IV's Persian Horses being taken out for exercise* (they are, in fact, Arabian horses), on view in the Tate Gallery, London. In this picture, the action of the bit is assisted materially by the attachment of a light nose chain. The arrangement is remarkably similar to that used on the American cow-pony, though, instead of a nose chain, the American horse wears a light rawhide 'bosal'. The connection, however, is very clear, which is not as surprising as it might at first appear. Further examples can be seen in Italy, where the horses drawing the *fiacres* are driven from a noseband fitted on each side with a ring set on a projecting metal shank to which the reins are attached. The assembly resembles a lungeing cavesson and employs no bit at all.

Origins of the hackamore

The apotheosis of the 'nose school' of riding (as opposed to that which concerns itself primarily with the mouth) came in the period following the Moorish conquest of large parts of the Iberian Peninsula in the 7th and 8th centuries and the long occupation which followed.

The Moors, who at one time threatened to engulf Europe until their decisive defeat by Charles Martel and his knights at Poitiers in AD720, established a highly sophisticated system of horse schooling based on the use of the sensitive nose area. It employed as a principal element an item termed *la jaquima*, from which the word 'hackamore' is derived. The system was a progression, which culminated in the production of a highly schooled, well-balanced horse. As a result of its training, the horse could perform 'practical dressage' movements—in combat or working with bulls—at full speed on the weight of a floating rein attached to a ported curb bit and the indications made by the disposition of the rider's body.

Above: 16th-century curb bit of German manufacture. The bit is unusual in the width of its mouthpiece, which is also jointed. Provision has been made for the bit to be used as a form of Pelham; there are top rings to which the reins can be attached. **Right:** Henry Bernard Chalon's picture, *George IV's Persian Horses*, from the Tate Gallery, London. The action of the bit is assisted by a light nose chain.

THE WESTERN HACKAMORE SYSTEM

Eight centuries later, the Spanish *conquistadores* took themselves, their culture, their horses and their horselore to the American continent, where horses had been extinct for millions of years. Settling in Mexico and California, which were to become cattle-ranching countries, it was their horse culture, ideally suited to cattle working, which was to become part of the Western legend. Their equipment and methods, modified and adapted to local needs, gave the world the culture of the Western horseman, which survives and is practised actively today all through the USA and on into Canada, as well as in Europe.

The true hackamore

In Europe, 'hackamore' often is used mistakenly to describe a bitless-type bridle, usually fitted with metal cheekpieces. The true hackamore consists of a heavy braided rawhide noseband, the shape of a *Réal* tennis racquet, with a large knot at the end which lies under the horse's chin. The noseband itself is called a bosal and is fitted to the horse by means of a lightweight latigo headstall. This may be slit at an appropriate point so that it can be kept in place by passing it over an ear, or may be made more secure by the addition of a browband, a *cavesada*.

The hackamore is completed by the addition of a rope made from mane hair, which is called the *mecate* and usually by a *fiador*, made from the same material or sometimes from cotton. The *mecate* is attached to the heel knot by a system of 'wraps' to produce a delicately balanced and sophisticated control device, the heavy rope reins and the heel knot combining to act as a counterweight to the substantial nosepiece. The *fiador* is used as a throatlatch and adjusted short enough to prevent the heel knot from bumping against the lower jaw as the horse moves.

The hackamore is adjusted so that the nosepiece of the heavy bosal lies at least 2in above the end of the nose cartilage, the cheeks sloping downward to the curb groove, behind and below which lies the heel knot. The cheeks of the bosal are scarcely in contact with the horse; at rest the hackamore barely touches the nose, so well is it balanced. The extent of the pressure that can be applied is determined by the number of 'wraps' taken with the *mecate* around the heel knot. Only when the hand is raised and the bosal tipped into contact is a momentary restraint put on the nose, which causes the horse to retract the head. Directional changes which, in common with all movements, are taught first at the walk, are made by a rein

Left: The finished Western hackamore horse, with the distinctive braided noseband ending in a large knot under the horse's chin and a rope of mane hair. **Below:** An Arab horse wearing a fairly powerful curb bit of Turkish design, which was probably introduced via a system employing a nose-chain.

CHAPTER FIVE · BITS, BRIDLES AND ADDITIONAL AIDS

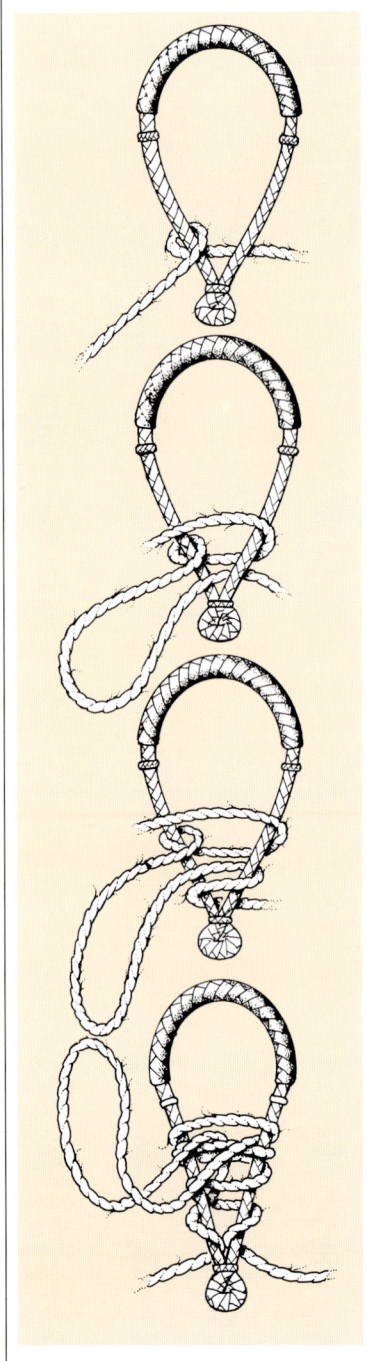

Above: The method employed to attach the mecate to the heel knot of the bosal in a series of wraps. The rope reins (mecate) and the heel knot act as a counterweight to the substantial nosepiece.
Right: The bosal fitted to the horse by the latigo headstall. It is so balanced as to lie clear of nose and jawbones while the horse maintains a steady and correctly positioned head carriage.

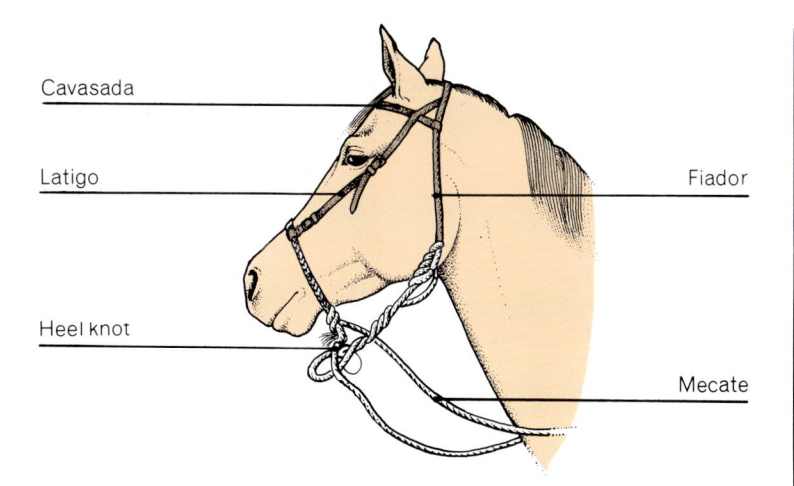

THE WESTERN HACKAMORE SYSTEM

Cavasada
Latigo
Heel knot
Fiador
Mecate

Above: The parts of the hackamore including the **fiador**, the throat-latch which prevents the heel knot from bumping annoyingly against the lower jaw.

Below: The rawhide **bosal**, the woven **mecate** and the simple **latigo** headstall which combine to make the hackamore.

THE CURB BIT

Above: The Western curb bit which is the last stage in the Californian system of bridling. In the trained Western horse it is sufficient to maintain contact with the mouth by the weight of the rein alone. **Left:** A selection of Western curb bits including one with 'pistol' cheeks.

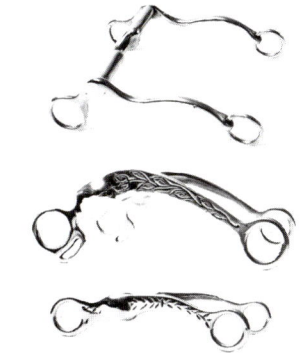

pulled out to the side required, supported by the opposite rein being laid on the neck. At all times the low-held hands operate on the act-and-yield principle—the hand acting to obtain the movement and yielding the moment the latter becomes evident. The action of the bosal on the nose teaches the horse to 'tuck in' or flex the head and neck, while the heavy heel knot acts in opposition to this when necessary to make sure it is impossible for him to evade the pressure on his nose by means of overbending.

From hackamore to bit
Initially, the hackamore is used with both hands, but, as the horse's schooling progresses, the reins are used in one hand only. The fully schooled hackamore horse can carry out all the movements required of him in a state of constant balance and at high speed. He can make the sudden stops, the pivots (the equivalent of the dressage pirouette, though not the same movement), the turns and the rein-backs all on a looping rein and without his mouth ever being touched.

The final stage is the graduation from the hackamore to the bit, usually, but not always, a fairly long-cheeked, high-ported curb (the port is the inverted U in the mouthpiece which allows room for the tongue and permits the bearing surface of the bit to rest directly on the bars). This transition is a gradual one, made with the help of a much lighter hackamore fitted with a pair of very light rein ropes. It is often known as a two-rein bosal. In the final stages, control passes to the bit, the latter being supported by a bosal of

143

CHAPTER FIVE · BITS, BRIDLES AND ADDITIONAL AIDS

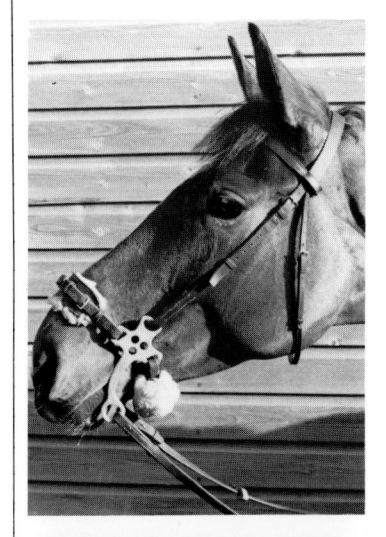

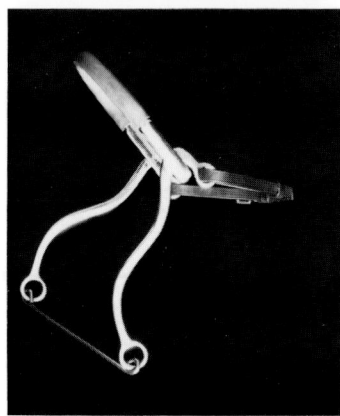

Top and right: Two variations of the bitless bridle, misnamed hackamore, now in general use. Both achieve their object by putting pressure on the nose. The sheepskin padding on the nose and rear strap is to prevent chafing. It is also necessary to vary the fitting frequently to avoid callousing the nose. **Above:** Another bitless bridle, acting as a form of curb on the nose and employing a single rein.

Below: This diagram shows the action of the European hackamore

A little pressure is exerted on the poll by the headpiece.

Pressure is exerted by a tightly fastened noseband. Care should be taken that it comes above the ending of the nose cartilage.

The tight back strap also exerts pressure and should be well padded.

The longer the cheekpiece, to which noseband and backstrap are fastened, the more severe the action.

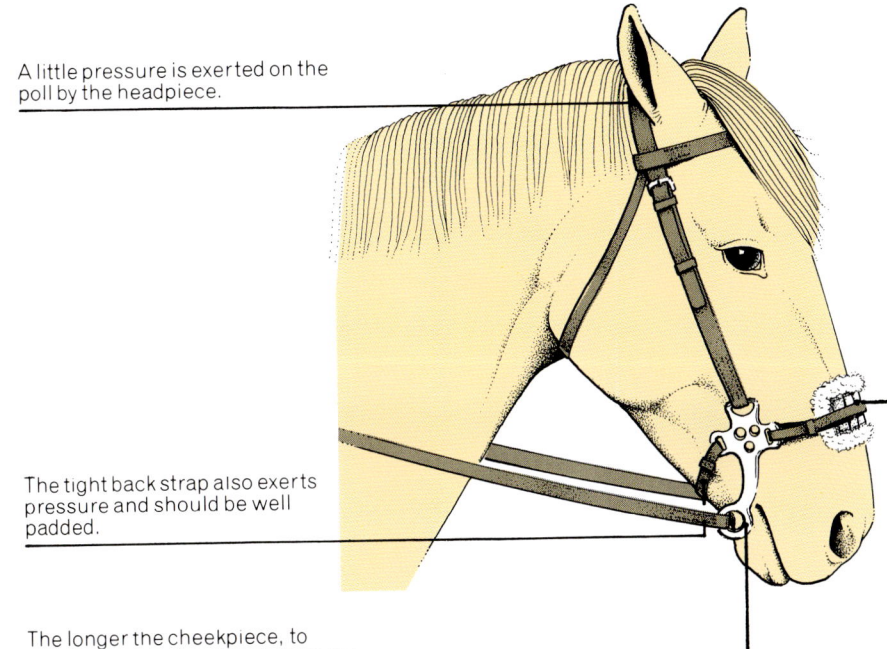

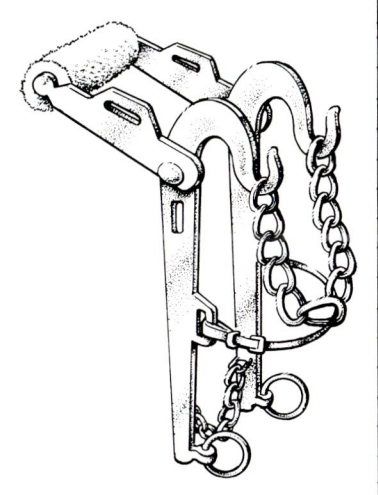

Above: The William Stone Bitless Pelham. It is relatively sophisticated and is used with two reins.

the very lightest proportions acting independently without reins.

The finished Western horse is ridden in a light curb bit bridle without a bosal or noseband of any sort, and a floating, or looping, rein, which exerts no more than a minimal contact on the mouth. Sometimes the reins are weighted by the addition of small decorative pieces of metal, but the ideal is for the horse to ride on the weight of a plain ¼in rawhide rein!

The European hackamore
The European equivalent of the hackamore is the variety of bitless-type bridles, deriving from the hackamore system. Of these, the best known is Blair's pattern. This bridle consists of the usual type of headpiece, a noseband, a curb or back strap, and a pair of long metal cheeks to which the last two items are attached. Control is effected by exerting pressure on the nose and on the back strap embracing the lower jaw, the potential severity of the action being dependent upon the length of the cheek. Since nosepiece and back strap must be adjusted tightly to be effective, both must be soft and well-padded. The nosepiece should rest, as in the case of the bosal, above the ending of the nose cartilage, so as not to restrict the breathing, and its position needs to be altered continually if the nose is not to become calloused.

Contrary to the general view, the bitless bridle is not suitable for novice use, since a novice could do far more damage with it than a metal bit. Nor will it produce sudden and miraculous results. It is the precision tool of the expert horseman with a pair of delicate hands. Ideally, it, too, should operate from a floating rein, changes of direction being made by carrying the required rein outward and combining that action with a shift of the body weight in the same direction. Less severe and often effective on a horse whose mouth, for whatever reason, precludes the use of a bit, are the far shorter cheeked bitless bridles, but they have little in common with the hackamore system.

An interesting bitless bridle is that perfected by William Stone, a loriner in Walsall, Britain. It is called the WS bitless pelham and the bridle employs two reins—hence the term pelham—the top rein acting on the nose and the lower one on the curb groove by means of a curb chain. The metal cheeks of the bridle, which are comparatively short, move independently and thus allow a certain finesse in the action which is not found in other patterns in current use.

The advantages of the hackamore system are obvious enough in the schooling of polo ponies, for instance, but perhaps less so in regard to the modern, competitive horse world. This is considered to be unfortunate by many, because there is much to commend to the present-day rider in this older and infinitely skilfull school of riding.

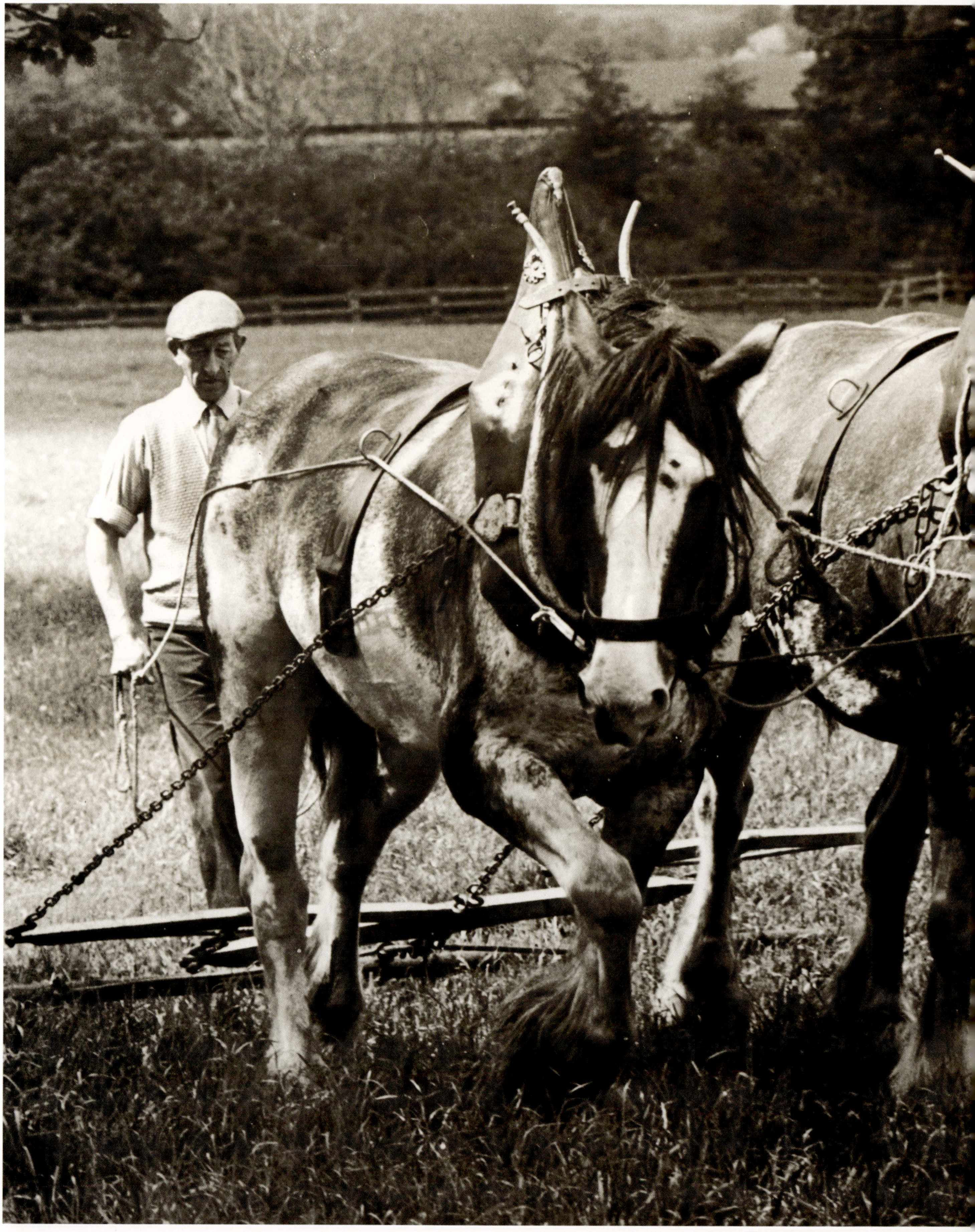

CHAPTER SIX

Driving and Farm Harness

Present Day
Whips
Trotting Equipment
The Farm Horse

A pair of work horses in farm harness with Scottish pattern peaked collars. The horse was the dominant factor in agriculture over the centuries.

CHAPTER SIX · DRIVING HARNESS

Driving Harness · **Present Day**

The driving harness of today is being produced, as it has been for centuries, to a large variety of designs, shapes and sizes to suit different requirements. Some basic factors have remained the same—the best harness is made of either black or brown leather—but, in certain instances, new substances have come into use alongside traditional ones. Materials such as plain webbing, plastic-coated webbing, canvas and buffalo hide are now used for some modern exercise harness, while rivets take the place of stitches on some sets. The harness furniture—that is, buckles and so on—can be made of brass, nickel or other white metal, or it can be silver plated. Gold-plated furniture is fashionable in parts of Australia for exhibition purposes.

Showing harness
The most popular harness for showing in private driving classes is made of black leather with patent trim on the blinkers, collar, saddle, false martingale front and

HISTORICAL ACCOUTREMENTS

Above: Accessories certainly not in evidence today: a sun bonnet; black silk bridle front for periods of mourning; decorative French flowers for horses' heads.

148

PRESENT DAY

Left: Single harness turnout to a four-wheeled vehicle at a driving meet. This light, black harness is plain and functional but very smart.

CHAPTER SIX · DRIVING HARNESS

Stages in putting on the collar. **Left to right:** The collar, turned upside down, is put over the head; hames are fitted to the collar while the latter is still reversed; collar turned around with the lie of the mane. **Below, left to right:** Hame strap tightened; check to see that it is possible to pass the hand between the bottom of the collar and the base of the neck; check to see that a flat hand can be inserted between collar and neck.

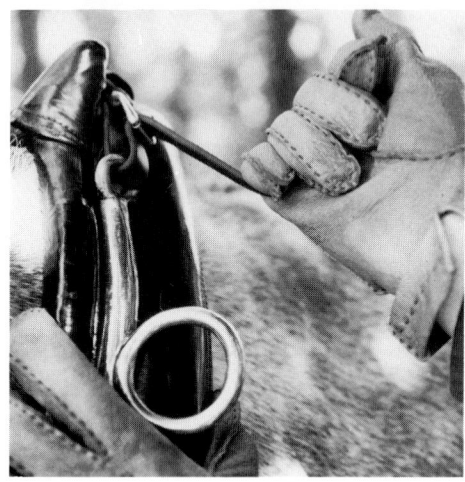

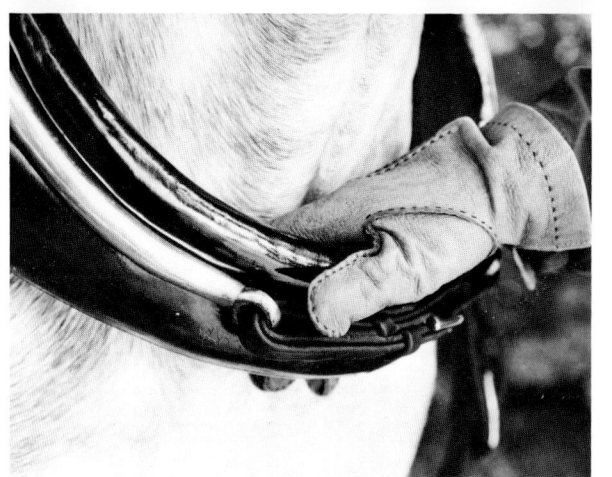

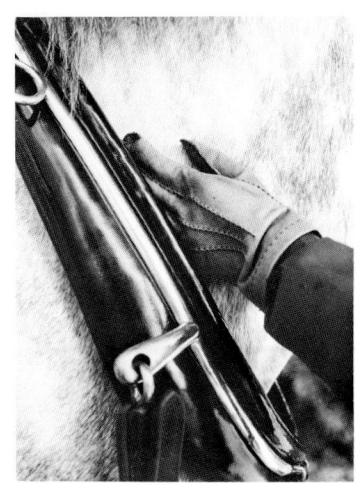

face drop. Brass furniture is favoured. The harness itself is as light and elegant as is practical. Two layers of fine quality leather are painstakingly joined by rows of hand stitching wherever possible. Such parts as the girth, belly band, loin strap and crupper have buckling adjustment on both sides so that perfect uniformity is obtained throughout the set.

Designs are broadly similar to those which were used 100 years ago, although some modern materials have been introduced. Some harness makers, for instance, now use fibreglass, instead of metal plates, for the blinkers. As a result the blinkers hold their shape better and do not rust. Saddle trees are now sometimes built with laminated wood to give them additional strength. Solid wood is more liable to crack and split and is more susceptible to woodworm, which dislike the glues that are used with laminated trees. Most modern patent leather is finished with polyurethane, which makes it very durable and less likely to crack. It is not, however, as easy for the harness maker to work as it is reluctant to mould and difficult to finish on the edges.

Single harness
Different types of harness are necessary for a single, pair, tandem and team. A set of single harness is designed for one horse to work between the shafts of a two- or four-wheeled vehicle. It consists of a bridle, collar, saddle, reins and a multiplicity of additional components. These can amount to as many as 35 separate items when the set is taken apart for cleaning.

When harnessing a single horse, the collar is always the first item. There is a strong superstition amongst driving people which holds that there will be an accident if any other part of the harness is put on first. This belief probably originated in the days of serious coaching, when teams were harnessed in great haste. The collar and hames were put on with the false martingale buckled around the collar. Then, when the pad went on, the martingale could be threaded through the girth as it was buckled. This was quicker than putting the pad on and girthing it before putting on the collar and martingale, because the girth would then have to be undone again to take the martingale. This coaching practice has remained a part of the technique to the present day.

When putting on the collar, there is sometimes a need carefully to stretch it slightly sideways, so that it is not forced over the animal's eyes. It should then be left upside down on the horse's neck while the hames are put into place in the groove between the fore- and afterwales. The top hame strap should now be buckled to fasten the hames lightly onto the collar. The latter can be turned around, at the windpipe, and pushed down into position against the shoulders where it should fit comfortably. The top hame strap must now be tightened, so that the hames fit firmly into place. They should lie well into the groove, so that there is no danger of them coming out.

The fit of the collar is also extremely important. There should be adequate room

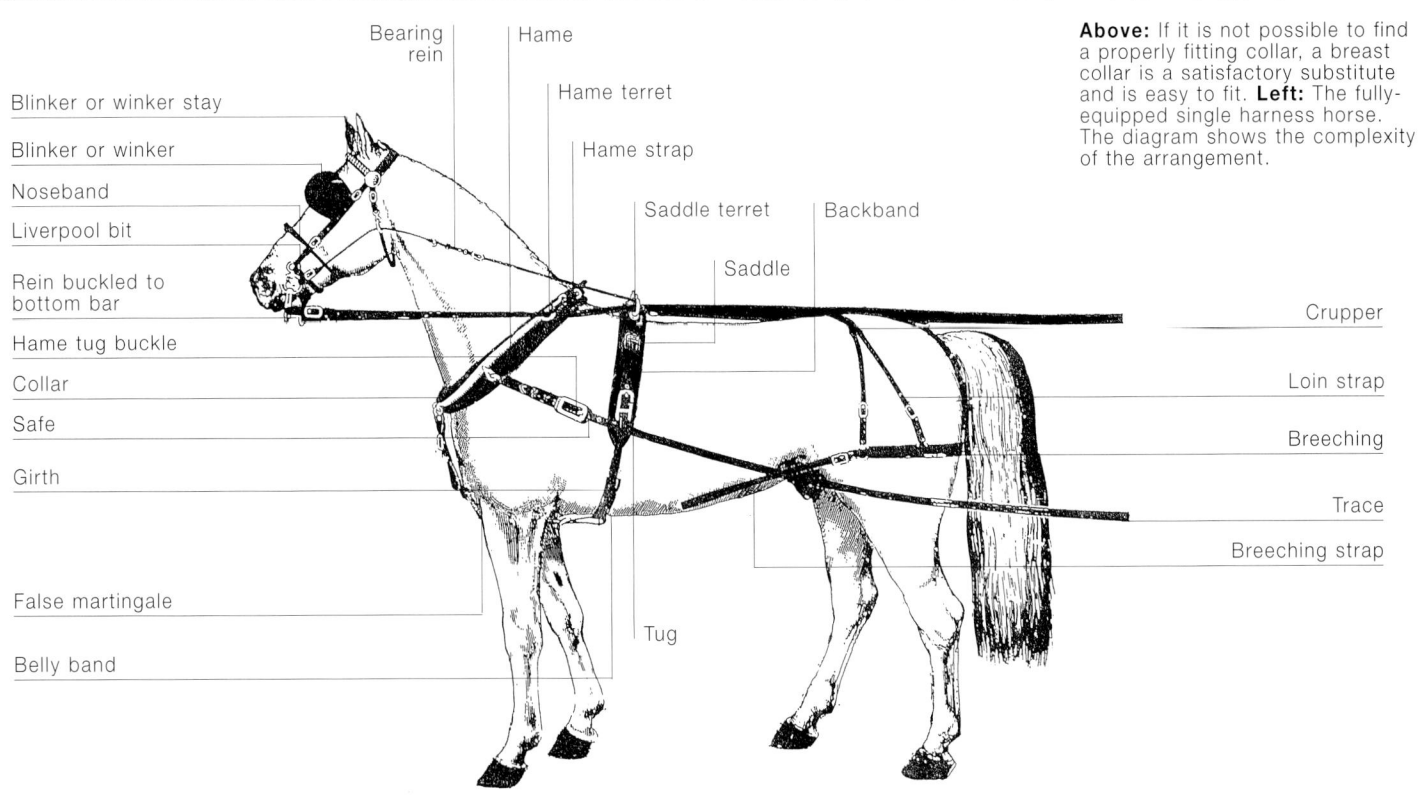

PRESENT DAY

Above: If it is not possible to find a properly fitting collar, a breast collar is a satisfactory substitute and is easy to fit. **Left:** The fully-equipped single harness horse. The diagram shows the complexity of the arrangement.

Labels on diagram:
- Blinker or winker stay
- Blinker or winker
- Noseband
- Liverpool bit
- Rein buckled to bottom bar
- Hame tug buckle
- Collar
- Safe
- Girth
- False martingale
- Belly band
- Bearing rein
- Hame
- Hame terret
- Hame strap
- Saddle terret
- Saddle
- Backband
- Tug
- Crupper
- Loin strap
- Breeching
- Trace
- Breeching strap

151

CHAPTER SIX · DRIVING HARNESS

Right: The saddle is built on a tree which, as in the case of the riding saddle, must fit the horse's back comfortably. **Below:** Placing the saddle in position on the back. It is most important, both from the point of view of looks and of the horse's comfort, that the saddle is not placed too far forward on the back.

at the side to permit the flat of the hand to lie between the horse's neck and the collar, while there must be enough space at the bottom to allow the whole hand to pass freely between the base of the collar and the bottom of the neck. A collar which is too wide will rock from side to side. One which is too narrow will pinch. One which is too deep will ride upward, while one which is too shallow will press against the windpipe. It can be very difficult indeed to find a collar which fits the horse properly. One which does not fit will probably gall the horse and make him sore. This, understandably, can lead to reluctance to work and may result in severe problems.

If it proves impossible to find a collar that fits correctly, it is better to use a breast collar, rather than compromise. A breast collar can be adjusted at the neckpiece to fit any horse or pony within a range of a hand (4in) or more. More importantly, it can be made to fit narrow, wide, muscular or scraggy necks; finding different collars for a horse whose neck changes shape and size, according to the time of the year and the amount of grass consumed, can be wearying. The breast collar itself should be fitted to the animal in question so that it lies below the windpipe and above the point of the shoulder.

The traces are buckled to the hame tug buckles if a full collar is used or to the tug buckles on the breast part of a breast collar if that is employed. Traces are generally made of two layers of leather which are stitched with four rows of stitching. Hand stitching is preferable, although this is naturally far more expensive than machine stitching. The advantage of the former is

Positioning the shaft tug: The shaft tug in position against the tug stop. The tugs are buckled onto the backband, which must take the weight of the vehicle if necessary.

Connecting the traces to the vehicle: The traces are attached firmly to the vehicle by hooking them over an open-ended loop known as a trace hook.

Attaching the breeching strap: The breeching strap is buckled round the shaft and the traces and also through the breeching dee which is found on the shaft.

152

Left: The crupper dock is sometimes sewn to the crupper back strap, and when fitting the crupper, the tail is folded carefully at the base of the dock and threaded through as shown.
Above: Buckles instead of stitches can facilitate fitting and adjustment of the crupper dock.

that if one stitch gets worn and breaks, the stitches will not run, as can happen with machine stitching.

A layer of leather lying under the hame tug buckle, known as a safe, saves trace wear from the buckle. It is cheaper to renew safes than to replace a pair of traces.

If a false martingale is used, it should be buckled around the collar and lower hame strap or hame chain. Its purpose, with a single horse, is to hold the collar down. Extravagantly moving horses, with big fronts and sloping shoulders, will tilt the collar upward when they are in action.

The saddle's additions of backband, tugs, crupper and breeching are added separately, and the completed assembly is put on next. It is important that the tree of the saddle fits the contours of the animal's back. Too narrow a tree will pinch the horse, while one which is too wide will press down on the horse's spine and make him sore. There should be adequate padding so that the horse can take the weight of the vehicle, if it becomes unbalanced for any reason. The backband is threaded through a slot in the saddle. The backband is normally made of double leather with four rows of stitching, similar to that of the traces. Its strength is essential as it may have to hold the weight of the vehicle through the tugs and shafts, both in going down hill, if the breeching is not tight enough, or if the balance of the vehicle is at fault.

The shaft tugs, which should have safes behind them, are buckled onto the backband. The terrets, which hold the reins in position, are screwed into threaded sockets in the saddle tree. The crupper back strap is passed through a dee at the back of the saddle. The point is then threaded back through its floating keeper before being buckled. The crupper dock, which is usually filled with linseed and well-oiled to keep it soft, is sometimes sewn to the crupper back strap, or sometimes attached by one or two buckles to make it easier to put on the horse. The loin strap of the breeching is passed through the slot in the back strap of the crupper, and the seat of the breeching is buckled to the loin strap on each side. The shaft straps are attached to rings at each end of the breeching seat, while the point should be passed through the keeper by the buckle in order to hold the strap on the ring.

The complete saddle unit should be placed on the middle of the horse's back. The tail is then folded at the base of the dock to take the crupper, like darning wool going through a needle. The crupper must then be carefully placed in position under the top of the dock, taking care to get all the hairs out from under the crupper. The breeching seat is left hanging loosely against the horse's hindquarters It should be adjusted so that it lies below the widest and above the narrowest part of the quarters. The saddle should then be lifted up and put down in a position the same as that of a stable roller. Novices tend to place the saddle too far forward. Not only does this make the horse look long, but the faulty positioning can give the animal a sore back and girth galls. The girth can now be buckled, taking up the false martingale. The belly band is passed through the loop on the girth. This prevents it from sliding back toward the belly.

The reins are put on next. It is best if these are made of brown leather, since reins with black leather hand-parts tend to leave their dye on the driver's gloves and apron. The reins are threaded through the saddle terrets and hame terrets (or breast collar terrets, if fitted) with enough left at the head end to buckle to the bit. The

CHAPTER SIX · DRIVING HARNESS

Top: The reins are passed through the saddle terrets.
Above: They are then passed through the hame terrets or breast collar terrets.

Right: The loose rein ends are folded neatly into the off-side saddle terret so that they can be picked up easily by the driver when mounting the vehicle.

loose, hand end should be folded into the offside saddle terret in such a way that it can be easily picked up for mounting.

The bridle is always put on last and should be fitted as carefully as a riding bridle. The browband must be of the correct size; one that is too short, for instance, will pull the headpiece against the ears and cause considerable discomfort. It is held in place on the headpiece by two rosettes, which are not purely for decoration. They are secured onto the browband by a dee at the back and the points of the headpiece are threaded down through the browband loop on either side of the rosette dee. This prevents the browband from rising upward and keeps the blinkers close to the sides of the horse's face so that he cannot see behind. The blinkers are permanently fixed to the cheeks of the bridle, the tops being held in place with stays coming from the centre of the headpiece. The noseband must fit correctly and should lie close to the nose so that the cheekpieces which are threaded down through slots in the noseband, and up through keepers on the outside, hang straight down the side of the horse's head. This again ensures that blinkers are kept in place.

Liverpool bits are most commonly used for private driving. They can now be obtained with a large variety of mouthpieces and have the advantage of providing a range of positions for the reins, allowing the bit to be used with greater or less severity. When the reins are buckled to the plain cheek, the action is that of a snaffle. Increasing degrees of curb action can be obtained as the reins are buckled down the cheeks, the bottom bar giving the greatest leverage on the curb chain. In this position the greatest degree of pressure is exerted on the horse's poll, through the eye of the bit, and on the mouth by the mouthpiece.

Tandem harness
Tandem harness is much the same as that for the shaft horse but with some necessary modifications. Basically, a set of tandem harness is made up from a set of single harness, with modifications, for the shaft horse, and a set of tandem leader harness.

The saddle terrets are divided by a horizontal roller bar so that the wheel and lead reins are separated. The hame tug buckles have protrusions at the lower sides with slots into which the lead trace spring

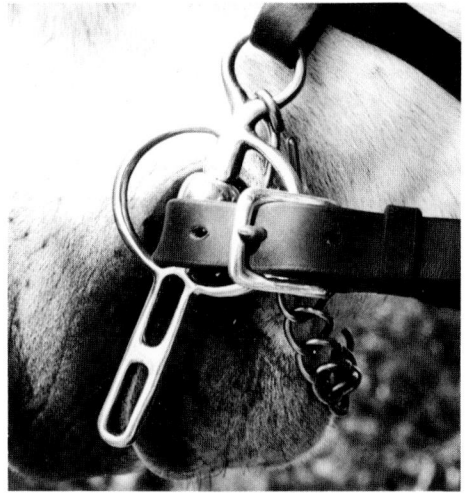

PRESENT DAY

Above left: The bridle in place, with the rein attached to the rough cheek of the Liverpool bit. **Top:** Detail of the rein attached to the rough cheek of the bit. **Above:** The rein buckled to the plain cheek. **Left:** The Liverpool driving bit which is in general use. **Below:** The Wilson 4-ring snaffle which is not so much in favour today.

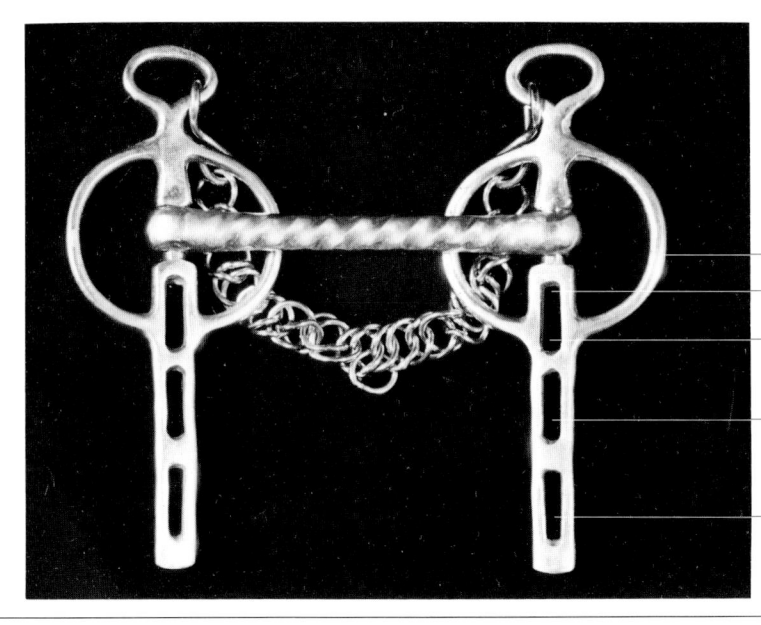

Plain cheek
Rough cheek
Upper bar
Middle bar
Bottom bar

155

CHAPTER SIX · DRIVING HARNESS

Right: Tandem leader in breast-collar harness. **Below, left to right:** Leader's saddle terret (also used for single and pair); hame terret; tandem wheeler's saddle terret; tandem wheeler's terret with leader's rein on top of the bar and wheeler's below. **Bottom:** 19th-century tandem harness which is an engraving from an American catalogue.

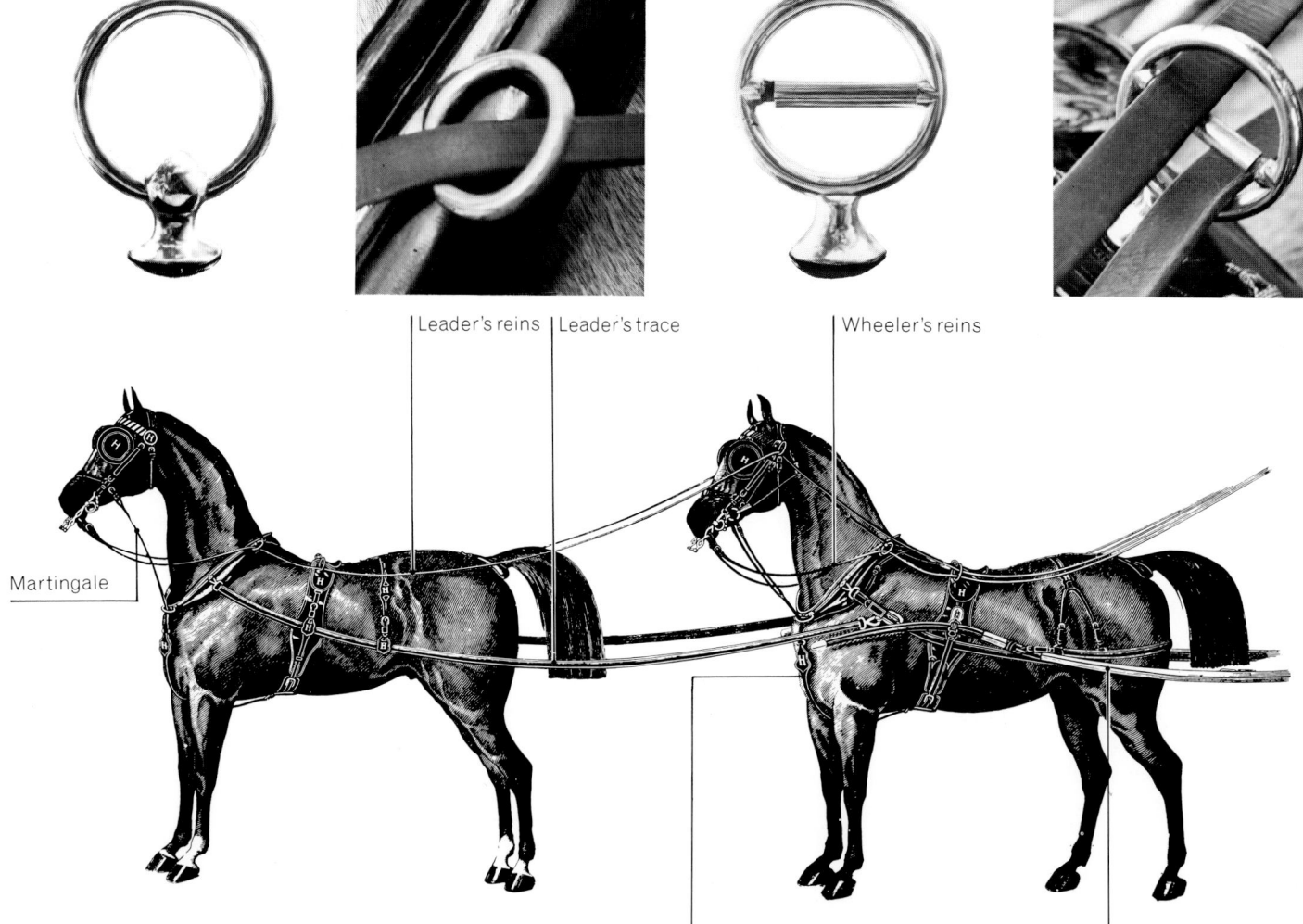

Leader's reins | Leader's trace

Wheeler's reins

Martingale

False martingale

Wheeler's trace

156

Above: Sallie Walrond, the first whip to complete a three-day driving trial with a tandem in 1975 at Lowther in England. It sets a splendid example in style and elegance, with black leather harness and brass furniture.

cockeyes are buckled, and the bridle has rosettes with terrets to take the leader's reins. It is also a good idea to have an additional strap in the form of an extra throatlatch to hold the bridle to the wheeler's head if the leader should come around suddenly. This can easily be made by putting an extended loop on the back of the browband. A strap with a buckle is put through the loop and passed over the horse's head before going down through the other browband loop. The strap is then passed through a double loop which is secured to the back of the noseband. It can be buckled far tighter than an ordinary throatlatch, because the pressure is put on the horse's cheeks instead of on his throat. As a result the horse will be more comfortable and more able to flex at the poll. It is essential to use a bar bit in tandem wheeler harness to prevent the leader's reins from getting caught inextricably in the cheeks. If this happens, the leader is pulled around and the result is that the driver is left helpless.

The leader can wear either a breast or a full collar, but, unless tandem bars are used, the leader's traces must be longer than usual traces and are passed through loops on the sides of the saddle. This latter matches that which is on the shaft horse in shape, but it has no slot through the top since there is no backband. The belly band points are threaded through dees on the lower sides of the traces. A false belly band is buckled to these and then passed through a loop at the back of the girth, while the traces are held up, at the back, by a trace bearer. This should be of the martingale type, so that there are no points

CHAPTER SIX · DRIVING HARNESS

Below: Tandem wheeler's bridle showing the extended loop on the browband, the additional throatlatch, a bar bit and leading eye terrets to take the leader's reins. **Right:** Bridle with Buxton pattern driving bit with the rein fastened to the middle set.

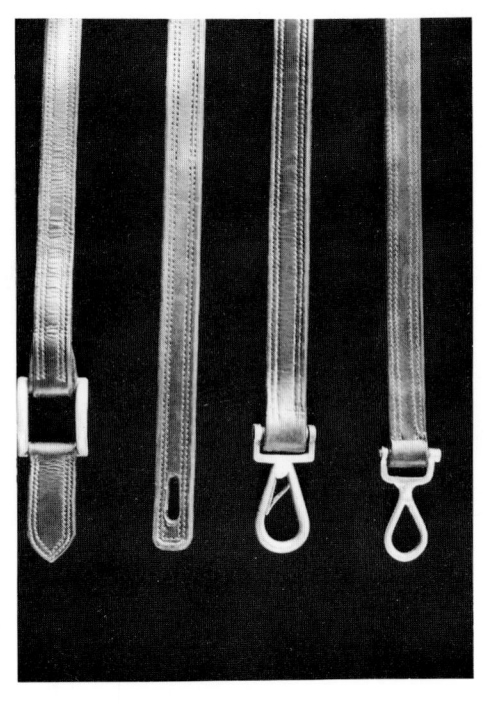

Above, left to right: A variety of trace ends. Pair, with link through which the trace passes to make a loop; single with a crew hole; tandem with spring cock-eye; team leader with cock-eye.

of leather under which the lead reins can get caught. For the same reason, the leader should wear a martingale-type crupper.

Pair harness

Pair harness has the same bridles and collars as single harness, but the hames are different. The bottom eyes, in this instance, are joined by a kidney-shaped link which has a floating ring on the lower side. It is onto this that the pole strap is buckled. Breast collars have a dee at the front for the same purpose. The hame tug in pair harness is longer than that on single harness, so that the buckle lies level with the pad. This buckle differs from that used in single harness in that it has a dee both above the buckle and below it. A short strap with a small buckle is sewn to the top dee and is fastened to a point strap coming down from a dee on the pad. A point strap, sewn to the lower dee on the tug buckle, is used to attach the false belly band. The pads used for pair work are very light because they do not have to take any weight, their purpose being as a securing point.

In putting a set of pair harness on the horses, the collars, hames and false martingales go on first, and the pads next. It is best to buckle the hame tug buckles to the points on the pad dees on both sides before putting on the cruppers, so as to prevent the pads from falling to the ground; the latter are then girthed with the false martingales threaded through. The false belly band should be buckled next after it has been passed through the false martingale. The traces should be passed through the trace carriers and thrown over the horses' backs in preparation for putting to, with the outer trace lying on top of the inner one. The trace ends for pair harness are usually designed to go around roller bolts on the splinter bar, some of which are made with a curving square metal link at the end through which the trace is passed to form a loop, while others have a quick-release system of two metal fittings, and still more have a simple loop at their end. Those that are used with swingle trees, which are necessary when breast collars are worn, have crew holes at their ends. If breeching is used it is buckled into the hame tug buckle alongside the trace on each side. When the vehicle runs onward in going down a hill, or stopping, the pole goes forward, the weight being transmitted to the pole straps pulling on the bottoms of the collars, which, in turn, are held down by the false martingales. Unavoidably, a certain amount of pressure is taken on the top of the horses' necks through their collars. If breeching is worn, this tightens around the quarters as the hame tug buckles go forward.

The reins are the next items to be fitted. The draught rein, which is the continuous one, with about 11 holes punched in the centre to which the coupling rein is buckled, goes on the outside of each horse. It is passed through the pad and hame terrets in preparation for buckling to the bit. The coupling rein is passed through the inner pad and hame terrets. The secret of successful pair driving lies mainly in the adjustment of the coupling rein buckles. They must be fitted in such a way that both horses work evenly in their collars with their heads straight.

The bridles are then put on and the draught reins are buckled to the outer sides of each bit with the coupling reins being passed around the backs of the nosebands with the rein points secured in

PRESENT DAY

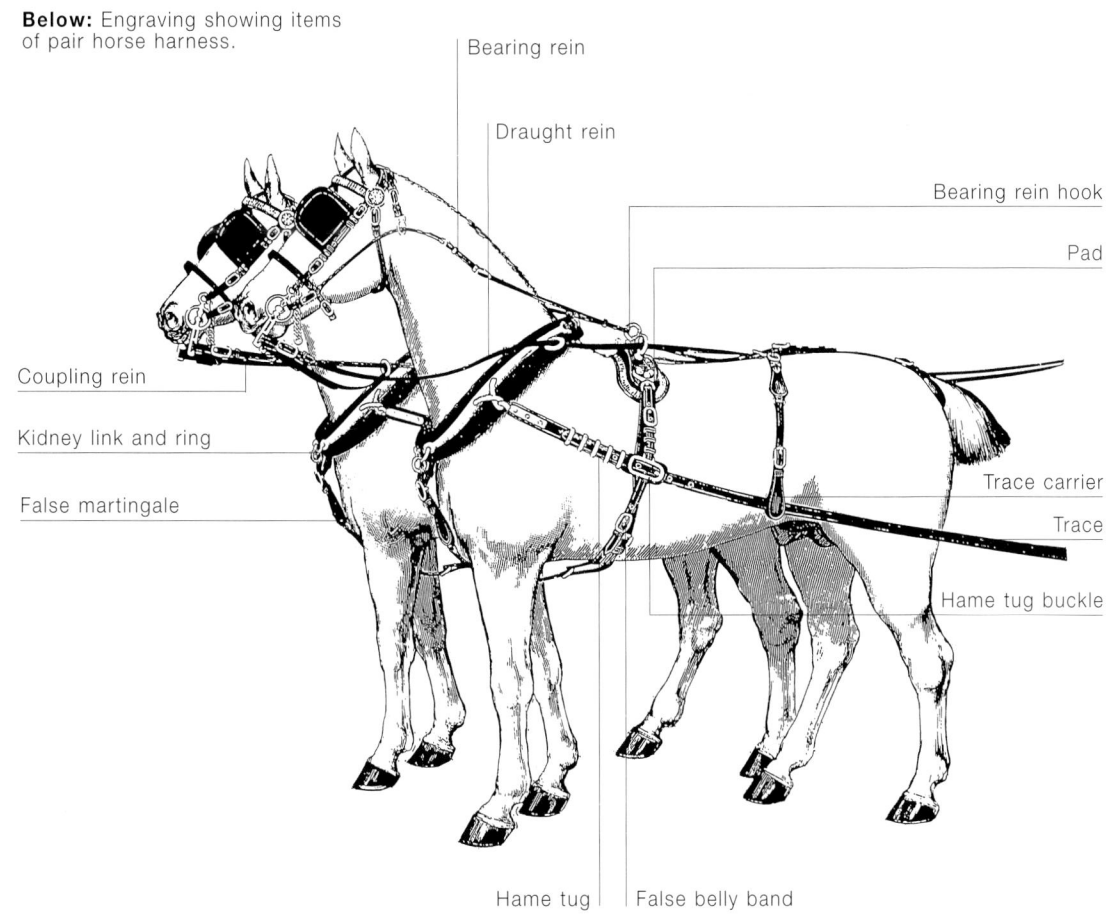

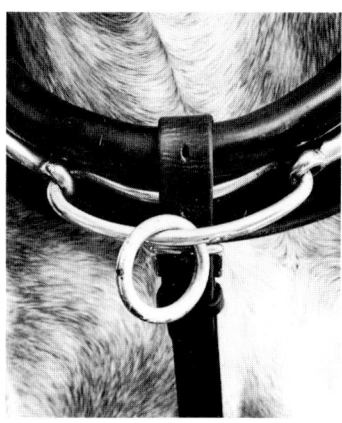

Below: Engraving showing items of pair horse harness.

- Bearing rein
- Draught rein
- Bearing rein hook
- Pad
- Coupling rein
- Kidney link and ring
- False martingale
- Trace carrier
- Trace
- Hame tug buckle
- Hame tug
- False belly band

Left: Pair horse harness. **Top:** Pair horse pad showing the hame tug buckle. This buckle lies level with the pad and has a dee both above and below it. **Above:** Pair horse hames showing the false martingale, which is passed around the collar and through the kidney link.

159

CHAPTER SIX · DRIVING HARNESS

Opposite: George Bowman driving a splendidly turned out four horse team. Yesterday's commonplace means of transport has become one of the more specialist forms of horsemanship. **Above:** A well turned out pair of bays. **Right:** The larger horse shows are ideal places to see a variety of types of harness. This example of the unusual Unicorn harness was photographed at the Royal Windsor Horse Show.

their keepers. They are then ready to be put across to their partners when the horses are put to the vehicle. Traditionally, pairs are driven in bar bits to prevent the coupling reins from getting caught in the cheeks. However, there is the grave danger of long-cheeked bar bits, on small ponies, becoming caught on the pole head. This can result in broken bridles and cause even more problems.

Team harness

Team harness is similar in many ways to pair harness. The leaders wear pair harness but have no breeching as there is no pole. Very often, the leaders wear trace

Left: Reins and whip held correctly for single and pair driving. The right hand is supporting the left.

Left: Holding the reins in the left hand so that the right hand is free to use the whip.

carriers and the traces usually have metal cockeyes at the ends which hook over the lead bars. False martingales, however, are not always worn by leaders. The reins are the same as for a pair except that the draught reins are longer so that they will reach back to the driver. The wheeler harness is similar to that of pair but with modifications. The bridles have leading eye terrets on the outer rosettes to carry the leaders' reins and the pads have central terrets through which these reins are passed.

Unicorn harness
Unicorn harness is a slightly different arrangement of team harness, employed when a unicorn—two wheelers and one leader—is being driven. It is made up from team wheeler harness with the bridle terrets put on the inner sides, as the reins run centrally from the single leader who wears one side of a set of lead harness. Tandem leader reins are best for this purpose, but if these are not available, then team lead reins, with the coupling reins off, can be used.

Handling reins and whip
The handling of the reins and whip follows the same principles, irrespective of whether one, two, three or four horses are being driven. As far as the reins are concerned, the only difference is of number; there are two reins in the hand with a single and a pair, while with a tandem, a unicorn or a team there are four reins.

For single and pair driving, the two reins are held in the left hand with the nearside rein lying over the index finger and the offside rein lying below the middle finger. They are secured in position by the finger tips against the palm. The right hand, in which the whip is held at all times, is placed on the reins in front of the left hand. The left rein lies over the middle finger and the right rein lies below the third finger. The right hand is then in a position to assist the left in turns and in pulling up. The left hand remains as an 'anchor' hand.

A turn to the right is made by increasing the pressure on the offside rein with the right hand, while making sure that the index finger is not still pressing on the nearside rein. At the same time the left hand can be turned slightly, so that the

Above: Method of holding reins and whip when driving tandem, team or unicorn.
Left: Making a gentle left hand turn.

palm lies uppermost and the nearside rein is slackened in consequence.

A turn to the left is made by putting pressure on the underside of the nearside rein with the right hand. The left hand can be turned slightly with the knuckles facing uppermost to slacken the offside rein.

If additional pressure is needed, it can be gained by bringing the left hand toward the right hip for a left turn and toward the left hip for a right turn, thus increasing the contact on the desired rein and loosening the opposite one. The reins are shortened by either sliding the right hand forward and following up with the left hand or by grasping the reins with the right hand, held behind the left, and sliding the latter forward the desired amount.

For tandem, unicorn and team driving the four reins are held in the left hand. The near lead rein lies over the index finger. The off lead rein goes under the index finger. The near wheel rein lies under the off lead rein on top of the middle finger and the off wheel rein goes under the middle finger. The right hand is placed with the middle and third fingers separating the nearside and offside reins, in front of the left hand. Simple, wide, turns to the left and right are made, as with a single or pair, by bringing the horses around as one with both left or right reins as desired. Tight turns are much more difficult, as it is essential to prevent the shaft horses, or wheelers, from cutting across the corner in an attempt to follow the leader by a shorter route. If this is allowed to happen, the vehicle will inevitably become caught on whatever may be in the way. Therefore, it is important to oppose the wheeler adequately before asking the leader to turn.

It is often necessary to take a loop in the relevant rein with a unicorn or team, but lighter opposition with a tandem is usually adequate. Then, when the leader has begun to come around, the opposition rein can be released to allow the wheeler to follow him.

The whip is held at all times between the index finger and thumb of the right hand. It should lie at an angle of 45° across the thumb muscle. One which is held at the wrong angle is likely to get caught in the wheel or it could touch the horse's quarters by mistake.

CHAPTER SIX · DRIVING HARNESS

Driving Harness · **Whips**

The driving whip is an essential piece of equipment for the driver of any horse-drawn vehicle. Its function is to urge on or correct the horse and its careful use adds to driving safety. It is to some extent, also a staff of office, the driver being known traditionally as the Whip. The aid should be carried at all times when on the move, held lightly but firmly in the right hand in such a fashion that the fingers of that hand are free to assist the left hand with the reins when necessary. An approximate angle of 45° forward and a similar angle upwards should be maintained so that the whip is ready for use without putting the passenger's hat at risk. Whilst a sharp stroke is occasionally necessary a light touch between collar and pad is often sufficient. The whip, however, should not be used whilst the whip hand is on the reins because of the resultant jerk on the horse's mouth.

Signals to other road users are also made with the whip. Held vertically aloft it indicates slowing down or stopping. A similar position with a circular movement of the point followed by a horizontal gesture to right or left indicates a turn in that direction. When not in horse-drawn company it is probably prudent to use motoring hand signals so as not to confuse motorists whose knowledge of horses can be extremely limited.

Types of whip

In the main, there are two traditional types of driving whips still in use and the survival of so many, a number having been made around the turn of the century, testifies to their popularity and quality. Firstly, there is the Dealer's whip, or 'dropthong', and secondly the Coach, Carriage or Gig whip, sometimes called the 'bow-top'.

The Dealer's whip, both flexible and enduring, lacks the reach, balance and elegance of the Coach whip, but it has withstood the test of time for commercial and general use. Such whips were familiar pieces of equipment at the fairs and similar gatherings depicted by the British painter Sir Alfred Munnings and described by the writer George Borrow.

The stock of the whip, in the best examples, had a whalebone core or lining about ¼in square, whilst the less expensive types, which are still made today, were lined with spring-steel wire. In both cases, the lining is enclosed within split cane to provide taper and substance and covered, by means of a machine, with woven waxed thread. This ingenious and unlikely combination of materials produced a stock as resilient as it was strong, but today as a result of the restrictions on the slaughter of whales, the whalebone-lined type is no longer made.

The hand-part of a Dealer's whip is sometimes leather-covered with white metal mounts at top and bottom, stamped or engraved with an attractively florid design. The occasional absence of a normal stitched seam on the underside of the leather hand-part may puzzle post-war drivers, but it was thus because it was made from a calf's tail pulled over the stock! The four-plait thong of split horsehide was secured to the stock by means of a loop or keeper from which it hung down (hence the name 'dropthong').

A longer-stocked version of this whip with a very short rawhide thong was also produced for heavy horse teams. The bottom of the butt mount (or cap) was usually sealed with a Victorian copper coin and the thread-covered cane stock deco-

Left: A selection of ornamented Victorian whips, the mounts being of silver, brass and gilt. The parasol driving whip belonged to Queen Victoria. **Above:** Detail of an elaborate turquoise-studded whip butt. Whips of the Victorian period were frequently intricately decorated. **Opposite, left to right:** A selection of driving whips: pony size holly whip; horse size holly whip; gig size braided cane whip; pair horse size braided cane whip; drop thong whip.

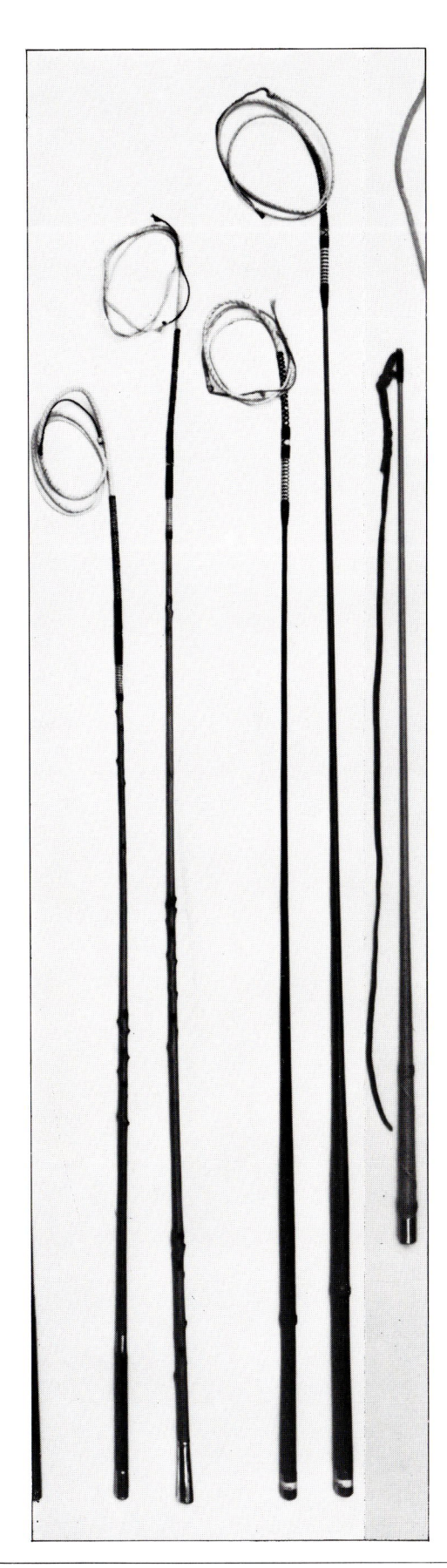

rated with closely spaced brass collars, or ferrules.

Whilst this whip is well suited for its original purpose—modern hybrid versions serving well enough for exercising or informal occasions—the 'dropthong' type should not be used at any event where a stylish appearance is required.

The Coach whip is the whip for the elegant well-appointed private turnout and discrimination is needed in its selection. The whip must suit the driver, the horse and the vehicle—in short, the whole turnout. An important factor in selection is that of utility. The ideal is to have a light whip with sufficient reach for the job and for it to be well-balanced. There has to be a limit so far as weight is concerned, as a wet 12ft thong swishing through the air cannot be carried on a twig. The point of balance should be just above the collar of the hand-part and is achieved by tapering the body and sometimes counter-weighting the stock. Examination of the hand-part of an old whip will sometimes reveal a quantity of lead-foil wrapped around under the leather so as to fix the balance.

Specialist whips and decoration
As far as standard whips are concerned, the achievement of a satisfactory end product can be more or less assured. When, however, a screw-jointed or dog-leg whip is required—or a custom-made whip of unusual design—then much preliminary work has to be done until the whip comes to life, as it were, with an easy balance in the hand and increasing flexibility towards the top of the stock.

Various woods are used for the stock, the most usual being holly and blackthorn, but other woods are occasionally substituted, such as hickory, bamboo, greenheart, yew, and, very rarely, solid whalebone. It is probable that the finest quality whips, and the greatest number, were produced around the turn of the century, when the fashion in design was to make things look like something else. Ivory hand-parts were, for example, sometimes decorated with a pattern of wood knots and a simulated wood grain. Some manufacturers went even further and produced a type of celluloid which, posing as ivory, was also moulded to resemble knotty wood.

Many of the old whips described today as 'ivory-handled' are, in fact, made from a composition which has the even, opaque, and yellowish tinge of dairy cream, but lacks the slight translucence and the subtle graining of ivory. An infallible test is to file off a little powder and sniff—no genuine elephant's tusk smells strongly of camphor.

Whip maintenance
Whips are subjected to much misuse. They are walked on, run over, leaned up against corners, caught up in tug-buckles or roadside bushes, picked up and 'cracked' by non-drivers or left in whip-holders and pushed, to their detriment, under coach-house lintels as the vehicle is being housed.

The most usual damage to a whip is a cracked or broken stock, a broken thong or crippled quills. When quills are badly bent or broken, it is almost certain that the whalebone or cane core will also be damaged. Replacement of this with renewal of quills and the whipping necessary to refix the thong is difficult, but a neat and effective repair can be made by leaving the original work alone and, with adhesive, fitting a pair of short goosequill splints on each side of the thong, at the site of the break, and whipping, or binding, the whole tightly with black thread. The alternative is to fit an entirely new thong.

The bow-top thong, which nowadays is six-plait at the thicker end reducing to four-plait at the thin end, usually gets broken at the latter part, where splicing is difficult. A knot is ugly and catches up in use, so the best repair method is to taper off the broken ends, overlap them by an inch, moisten with adhesive and whip tightly with matching cotton.

The elegant bow which distinguishes the Carriage whip is formed by the curved whalebone or cane core, which will revert to its original straightness if it is allowed to do so. It is therefore essential when the whip is not in use to keep the bow part of the thong curved round a 'whip-reel' (or can about 4in diameter—the base of a saddle-soap tin makes an excellent reel).

This treatment is only effective if the thong is in the correct position—that is, with the end of the cross-threading at 3 o'clock on the reel. This position on an average thong will bring the tip of the core (which may be felt with the fingers) to about 12 or 1 o'clock. The thong must be prevented from slipping round the reel by securing the thin end with a loop of string tied to a nail.

CHAPTER SIX · DRIVING HARNESS

Driving Harness · **Trotting Equipment**

TROTTING EQUIPMENT

Harness racing, the racing of trotters and pacers, is a highly specialized sport. The basic item of equipment is breast harness. This consists of a breast collar, traces, a saddle and girth, plus a bridle fitted with long driving reins. The collar itself is a broad leather strap that passes round the horse's breast and is supported by another strap fitted over the shoulders. Long leather straps, called traces, run back from each side of the breast collar and are fastened to the shafts of the sulky, which the animal draws and the jockey sits.

The saddle sits in the normal place behind the withers; it usually has a pad or towel placed underneath it to prevent chafing. It is girthed, in the normal way around the horse's belly. To prevent it riding forward, a crupper may be fitted around the horse's tail and attached to the rear of the saddle by means of a back strap. Fitted to either side of the saddle are small leather loops, known as shaft tugs, through which the shafts are passed and which support their weight. Each shaft is inserted into a shaft thimble (also known as a point strap), a thimble-shaped device which fits over the end of each shaft and is connected to the side of the saddle by a strap. Point straps control the positioning of the sulky and prevent it from riding forward, too close behind the quarters.

The traces, which enable the horse to pull the sulky, are slotted through leather loops, specially positioned on the inside of the shafts, and attached to hooks set on the inside of the rear of each shaft. On either side of the girth is a strong strap called a wrap strap or tie down. Each of these is wound round the corresponding shaft and fastened with a buckle. These straps must be properly adjusted to hold the shafts firmly in place.

The driving bridle and bits
The basic driving bridle is open—that is, not fitted with blinkers—and consists of a headpiece, throatlatch, browband, cheekpieces, noseband (known in the USA as a head halter), snaffle bit and reins, or lines, which pass through rings, or terrets, on the saddle and then back to the driver's hand.

Driving bits come in two main varieties—the jointed and the unjointed

Left: The exhilarating sport of trotting, which is immensely popular in America, Australia and the Continent of Europe but has only a comparatively small following in Britain.

CHAPTER SIX · DRIVING HARNESS

snaffle. A leather- or rubber-covered mouthpiece and rubber bit guards are frequently used to prevent soring of the mouth and cheeks, while special bits are employed for schooling young horses. Since the young horse takes time to develop his balance and steering, there is a tendency for him to lean to one side or the other, thus pulling the bit through his mouth. This soon leads to soreness. To guard against this, a youngster is usually schooled in a special colt-breaking bit. This has a strap attached to the rings which fastens under the chin and is also fitted with large leather cheekpieces to guard against chafing. One variety of colt-breaking bit, the Frisco June, has the chin strap built in as an integral part of the bit; others have detachable straps.

Keeping a straight course
It is a prime requisite for harness racers to hold their heads absolutely straight in front of them. If a horse does not do this, he will not only be unable to achieve his maximum speed, but also will almost certainly strike into and injure himself when moving at racing pace. Various devices have been invented to cope with the problem of the horse who persistently leans to one side or the other. One is the side-lining bit which has an extension—a steel bar 2 to 4in long and about ¼in in diameter—protruding from one side. The rein fastens to a ring at the end of the extension. The extra leverage this arrangement produces is often sufficient to keep the horse straight.

For horses who tend to pull on either side at different stages of a race, the slip-mouth side-lining bit is the answer. Here the straight, leather-covered mouthpiece is hollow, with a bar running through it and protruding on either side of the horse's mouth. The bit automatically adjusts to extend on one side or the other, depending which is favoured.

Another device for keeping the head straight is the head pole, a small pole running alongside the neck and head from the saddle to the noseband. Head poles are telescopic, so that they can be adjusted to exactly the length required. The pole is attached to the saddle by a strap running from the terret, through a slit in the pole, to the overcheck hook, which is positioned on top of the saddle pad. The front of the pole fastens to a ring on the noseband. Even with this arrangement, some horses still find it possible to lean in a little towards the pole. To discourage this, a small rubber ball or a burr—a length of leather studded with little rivets—can be fitted around the pole where it runs alongside the neck. The poles can be fitted on either side of the neck, or on both, depending on the idiosyncracies of the particular horse.

Some horses object to the presence of a head pole, so an alternative means of straightening the head has to be employed. One way is to fit a burr, appropriately

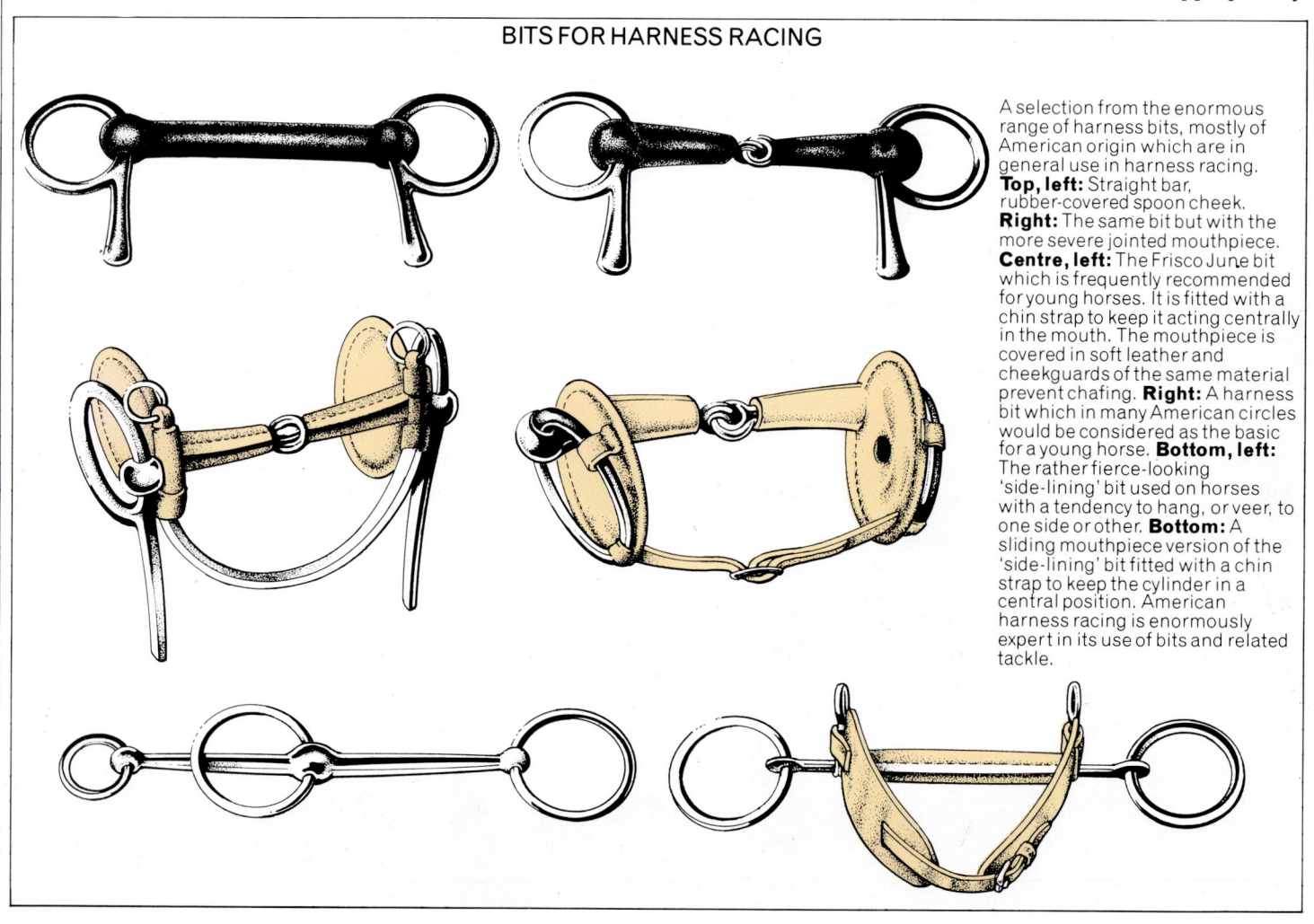

BITS FOR HARNESS RACING

A selection from the enormous range of harness bits, mostly of American origin which are in general use in harness racing.
Top, left: Straight bar, rubber-covered spoon cheek.
Right: The same bit but with the more severe jointed mouthpiece.
Centre, left: The Frisco June bit which is frequently recommended for young horses. It is fitted with a chin strap to keep it acting centrally in the mouth. The mouthpiece is covered in soft leather and cheekguards of the same material prevent chafing. **Right:** A harness bit which in many American circles would be considered as the basic for a young horse. **Bottom, left:** The rather fierce-looking 'side-lining' bit used on horses with a tendency to hang, or veer, to one side or other. **Bottom:** A sliding mouthpiece version of the 'side-lining' bit fitted with a chin strap to keep the cylinder in a central position. American harness racing is enormously expert in its use of bits and related tackle.

TROTTING EQUIPMENT

Above: Using a head pole on an American pacer. (Pacers move their legs in lateral pairs while trotters use diagonal pairs.) The head pole is a salutary aid in keeping the horse straight. Poles can be fitted on one side of the neck or on both as necessary and can be reinforced with a burr. **Right:** Yet another piece of American equipment designed to keep a horse running straight. This is the Murphy blind which can be adjusted to counteract a tendency to hold the head on one side. In this instance, the horse holds his head to the left and the blind is therefore fitted over the right eye.

positioned, to the rein, another is to use a Murphy blind, a type of blinker. Some drivers prefer a blind to a pole in any case, since it is less cumbersome. The Murphy blind, named after the notable American trainer and driver Thomas W Murphy, is a piece of stiff leather that fits on to the cheekpiece of the bridle. It is shaped so that it cups inwards slightly at the front of the eye. The principle of operation is simple; with a horse who turns his head to the left, the blind is fitted on the right, so that too acute a turn of the head will bring the blind in front of the right eye, thus obscuring his vision. A horse quickly appreciates that if he keeps his head straight he can see straight ahead perfectly well, but that if he turns it his vision will be obscured.

Shadow rolls and hobbles

Other items in common use on harness horses, particularly pacers, are shadow rolls and hobbles. The shadow roll is basically a sheepskin-covered noseband, fitted so that a horse can see straight ahead but cannot look down at the ground immediately in front of him. It is used on horses who have a tendency to shy at shadows, marks on the tracks, bits of paper and so on. Pacers are particularly prone to spookiness, something which, it is believed, is the result of their wearing hobbles. Because they do not have free use

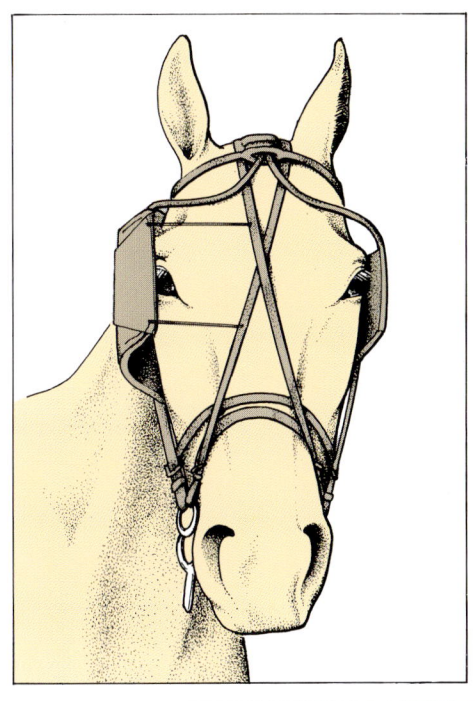

CHAPTER SIX · DRIVING HARNESS

A SELECTION OF SHADOW ROLLS

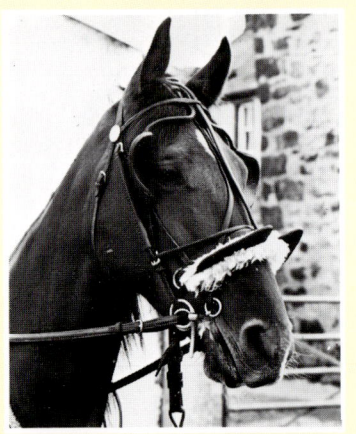

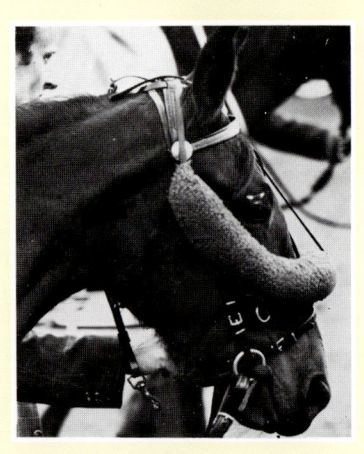

The shadow roll is virtually integral to the equipment of the harness-racing horse and its shape and adjustment can be critical to the horse's performance. The type of roll employed depends upon the idiosyncrasies of the individual horse and on the preference of the particular trainer. Whatever the type employed, and a selection is reproduced on this page, the object of the shadow roll remains unaltered. Its purpose is to prevent the horse seeing the ground directly to his front and thus to prevent him from checking and breaking his gait at the sight of a shadow (hence the name), a discoloration on the track, a piece of paper or any other object. The roll, however, must not prevent the horse from seeing straight ahead. If it does he will only twist his head and thus affect his action.

of their legs they seem to be much more fearful of stepping in a hole or of tripping up than are other horses. As a result, they are likely to shy violently at real or imagined objects on the ground, something which is extremely dangerous when they are racing alongside other sulkies. There are various designs of shadow roll, all of which fit across the nose below the eyes, buckling under the jaw. They must be adjusted with great care, so as not to obstruct the horse's vital forward vision.

Hobbles are used on pacers to keep them steady and enable them to maintain their lateral gait. The traditional material used was leather, but nowadays lightweight plastic and nylon are frequently substituted. Hobbles are adjustable straps fitted with padded loops at each end. One loop encircles the front leg and the other the hindleg on the same side of the animal. At the front and back of each leg loop is a vertical strap which fits on to a set of four hobble hangers. The front hangers on each side pass up over the neck just in front of the withers—the rear ones rest on the horse's quarters, either side of the tail—joining up and fastening to the back strap some way in front of the top of the dock. The two centre hangers are also fastened to the back strap, the forward one immediately behind the saddle and the rear one a little in front of the hips.

Alternatively, the two centre hangers can be replaced by a single one which divides halfway down the horse's sides into a Y shape. Although this arrangement looks neater, it can cause chafing.

The fit of hobbles is critical and must be constantly corrected, since the straps stretch with use. If they are suspended too high, they will restrict the action of the muscles at the top of the legs; if they are too tight, they will prevent a horse extending properly and will tire his legs; if they are too loose, a horse that is used to them may start to roll about in his gait as he seeks their support.

Cross hobbles, which, as their name suggests, are fitted from one foreleg to the opposite hindleg, used to be employed on trotters to prevent them from breaking into a faster pace, but their use has considerably declined, probably because of their tendency to make a horse hit his knees and shins. Half hobbles can be used on both trotters and pacers. These are made of two loops joined by rope which runs through a pulley. Although they can be employed either on the front or the hindlegs, they are most usually seen on the front legs of a trotter. The pulley is positioned under the horse's belly just behind the girth and is kept in place by means of two straps attached at right angles to the shafts. Two further straps prevent the pulley from riding forward. It is difficult to maintain the desired tension and, therefore, the desired effect of half hobbles because of the tendency of the vehicle to move forward a bit when the horse begins to take a strong hold.

Coping with pulling

A great many harness racers are inclined to hot up in excitement and pull. Various

Below: Many harness horses pull quite strongly and to counteract this difficulty an overcheck or check rein is used. This will prevent the horse lowering his head below a certain level and becoming out of full control.

CHAPTER SIX · DRIVING HARNESS

COPING WITH PULLING

Top: The side pole in position, to keep the horse straight, and also an overcheck to fix the head vertically and to combat excessive pulling. **Above:** Three types of overcheck bit. Plain standard overcheck (**top**), Speedway overcheck (**centre**) and jointed overcheck used with a snaffle (**bottom**).

Above: The jointed overcheck bit in position. The reins are fastened to both driving bit and overcheck; the bridle head to the driving bit only. This constitutes a fairly mild restraint.

Above: The Raymond overcheck, a device which operates on the nose and is considered to be very effective, particularly in the case of horses with sore or injured mouths. It can be kept in place either with a chinstrap or a curb chain.

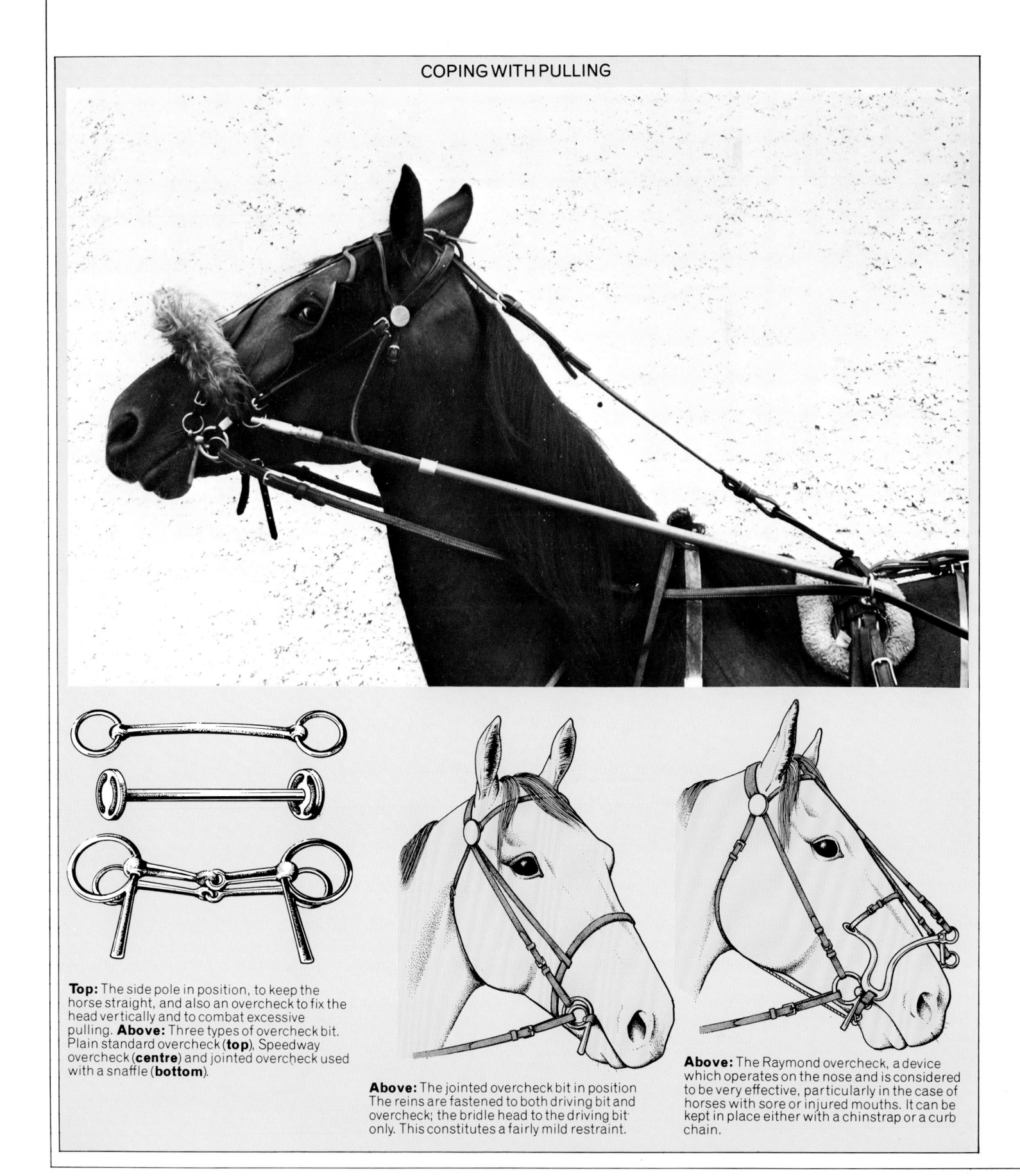

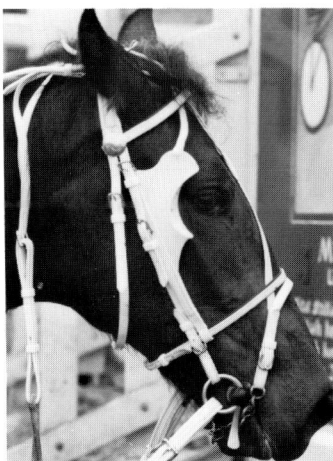

Far left: Blinkers are used to restrict the horse's lateral and rear vision and to concentrate his attention to the front. This form of closed bridle allows good forward vision and some lateral vision also.
Left: The modified 'Kant-See-Back' type of blinker, which is less restrictive.
Right: Full protection for the legs and heels is given by bell boots, ankle boots and knee boots.

ingenious devices have been invented to cope with this, including the jointed overcheck bit, the lip cord and the overcheck or check rein. A jointed overcheck bit is simply a second jointed snaffle, used in conjunction with the usual driving bit. The reins are fastened through the rings of both the driving and overcheck bits; the extra pressure exerted on the mouth is often sufficient to control a mild puller.

The lip cord is much more severe. This is a cord fitted around the top gums below the upper lip, behind the mouthpiece of the bit and out at the corners of the mouth, fastening under the chin. It is an effective deterrent to a pulling horse, but it requires a very light hand, otherwise the mouth might be damaged.

The overcheck or check rein is more common. The rein is a strip of leather that runs from the saddle, to which it is attached by a hook, up over the horse's neck where it divides into two. Each strap passes through a separate loop provided in the headpiece of the bridle and runs between the ears and down the front of the face, fastening to each side of a check bit or chin strap. The overcheck is used to prevent a horse lowering his head below a certain level, ensuring that it stays at a height where he can be most easily controlled and where he can use himself to best advantage.

Further controls
Horses with basically good head carriage who just occasionally pull down with their heads at moments of excitement—perhaps before the start of a race—or those who have particularly light mouths can be fitted with a simple chin strap, which has a ring at each end to which the overcheck buckles. The chin strap is usually connected to the throatlatch by a strap running under the jaw. This ensures that the chin strap stays in the correct position. When a chin strap is insufficient to control the position of the head an overcheck bit is used. The basic bit is a straight piece of metal with small rings at either end, but there are many variations, some of which are quite severe and only suitable for horses who are otherwise uncontrollable. An overcheck bit can also be used in conjunction with a chin strap, an arrangement which will help to keep a horse's mouth closed. In this case, a bit called a Speedway is usually employed, since it has special slots into which the chin strap can be fitted.

A horse who persistently puts his head down can be fitted with one of the many leverage devices on the market, such as the Raymond overcheck. This may look clumsy, but it is most effective. The equipment is somewhat like a sophisticated version of the chin strap, since it employs no bit. It works by lifting the chin and at the same time pressing down on the nose. Many horses seem to perform better in it than in an overcheck bit.

Other additions to the harness racer's wardrobe include standing and running martingales and various nosebands, including the figure-of-eight and a version of the drop noseband. Some horses, particularly those inclined to be lazy or lacking in concentration, are fitted with closed bridles—that is, bridles with blinkers. The latter come in a great variety of shapes and sizes, but they share the same basic principle—to concentrate the horse's attention to the front.

A horse who tends to swing his quarters over towards one shaft or the other can be fitted with a gaiting strap or gaiting pole. It runs parallel to the horse's body from the tip of the shaft back to the crosspiece or arch of the sulky and acts on the quarters in the same way that a head pole acts on the neck and head.

Boots for protection
Finally there is a large selection of boots designed to protect various parts of the racer's limbs. Trotters often strike their elbows with their feet; to guard against this special elbow boots are fitted to cover the vulnerable area. Knee boots are most often used on pacers, who are prone to striking the inside of the knee with the opposite forefoot. Both elbow and knee boots are fitted with suspenders.

There are many other forms of boot designed to protect the shins, ankles and coronets, all of which can be injured when a horse is moving at high speed. Trotters tend to need shin boots and scalpers behind and quarter boots in front, while pacers normally need tendon and pacing quarter boots in front.

Quarter boots are designed to protect the heels and coronets of the front feet at the rear or both the rear and the inside. They are usually made of felt or leather. Many pacers need this type of boot because of their tendency to cross-fire—that is to hit the front foot with the opposite hind foot.

Scalpers are similar to rubber overreach or bell boots and are pulled on over the foot. The front part curves upwards to give protection to the coronet and the area above it. They are used on horses who are prone to speedy cutting and on passing-gaited trotters, horses whose hindlegs pass outside their front legs.

CHAPTER SIX · DRIVING HARNESS

Harnessing a trotter. **Right:** The first fitting is a light halter. **Far right:** The crupper being placed in position. **Below, left:** Pad, backstrap, etc in place. **Centre:** Putting on the bridle. **Right:** The bridle correctly adjusted and the breast girth in position.

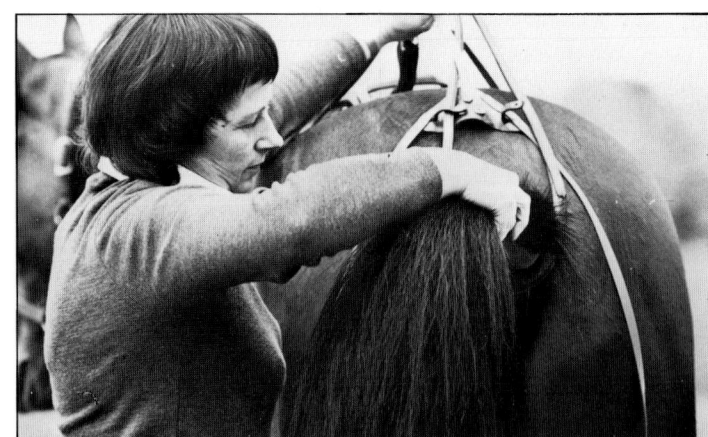

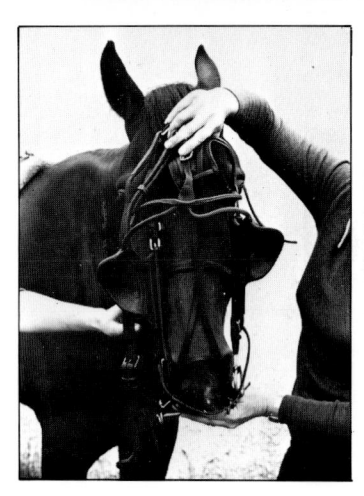

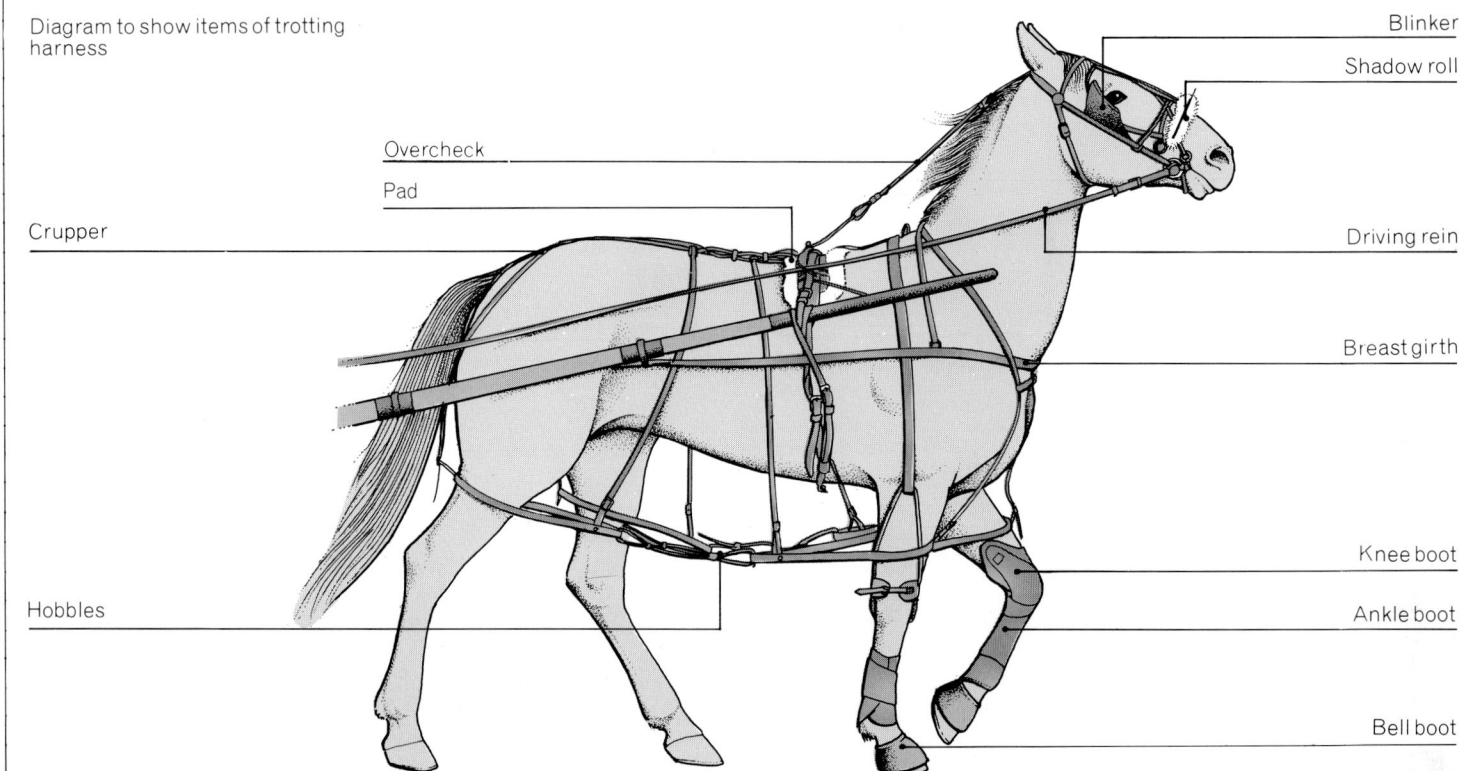

Diagram to show items of trotting harness

- Blinker
- Shadow roll
- Overcheck
- Pad
- Crupper
- Driving rein
- Breast girth
- Knee boot
- Ankle boot
- Hobbles
- Bell boot

TROTTING EQUIPMENT

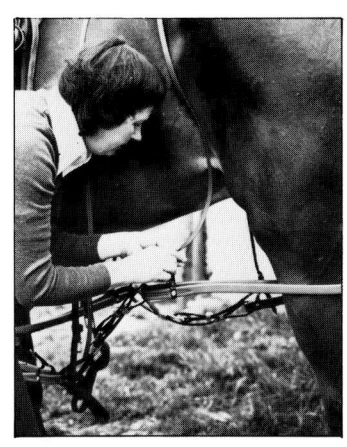

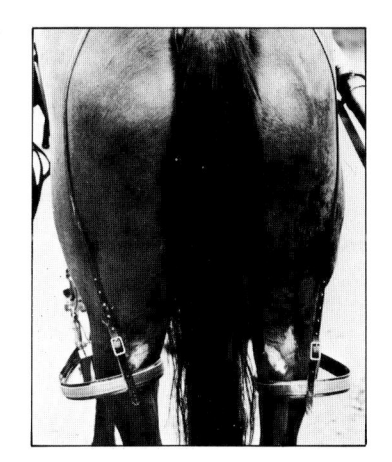

Far left: Getting the horse to step into the hobbles. **Centre left:** Connecting and adjusting the hobble straps. **Left:** Rear view of the hobbles hanging equally and adjusted correctly. **Below, left:** The harness fitted and the horse ready for putting to. **Centre:** Detail of shaft holder. **Right:** Detail of pad/shaft fastening.

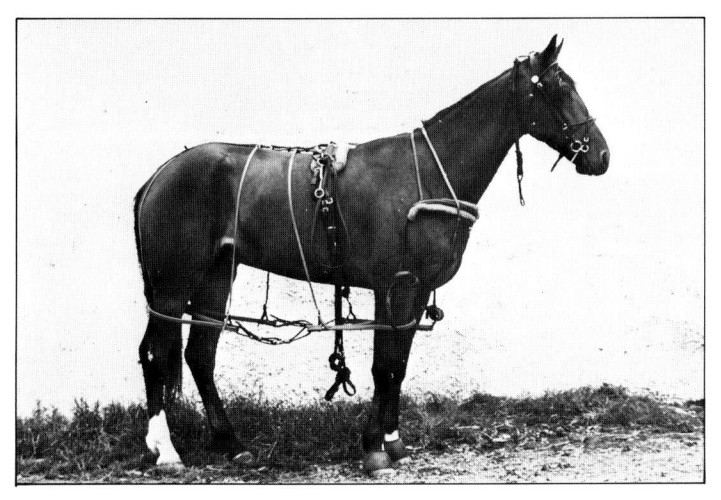

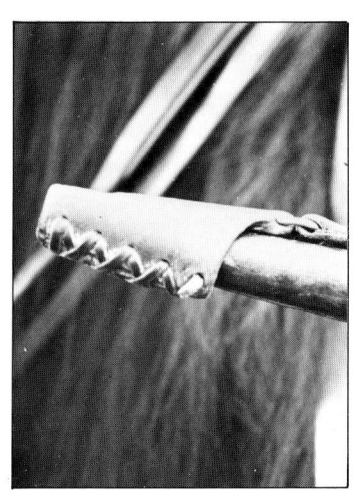

Left: The harness pacer in racing harness with booted forelegs, hoobles, light shadow roll, closed bridle and overcheck. The harness racing trainer takes infinite pains with the correct bitting of his charges and the minute adjustment of each part of the harness.

175

CHAPTER SIX · DRIVING HARNESS

Driving · **Farm Harness**

When horses were first domesticated by man some 3,000 years ago, their small stature made them more suitable for pulling some sort of vehicle or load than for carrying a rider. Since the ox had already been successfully pressed into service as a draught animal it seemed natural enough for the horse to be utilized for the same purpose.

In practice, however, this was not as simple as it sounds in theory, since the horse's conformation differs a good deal from that of the ox. The latter was attached to a vehicle by means of a simple wooden yoke, which rested on top of the beast's shoulders—an arrangement which worked admirably and is still to be seen in many parts of the world where agriculture has yet to be mechanized. The structure of a horse's shoulders, however, makes it not only difficult to secure a yoke, but the method of haulage required is actually detrimental to the animal's pulling ability. The only way to keep a yoke in place on a horse was to employ some form of neck strap which, as soon as the horse began to pull against a heavy load, had the undesirable effect of putting undue pressure on the windpipe.

The first farm horses
In the course of time, breast harness was developed, which was a considerable im-

provement on the yoke arrangement. Breast harness consists of a broad band of leather passed round the breast of the horse, parallel to the ground, attached at either end to a pad and girth and kept at the correct height by means of a strap passed over the neck. Such harness is still popular in many countries, but it is not really ideal for heavy work, such as ploughing and pulling large farm implements, since it tends to interfere with the action of the shoulders and can also ride up and exert pressure on the windpipe.

Because of the imperfections of early harnessing devices, therefore, the horse was, of necessity, restricted to pulling light loads, such as chariots. Then, when the horse had grown large enough to carry man into battle, his use as a draught animal dwindled, leaving the ox to its traditional role. It was not for many centuries that widespread use of the horse on the land occurred and, even then, this varied from area to area and depended on many factors.

Available evidence points to Scandinavia as the first area to use horses as farm animals. The most likely reason for this development was the invention of the collar, a piece of equipment which revolutionized draught work just as the coming of the stirrup revolutionized riding itself. Although it is possible that the nomads of

There is a tradition of decorated horse displays throughout Europe and at some horse shows classes are held for the best-decorated horse. **Above:** An English Shire horse. **Left:** A Scottish Clydesdale, wearing a very good example of a Scottish peaked collar. **Far left:** A pair of highly-ornamented German horses wearng the collars peculiar to the Bavarian area from which they come as well as such accessories as bells and ear caps. The muzzles have a purely practical purpose and prevent the horse from biting or eating.

CHAPTER SIX · DRIVING HARNESS

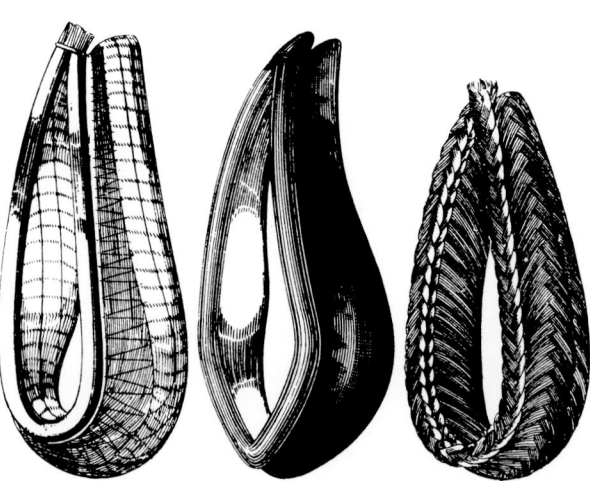

Far left: Reproduction of a page from the illuminated Apocalypse of Trèves (c. 880 AD) which shows a horse collar of the period. **Left:** Three collars, the illustrations taken from a trade catalogue of the early 1900s. They are (left to right) a bodied country cart collar, a piped van collar and a straw-woven segg or plough collar.

Central Asia used collars, the earliest tangible evidence for their introduction lies in the frames of metal collars unearthed from Swedish tombs of the middle and late years of the 9th century AD. Towards the end of that century King Alfred of Wessex, writing of voyages to the north, expressed surprise that in northern Norway the horse was used for ploughing, while a picture of a horse collar exists from about the same period in the illuminated *Apocalypse* of Trèves (*c*.880).

The link with Scandinavia is apparent in England, too. The earliest instances of the horse being used as a farm animal there occur in the eastern counties, areas which most felt the influence of the Vikings and other north European invaders. Although there seems as yet to have been no organized breeding of horses specifically for agricultural work, by the time of the 12th century there was an increase in their use on the land. However, it was not until Tudor times that the horse began to share with the ox the job of pulling wagons and ploughing the land. The changeover from ox to horse power was thus a very slow one, spanning a period of several centuries. Only as the weight-carrying war horse became obsolete in its original field, did farmers begin to appreciate their tractive powers and, additionally, the advantages of breeding horses of a certain type to carry out specific tasks. One such example is the Suffolk, bred in the East Anglian region of England and ideally suited to working the area's heavy clay soil.

The working collar
The item of equipment which enabled the horse to become the agricultural worker *par excellence* of the 18th and 19th centuries, especially in Europe and the USA, was the final version of the collar. As can be seen from paintings and various other records of the day, it and the other items of horse harness have changed little since those dates.

A collar is made of a tube of leather, called a forewale, which is stuffed with straw until it is stiff. The body, known as the afterwale, consists of padding made from stout woollen cloth filled with rye straw, with leather side pieces to protect it from weather and wear. The design is planned to avoid putting pressure on the windpipe and the withers; horses who are particularly prone to choking can be fitted with a special variant as a further precaution. This is made with a pipe, a device which is placed in the forewale at the stuffing stage, so changing the shape of the collar slightly. To ensure a good fit, the collar is made narrow at the top and wide at the bottom to correspond with the shape of the horse. However, because the collar must be passed over the horse's head, which is small at the lower end and broad at the top, it is necessary to put the collar over the horse's head upside down and to turn it round once it is on the neck.

Horses who are head-shy may be fitted with an open-topped collar, a regional design, confined mainly to south-west Britain and Ireland. This, as the name suggests, is not closed at the top but can be pulled open and slid over the neck. This, however, is not wholly satisfactory, since, with constant use, it tends to lose its rigidity and is then liable to produce shoulder sores. Over the years, many other types of 'improved' collars have been tried—pneumatic (with air instead of stuffing), elastic steel, collars stuffed with cork and ones with removable, washable linings—but none has succeeded in replacing the basic model.

The implement to be pulled is attached by chains to the hames, a rigid frame which fits round the collar. Hames used always to be made of wood—either ash or beech—but, by the end of the 19th century, iron hames had largely superseded wooden ones. Today, this process has gone one stage further, with steel. The hames are fastened together at the top by a strap, or leather thongs, and usually by a chain and hook at the bottom.

The draught bridle
The other essential piece of equipment is the bridle, which, in principle, is the same as that of a riding horse, with a headpiece, throatlatch, cheekpieces and a bit (usually a simple snaffle). In some areas, nosebands are used; in others they are not. Some horsemen, too, favour blinkers, while others are opposed to their use. Blinkers probably derive from the days of horse armour, when protective devices were worn to save the horse's eyes from injury during combat. The chief justification for their use on a farm horse is that they prevent his catching sight of the implement he is pulling and taking fright. However, since most young horses are trained without blinkers and many older ones can be seen working calmly in 'open'—that is, blinkerless—bridles, it seems likely that blinkers are something of an anachronism. Many people, however, still favour them. Blinkers can be made in different ways. It

is possible, though wasteful, to cut the blinker and the cheekpiece of the bridle from one piece of hide. However, it is more usual to cut the blinkers and the cheekpieces separately and then stitch them together.

Leather reins are usually used for driving with cart harness and rope 'lines' with plough harness. In addition, the horse may wear a shorter rein fastened to the bit rings and hooked over the hames. This is a useful device which acts like a mild bearing rein, stopping the horse from putting his head down to graze while at work.

Harness types
Equipped with the basic essentials of bridle and collar, the farm horse is worked in one of three types of harness—cart harness, plough harness or trace harness. Cart harness is used with all vehicles or implements equipped with shafts. These include a variety of wagons and carts, as well as some horse-drawn hoes and rollers and one or two other devices, such as manure spreaders. In order to work in shafts, the horse must be fitted with the usual collar and bridle, with long leather reins, plus a pad, or saddle, and breeching.

The cart pad or saddle is made on a tree of elm or beech, consisting of two boards fixed either side of a grooved arch. It occupies the same position on a horse's back as a riding saddle and is secured in a similar manner by means of a girth. A strap is fastened to the front of the pad and secured to the collar, thus guarding against any backward movement of the pad. This item of equipment is known as a meeter strap.

In bad weather a piece of stout leather called a housen may be attached to the collar and positioned so that it bridges the gap between the collar and the pad, the idea being to prevent rain from running between the horse's shoulder and his collar. In most areas, however, the housen is no longer used.

To stop the pad riding forward, the horse may be equipped with a crupper, a padded leather loop which passes under

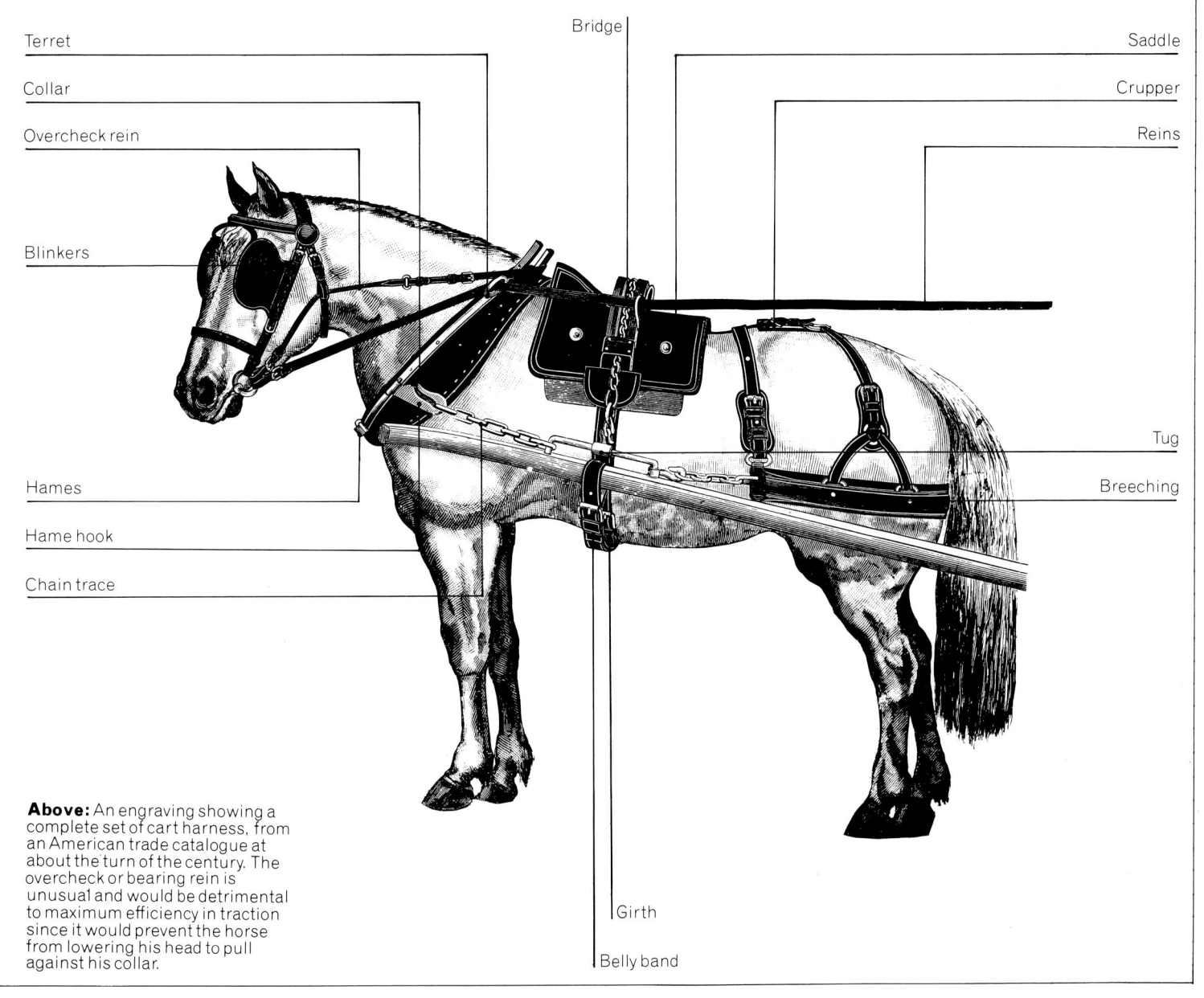

Above: An engraving showing a complete set of cart harness, from an American trade catalogue at about the turn of the century. The overcheck or bearing rein is unusual and would be detrimental to maximum efficiency in traction since it would prevent the horse from lowering his head to pull against his collar.

CHAPTER SIX · DRIVING HARNESS

Right and opposite: These illustrations show the stages followed when harnessing a cart horse. The collar is always put on first and upside down so that it passes easily over the head, being turned into place at the thinnest part of the neck. Apart from the logic of beginning at the front and working backwards, there is an element of superstition in the practice and no horseman would put on the saddle before the collar. Once the collar is in position the hames are put on and fastened with the small hame strap. The driving reins are put on last and looped over the near side hame preparatory to the horse being put to.

the dock and is kept in place by means of a broad leather strap attached to the rear of the collar. However, such a precaution is not usually necessary and the tail loop is often dispensed with, the back strap being retained merely to suspend vertical hip straps and breeching.

The purpose of the pad is to support the back chain, or ridger. This chain passes over the horse's back and is attached to both shafts, thus keeping them at the correct elevation for easy forward movement. In the case of a two-wheeled vehicle the horse supports a portion of its weight, but when a four-wheeled vehicle is used the ridger merely takes the weight of the shafts. The deep groove on the upper side of the pad houses the ridger when it is in position, the ends being attached by hooks to a metal ridger bar fitted to the top edge of each shaft.

The shafts of a vehicle are attached to the horse's collar by means of strong chains known as tugs. It is important to ensure that, when in position, the offside and nearside tugs are of equal length or the horse will not be able to pull effectively. Forward movement of the vehicle is effected by the horse leaning into his collar and exerting a pull on the shafts via the tugs.

Sometimes, it may be necessary for the horse to back the vehicle. This is where the device known as breeching comes into play. Breeching consists of a broad band of leather which passes round the hindquarters and is suspended from the crupper strap by vertical hip and loin straps. Chains are used to fasten the ends of the breeching band to a bar on each shaft. By pushing back against the breeching a horse can put a cart into reverse or help to steady a load when travelling downhill.

An additional strap or rope may be attached to each shaft, passing under the horse's body. This is a belly band; it is not fastened tightly under the horse's belly like a girth but is left fairly loose. Its role is to help prevent the vehicle tipping backwards, should it become tail-heavy for any reason. The weight of the horse's body counteracts the upward swing of the shafts.

Sometimes a strap is passed between the horse's forelegs and attached to the girth at one end and at the other to the collar. This, the martingale, is often decorated with horse brasses. The latter ornaments are believed to be of pagan origin and legend has it that they are efficacious in bringing good fortune.

The process of harnessing a horse to a cart or other shafted vehicle is termed shutting in. Collar, bridle, pad and breeching are fitted on the horse. He is then lined up square with the shafts of the vehicle and backed between them. Once the horse is correctly positioned, the shafts can be lifted and held in the raised position by one of the tugs while the ridger, breeching chains and second tug are all fastened.

When removing a horse from shafts—

FARM HARNESS

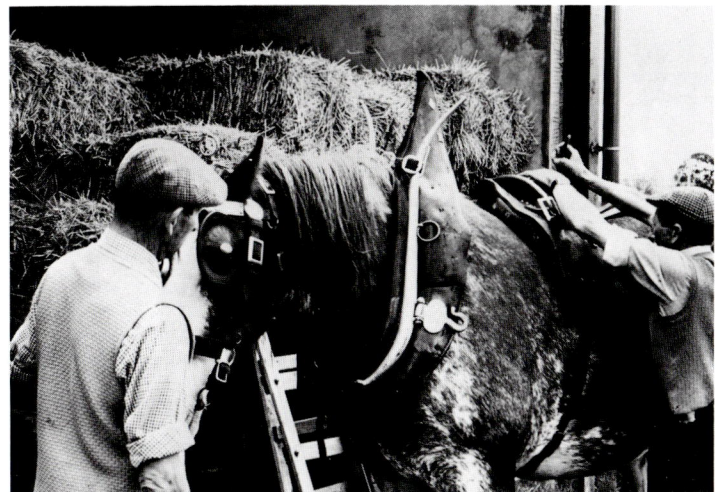

Left: A Shire in cart harness and ready to move off. The hame strap, keeping the hames on the collar, can be seen clearly at the top of the latter. When the size of the Shire is considered (some of them measure 18 hh and may weigh nearly a ton), and the weight of a loaded vehicle, the necessity for harness of the greatest strength is appreciated.

181

CHAPTER SIX · DRIVING HARNESS

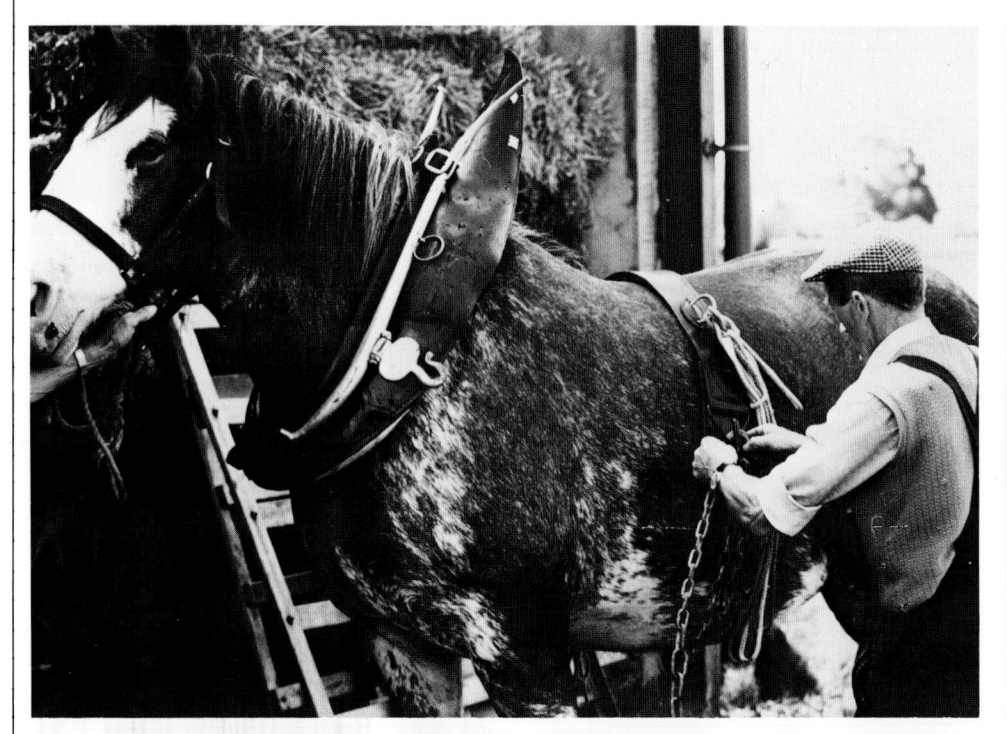

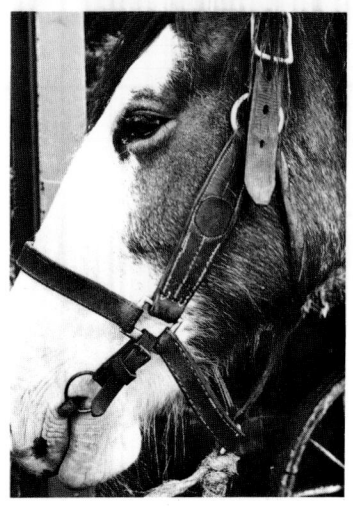

Above and left: Detailed illustrations of plough harness, in which such items as breeching are unnecessary and cord plough lines are used in place of the leather driving reins in a cart harness. These lines are secured to the open bridle (no blinkers) by means of a ploughmans knot, illustrated left. **Opposite:** A pair of Shires in plough harness.

shutting out—the breeching is unfastened first, followed by the tugs and finally the ridger. After this, the shafts can be lowered to the ground and the horse led forward and clear of the vehicle.

Plough harness
Plough harness, also known as chain harness or sling gear, is employed for implements such as ploughs and harrows. The horse wears a bridle and collar as for cart harness, but dispenses with the pad and breeching. The traces, or chains, which are used to pull the implement are attached to the hames of the horse's collar, one on either side, the other ends being fastened to either end of a piece of metal or wood called, variously, a whipple-tree, a swing-tree or a billet. This must be long enough to ensure that the chains do not touch the horse's sides, otherwise galling will occur. The whipple-tree is attached by means of a chain and hook to the implement.

Various devices are employed for supporting the weight of the chains and preventing the horse stepping on them when they are slack. Sometimes a backband is used. This is fitted in the same place as the pad; no girth is necessary, however, since the downward pull of the chains keeps it in place. Hip straps, suspended from the crupper strap, are also used as an alternative way of performing the same function as the backband.

When two horses are harnessed abreast, each horse's traces are fastened to separate whipple-trees. These are attached by chains to the ends of another whipple-tree, which in turn, are chained to the implement. Things become more complicated when three or more horses are used, since the combination of whipple-trees has to be calculated carefully. Various combinations of whipple-trees and compensating whipple-trees can be used for such teams, care being taken to ensure that the leverage is the same on each side of the implement. When unhitched from the whipple-trees the chains are hooked up on to the hames.

When working two or more horses abreast it is usual to employ couples, made of leather, rope or chain. These are fastened from one horse's bridle to the next, preventing a horse moving too far in front of, or away from, his neighbour.

The reins
The reins used for ploughing, harrowing etc are usually made of rope and are termed lines. Because there is a danger of lines of the necessary length becoming entangled with the horse's harness, some means must be employed to keep them clear. How this is done is largely a matter of individual preference. One method is to pass the lines through rings on either side of the hames; another is to suspend two rings on lengths of cord—one on either side of the horse's quarters—the cords being attached to the crupper strap. The lines are passed through these rings and thence to the driver's hands. The lines are held one in each hand and the driver walks behind the implement along the mark left by the last bout—each trip across a field is known as a bout.

When not in use the lines are neatly wound up to prevent tangling and hung on the end of the hame. One method is to take the two leather straps which fasten the lines to the bit rings in one hand and wind the doubled line round the wrists in a figure of eight holding it rather like a skein of wool. To finish it off neatly, the spare end of the line—that is, the looped end—is wound several times around the centre of the coiled line, passed through one of the loops in the figure of eight and then hung.

Harnessing variations
When working on heavy ground it may be necessary to use three or more horses and there are a variety of ways of harnessing them to the implement. One is the unicorn method, where two horses are yoked

CHAPTER SIX · DRIVING HARNESS

Above: Drawing a harrow in conventional harness. **Right:** Detail of the swingle tree which acts to direct the pull and to prevent the horses becoming entangled in the chains and implements.

Above: A team of four Shires at work in the harvest field and wearing traditional English harness. **Left:** An American engraving of horses in tandem showing clearly the wheel and lead harness.

abreast, and the third placed between, but in front of, the pair and attached to the whipple-tree by a long chain called a soam. In some regions three horses are sometimes yoked in what is termed Bodkin fashion, the third horse being placed in front of the furrow horse of a pair. For exceptionally heavy implements, four horses can be yoked abreast, but this is impossible where ploughing is concerned, since they would ruin the farrow. Where heavy ground warrants it, either two pairs are yoked one in front of the other, or four horses are used in line.

An implement fitted with a pole requires a pair of horses to draw it, one on either side of the pole. Basically the harness is the same as chain harness, but with the addition of a broad leather collar or neck strap, which is fitted to the front of the collar and supports the front end of the pole.

Trace harness
A trace horse is sometimes needed to help a single horse pull a heavy load, particularly when steep hills have to be negotiated. In this instance the lead horse wears a collar and bridle and usually a backband and crupper. Long chain traces are attached to the collar of the trace horse, the other ends being fastened to hooks on the underside of the shafts. The backband and hip straps take the weight of these chains, with a spreader—a bar of wood or metal—placed between the chains behind the horse's quarters to keep them apart and prevent them from chafing his sides. To prevent the horizontal pull of the cart traces pulling the collar up so that it presses on the windpipe, a belly band can be fitted to the traces slightly forward of the backband. An implement like a plough does not present this problem, since its pull is downward.

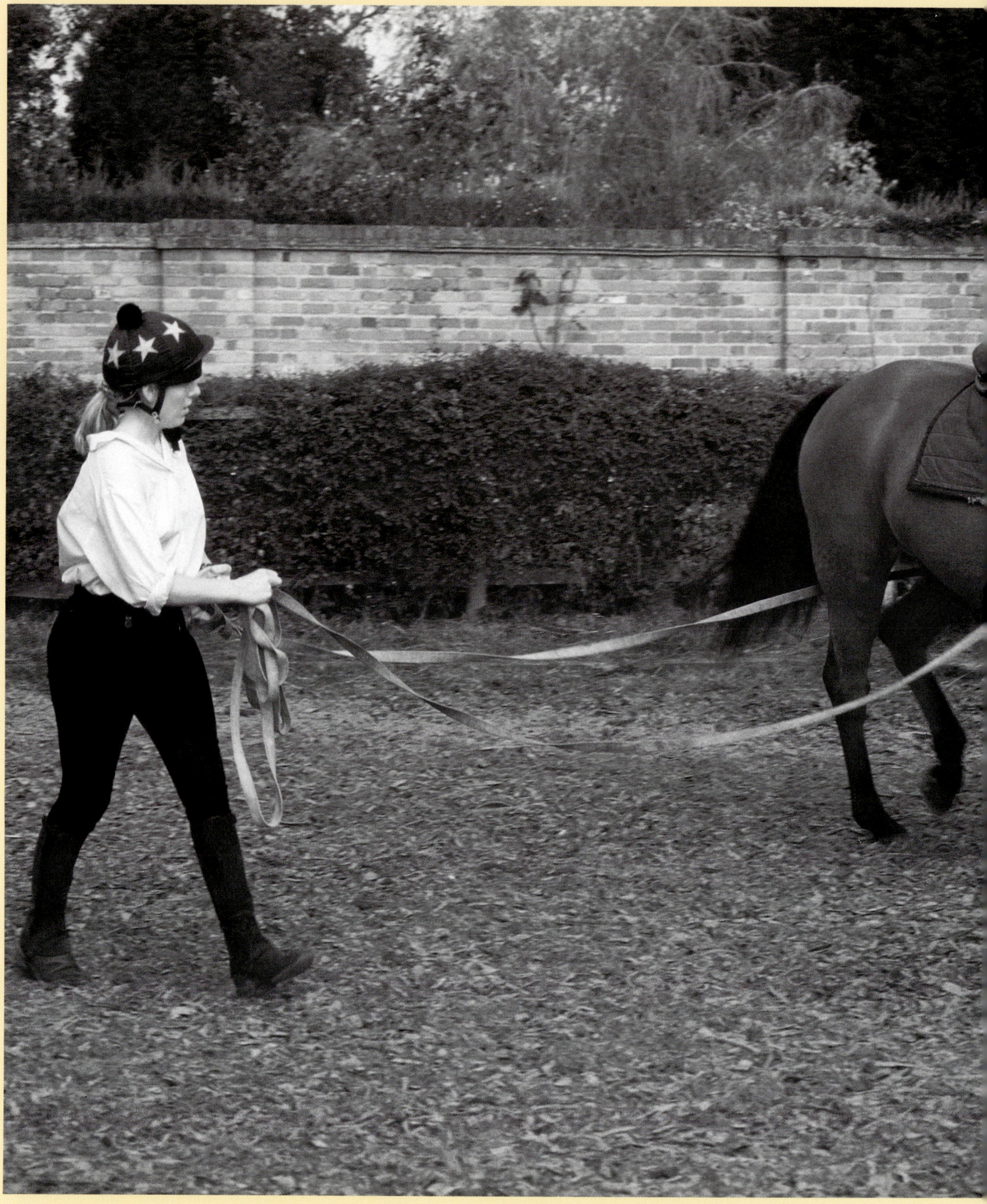

CHAPTER SEVEN

Training Aids

Schooling

Breaking

Lungeing and long reining are skills that can be used when starting a young horse's education, and also to improve the way of going of older animals.

CHAPTER SEVEN · TRAINING AIDS

Training Aids · Schooling

Left: Side reins run from the bit to a roller or saddle. They can be fitted higher or lower depending on the horse's state of training and the effect the trainer aims to achieve. This helps a trainer to obtain a steady head position, which can be more or less fixed by adjusting the rein's length. By fixing the head position, it also assists the effective action of the bit.

Below: The French chambon: a training device used to induce a lowering of the head and neck accompanied by a raising of the base of the neck. This will result in a rounded topline and greater engagement of the hocks under the body.

Training aids—or gadgets, depending on your point of view—are a controversial subject. In an ideal world, all horses would be schooled correctly right from the start and would learn to work on the bit as their physical and mental development permitted; but unfortunately, things do not always work out that way. If a horse has been trained incorrectly or has learned to resist, his rider may need help to break through the communication barrier.

Training aids are designed to encourage a horse to adopt a correct head carriage. However, he must still be encouraged to work from behind: his 'engine' or driving force comes from behind the saddle, and the fact that he arches his neck does not necessarily mean that he is working correctly. If fitted and used correctly, so that the trainer is using persuasion rather than force, training aids may help; in the wrong hands they can cause resistance and discomfort.

Whatever the equipment used, there are rules to follow. The first is that training aids should only be used by those who understand their action; obviously everyone has to learn, so less experienced trainers should use them under supervision to start with. The second rule is that they should only be used when you are sure that the horse is free from physical problems causing him discomfort. They should be used with a snaffle rather than curb bits, and they should be adjusted loosely, and used for only short periods to begin with, so that the horse gets used to their action and so that muscles which are perhaps being asked to work for the first time do not become overtired. Finally, training aids used for riding should be used in the short term, perhaps with occasional 'refresher' periods. If you can only ride your horse successfully or safely when equipped with draw reins or other aids, they are masking the symptoms rather than helping to bring about a cure.

Training aids for lungeing, such as side reins or a chambon, are usually fitted as standard to influence the horse's way of going, and the same rules apply. Some equipment, but not all, can be used for both lungeing and riding.

Side reins

Side reins are probably the simplest training aid and are used for breaking and schooling. They should only be used for lungeing—there have been cases of horses rearing when ridden in side reins and falling over backward, with horrific consequences.

Side reins can be made from plain leather or nylon, or with inserts of either

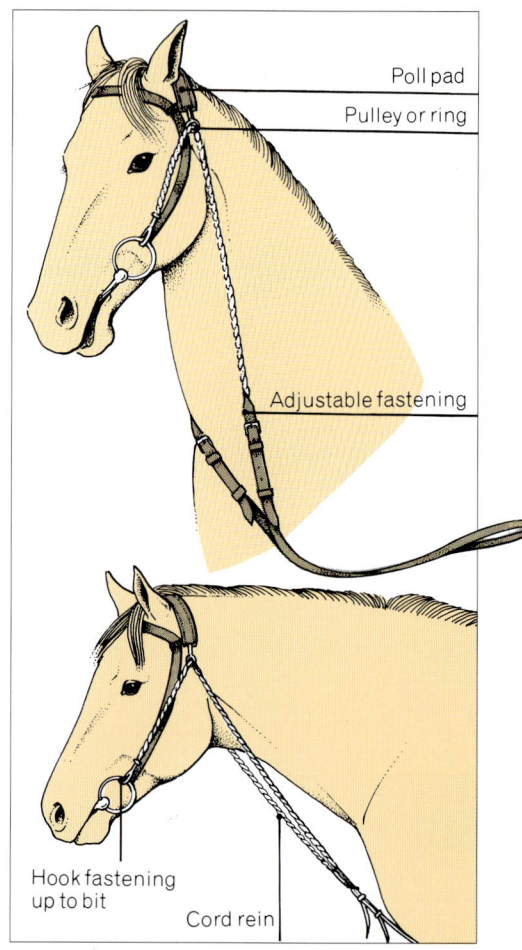

Poll pad
Pulley or ring
Adjustable fastening
Hook fastening up to bit
Cord rein

188

SCHOOLING

Left: Usually a draw rein is fastened from the girth and comes to the rider's hands through the bit rings. Draw reins must be used with tact and are not suitable for novice riders. They must always be used in conjunction with reins fitted directly to the bit.

CHAPTER SEVEN · TRAINING AIDS

strong elastic or rubber to provide a slight amount of 'give'. Some trainers prefer plain side reins because they feel this type encourages the horse to take a consistent contact; others believe that those with inserts mimic more closely the action of the rider's hands. Whatever you prefer, choose side reins with eyelet and buckle adjustments rather than those with sliding buckles, because with the latter it is more difficult to adjust the reins equally. They can be fastened either to a roller, or if the horse is being lunged in a saddle, to the girth straps.

The reins should be adjusted according to the horse's level of training, but always according to the principle that he should be encouraged to seek a contact with the bit rather than being pulled into a contact. Start off with them fairly loose and if necessary, adjust them as the horse warms up.

Draw reins and running reins

Draw reins and running reins are the most commonly used training aids—and many would say that they are also the most commonly abused! Invented by the Duke of Newcastle, a 16th-century British riding master, they can be used to great effect by riders who are masters in the art of their use … but as American coach Bert de Nemethy is often quoted as saying, in the wrong hands they can be like 'razors in the hands of a monkey'.

The terms 'draw reins' and 'running reins' are often used indiscriminately, but there is a difference. Standard draw reins start at the girth, pass through the bit rings and go back to the rider's hands. They have a more definite action than running reins, which fasten to the girth straps under the saddle flaps, then again pass through the bit rings and to the rider's hands. Usually they are fitted so that they run from the inside to the outside of the bit rings, which gives less of a squeezing action against the bit. American breastplate draw reins clip to the centre ring of a breastplate neckstrap, so leverage is therefore more direct.

Both draw reins and running reins should always be used with a direct rein to the bit ring, and only brought into play with light pressure if the horse fails to respond to the direct rein. As soon as he responds to the pressure, it should be released and he should be ridden on the direct rein again. The danger of using these reins—and many other devices—is that the horse learns to overbend. Even worse, the ligament at the poll may be stretched permanently.

The chambon

The chambon is a standard part of many European trainers' lungeing equipment, the latter stages of schooling, however, the rein is fastened from the girth to the mouth. Many riders use only this fitting.

Opposite, above: PJ nose reins, developed by Olympic trainer Pierre Jolicoeur, rely on a combination of nose pressure and rein contact.

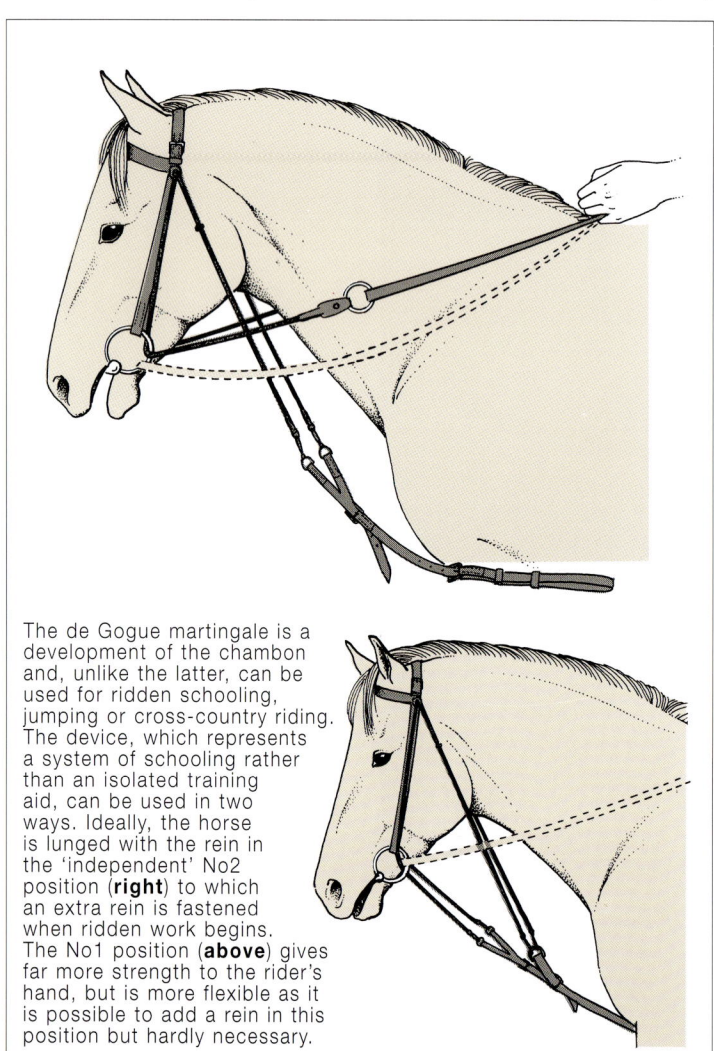

The de Gogue martingale is a development of the chambon and, unlike the latter, can be used for ridden schooling, jumping or cross-country riding. The device, which represents a system of schooling rather than an isolated training aid, can be used in two ways. Ideally, the horse is lunged with the rein in the 'independent' No2 position (**right**) to which an extra rein is fastened when ridden work begins. The No1 position (**above**) gives far more strength to the rider's hand, but is more flexible as it is possible to add a rein in this position but hardly necessary.

Above: The Abbot-Davies Balancing Rein. Its object is to develop the muscles of the back and hindlegs by raising the base of the neck. Theoretically, a connection is made from the tail to the mouth between the forelegs, the action on the mouth being initiated by an ingenious spring and pulley arrangement. In

and has become increasingly popular in Britain and North America. Some horses find it easy to evade side reins by coming above or behind the bit, and in these cases the chambon is more effective. It also encourages the horse to stretch his topline and work from behind, as long as he is lunged correctly and not allowed simply to run around in circles.

The chambon starts at the girth, like a martingale, then splits into two cords or straps, each with a clip at the end. A separate poll strap with a ring at each end fastens to the bridle headpiece, and the cords/straps pass through these, down the sides of the horse's face and clip onto the bit rings. When the horse raises his head, pressure is applied on the poll and the mouth; when he lowers his head, the pressure disappears. The horse soon learns that the most comfortable way to work is with a rounded back and a lowered head and neck, at a balanced pace.

The de Gogue

The de Gogue is related to the chambon and can be used in two positions, one for lungeing and one for riding. The chambon is designed as a lungeing device, but unfortunately riders who do not understand its use sometimes use it while riding, when the same dangers apply as to side reins. The lunge fitting—often called the independent fitting, and which can also be used for loose schooling—is similar to that of the chambon, but instead of clipping to the bit rings, the cords or straps go back to the girth. In the riding or command fitting, they pass down the sides of the face and through the bit rings and then fasten to special reins with rings at the end to take the clips. As with draw reins, an ordinary pair of direct reins attach to the bit so that the rider can use whichever pair is required.

The Abbot-Davies balancing rein

The Abbot-Davies balancing rein was developed in the 1970s by Major Peter Abbot-Davies, a former British army officer. At first it attracted much controversy, because its introduction relied on fastening the horse's tail to the bit via a system of reins and pulleys. This is a schooling device that dates back to ancient Egypt when Rameses III drove his chariot horses in a similar fashion, and it has come full circle with problem horse specialists such as Britain's Richard Maxwell, who in certain circumstances will use a similar but humane system to encourage horses to use their back ends more effectively.

Although such techniques must be used with great care, horses appear to accept them quite happily. Ironically, modern users of the Abbot-Davies balancing rein often omit the head-to-tail stage and go straight to the riding or lungeing positions. The rein attaches at the girth, and then separates into rolled leather straps with clips at each end which fasten to special reins with small D-rings sewn along them. The key to the system lies in the pulleys which clip to the bit rings, so that the horse is rewarded as soon as he works in a round shape. With this system, the horse is deliberately encouraged to overbend, the theory being that when the rein is taken off, he will adopt a correct outline. As with all training aids, however, it is very much a matter of what works best.

New ideas

Although most training aids are based on one or more of the above systems, new ideas have been developed in recent years, although as yet they have perhaps not had enough use to stand the test of time. For instance, there is the Harbridge, which starts at the girth and clips to the snaffle rings; it has elastic inserts, and although simple in design, it is claimed to be more effective than draw reins and to encourage a correct bend from the poll. The designer stipulates that it should not be used when jumping.

PJ Nose Reins, developed by Olympic trainer Pierre Jolicoeur, also seem to be a humane way of encouraging a more controllable head carriage. These combine nose pressure—once an important facet in training but now usually neglected in favour of direct contact with the bit—with rein action, and they incorporate a pulley system to allow enough freedom of the head and neck.

Then there is the Schoolmasta, developed by Hilary Janion, a British producer of show horses, to help overcome the problem of pulling or leaning on the bit. There are two versions: one for riding, which incorporates a specially strengthened numnah with pulley attachment and reins with a rolled connecting strap, and the other for breaking in, which uses a roller. The idea is that the horse pulls against himself rather than the rider's hand, but is still able to bend and flex to either side.

Training Aids · **Breaking**

Starting a young horse's education has traditionally been called 'breaking' or 'breaking in', terms from the times when it was accepted that a rider had to break the horse's will or spirit to make him carry a rider. They have remained part of equestrian language until comparatively recently, even though it is generally accepted that animals are best trained by humane rather than forceful methods. However, California horseman Monty Roberts has demonstrated dramatically the benefits of working with the horse's instincts and body language, and he has had a revolutionary effect on handling and training practices; many riders now follow not only his approach, but his preference for 'starting' rather than breaking a horse. Those inspired to use his technique of 'join-up', where the trainer's body language is used to make the horse advance, retreat and eventually decide that the most comfortable place to be is *with* his handler, will put a round training pen with high sides and a safe footing at the top of their equipment list.

Basic equipment

The first piece of tack worn by a young horse is a headcollar, or halter, and many breeders introduce a foal to a lightweight version of this, often known as a foal slip, when it is just a few hours old. Headcollars are made from leather or nylon webbing; expensive leather headcollars with brass fittings are used for show and for travelling, while cheaper chrome leather versions are suitable for use in the field. Nylon headcollars are fine for everyday use when someone is with the horse, but they should not be used for travelling or field turnout because if the horse gets caught up, leather will break but nylon could cause injury or worse. Having said this, you can now buy nylon headcollars with special inserts designed to break under stress, which makes them safer to use.

Control halters such as the Be Nice are an excellent way of teaching unruly animals—particularly youngsters that have not been bitted—that they cannot drag their handlers around. These tighten and put pressure on the nose when the handler pulls on the leadrope, but the pressure is relieved as soon as the horse yields and the leadrope slackens. It is important that the handler uses a 'give-and-take' technique so that the horse understands that good behaviour is more comfortable than bad.

Lungeing and long reining

Young horses are lunged and long reined, or long lined, as a prelude to being ridden. Monty Roberts and the accredited teachers of his system prefer to long rein rather than use the traditional method of lungeing. However, lungeing is still regarded as a valuable training method by most trainers throughout Europe and North America

An early example of the schooling device that came to be known as a 'dumb jockey' in action at the Spanish Riding School, Vienna.

Left: This headcollar has a 'panic insert' that will break if it gets caught on something. It is safe for use in the field.

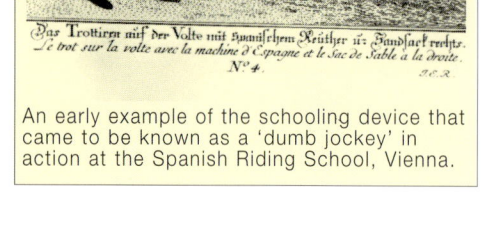

Left: A smart leather headcollar suitable for travelling, or to present a horse at his best.

LUNGEING TECHNIQUES

Right: A lungeing cavesson correctly fitted to the horse, with the lunge rein fitted with a swivel fastening to the central nose ring. **Far right:** A cavesson fitted with side rings to which side reins can be attached, or from which the horse can be lunged if the trainer follows the practice of lungeing from the inside ring. **Below:** A long lunge whip is an essential part of schooling equipment.

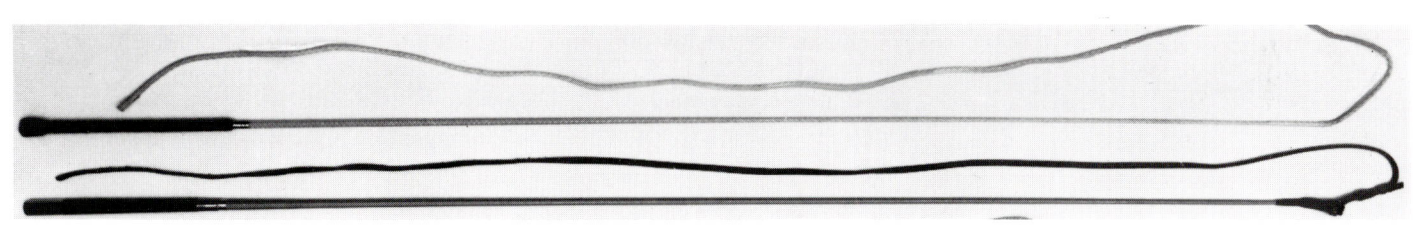

Below: The diagram shows the correct positioning of the trainer in relation to his pupil. Here, the horse is circling left on the lunge. The trainer stands a little behind the shoulder controlling the head with his left hand and maintaining impulsion through the presence of the lunge whip. The aim is to get the horse to walk, trot and halt correctly and respond to verbal commands.

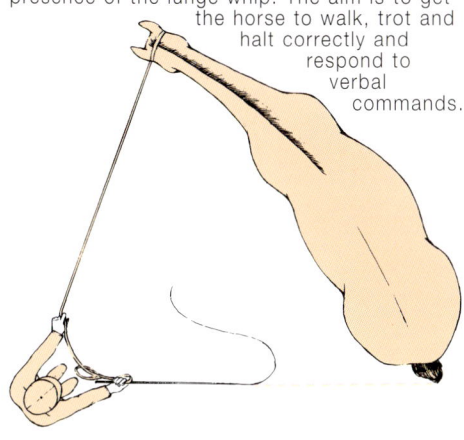

Above: A horse correctly equipped for lungeing and working well. The trainer uses a mixture of voice and whip aids and body language to work the horse, although the lunge whip is never used to hit the horse.

because it teaches the horse to respond to the trainer's voice and, when carried out correctly, to his body language. Unfortunately, many people do not understand correct lungeing techniques and are unable to influence their horse's way of going.

Traditionally, horses are taught to lunge wearing lunge cavessons so that the control point is the nose rather than the bit. These look rather like headcollars, but are designed so that they do not pull round onto the horse's eyes; they can be made either from leather—the best, but the most expensive—or nylon. The noseband is reinforced and padded and has three rings, thus giving a choice of positions for attaching the lunge rein. Most lunge cavessons fasten above the bit, similar to a cavesson noseband, but there are also designs which fasten below the bit and have a similar effect to that of a drop noseband.

One school of thought maintains that lunge cavessons have a basic design flaw in that the lunge rein is attached to the front of the horse's face. As horses 'back off' from anything in this position and the idea of lungeing is to encourage him to go forward, there is some logic in this.

CHAPTER SEVEN · TRAINING AIDS

Left: Long reining, or long lining, enables the trainer to introduce the idea of starting, stopping and turning without the complication of a rider's weight affecting the horse's balance. A skilled trainer can encourage the horse's acceptance of the bit.

Lungeing from a ring at the back of the nose uses a control point that the horse should already be accustomed to, from being led—but ordinary headcollars tend to slip round. As soon as side reins are introduced (see previous section on schooling equipment), the horse will need to wear a bridle as well as a cavesson. The noseband is then superfluous and should be removed, and the resulting half-bridle fitted so that the cavesson does not interfere with the bit.

The best lunge reins are made from cotton webbing, which is easy to handle and does not cut or burn the trainer's hand—which nylon can do even when the trainer wears gloves, one of the basic safety rules for lungeing. Nylon is also too light and unstable. Lunge reins fasten with either buckles or swivel clips; the latter are less complicated, but must be of good quality. For some reason they are always made with a loop at the other end, but in fact it is important not to put your hand through this in case the horse takes off and traps your fingers.

Perfectionists say that you should always lunge from a cavesson, never from a bit, but there are some situations where lungeing from the bit is the only safe way to make sure you are in control. However, this should not be done until the horse has been introduced to the bit and accepts its action. The lunge rein should be passed through the nearside (left) bit ring, under the chin and clipped to the offside (right) ring when lungeing in the left rein and the position reversed when the rein is changed. Some trainers like to pass the rein through the inside bit ring, over the poll and then fasten it to the outside ring, generally when lungeing an experienced but uncooperative horse, but this position has a potentially severe action similar to a gag snaffle and should only be used by the more experienced.

The lunge whip is used to encourage the horse forward, never to hit him—though cracking a lunge whip behind a lazy horse which takes a long while to obey voice commands should encourage him to buck up his ideas. Whips come in different weights, so choose one which you find easy to hold in balance.

Long reining is a valuable part of any horse's education, whether his future is to be ridden or driven. It teaches him to go forward, to stop, start and steer and to obey the trainer's voice commands, all without the extra complication of a rider on his back, which inevitably affects his centre of gravity and therefore his balance, or a vehicle behind him. As long as it is carried out correctly, by a trainer with sensitive hands, long reining also helps to 'make a mouth'—that is, to develop an acceptance of the bit and a sensitivity to rein commands.

Most veterinarians recommend that lungeing is not started seriously until the horse is three years old, as working on even 60-foot circles puts strain on young joints, particularly the hocks. Long reining, which can be carried out on straight lines or circles, is less physically stressful and helps to teach the horse to go forward and straight, the basic principles his rider will be aiming at! Short periods of long reining often benefit two-year-olds, especially the precocious kind which, if not given plenty to think about, find ways of amusing themselves that are not necessarily so appealing to their owners.

In the days when horses were used to work the land, youngsters would be driven in 'plough lines' made from tapered ropes. Modern trainers use two lunge reins, which again are best made from easy-to-hold cotton webbing that is not so lightweight that it blows around. Some trainers like to attach the long reins to the two outside clips of a cavesson to start with, and only graduate to attaching them to the bit when the horse has a basic idea of what is required of him.

Some trainers like to use side reins, adjusted on the loose side, when the horse is being long reined because they consider these give extra control and prevent the horse from throwing his head in the air or putting it down to eat when he is being long reined in the open—and long reining on roads or trails is a good way of giving the horse confidence.

The horse can wear either a saddle or a roller. If a saddle is used, the stirrup irons can be removed, or let down to a shorter-than-normal riding length so that the long reins can be passed through them on each side; this prevents the latter from trailing too low. The stirrup irons should be secured to prevent them from banging on the horse's side and startling him, either by fastening each iron to the girth with a separate strap, or linking both irons with a long strap under the belly.

Rollers have three sets of rings; which ones the trainer will pass the reins through will depend on the horse's stage of training, lower fittings being best for young horses which are expected to take a naturally lower head carriage. Advanced movements such as piaffe can be taught to and carried out by very advanced, experienced horses on long reins, as long as their trainers are equally experienced. At the Spanish Riding School in Vienna, one of the world's great centres of classical horsemanship, spectacular 'airs above the ground' are performed on long reins.

Introducing a bit

Some trainers do not ask a horse to wear a bit until he is ready to start his real training, at about three years old. Many more prefer to introduce a bit much earlier, when the horse is two or even as a yearling. Whatever approach you take, it is vital that the horse's mouth is checked and his teeth rasped, or floated, to smooth any sharp edges; if his first experience of wearing a bit involves discomfort, you are starting his education on a bad note. It is also important to remember that young horses grow rapidly, and that their mouths grow along with the rest of them. Thus a bit that fits your two-year-old perfectly may be too small when he reaches three.

The traditional breaking or mouthing bit, which has 'keys' attached to the centre of the mouthpiece to encourage the horse to mouth or play with it, is liked by some trainers and disliked by others. Those who dislike it maintain that it encourages the horse to fiddle with the bit rather than to accept it. Perhaps the sensible approach is to look at each horse as an individual: if he is too fussy with a mouthing bit, use some form of ordinary snaffle instead, but if his mouth remains dry in an ordinary snaffle, try a mouthing one to start with. A horse's mouth must be fairly wet if he is to be comfortable with a bit, as saliva makes it slide over the bars rather than drag over the skin that covers them. Suitable early bits to choose from include single-jointed or French link snaffles, or mullen-mouth (half-moon) designs made from metal, nylon or plastic. Nylon and plastic are lightweight and some horses seem to find them more comfortable at first.

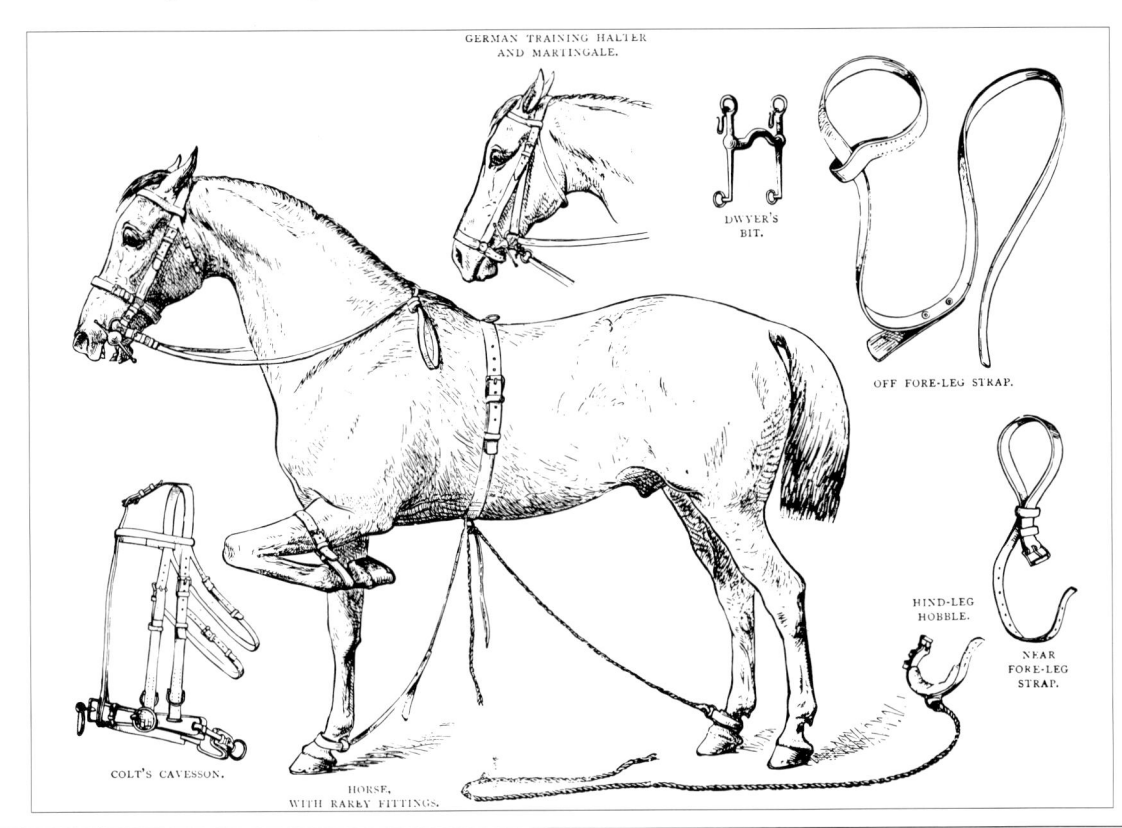

Left: John Rarey, possibly the most famous of Victorian horse tamers, specialized in difficult subjects which he subdued by tying up legs, throwing the horse and so on. Modern trainers rely more on understanding the horse's body language and psychology than on using force. The German training halter shows the use of the drop noseband which was generally employed in Europe during this period, but was not much used in England.

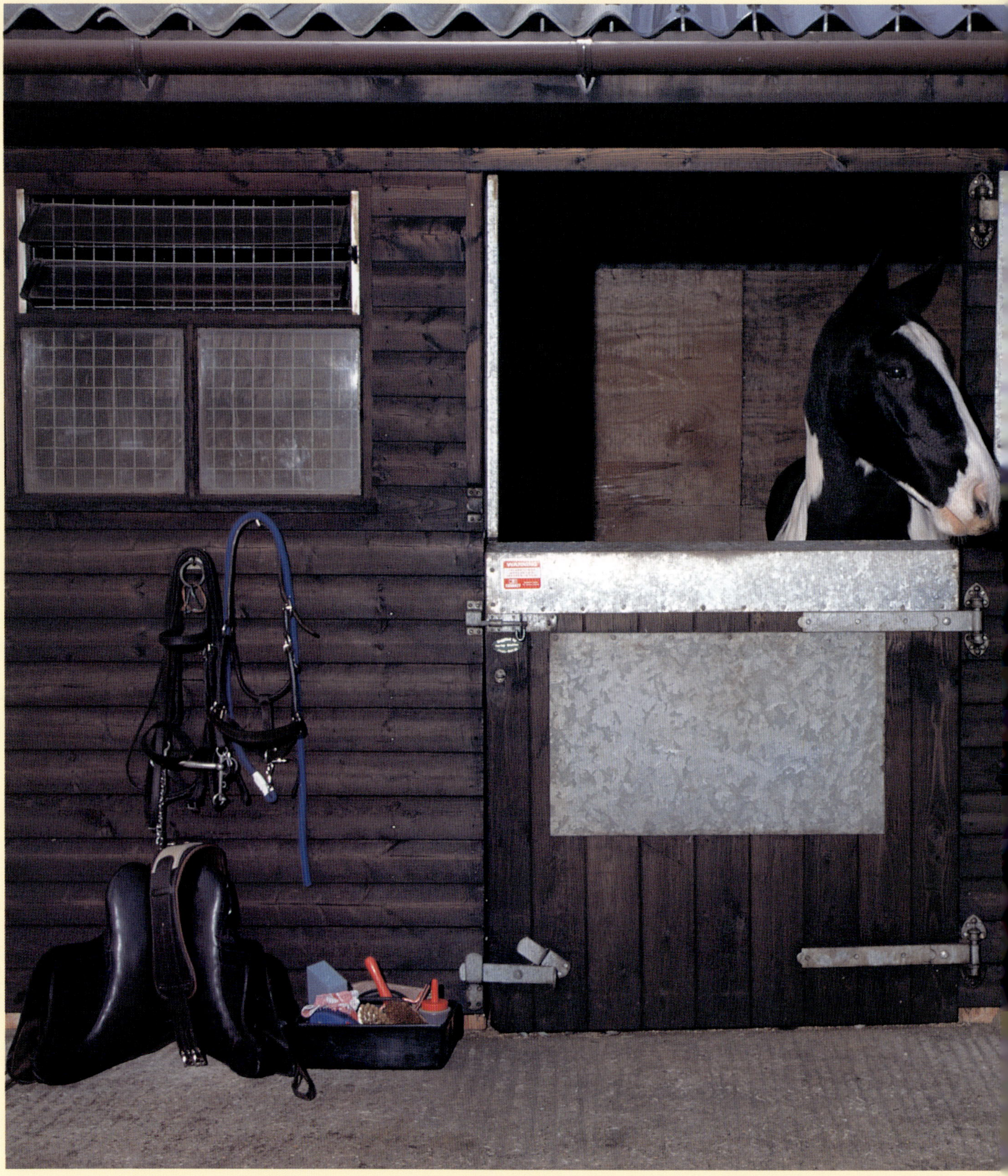

CHAPTER EIGHT

The Well-Equipped Stable

Tools and Fittings
Tack Cleaning
Grooming
At Home in the Horsebox
Show Tack
At Stud
Rugs and Travelling Dress
Bandages and Boots

Equipment in the stable is not confined to the horse's box. It also involves rugs, bandages, boots, grooming equipment and, if there are young horses or breeding stock, halter and service equipment.

CHAPTER EIGHT · THE WELL-EQUIPPED STABLE

Stable Equipment · **Tools and Fittings**

Horses have evolved with a system which is best suited to a nomadic lifestyle, to roam wide areas, not to be shut up in enclosed spaces. It is therefore important for their health and happiness that stables should be large, light and airy, and that they should be turned out as much as possible. Horses in the wild do not demonstrate so-called stable vices, more accurately described as stereotypic behaviour, such as cribbiting, windsucking or box-walking; these develop only when they are confined.

Stables can be either individual looseboxes, or looseboxes built within a barn with a central walkway (known as the American barn system). The most important factor is that there should be a constant free flow of air so that the horse's respiratory system is not at risk from dust, spores and ammonia; this also means that good stable design should always go hand in hand with a management system designed to keep his environment as free from such hazards as possible. In general, the more room you can give your horse, the better: 12 x 12 feet is the minimum, while mares with foals at foot need much more.

Doors should be in two halves, and the top half should be kept open except under emergency conditions; the bottom door should fasten at the top and at the bottom. If the weather turns cold, it is far better to put extra rugs on your horse for warmth than to shut the top door. Dividing walls are best designed with grilles along their top halves; horses are companionable, and this allows them to see and touch noses with their neighbours, which keeps them much more relaxed and happy than being cooped up alone. Obviously this would not be wise with horses suffering from infectious or contagious conditions. Stallion accommodation should be designed with safety in mind, although they should still be treated as horses, not as wild animals.

Ideally, all stables should have windows at the front and at the back to encourage the free flow of air, though standard commercial designs often provide only a single window on the same side as the door. Windows should be made from unbreakable materials and protected by safe mesh or grilles when necessary. Electric wires and switches should be enclosed so that neither horses nor rodents can chew them.

Horses should have clean, fresh water available at all times. Automatic waterers are labour-saving in large yards, but their disadvantage is that it is not possible to see how much your horse is drinking. Both water and feed containers should be free from sharp edges, and they should always be kept clean. Research shows that some horses are happier to drink from buckets or containers in wall holders than from those placed on the ground.

Mangers can be mounted in the corner, they can be free-standing, or designed to clip on the stable door. Corner mangers

Above: A swing-over safety bar at the bottom of the stable door is a necessary and important additional fastening. **Left:** The American barn system means that those looking after the horses can work in comfort even in bad weather, but buildings must have correct ventilation.

TOOLS AND FITTINGS

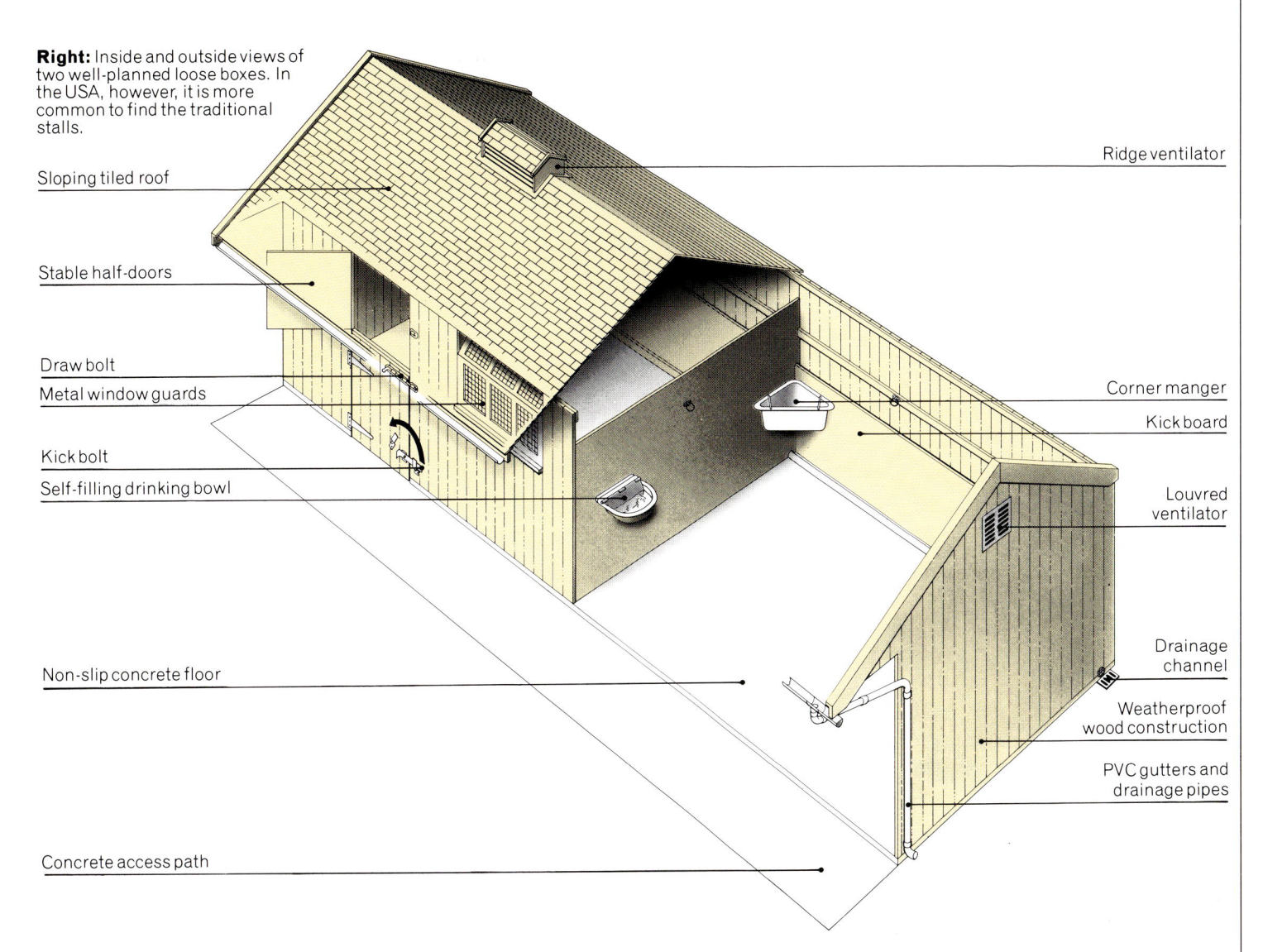

Right: Inside and outside views of two well-planned loose boxes. In the USA, however, it is more common to find the traditional stalls.

- Sloping tiled roof
- Stable half-doors
- Draw bolt
- Metal window guards
- Kick bolt
- Self-filling drinking bowl
- Non-slip concrete floor
- Concrete access path
- Ridge ventilator
- Corner manger
- Kick board
- Louvred ventilator
- Drainage channel
- Weatherproof wood construction
- PVC gutters and drainage pipes

must be at an appropriate height for the size of the horse so that he can eat in a comfortable position. If you prefer to use a free-access salt/mineral lick rather than adding salt to your horse's feed, choose a heavy-duty plastic holder with rounded corners rather than a metal one.

Hay can be fed from the floor or put in a net or hayrack. The first method is more wasteful, because the horse tends to tread some of the hay into his bedding, but it is the way of feeding which accords most closely to his natural manner of grazing. It also avoids the risk of seeds falling into his eyes or ears. Alternatively a hay-box can be made by squaring off a corner of the stable with wooden slats. Haynets can be made from large or small mesh; small-mesh nets encourage the horse to eat more slowly and are more suitable for certain forms of bagged silage where lesser amounts are fed and so where again, the horse might be discharged from eating too quickly. They should be tied to a wall-mounted ring, high enough so that there is no danger of the horse putting his foot through the net as it drops down or it empties, but not so high that he has to struggle to reach it.

Mucking out tools will vary depending on the bedding materials used, and also according to personal choice. An all-round selection would include a four-pronged fork, stable and yard brooms, a shovel, a wheelbarrow or muck cart, and a fork designed for use with shavings or hemp if necessary. Many owners use heavy-duty rubber gloves and pick up droppings by hand, although equine 'poop scoops' are available for those who prefer not to do this! Large yards sometimes use motorized 'vacuum cleaners' to remove droppings and soiled bedding from stables and fields.

Above: Essential equipment for mucking out. On the wall, a stable fork, a rake for boxes laid with wood shavings or peat, a shovel and a broom. In the foreground, a wheelbarrow and a muck box for collecting droppings.

199

CHAPTER EIGHT · THE WELL-EQUIPPED STABLE

Stable Equipment · Tack Cleaning

Ideally, saddlery and tack should be cleaned each time it is used; at the least, it should be given a quick cleaning after use, with a thorough one once a week. If the leather is allowed to dry out, it will become brittle.
Right: Equipment for tack cleaning consists of: 1. Bucket of warm water; 2. Towelling cloth for removing grease and dirt; 3. Leather dressing and application brush; 4 and 5. Sponges; 5. Saddle soap in bar form; 6. Brush; 7. Liquid saddle soap.

Cleaning a saddle: 1. Strip the saddle into its component parts: girth, irons, leathers and girth guards.

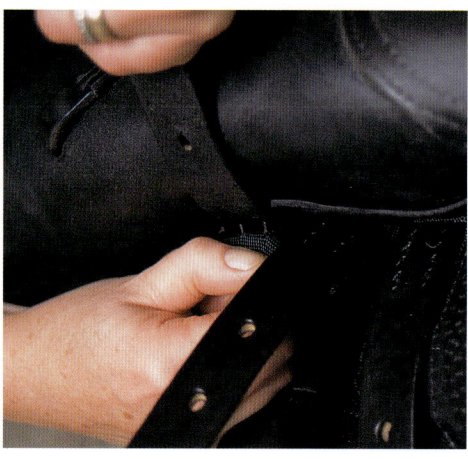

2. Check all areas where there is stitching, especially on the girth attachments, for signs of wear.

3. Check the holes on the girth straps and stirrup leathers, as excessive wear or splits around holes will weaken leather.

4. Check any areas where metal rests on metal, such as where stirrup irons rest on stirrup leathers.

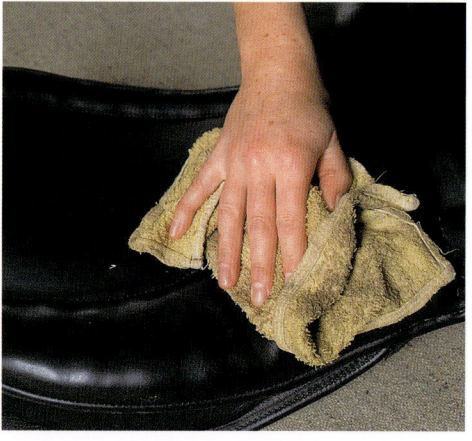

5. If using traditional saddle soap, remove grease and dirt with a damp cloth, which is more effective than a sponge.

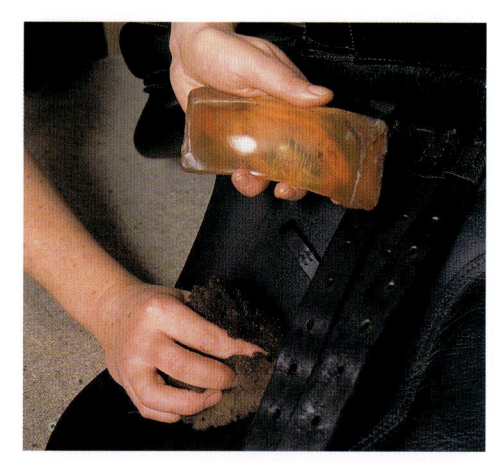

6. Apply saddle soap to both sides of the leather, particularly the flesh (rough) side. If the soap foams, you have used too much water.

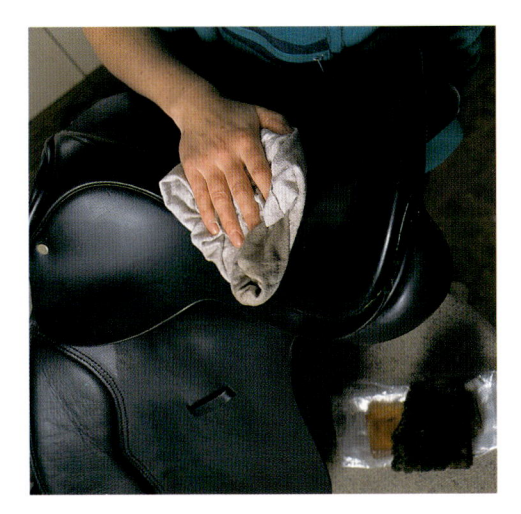

TACK CLEANING

7. Polish the top (smooth) surface of the leather with a cloth to remove excess soap. Pay particular attention to the seat and flaps.

8. Apply leather dressing or oil when necessary. Girth straps take a lot of strain and must be kept supple.

9. If you use a machine-washable girth, put it in a net bag or tie it in an old pillowcase to prevent buckles from damaging your machine.

CLEANING BRIDLES AND BITS

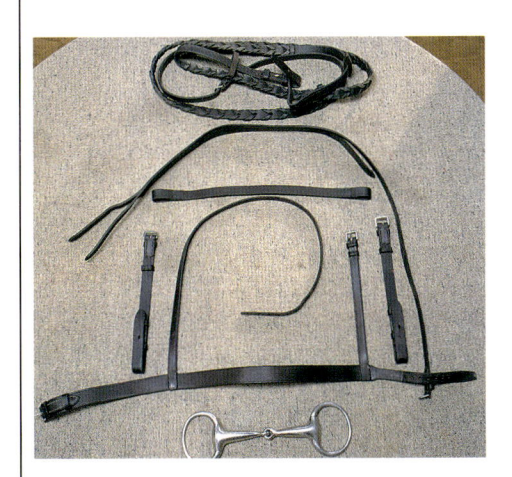

1. Strip the bridle into its component parts: headpiece, cheekpieces, browband, noseband, reins and bit.

2. Some modern saddle soaps clean off both grease and dirt. If using a traditional saddle soap, remove any dirt first with a damp cloth.

3. A nailbrush is useful for easing dirt out of fiddly areas such as laced reins. Try to do this as thoroughly as possible.

4. Apply leather dressing or oil as necessary to the flesh (rough) side of the leather.

5. Clean the bit with a brush and water, then rinse and dry. Do not use metal polish.

6. Finally, check the bit for wear and rough edges, especially around joints.

201

CHAPTER EIGHT · THE WELL-EQUIPPED STABLE

Stable Equipment · Grooming

Daily grooming helps to keep your horse looking good, and it also gives you a chance to check his health because while you are grooming you can feel for unaccustomed heat, lumps, bumps, minor wounds and irritations such as insect bites. Every horse should have his feet cleaned out twice a day, to remove dirt and any stones that might have become lodged, and also so that you can check the condition of his feet and shoes. The equipment used for grooming and the routine followed will depend on the horse's lifestyle: a pony or horse who lives out all the time needs to retain the natural grease in his coat to help protect him from cold and wet, even if he wears outdoor rugs in the worst conditions, so it is best not to brush him too assiduously. A horse who is stabled part of the time and is clipped during the winter may be groomed more thoroughly.

A grooming kit to cover most eventualities would include a hoofpick to clean out the feet; a rubber or plastic curry comb to brush off dried mud and stains; a dandy brush with long, stiff bristles to brush dried mud off a thick coat, and to tease through a thick tail; a version with softer bristles; a body brush with short, fairly soft bristles to remove dust and grease from a thin summer or a clipped coat; a curry comb on which to clean the body brush; a cactus cloth to remove stains; cotton wool for cleaning the eyes, nose, mouth and dock; and a pulling comb for pulling the mane and tail if necessary. Metal curry combs are useful for cleaning brushes, but should never be used on the horse. Which brushes you use will vary according to your horse and the state of his coat: thus a thick-coated Welsh Cob might stand quite happily while you brush off dried mud with a stiff-bristled dandy brush, but a thin-skinned Thoroughbred would probably explode!

Everyone develops his or her favourite grooming items; for instance, some owners find that hairbrushes for humans are effective on manes and tails and less likely to damage the hair. You will want to add hoof oil or polish for special occasions, trimming scissors, fly repellent, a plastic sweat scraper for removing excess water when you have washed your horse, and a rubber grooming brush with soft 'fingers' to remove dried mud. A soft cloth or sheepskin glove gives a final polish, and some people like to use traditional water brushes to dampen the mane and tail to encourage the hair to lie flat. If you are applying a tail bandage, dampen the hair, not the bandage, because bandages will shrink and become tighter as they dry, and this can affect the circulation.

Opposite: A comprehensive grooming kit. 1. Grooming brush which attaches to household vacuum cleaner—an alternative to an electric grooming machine; 2. Hoof oil and brush; 3. Body brush; 4. Water brush; 5. Dandy brush; 6. Cotton wool for cleaning eyes; 7. Plastic curry comb; 8. Rubber curry comb; 9. Cloth for wiping over coat to remove dust; 10. Hairbrushes are preferred by some grooms for brushing out tails; 11. Mane comb; 12. Pulling comb for thinning and shaping manes and tails; 13. Hoofpick; 14. Round-ended trimming scissors; 15. Grooming mitt with cactus cloth on one side and sheepskin on the other; 16. Electric clippers; 17. Battery-powered clippers for trimming small areas; 18. Shampoo/massage glove; 19. Sponge for dock area; 20. Sweat scraper.

Electric grooming machines are useful in large, busy yards but the job should always be finished by hand. Whenever possible, the horses should not be groomed in their stables, as in doing this you are polluting their living environment with dirt and dust. Grooming equipment should be cleaned regularly, and each horse should have his own kit. Conditions such as ringworm are easily spread if brushes used on an infected horse are then used on others.

As well as a grooming kit, you should have separate first-aid kits for horses and humans. It is possible to buy complete kits, or you can put together your own.

Whichever you prefer to do, always check with your veterinarian and doctor that you have included everything necessary.

If you decide to clip your horse yourself, rather than paying a professional to do it for you, you will need a set of electric or battery-operated clippers. Battery-powered clippers are often quieter, which can be an advantage with an inexperienced or nervous horse, but only the full-size versions will have the power to tackle a woolly coat successfully, or to clip a big horse right out without overheating. Small battery-operated trimming clippers can be useful for trimming awkward areas such as faces and heels.

Left: A groom in the stable of King Ashurbanipal of Assyria attending to his horse and adopting a stance that would have the approval of modern instructors. **Below:** An early American grooming machine of the late 19th century in action. The brush revoled at the rate of 500 to 600 times per minute and was driven either manually, through a system of belts, pulleys and counterweights, or by a small gas engine. It was claimed that 'so searching and vigorous is its action that a perfect cloud of dust is raised from the horse's skin'.

CHAPTER EIGHT · THE WELL-EQUIPPED STABLE

Stable Equipment · **At Home in the Horsebox**

Right: A well-equipped horse being loaded into a well-designed horsebox—the recipe for successful travelling. If horses are to load happily and travel comfortably, ramps should be non-slip. This also dampens the noise from clattering hooves, which can frighten horses when entering a horsebox. **Below:** Going to a show or competition means taking a lot of equipment with you. 1 and 2. Your horse's tack and protective boots if needed; 3. Lunge rein in case you want to lunge your horse to settle him or need extra control when loading; 4. A selection of rugs for varying temperatures and conditions; 5 and 6. Water container and bucket; 7 and 8. First aid kits for horses and humans; 9. Filled haynet.

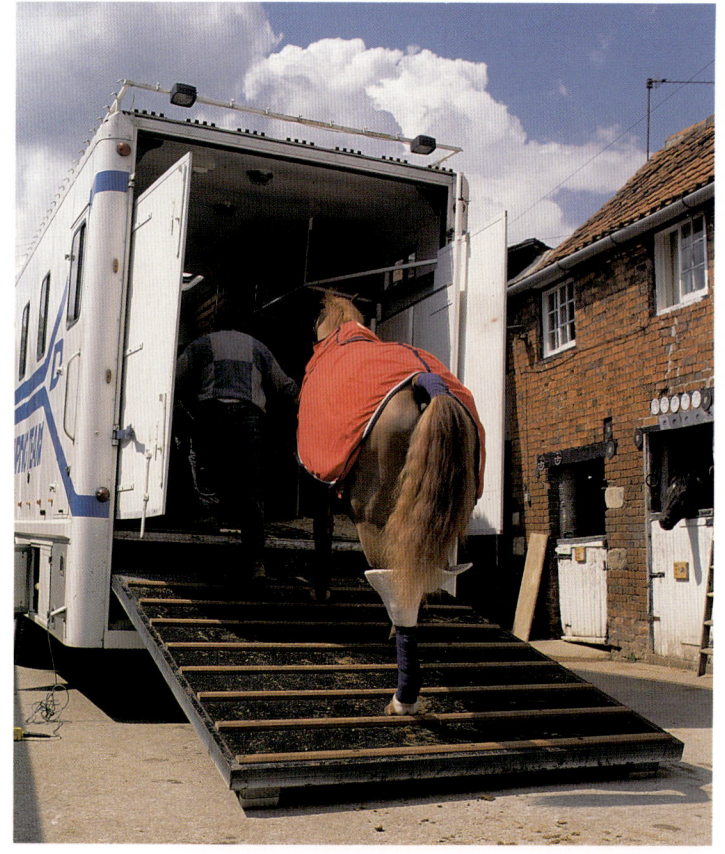

AT HOME IN THE HORSEBOX

Above: A two-horse trailer. As well as accommodating the horses, their fodder and saddlery, this horsebox is also equipped with a dressing room for the riders. **Left:** A modern American gooseneck trailer. Vehicles must be light and well-ventilated, but not draughty.

CHAPTER EIGHT · THE WELL-EQUIPPED STABLE

Stable Equipment · Show Tack

The show ring provides a shop window for breeders and producers of all types of horses, be they English hunters, American Saddlebreds or native ponies. While traditions and practices regarding showing vary on each side of the Atlantic, basically the objective is always for horse and rider to be equipped and turned out to the highest possible standard. Fashions are not universal either: for instance, English show hunters traditionally wear workmanlike bridles with broad, flat nosebands, while American riders prefer less substantial bridlework, usually with padded nosebands, for equivalent classes.

The best way of deciding how to present your horse is to study the top competitors in the category in which you intend to specialize; you will soon develop an eye for the styles which would complement your horse and will thereby avoid making obvious mistakes. There are many pitfalls for the unwary, particularly in the English show ring—for instance, a browband covered in velvet ribbon would be in perfect style for a hack, but it would be frowned upon for a hunger or cob. Breed societies will also offer guidance, and these have their own fashions and traditions: for instance, Welsh Cob mares and young stock are traditionally exhibited in white webbing halters; and Arabians wear fine bridles and halters made from reinforced rolled leather, often with ornate silver inserts.

Showing falls into two broad categories: in-hand, or halter, classes, and ridden classes. In-hand classes are for breeding stock and young horses up to three years of age, and in many cases, young horses are expected to be shown in full bridle. Yearlings and two-year-olds are best equipped with mild, mullen-mouthed or straight-bar snaffles; these are equally suitable for three-year-olds, though some producers prefer to show these in double bridles.

The obvious risk is that a young mouth can be made insensitive or one-sided by poor handling. Double bridles are perhaps best avoided except by expert handlers, while a snaffle bridle should be used with a coupling that links the bit rings and also fastens to the noseband; this provides a more even pressure and means that the nose is also used as a control point rather than just the mouth. Stallions are always shown in a bridle to give the handler full control. Some breeds may be equipped with full stallion tack: a bridle with straight-bar bit and fancy horseshoe rings instead of plain ones, side-reins and crupper.

With ridden horses, the tack should complement the horse's conformation rather than detract from it. For example, saddles should be cut straight so as to show off the slope of the horse's shoulder, not cover it up. Although it is often correct—and advisable—for novice horses to be shown in snaffle bridges, double bridles are required

SHOW TACK

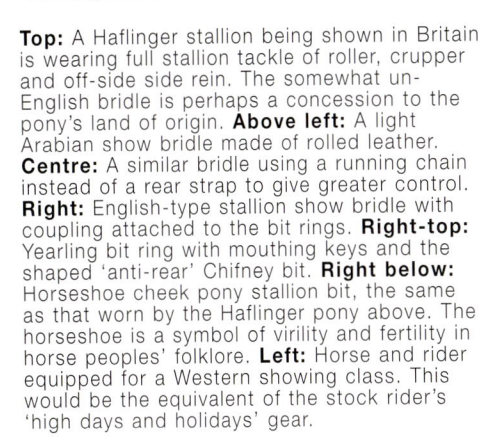

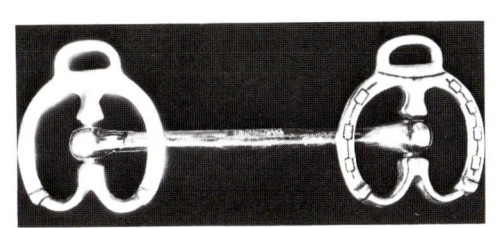

Top: A Haflinger stallion being shown in Britain is wearing full stallion tackle of roller, crupper and off-side side rein. The somewhat un-English bridle is perhaps a concession to the pony's land of origin. **Above left:** A light Arabian show bridle made of rolled leather. **Centre:** A similar bridle using a running chain instead of a rear strap to give greater control. **Right:** English-type stallion show bridle with coupling attached to the bit rings. **Right-top:** Yearling bit ring with mouthing keys and the shaped 'anti-rear' Chifney bit. **Right below:** Horseshoe cheek pony stallion bit, the same as that worn by the Haflinger pony above. The horseshoe is a symbol of virility and fertility in horse peoples' folklore. **Left:** Horse and rider equipped for a Western showing class. This would be the equivalent of the stock rider's 'high days and holidays' gear.

for seasoned campaigners in English categories and in American classes such as park horse and English pleasure. Equally, it is quite acceptable for English exhibitors to use a pelham bridle with double reins, but never with roundings and a single rein.

An important but often neglected aspect of showing the ridden horse is that the tack must be comfortable for the judge as well as for the exhibitor. This means paying attention to details such as the size of the saddle seat and stirrup irons, and the length of the leathers—the former must be large enough to accommodate a generously proportioned judge, if necessary!

207

CHAPTER EIGHT · THE WELL-EQUIPPED STABLE

Stable Equipment · **At Stud**

Relatively little equipment is required for stud purposes, beyond the items necessary to control the stallion and to protect him against a mare who may kick during the mating process.

The stallion has to be under control both when being led in the vicinity of mares and during the performance of his stud duties. At most studs, a strong stallion bridle is used; this, by tradition, is brass-mounted. The bridle is of particular importance, since a stallion will quickly come to associate it with the act of covering a mare and will be aroused sexually by its being fitted. The bit employed is usually a straight-bar metal one. A strong, leather lead, somewhat longer than usual, is also necessary. This can be fitted with a stout length of brass chain with a strong snap hook.

Twitches and hobbles
Slightly more equipment is necessary for the mare. At one time twitches were regarded as essential to keep the mare still and to prevent her from kicking at the stallion, but modern studs tend not to use them as standard. It used to be thought that twitches caused discomfort, but it is now known that the pressure they put on the horse's upper lip stimulates the production of natural 'calming chemicals' called endorphins. Having said that, there is still the occasional animal who will fight any form of restraint.

The traditional twitch is made from a loop of cord fastened to a short piece of wood—often a piece of broom handle. The metal 'humane twitch' is now more generally used and looks like a pair of large nutcrackers. Twitches should only be used on the upper lip.

At some studs mares are hobbled, so that they cannot kick. The hobbles on the hind feet are fitted with a central strap, which passes forward between the forelegs and culminates in a neck strap. Often such hobbles are fitted with a quick release device in case of emergency. Sometimes a thick strap is used to fasten up a foreleg,

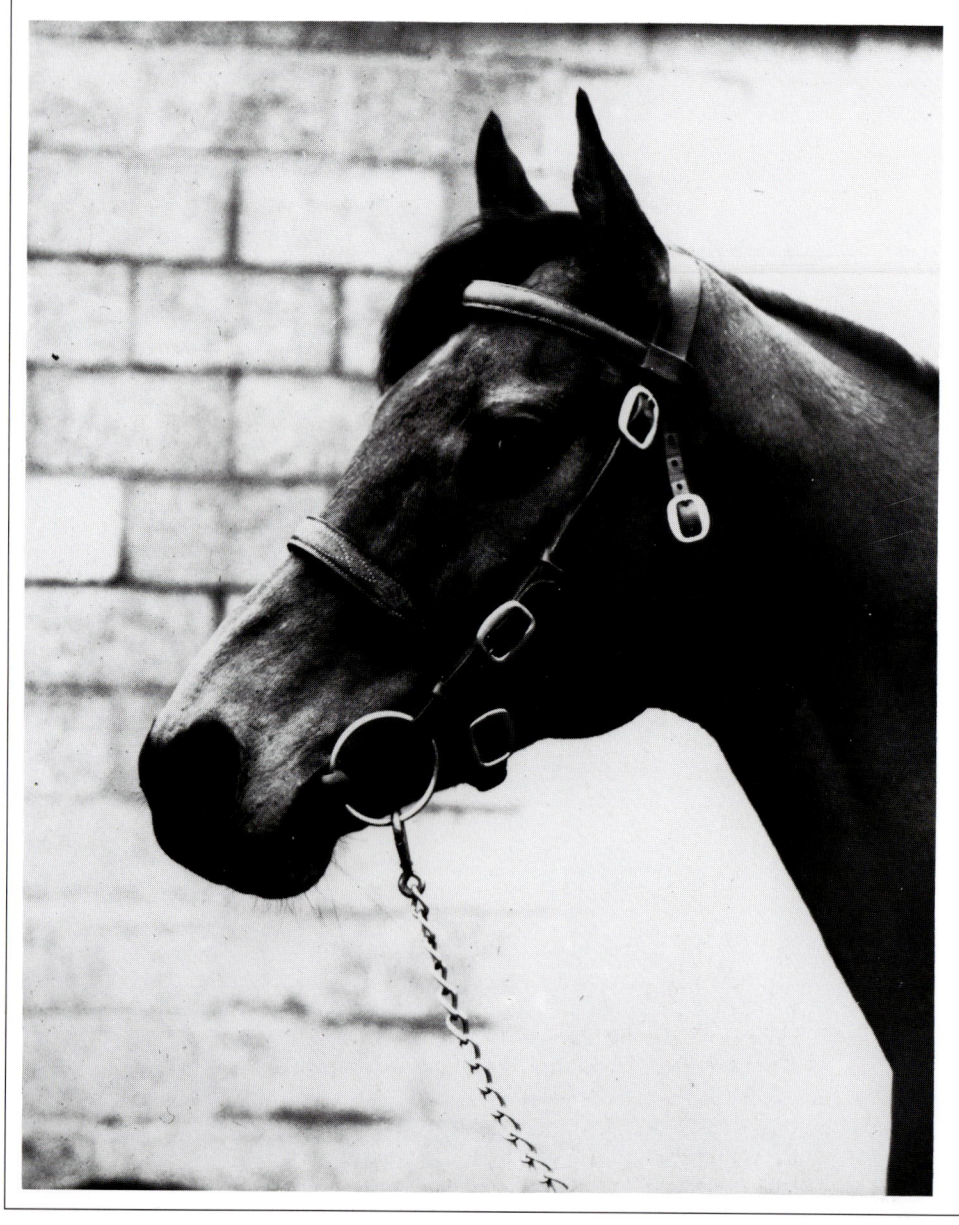

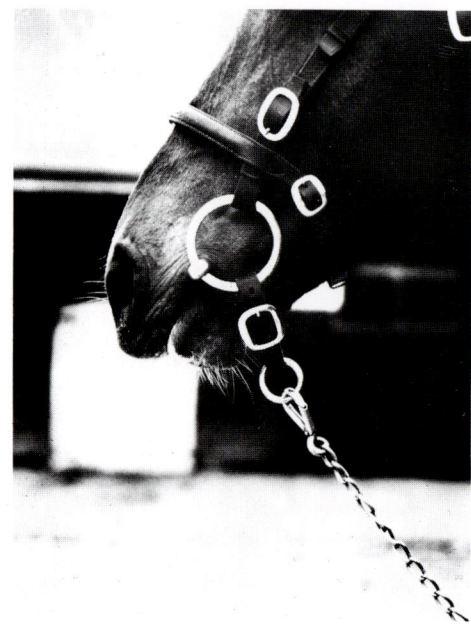

Left: A brass-mounted stallion bridle with chain lead. **Above top:** A straight-bar stallion bit. **Below:** A stallion bridle with a lead couple connecting the bit rings. The stud equipment of stallions falls into two categories—equipment to control the horse and that to protect him during serving.

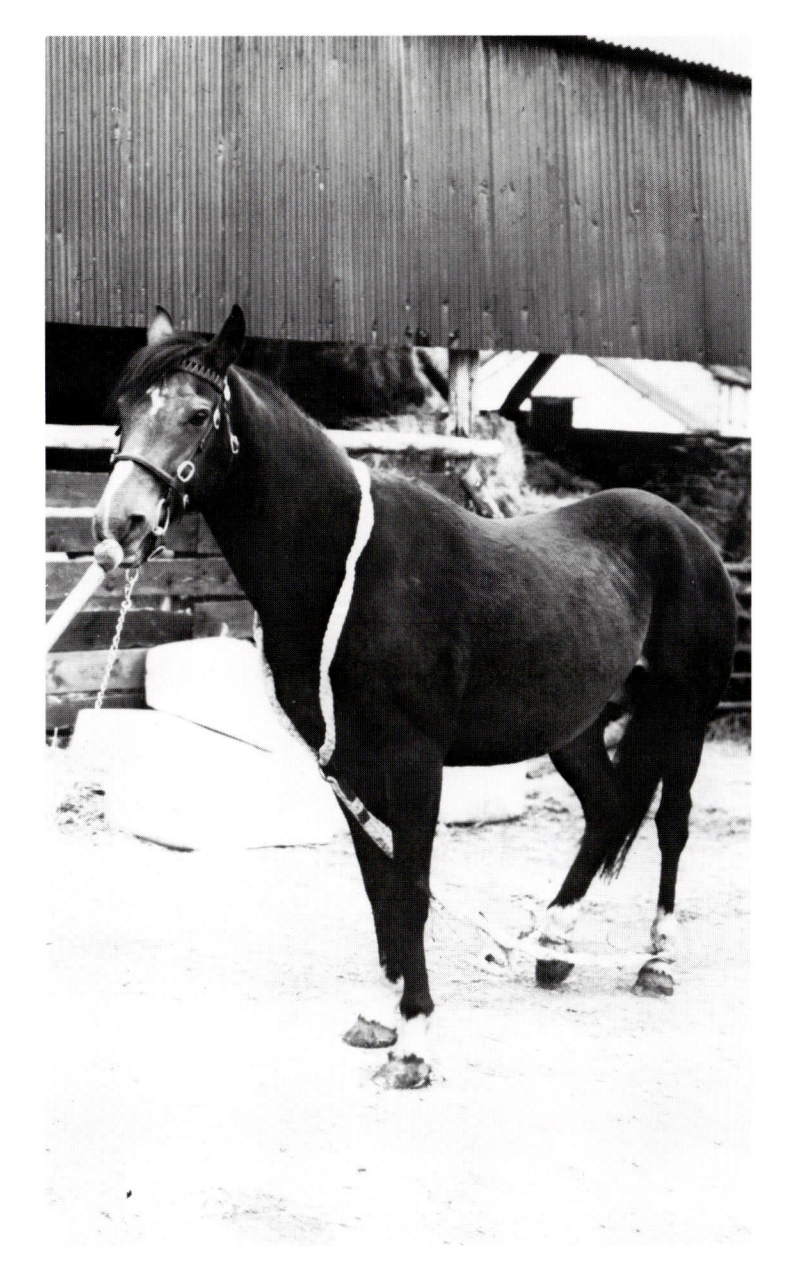

Left: Service hobbles are used as a precaution against the mare kicking the stallion as the latter attempts to serve her. **Above:** Thick service boots of felt. These are fitted to the mare's hind feet as another safeguard against her kicking. **Right:** A neck cover will prevent the stallion from biting the mare's neck during a service. **Below right:** It is standard practice to put a tail bandage on a mare that is to be served. **Bottom left:** The standard type of foal slip which can be made in soft leather, webbing or even in nylon.

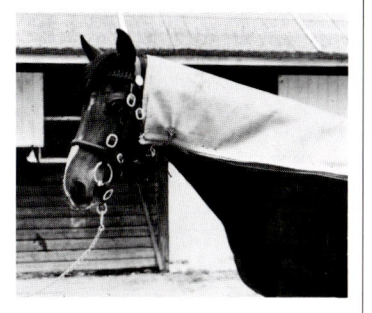

which is a common method of control. Many studs, however, prefer to rely on a pair of 'kicking' boots made from very thick felt and to dispense with hobbles and leg straps.

A tail bandage is almost always put on a mare who is to be served, so that her tail hairs will not cut the stallion's organ, while nervous mares can be fitted with a pair of blinkers, so that they cannot see the stallion's approach. These are often extremely effective. Some stallions, when they have mounted the mare, will bite her neck in front of the withers quite severely. To protect the mare from these love bites, she can be provided with a harness collar, which the stallion can bite, or a thick rope 'necklace'.

Foals are nearly always provided with a headcollar of the 'Dutch slip' pattern, which is easier to put on than other varieties and is easy to adjust. Such headcollars are made from either soft, tubular webbing or supple leather and are fitted with a lead tag.

CHAPTER EIGHT · THE WELL-EQUIPPED STABLE

Stable Equipment · Rugs and Travelling Dress

Rug design and manufacture have been revolutionized by lightweight, breathable materials that make both horses' and owners' lives more comfortable. Gone are the days when rugs were inevitably heavy and difficult to clean, and many modern designs can be washed in household washing machines. Fabric technology also means that some rugs can be multi-purpose—for instance, rugs made from lightweight, thermal fabrics can be used in the stable, for travelling and to dry off a sweating horse or one that has been bathed.

However, high-tech materials can only do their job if the rug is well designed and of the right size and proportions. Cheaper rugs are usually not shaped as well as the more expensive ones, which means they are less likely to stay in place and more likely to cause pressure points and rubs. Fastenings should also

Left: An exercise sheet helps keep the quarters and loins of a clipped horse warm. **Below:** A New Zealand rug with cross surcingles, cut to allow freedom of movement at the shoulder.

210

RUGS AND TRAVELLING DRESS

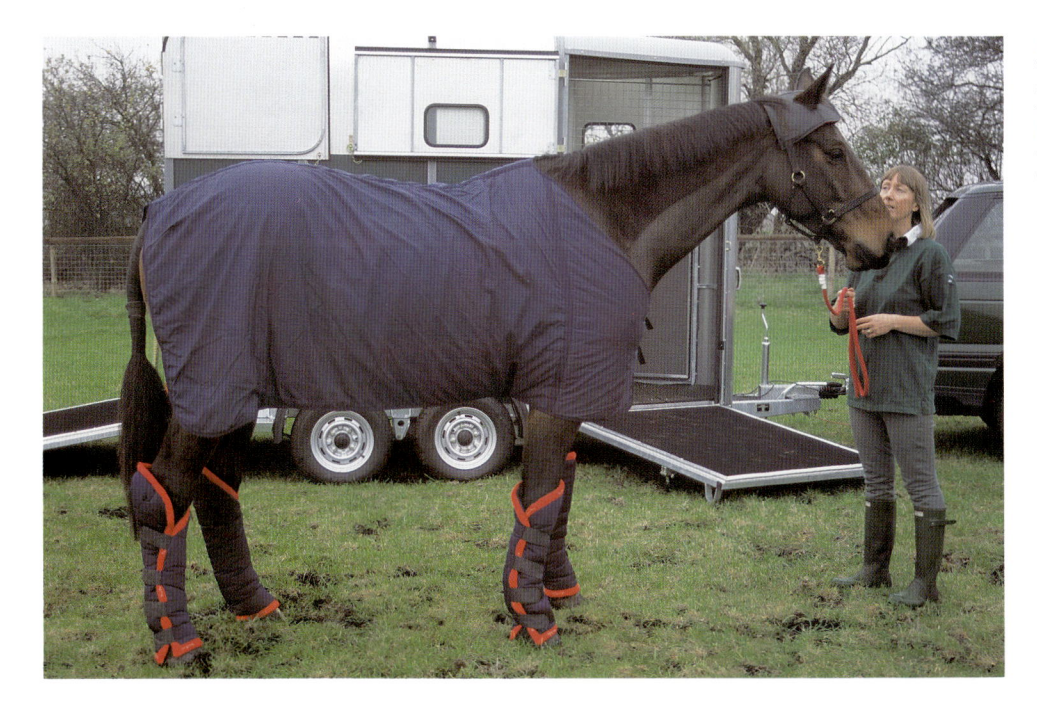

Left: A horse correctly equipped for travelling. Note the poll guard, which is a sensible precaution for big horses or those who tend to throw their heads up.
Below: New Zealand rugs such as this one should stay in place when the horse gallops or rolls.

be of good quality and design; metal which rusts or cross-surcingles anchored at a single, narrow point will not stand up to the strain of a galloping or rolling horse. Having said that, for safety's sake there must always be a breakage point because if a horse manages to get his rug caught up on something, it is better for the rug to break than for him to risk injury should he panic.

Fitting a rug

To find out what size rug your horse needs, measure him from the centre of the chest, along his side to the back of the quarters. Measuring from just in front of the withers, along the centre of the back to the top of the tail gives an additional guideline when comparing one design with another. The neck should be cut high to prevent the rug gaping and slipping back. A badly fitting rug can cause as much damage as a badly fitting saddle: white hairs on the withers are often a sign that the horse has worn a rug which pulls across this area. No matter how well the rug fits, it must be removed and replaced at least once a day so that you can check the condition of the horse and make sure it is not putting pressure on a particular point.

Types of rug: outdoor rugs

Rugs fall into two basic types, indoor and outdoor, although there are some which can be used for both purposes; there are

CHAPTER EIGHT · THE WELL-EQUIPPED STABLE

VINTAGE AMERICAN HORSE CLOTHING

A selection of clothing from an American trade catalogue of the early 1900s. **Top left:** A 'cooler' or 'round blanket' used when walking out horses after exercise. **Top right:** A jowl or throat sweater employed to reduce fat in those areas. **Centre right:** A full-neck sweating hood. **Bottom left:** A set of hot weather net clothing. **Bottom centre:** Complete English-style suit of walking clothing including a breast cloth. It was used when stallions were walked round the countryside to serve mares at pre-arranged points and also as hunter clothing when the latter were walked to meets. **Bottom right:** A heavy sweating blanket. It was once the practice to sweat horses as part of their conditioning programme. It is possible that this practice originated in the Middle East, where it still takes place.

also many styles within each category. For instance, some outdoor rugs—often called New Zealands, as this is where they originated—are designed to withstand harsh conditions for long periods, whereas others simply give enough protection to the horse turned out for just a couple of hours, and it is unrealistic to expect the second type to do the job of the first.

Traditional New Zealand rugs are made from canvas, which only reaches its maximum efficiency when it has become wet and then dried again two or three times so that the fibres swell; it may need reproofing at the start of every season. Because of this extra bother and cost, machine-washable, breathable rugs have become increasingly popular. Many of the latter are made from fabrics with a special coating, and it is important to follow the manufacturers' cleaning instructions, as washing at too high a temperature may destroy the rug's waterproof qualities. Lightweight rugs must be well shaped around the quarters, as horses will always turn their backs to wind and rain, and a rug which blows up results in a cold, wet horse. Some have a fillet string, which fastens from one side of the rug to the other underneath the tail and helps to prevent this; generally, however, the rug will have leg-straps and an elongated tail-piece to keep it in place over the quarters.

Stable rugs

Indoor or stable rugs for everyday use were at one time made from jute, which was heavy, difficult to clean and soon became smelly. Quilted fabrics with cotton linings have made life much more pleasant and are available in different weights. Some manufacturers offer a 'layer' system, whereby different linings can be added or taken off according to the weather conditions.

Wool or wool-mix day rugs were once traditional in stables; they would be worn in the daytime, when boxes would be cleaned regularly and they were therefore less likely to become soiled. They have been superseded by more practical fabrics, although some owners still like to use them for travelling; they are often embroidered with the owner's or sponsor's name or logo, and act as an advertisement.

Thermal rugs have become increasingly popular; these are made from knitted fabrics which absorb any moisture from the horse's body and allow it to evaporate on the outside of the rug. Because they mould more readily to the horse's shape, they are often more successful on horses of

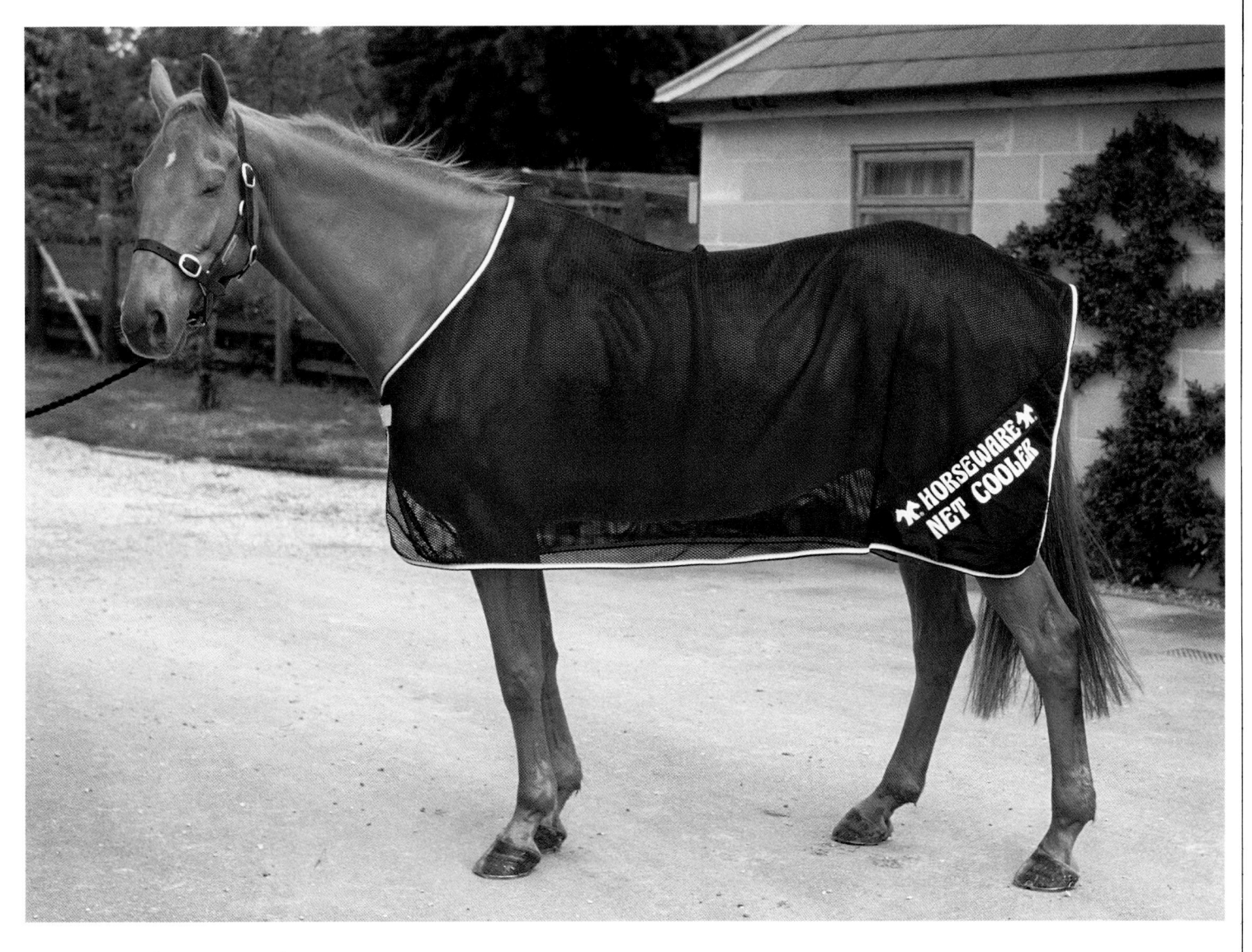

Above: A cooler rug can be used to prevent a hot horse from catching a chill, or when travelling. **Right:** A tailguard in position over the tail bandage.

difficult conformation, where conventional designs often fit badly. As this sort of fabric stretches, it is important that the neckline is well bound to give stability, or that the thermal fabric forms a lining stitched to a tough, lightweight outer layer such as Cordura.

The traditional summer sheet is generally made from strong cotton, and protects the horse from draughts and flies in the summer, particularly when travelling. Such sheets can also be used to protect horses who are photosensitive—that is, suffer adverse effects from strong sunlight when turned out; but obviously they are not particularly hard-wearing. Tougher designs made from white nylon mesh, which reflects the heat and gives protection from insects, were developed (by Thermatex Ltd.) for British horses competing in the 1994 Olympic Games in Atlanta.

There are several styles of anti-sweat rug, or cooler, currently available; these are designed to help a horse which has worked hard to cool down gradually. The racing world still uses traditional mesh rugs—rather like string vests—but these are only effective if a second, lightweight sheet is used over the top because they will only cool the horse by virtue of the layer of air trapped in the mesh holes beneath the sheet. Lightweight thermal fabrics are more effective and simpler to use, however, and some designs incorporate neck covers.

Hoods with eyeholes or neck covers add extra warmth to both outdoor and indoor

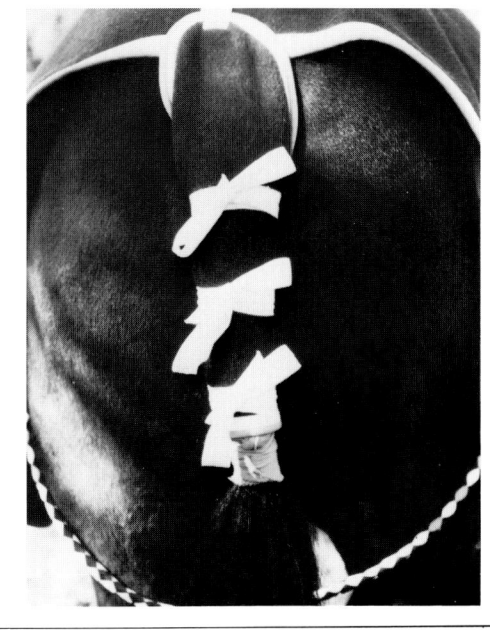

CHAPTER EIGHT · THE WELL-EQUIPPED STABLE

Above and right: Outdoor and stable rugs must be cut high up the neck to prevent them from slipping back and rubbing. The quilted stable rug has a tailflap to give extra warmth.

rugs, but hoods in particular should be used with caution. If they slip and the horse's vision is restricted, he may panic, with potentially disastrous consequences. Neck covers are perhaps a safer bet. One company (Ireland Horseware) has developed a cleverly designed rug which extends farther up the neck than usual, providing extra protection without the need for a separate neck cover.

Clipped horses, particularly racehorses, are often worked in exercise or quarter sheets. These are worn while the horse is being ridden and help to keep the muscles of the back and loins warm. They can be made either from wool, thermal knitted fabric, or fabric with a waterproof outer layer; bright, fluorescent waterproof exercise sheets are a good safety measure in bad weather, as they make the horse more visible to drivers. Some exercise sheets are fitted underneath the saddle and folded back at the front, while others are cut to fit around the saddle and fasten over the pommel.

Fastenings
At one time rugs were held in place by surcingles or rollers which fastened around the horse's body, but even the best designs put unwanted pressure on the withers and spinous processes. Modern fastenings are much safer, and among those more commonly used are cross-surcingles, under-belly harnesses—sometimes called spider fastenings—and leg-straps.

Cross-surcingles fasten diagonally under the horse's belly, crossing in the centre. They should be fastened to allow a hand's width between each surcingle and the belly. Some are made from elasticized materials, which 'give' as the horse moves and breathes and are probably more comfortable for him.

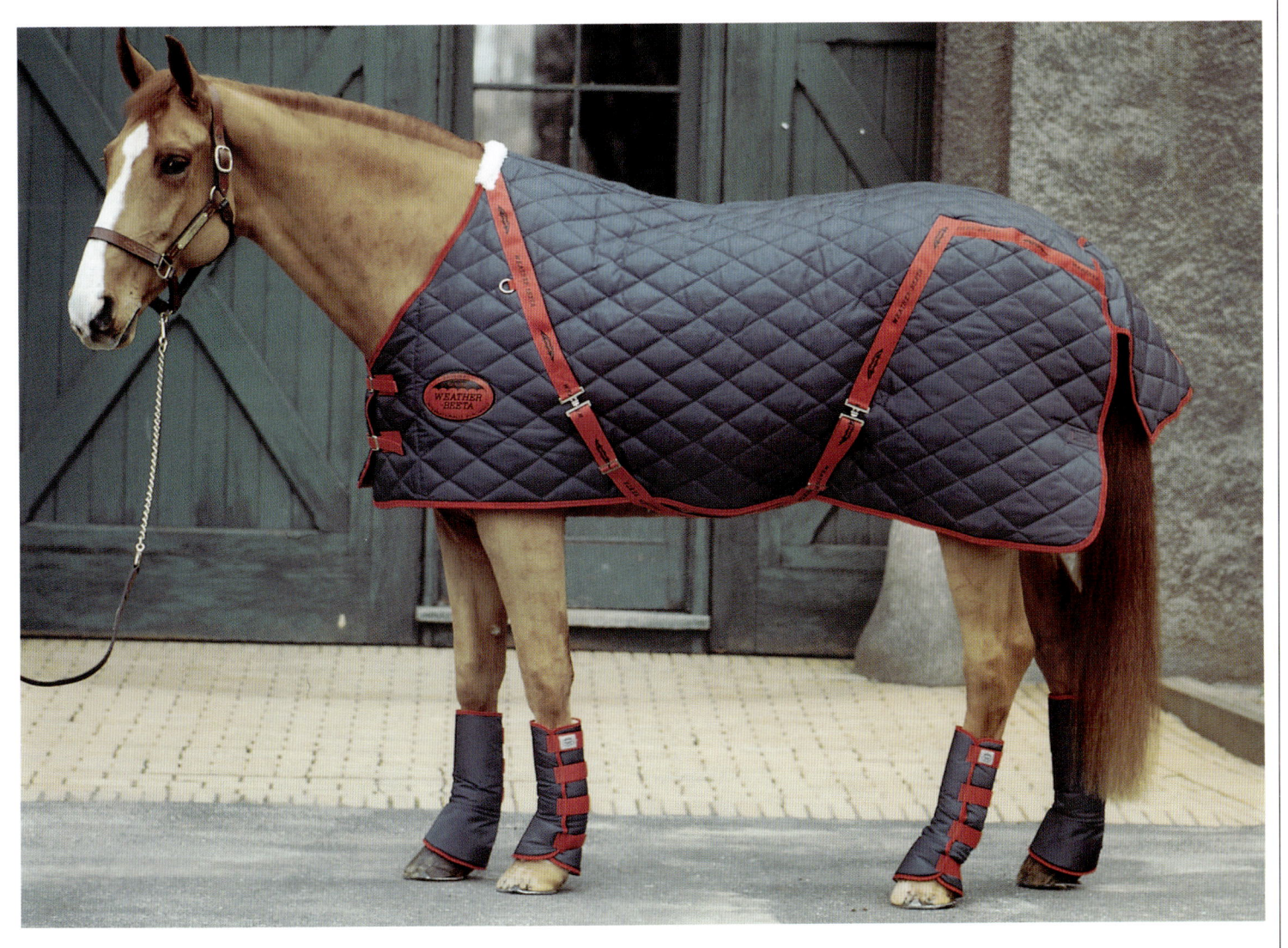

Under-belly harnesses are particularly effective and must be adjusted according to the manufacturer's instructions. Some, but not all, are designed to link between the horse's hindlegs. Rear leg-straps are usually linked between the hindlegs: to secure them, take the left leg-strap, pass it between the hindlegs and through the left strap and finally fasten it to the right-hand side. To fit comfortably, there should be a hand's width between each leg-strap and the horse's thigh.

Dress for travelling
Travelling horses should be rugged according to the vehicle and the weather conditions, and their vulnerable areas—limbs, dock and poll—need protection. Bandages over padding or travelling boots protect the legs and are described in the next section, while a tail bandage and if necessary a tailguard prevents the hair at the top of the tail from being rubbed and broken. The bandage should be applied all the way down the dock, then fastened with tapes or Velcro fastenings.

Tailguards wrap around the dock and are fitted over tail bandages; some designs fasten to the centre back of the horse's rug with long tapes, while others close with a Velcro fastening and are meant to stay in place without extra attachments. An alternative method is to put on a tail bandage as normal, then place a piece of thick foam at the top of the dock and apply another bandage over the top. Enclose the rest of the tail in an old stocking to prevent it from getting dirty on route.

A pollguard is a sensible safeguard for travelling, especially on a big horse and those who tend to throw up their heads. The most effective design is a padded 'cap' with earholes and slots through which the headcollar passes. Horses should always travel in leather headcollars, or halters, or headcollars designed with 'panic inserts' to minimize the risk of injury, and the leadrope should be tied to a string loop, not directly to a metal ring.

Horses should not wear a bit while travelling, as the rings could get caught up and this could lead to injury. However, a horse which is difficult to load is easier to handle and control if he wears a bridle over the headcollar until he is on board. The bridle can then be removed and the horse secured. A Chifney or anti-rearing bit, incorporating a ring which encircles the lower jaw, gives even more control; its effect can be severe, however, in inexpert hands, so it must be used with care.

CHAPTER EIGHT · THE WELL-EQUIPPED STABLE

Stable Equipment · Bandages and Boots

Horses wear bandages for a number of reasons. Principally, bandages are used to protect the horse's tail and legs when travelling; to prevent injury to the limbs should the horse knock itself in the field or when being ridden; a support for the tendons during exercise; to keep the horse warm in the stable; to hold dressings in place when veterinary treatment is required.

The type of tail bandage commonly used is made of a strip of elastic crepe, about 8ft long and 3in wide. This is bound around the tail to keep the hair flat and in place. Such a bandage should always be worn during travelling to prevent the horse from breaking his tail hairs if he rubs his tail on the back of a trailer or against the side of a fence. The tail hair should be dampened before the bandage is applied; the bandage itself, however, should not be wetted, as it might otherwise shrink when in place, causing both discomfort to the horse and damage to the tail. It should be wound around the tail, from the top down to the end of the dock, and then up again for a few inches before being secured.

The same 3in-wide crepe bandages are also used as exercise bandages to support the tendons. Here, they are usually worn over a layer of Gamgee tissue, thick cotton wool, pads of cotton, felt, or other similar material. Such bandages are applied at the top of the cannon bone under the knee and extend down to above the fetlock joint. The tapes of the bandage are fastened securely on the outside of the cannon bone with a knot. Bandages fastened on the inside of the leg are more likely to come undone while the horse is working, since the knot can be caught by a blow from the opposite leg.

The purpose of the bandages is to help in absorbing concussion and to ensure that the pressure ridges, which could damage the tendons, are evened out. When used on horses taking part in strenuous activity, such as competing across country, show jumping or hunting, it is advisable either to sew the bandages in place after tying the tapes, or to bind them with surgical tape. This ensures that the bandage will not come undone, while if surgical tape is used, this will also supply a waterproof covering.

Support must be given to each pair of legs, if it is to be effective—that is, both forelegs have to be bandaged, or both hindlegs. The horse can be bandaged all around if this is considered necessary.

Crepe bandages can also be used to keep dressings in place, or as a cold water bandage for sprains and swellings. A type of ready-made elastic sock can also be used for this purpose. Another innovation is the 'self-stick' variety of crepe bandage. Its use removes the necessity of using tapes.

Wool stable bandages, approximately 5in wide and 8ft long, are particularly useful for keeping a stabled horse warm in winter and protecting the legs of horses in a box or trailer. In the second case, it is particularly important to ensure that the bandage and its padding come down well over the coronet, thus affording protection to the heel. Gamgee or similar padding is again used, though in the case of some bandages, this is unnecessary. This type is made of thick, padded wool, with stockinette at each end.

The bandages are applied between the knee or hock and continue down over the fetlock joint, thus affording more warmth and protection than exercise bandages. They are fastened with strips of Velcro (as in the case of the padded bandages

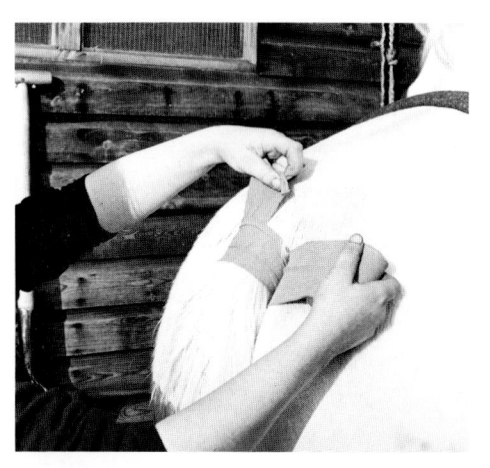

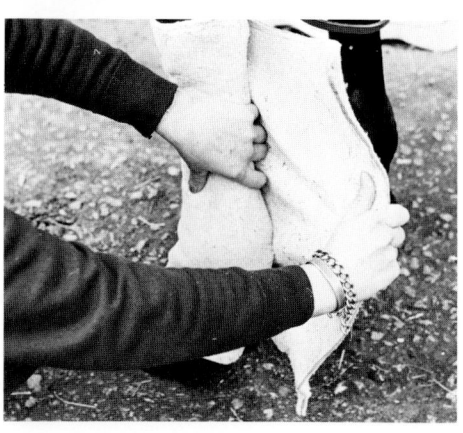

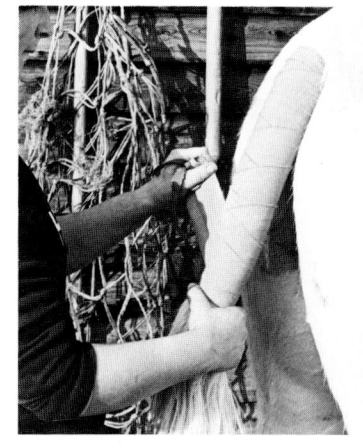

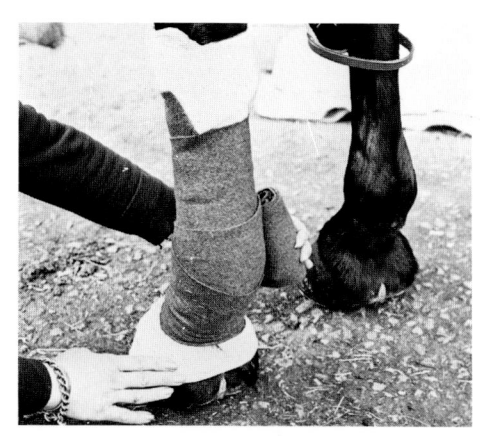

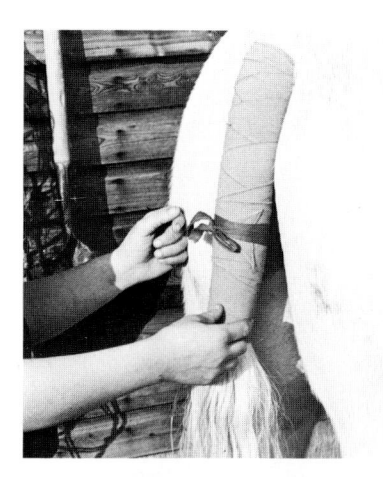

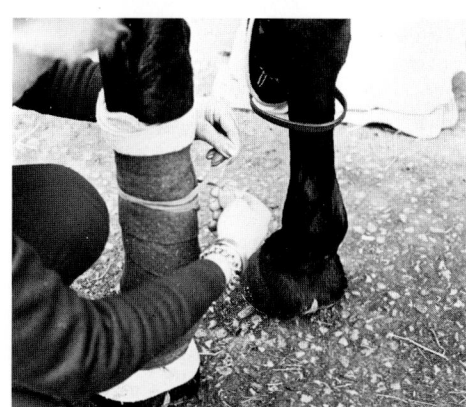

BANDAGES AND BOOTS

Right: Exercise or working bandages in position. These are used to give support to the lower limbs and do not cover the fetlock joint. **Far right:** Travelling bandages, covering the joint, worn with protective hock boots.

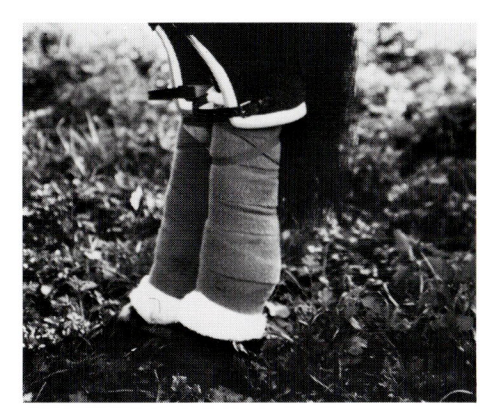

Opposite, top row: The stages involved in putting on a tail bandage. The end of the bandage is held against the tail and turned once to secure it. The process continues evenly down the tail, stopping just short of the last bone. The remaining bandage is wound upward and secured. The bandage shapes the tail and keeps the hairs in place. **Bottom row:** Leg bandages being put on for wear in the stable or when travelling. The bandage, wound over the fetlock joint, is put on over a layer of Gamgee tissue or a felt pad. Not only do they give protection against blows, they also keep the extremities warm.

Above: Anne Kursinski, riding Eros at the Atlanta Olympics in 1996. He wears the open-fronted tendon boots favoured by most show jumpers.

217

CHAPTER EIGHT · THE WELL-EQUIPPED STABLE

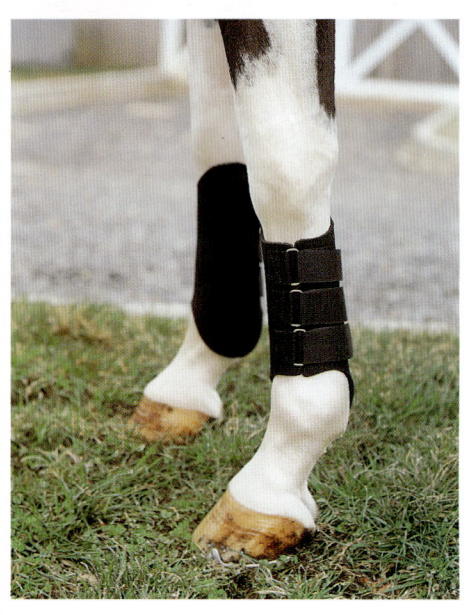

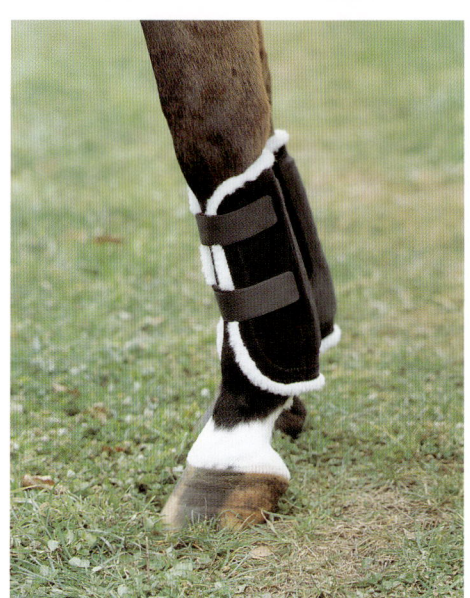

Top row: Side view of knee caps; hock boots designed to protect the joints when travelling; knee caps, also for protection when travelling; skeleton knee boots used for exercise on the roads; hind brushing boots; woof brushing boots. **Middle row:** Foreleg brushing boots with Velcro fastenings; padded travelling boots shaped to cover the hocks; fleece-lined tendon boots; two designs of fetlock boots. **Bottom row:** A very good leather boot, lined with strong foam plastic to protect the inside of the legs and encompass the joint; the cup fetlock boot, lined with foam plastic; the basic, but very effective, brushing ring; modern boots made from lightweight but impact-absorbing materials, comfortable for the horse and easy to clean.

218

BANDAGES AND BOOTS

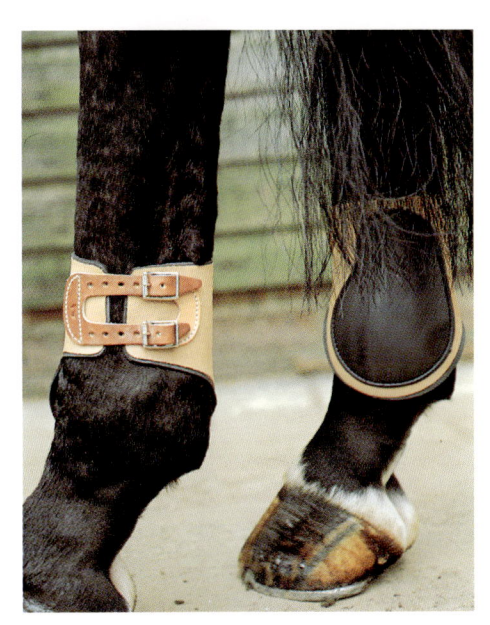

described above), or tapes. Velcro strips are quick and easy to apply, but their use can present a problem. The noise of the Velcro being unfastened can startle a young or nervous horse and care should be taken accordingly. If tapes are used, they should again be fastened on the outside of the cannon bone.

Boots
Protective boots are used when working or travelling horses to prevent injuries to the limbs. Travelling boots are quicker to put on and remove than bandages, but some designs have a tendency to slip. As long as they are well shaped and cover the leg from above the knee or hock to the coronet, boots can be efficient and convenient; but for long journeys, or if a horse is a restless traveller, bandages are the safest option. Some of the cheaper varieties of travelling boot are no more than padded oblongs with Velcro fastenings and usually do not give either the stability or protection that is necessary.

Alternatively you can use bandages together with reinforced knee and hock boots to protect the joints. The main advantage is that these boots need very careful fitting: each type has a strap at the top and the bottom; and the top strap must be fastened tight enough to prevent the boot from slipping down the limb, but the bottom one must be loose enough not to interfere with the flexion of the joint.

There are many types of boots for use on the ridden horse, all aimed at preventing specific sorts of injury. Some riders use boots as a matter of course on all animals, even when they are turned out in the field; others prefer to fit them only for specific reasons—for instance, to protect the

CHAPTER EIGHT · THE WELL-EQUIPPED STABLE

Above: Coronet boots, giving protection against blows or treads. **Left:** A selection of modern boots to give all-round protection.

tendons while jumping or to safeguard a horse with faulty action from knocking one limb against another. However, it surely makes sense at least to put boots on young and/or unschooled horses who lack balance, and on those who are jumping or doing fast work.

In some circumstances boots can *cause* rather than prevent problems. For instance, if they are worn frequently and for long periods, the horse may sweat underneath them and eventually the skin may become irritated or softened and consequently be more prone to infection. Furthermore, sand or mud may work its way underneath the boot, causing similar problems; this is why endurance riders often prefer to work their horses without boots even if competition rules permit them. Badly fitting or dirty boots may rub and cause sores in many circumstances.

Boots were originally made from leather, felt and canvas. Leather is still a good material but it must be kept clean and supple—and of course it inevitably suffers if it becomes soaked. Boots made of modern lightweight, washable materials are much easier to keep clean.

Such materials range from plastic and neoprene to Kevlar, which absorbs impacts so well that it is used in bulletproof vests! Some designs can be immersed in hot water and fitted to the horse while still malleable; this allows the boot to mould to the contours of the individual leg, allowing room for, and so avoiding pressure on, lumps and bumps such as splints. These boots can usually be remoulded by placing them in hot water again and repeating the process.

Fastenings can be strap and buckle, strap and clip, or Velcro. Buckles take longer to adjust but stay secure; clips are quick and easy, but some styles loosen or even come undone in use. Velcro is quick and effective, particularly if the straps have a double fastening, but it needs to be kept clean to preserve its adhesive qualities.

Boots should always be fastened on the outside of the leg, so that they are not pulled undone if the horse knocks them. They should fit snugly, but not tightly; for instance, you should be able to fit a finger between the top of a brushing boot and the horse's leg. Boots are usually sold in the following sizes: small, medium and large, or pony, cob and full size—but as with bridles, size often depends more on type than breeding; thus a stocky 14.2hh cob may need larger boots than a lightweight 16hh Thoroughbred.

Type of boot
The most basic type of boot is the brushing boot, which, as its name suggests, is designed to protect the horse who brushes—that is, knocks the inside of one leg with the opposite foot or limb, either because he is unbalanced or because he has faulty conformation leading to poor movement. Brushing boots fit from below the knee or hock to the bottom of the fetlock and have reinforced strike pads down the inside. As with all boots, they must be the correct size for the horse so that they do not interfere with the flexion of the joints or cause rubs. Fetlock, or ankle, boots are specifically designed to protect this particular joint, while polo boots and speedicut boots are similar to brushing boots, but slightly longer.

Skeleton knee boots are often used on young, unbalanced horses when they are

Above: Professional's Choice boots are claimed to support as well as protect tendons. The white overreach, or bell, boots protect the heels.

Above: Overreach, or bell, boots are a sensible precaution for fast work and jumping. They should not be so long that the horse trips over the bottom edge.

first ridden on the road to protect the knees from injury if the horse trips and comes down on a hard surface. They have a reinforced circular pad, and fasten at the top and bottom in a way similar to travelling knee boots, but they are open at the sides instead of being blocked in. Their use is very much a matter of personal choice: some trainers feel they provide essential protection, while others dislike their tendency to slip down the leg.

Overreach, or bell, boots minimize the risk of the horse overreaching—that is, striking the heel of the front foot with the toe of the back one. Even small overreaches can cause problems, as the wounds can be deep and they are in an area that is difficult to stitch. They can also be slow to heal, as they open and close every time the horse takes a step. These boots can be one-piece designs, either pull-on or fastening at a side opening with Velcro or straps, or made from replaceable 'petals' which are threaded along their top edge to a strap which fastens around the pastern. The idea is that if the horse overreaches, individual petals will pull off and can be replaced with new ones. Both types have disadvantages: some bell boots invert occasionally, though there are designs claimed not to succumb to this eventuality, while petal boots can flap in an irritatingly noisy fashion. It is important that bell boots are low enough to give protection, but are not so low that there is a risk of the horse treading on the bottom edge and tripping.

Tendon boots are a sensible precaution for horses who are galloping or jumping—it is all too easy for a back shoe to strike into a front tendon, with horrific effects. Although it is often said that tendon boots support weak tendons that have suffered a previous injury, veterinary surgeons maintain that most designs provide protection rather than support. There may be exceptions: one American design (Professional's Choice Sports Medicine Boots) is claimed to be able to provide support to the deep digital and superficial flexor tendons. Basic tendon boots have a strike pad down the back of the leg and may have closed or open fronts. Show jumpers often prefer open-fronted tendon boots because they believe that if the horse rubs a pole in front, he will be more careful next time. Event riders sometimes choose leg protectors rather than boots—that is, shaped pads which fit over the tendon and are held in place with bandages.

The Yorkshire boot is a simple design that gives light protection, though it would certainly not provide enough for the horse who moves badly. It comprises an oblong-shaped piece of felt with a tape on the outside, and the tape is then tied just above the fetlock and the material doubled over.

Ring boots are substantial rubber tubes with a strap running through the centre. They fasten just above the fetlock and are designed to prevent one leg from coming too close to its pair. Sausage boots, a similar but thicker design, fasten around the pastern and protect the horse who bruises his elbow on the heel of his shoe when he gets up.

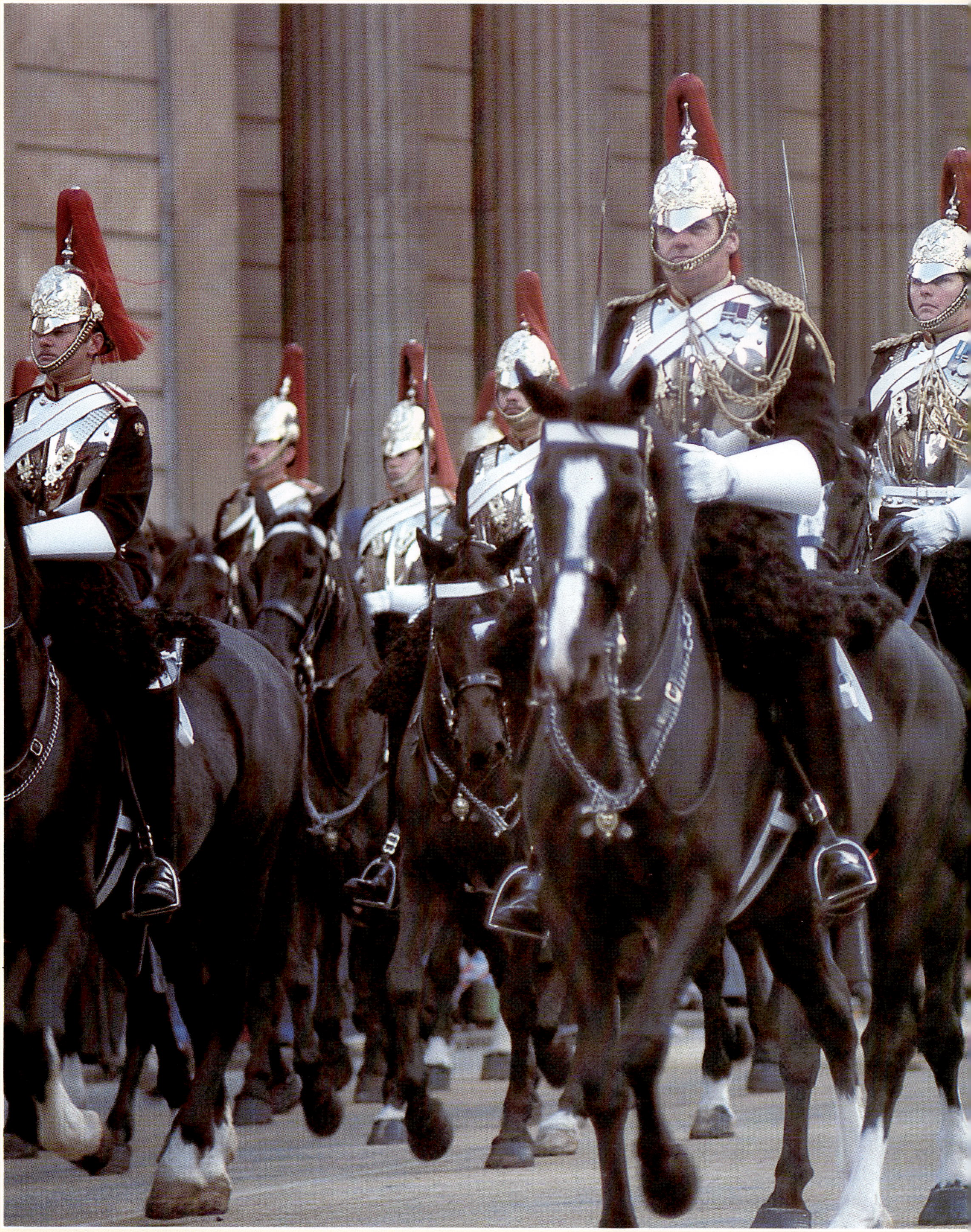

CHAPTER NINE

Ceremonial Trappings

The long tradition of decoration, military and mythological.

Britain's Household Cavalry, the Queen's personal guards, provide an integral part of British ceremonial, attending the Royal family on all state occasions.

CHAPTER NINE · CEREMONIAL TRAPPINGS

Ceremonial Trappings

From the start of man's association with the horse, display and decoration have been a virtually integral part of the relationship. There are two main traditions, one linked to demands of war and the other to the more indefinite areas of custom, myth and ritual.

In India, for instance, at the time of the feast of Dasshera, horses are garlanded and colour applied to their feet and heads as part of this religious festival. Similarly in the east, the horse bearing a bridegroom to a wedding is extravagantly caparisoned in honour of the occasion. In the west, the harness of heavy horses is frequently decorated with brasses. Though considered as decoration today, these owe their origins to something far deeper than mere display. In their various forms and designs, horse brasses are good luck charms, often deriving from pagan beliefs. They were thought to combat the effects of an 'evil eye'. The eastern counterpart is the necklet or anklet of coloured silks or wool, worn for good luck by racehorses and humble tonga ponies alike.

In the past, too, horses have been deified. There have also been times when the horse was considered the most acceptable of sacrifices and the creature most worthy to accompany a noble or royal master to the tomb. Such horses were buried with the accoutrements befitting the station of the late owners. Such trappings, in fact, were the owner's badges or rank, an aspect which often persists in the ceremonial saddlery of today.

Mogul saddles of northern India, for instance, are sometimes decorated with as many as seven yak tails. This practice originated with the Mongols; under Genghis Khan, the *orkhons* (leaders) of the *tumans* (divisions) of the great Mongol horde used a standard adorned with yak tails to mark the position of their horse-borne headquarters in battle. In time, this insignia of authority was transferred to the saddles of high-ranking officers.

Survival on ice

The finest surviving examples of regalia of the early horse peoples are those from the Siberian tombs of Pazyryk. The finds are not only important in themselves; since it is from Central Asia that all subsequent horse cultures derive, the debt extends to much of ceremonial saddlery,

Right: The decoration of working horses is of long standing. Farm horses were turned out in a colourful way for market days, braided and plentifully adorned with horse brasses. Harvest time was also an occasion for decking the horses out in every possible sort of finery. The tradition survives to the present day in show ring classes and in public parades.

CHAPTER NINE · CEREMONIAL TRAPPINGS

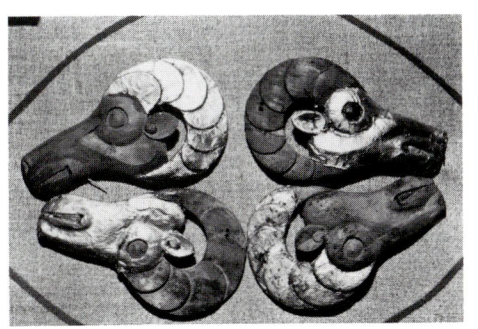

Left: Ornamented bridle from the Pazyryk tombs (5th-4th century BC) in the Hermitage Museum collection, Leningrad. **Above:** Carved moufflon heads used as saddle ornamentation, also from the Pazyryk tombs.

as well as the more utilitarian items of saddlery and horse equipment.

The tombs, situated high in the Altai Mountains of western Siberia, were first opened in 1929 by Dr S I Rudenko, a curator of the Hermitage Museum, Leningrad, the last one—Kurgan (barrow) 5—being explored in 1948, after the Second World War. Because of the climatic conditions peculiar to the area, the contents had been frozen in a bed of ice and thus preserved for over 2000 years.

The probable date when these once nomadic, but then settled, horse people were buried is around 423 BC. Who they were is unknown, but they were obviously of high rank, possessing much wealth, What is very clear is that they belonged to an extremely sophisticated horse culture, in which the ceremonial apparelling of horses in items of leather and cloth, most sumptuously embroidered in gold and silver, was a highly-developed skill. Rudenko himself suggested that these people were the inheritors of a tradition of horse husbandry that might have extended back to about 3000 BC, when their ancestors gave up reindeer in favour of horses.

The equipment found in the tombs was varied and gorgeous. It included, for instance, magnificently embroidered 'saddle' pads of felt and leather, with intricate appliqué designs. One pad fitted on each side of the horse's spine, joined front and rear by a wooden arch. The assemblage was kept in place by a form of belly girth, a breast plate and a sort of breeching passed around the quarters. The early form of military shabraque incorporated into this elaborate piece of equipment was decorated with pictures of birds, beasts and mythical monsters and studded with gold and silver.

Bridles, similarly decorated and of remarkably modern design, were also found on the horses, which were naturally preserved by the ice exactly as they had been at the moment of death. Much ingenuity had been expended on the mane and tail. The former was hogged—a natural development for a race of horse archers, since a flowing mane would obstruct the drawing of a bow. It was provided with a most elaborate case. The tail was also encased in an embroidered sheath, the lower end being plaited and worked with coloured fibres and thongs. Today, tail cases can still be seen at the classical riding schools of Saumur and Vienna and mane covers are in use in Asia and other parts of the east. In addition, the custom of plaiting manes and even tails for special events is commonplace in many regions of the world.

Possibly the most remarkable decoration was the face mask. This could have been a pattern for the medieval chamfron, but for the animals which it simulated. When in place, the mask transformed the head into that of a reindeer, a bird, or beast of prey. The effect was not only to make the horse more impressive, or terrifying, but also taller. Similar devices in the shape of plumes and other head decorations have been used for the same purpose down through the centuries.

The military tradition
Nevertheless, saddlery developed for military use has been the principal factor in the development of ceremonial equipment. This equipment was not entirely the result of what might appear to be the horseman's superficial need for bright display. It was also based on practical

225

CHAPTER NINE · CEREMONIAL TRAPPINGS

necessities, at least in theory. Flattering uniforms, richly decorated, and accoutrements which distinguished one unit from another were undeniable morale boosters for the rank-and-file, as well as providing easily recognizable badges of rank for the officers. The effect of gaily caparisoned bodies of mounted men also had an influence upon enemy infantry standing in stubborn ranks with feet planted in inches of cold penetrating mud.

The very early horse soldiers, such as the Assyrians, fully appreciated the advantages to be gained from impressive accoutrements. Assyrian bridles were richly decorated and studded, as were their chariot fittings. Such equipment was by no means an idle extravagance. The metal decorations were strong enough to withstand a blow from a sword, while the magnificent collars and necklaces also provided positive protection.

In modern terms, however, the military saddlery from which today's ceremonial equipment derives, has a dual origin. One important influence was the saddle used by the medieval knights. It could be argued that the world's military saddles are simplified, cut-down and improved versions of these. This, however, would be an over-simplification, since another influence came from the Mongol warriors and the two combined to affect the whole course of equestrian evolution.

The mercenary pioneers

There is little doubt that the pioneers of the military saddle were the Hungarians. Not only did their designs have the greatest influence on the cavalry of Europe, but also on that of the USA. It is possible, too, that the sartorial example of their dashing hussars set the pattern for innumerable European cavalry regiments.

Hungarian horsemanship contained much that was eastern, or Asian, in concept. There had been for centuries a regular trade in Oriental horses, on which the Hungarian cavalry was almost entirely mounted. In fact as well as by reputation, the Hungarians were Europe's light cavalrymen *par excellence*, following the traditional pattern of eastern and Asian horsemen. Similarly, they adapted the high-peaked Oriental saddle, which held the rider high off the horse's back, merging its design into the less sophisticated, but earlier, Mongol-type saddle, which was well established in eastern Europe.

The Hungarian example deeply influenced some of the chief military thinkers of the day. Surprisingly enough, these were frequently mercenaries. European armies had traditionally employed mercenary troops of other nationalities. Such officers were the true professionals of the day, making deep studies of warfare and acquiring an exceptional level of competence. In this respect, they were excep-

CHAPTER NINE · CEREMONIAL TRAPPINGS

Left: Russian saddle at the Royal Mews, London. It shows a pronounced Asian influence and it is interesting to note that the cushion-shaped seat is not dissimilar from that used by the Argentine gaucho. **Above:** The same saddle with its woven covering of Eastern design. This cover could double as a mat on which to sit or as protection from the cold.

Opposite: Detail of an embroidered saddle cloth from the Pazyryk tombs. **Right:** Another Russian saddle from the Royal Mews collection, which was presented to Queen Elizabeth II by the Russian statesman Nikita Khrushchev. Eastern in concept, the covering is heavy woven silk.

tions to the general rule. Many cavalry officers looked upon their commissions as no more than an agreeable pastime suitable for gentlemen. Although dashing, some were positively incompetent.

The mercenary was largely a European phenomenon and there a high proportion was of Anglo-Irish descent. Celebrated mercenary officers included MacMahon, who became a Marshal of France and President of the Third Republic; O'Dwyer, who served in the Austrian cavalry; and Nolan, who served with the Hungarians. The last was arguably one of Europe's most advanced cavalry thinkers and his death at Balaclava in 1854 ended what might have been a remarkable military career, had he been able to win acceptance from the conservative establishment.

It was largely due to the detailed studies of experts of this sort that the prototype of a near-universal military saddle came into being. Both O'Dwyer and Nolan went into print to explain their theories and the former, in his 'On Seats and Saddles, Bits and Bitting, Draught and Harness', published in the mid-1800s, provided a clear exposition of the Hungarian light cavalry saddle. This consisted of two wood bars, suitably reinforced, which lay on either side of the spine, being placed over a blanket or numnah. The bars were joined front and rear by arches, between which was stretched the bearing strap. This, in

CHAPTER NINE · CEREMONIAL TRAPPINGS

turn, was laced to each bar. The saddle's beauty was that it not only held the rider well clear of the horse's back, but, by adjusting the laces, it could also be fitted to the conformation of the individual trooper, so he was made to sit centrally.

O'Dwyer commented: 'It is just as necessary, or more so, to make the saddle fit the man's seat as to make his coat or boots fit his body or feet; and this is done, after careful observation of the seat, by shortening or lengthening the bearing strap of the seat, or by altering the lacings, till the seat comes right of itself, when you don't need to correct it in the riding school.'

Such consideration for the rider was not

Above: A magnificently worked ceremonial saddle from the Royal Mews, London which is fitted with ornamented holsters. **Above left:** An officer's saddle from the same collection with pouches in place over the front arch.

CHAPTER NINE · CEREMONIAL TRAPPINGS

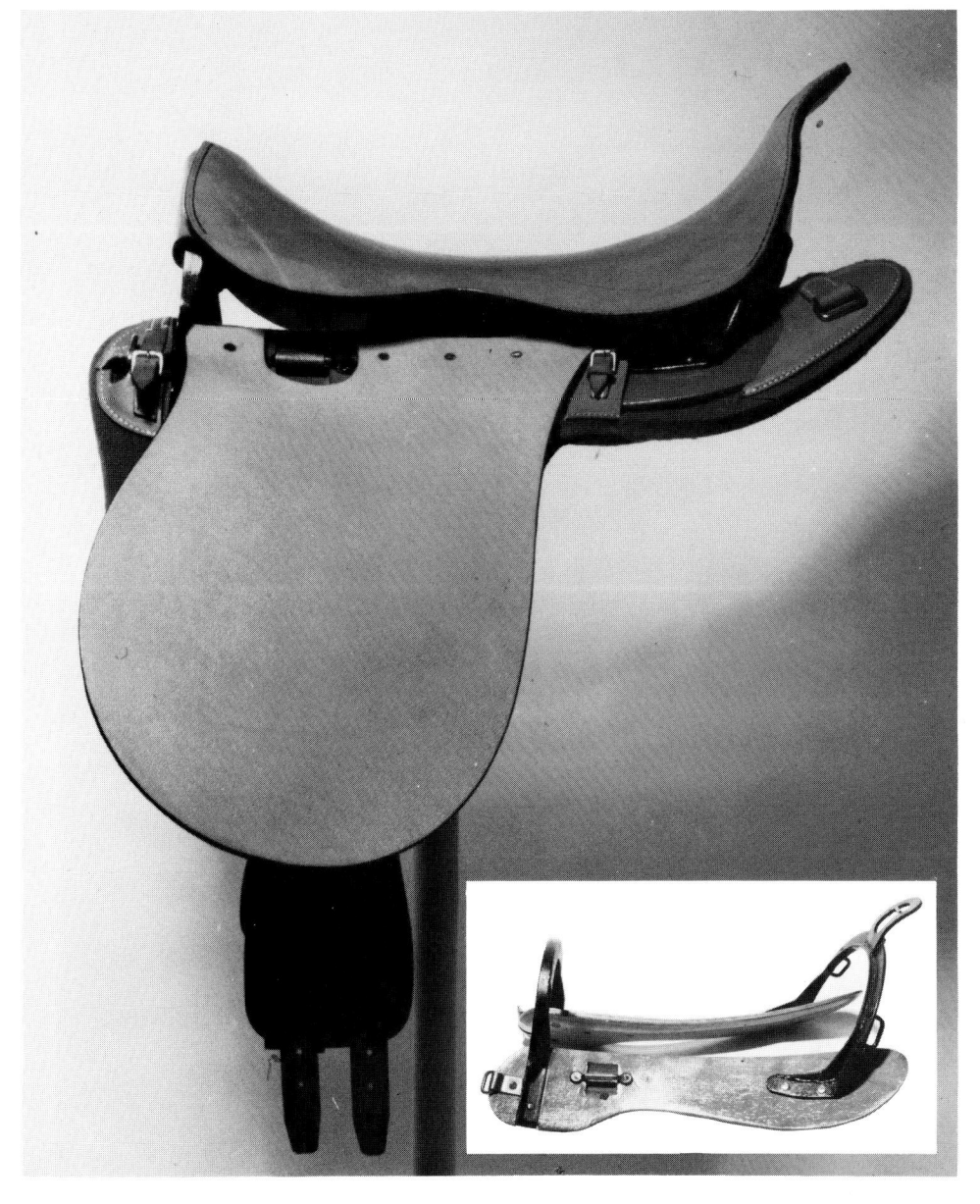

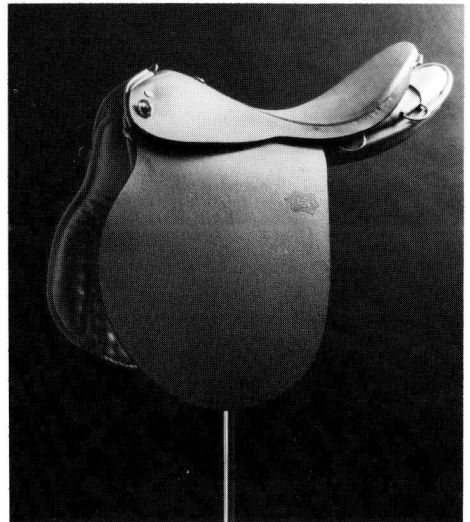

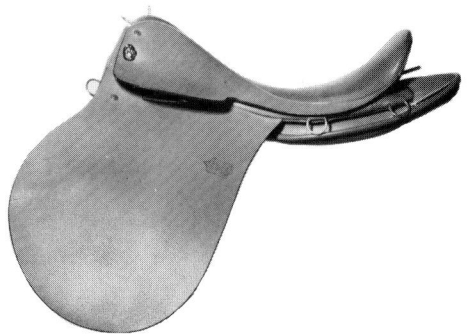

Left: The British Army Universal pattern saddle, developed following the Crimean War and first known as the Nolan saddle. It had its origins in the Hungarian cavalry saddle. **Inset:** The tree, an infinitely practical item which was easily maintained. **Top:** Modern version of the army officer's saddle, recommended for such activities as trekking and long distance riding. **Above:** A modern saddle made for police work which follows the same basic military pattern.

as much in evidence elsewhere, as most of the European derivatives had no such means of adjustment, but the Hungarian principles were followed nonetheless. Following the Crimean War, much attention was given to saddle design. In Britain, the result was the Universal Pattern Saddle (first known as the Nolan saddle), which survives in its essentials today, despite numerous and inevitable modifications. Though other European saddles varied in detail, they followed the same basic form for the most part.

The UP weighed 15lb. It had panels that could be adjusted to fit any back, either with or without the folded blanket or numnah. The dipped seat positioned the rider centrally well above the back, while the stirrup bars were positioned so as to allow the use of a shorter leather if the need arose. It was fitted with an assortment of buckles and slits for the attachment of extraneous gear, while it could be repaired easily—the basic repair kit was a piece of twine, a knife and a screwdriver. Just as important, it had a regulation life of between eight and 14 years, though usually it was serviceable after as much as 30 years of use.

The UP was the trooper's saddle. In almost every other army, except for the US cavalry, officers preferred to use the conventional type of English hunting saddle, possibly with individually designed fittings for attaching various pieces of equipment. Such saddles, though, were not as hard-wearing as the UP; in arduous conditions, they could become unserviceable after as little as a year.

The pack saddle

Almost as important as the riding saddle was the pack saddle, for armies depended upon pack transport for the movement of supplies well into the 1900s. Again, the British version, known as the Universal Purpose Pack Saddle, had the same basic pattern as that used throughout Europe. The saddle was really no more than a pair of side bars joined by a strong metal front and rear arch, to which were fitted hooks

229

CHAPTER NINE · CEREMONIAL TRAPPINGS

Left: This richly embroidered saddle is to be seen at the Royal Mews, London. It is of Iberian origin and close to the **Selle Royale** in design. The heavy stirrup irons are a relic of the long Moorish occupation of the peninsular. **Right:** A North African, or Arabian, saddle from the same collection. Both are reminiscent of the much earlier saddles of the Middle Ages.

for attaching the load. The bars were fitted with large, well-stuffed, square panels, covered with either serge or linen. The whole was kept in place by two girths, a surcingle, crupper, breastplate and breeching. Frequently, mules were preferred to horses, since their relatively long and straight backs were better suited to the saddle's construction.

Bridles and bitting
Most 19th-century armies employed a type of Pelham bridle, that is, one operating a single mouthpiece with two pairs of reins. Nolan had produced just such a bridle in the years prior to the Crimea, incorporating with it a headcollar which doubled as a noseband. This was an attempt to suit the equipment to the standard of riding, for cavalry recruits were by no means good horsemen. The standard of riding in Napoleon's cavalry at Waterloo (1815), for instance, was extremely low; indeed, for many years afterwards, there would have been no more than a handful of troopers who could have persuaded their horse to leave the ranks and act independently of their comrades.

Bitting under such circumstances was a matter of prime concern, particularly in regiments obsessed with uniformity of appearance in men and horses. The Spanish authority Don Juan Segundo devoted much time and no little ingenuity to his 'Complete System of Bitting,' which involved the interchange of mouthpieces, cheeks, curb chains and so on in accordance with the construction of the horse's mouth, plus the general conforma-

CHAPTER NINE · CEREMONIAL TRAPPINGS

tion of the head and neck. It was probably the British, however, who came up with the most satisfactory solution.

This was the Army Universal Pelham. The angled cheek of this bit permitted the use of a single rein in one of three positions. For a light-mouthed horse, the rein was fastened to the top ring; for an average mouth, on the centre slot; and for a hard one, on the third slot.

Ceremonial saddlery
Though ceremonial saddlery reached the peaks of extravagance in the 19th century, it was not, in fact, much more than an adaptation of that used in the field. Indeed, for some time, there was little, if any, difference between the two.

The most impressive item of cavalry furniture was the shabraque, ornamented in gold and silver lace and embroidered to show the regimental crest, or, in the case of general officers, the rank of the rider. Laid over the saddle, with its shape varying considerably from one regiment to another, the officer's version was usually lined with moleskin and the trooper's with leather or rawhide.

The housing was scarcely less eyecatching, even though it lacked the dramatic rake of the shabraque. The general tendency was for it to be a more rectangular shaped cloth, covering the horse's back behind the saddle, but it was often as beautifully worked and coloured. The essential difference between the two was that, whereas the shabraque was laid over the saddle, the housing was laid, or joined, under it to connect with the weapon

231

CHAPTER NINE · CEREMONIAL TRAPPINGS

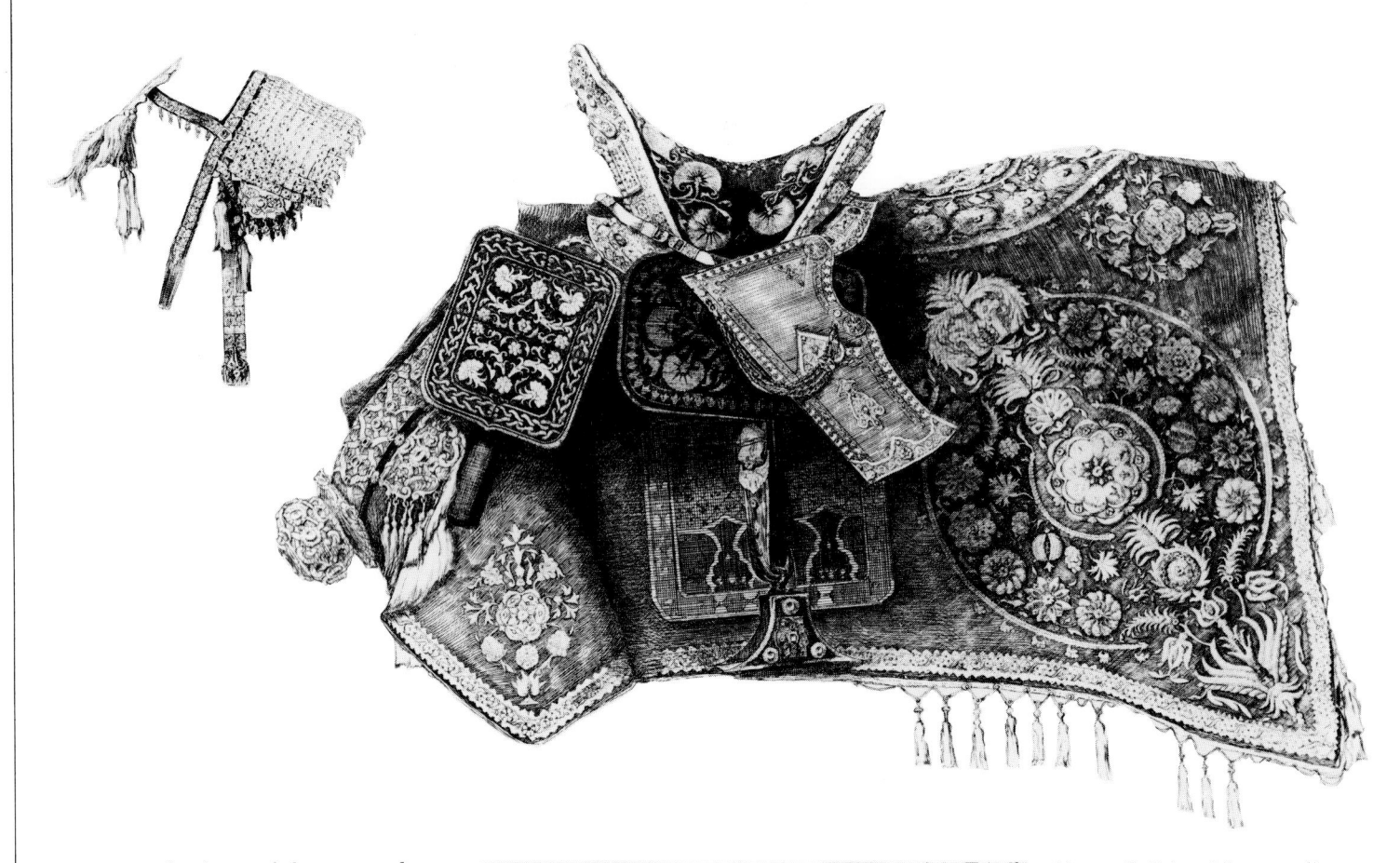

Above: Polish saddle, mountings and bridle of the 17th century. The Poles had an Eastern connection and their cavalry made much use of Arabian horses. The influence is evident in this superb example of a ceremonial saddle. **Left:** The saddle and accoutrements, from the Royal Mews collection, made for King Christian IV of Denmark on the occasion of his son's marriage in 1634.

coverings to the front of the pommel.

These fur-covered holsters (also called caps or flounces) were first in evidence when firearms were introduced to the cavalry proper in the early 18th century. They were only replaced by similarly covered wallets just before the Crimea to carry pistols, carbines and similar weapons. None of these coverings was of much practical value.

Traditionally, hussar officers laid leopard or cheetah skins (troopers used sheep skins) to cover the shabraque from pommel to cantle. This gave them a more secure seat than they would have enjoyed on the slippery leather of the saddle when riding in the then fashionably long manner. Both shabraque and skin were secured by an ornate surcingle.

A contemporary description of a 'furnished' British officer's charger of around 1860 gives a fascinating glimpse of the grandeur of ceremonial cavalry trappings of the period. 'The shabraque is of fine blue cloth made to fit the seat of the saddle, with a hole to let the cantle through. It is ornamented with two rows of gold lace all round, with ' V.R. ' and an Imperial crown embroidered in gold upon the front corners. The hind corners, or points, have the Prince of Wales feathers with motto surmounted by an Imperial crown; under that a scroll, with 'The Prince of Wales Own' on it, and a ' 10 ' in the centre; below that, at the extreme point, the letter ' H '; the whole handsomely embroidered in gold and silver. The shabraque is lined with strong fustian enamelled gold cloth and leather at the wearing points, and made up with straps, loops and strings where required. With this a cheetah skin is used, cut to regulation shape to cover the cloak (rolled) and valise, edged all around with cloth and gold fringe; these together are used for review and dress purposes. The surcingle buckles over the whole. For marching order, an entire cheetah skin is used—the head, paws and tail being stuffed soft; the head has a false tongue and glass eyes and is tied on the crupper, a hole being cut in the shoulder of the skin to let the cantle through and two holes over the holsters, the forelegs hanging on both sides. The hind legs hang on each

CHAPTER NINE · CEREMONIAL TRAPPINGS

Top left: Gericault's exciting picture shows the officer's accoutrements to perfection, in particular the leopard skin shabraque and the bridle. **Above:** French cavalryman of the late 19th century in marching order. **Left:** Officer's charger, Royal Horse Artillery 1890.

side in front and are tied to the breastplate straps. The tail hangs loosely on the near side of the neck, the whole also secured by the surcingle. On all occasions, the troopers use a shabraque, with woollen embroidery and lace with a black lamb-skin seat kept in place by the surcingle.'

Small wonder that one officer of the regiment described above was not amused when he was caught in the rain while on sovereign's escort duty between London and Windsor. His own uniform, as well as his charger's trappings, was ruined and he had no option but to have everything replaced, paying from his own pocket.

Finally, there was the valise. This was an oval or square cloth case, worn behind the saddle with the centre hollowed out to keep it off the back of the horse. It would bear an abbreviated regimental title and it held spare clothing, cleaning materials and the like. By the end of the 19th century, however, it had been largely replaced by the more practical saddlebag.

Ceremonial bridles retained the metal covered headpiece, originally a guard against a sword cut, and were often fitted with a chain replacing the leather rein in the first part of its length. This, too, was a preventative measure against the rein being cut and the rider being unable to control his mount as a result. Bits bore bosses bearing the regimental crest, or, in the case of general officers, bosses indicating the rider's rank.

The US tradition

Across the Atlantic, the US cavalry was unfettered by the conventions of Europe. It used practical saddlery suited to its method of operation and disdained, almost entirely, any sort of ceremonial trappings along European lines.

The US saddle was the McClellan, brought from Hungary in its original form by the future General George B McClellan in 1858. It remained in service until 1940. It was a simple saddle worn over a blanket, the two pads joined by the arches and the seat made from a piece of stretched rawhide. The stirrups were shaped wooden ones, following Western convention, while the girth was often of the Western type. The whole thing was very light—in this respect, it scored heavily

CHAPTER NINE · CEREMONIAL TRAPPINGS

Top: The saddle pad and terrets from a set of State Coach driving harness. It is made of red Moroccan leather, with elaborate gold mouldings. **Above:** The complete set of harness, except of course for the bridle. Elaborately decorated harness of this type makes quite a weight for the horse even before he starts to pull the coach.

Far left: Detail of the names and the decorative boss on a set of harness worn only by horses pulling a carriage carrying H.M. the Queen. **Left:** The saddle pad and terret from this same set of harness. **Below:** The harness ready for use in the procession for the celebration of the silver wedding of H.M. the Queen. All these photographs were taken at the Royal Mews, London.

CHAPTER NINE · CEREMONIAL TRAPPINGS

over its European counterparts—but it was a saddle for horsemen. In this respect, the USA was more fortunate than Europe, for its cavalrymen were certainly better and more experienced riders.

Though the US cavalry tended to eschew the fripperies of ceremonial, this was certainly not the case with its chief opponents—the American Indians. The latter had an innate love of colour and decoration. Clearly the pattern for the early Indian saddles was set by the saddles used by the Spanish explorers, but, given this, it is also evident that the Indians developed them to accord with their intricate and colourful art forms.

The Indians produced two distinct types of saddle—a pad saddle and one made on a wooden frame, which was usually, but not always, a woman's saddle. The pad was a skin bag divided so as to lie on either side of the spine and filled with grass. It was kept in place by a girth and fitted with stirrups set centrally. The stirrups were made from shaped pieces of willow wood. Such a saddle was an ideal

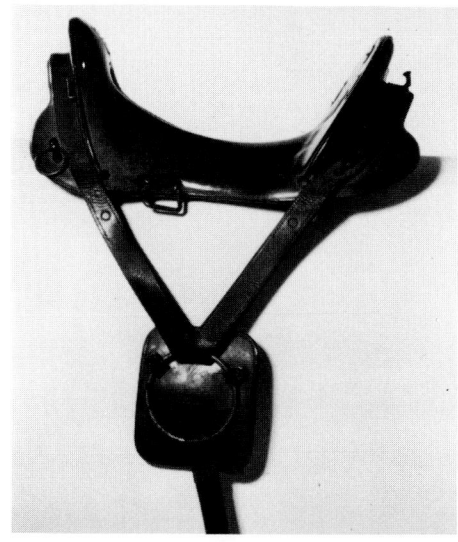

Top: An Indian artist's view of Custer's last stand at the Little Big Horn. The cavalry horses galloping away from the battle show the simplicity of the McClellan saddles to perfection. **Above:** The US Army McClellan saddle which was brought from Hungary and adapted by General George B. McClellan in 1858. It remained in use until 1940. It was a very light saddle but not particularly comfortable other than for experienced horsemen.

tool for horse stealing, since, when emptied of its stuffing it weighed very little and could be rolled up easily. The frame saddle, made of wood or antler horn, resembled the Hungarian cavalry saddle, or, more particularly, the saddles found in the Pasyryk tombs.

Saddle clothes and saddles were frequently ornately decorated in beadwork and, sometimes, with coloured porcupine quills. Often, there were fringes of buckskin hanging from intricately fashioned discs. The Cree, in particular, specialized in beautifully worked quill cruppers, which lay over the whole of the back, falling well down the flanks. Horses were given coats of paint, like their warriors.

Surprisingly enough, these saddles bear a remarkable resemblance to the saddles made by primitive peoples across the world. Such equipment once again demonstrates the universal nature of the development of horse culture and horse equipment. It also serves to demonstrate how the horse has always been essential in the development of human civilization.

CHAPTER NINE · CEREMONIAL TRAPPINGS

Left: The Alamo saddle, presented to H.M. the Queen by the film actor John Wayne and displayed at the Royal Mews, London.

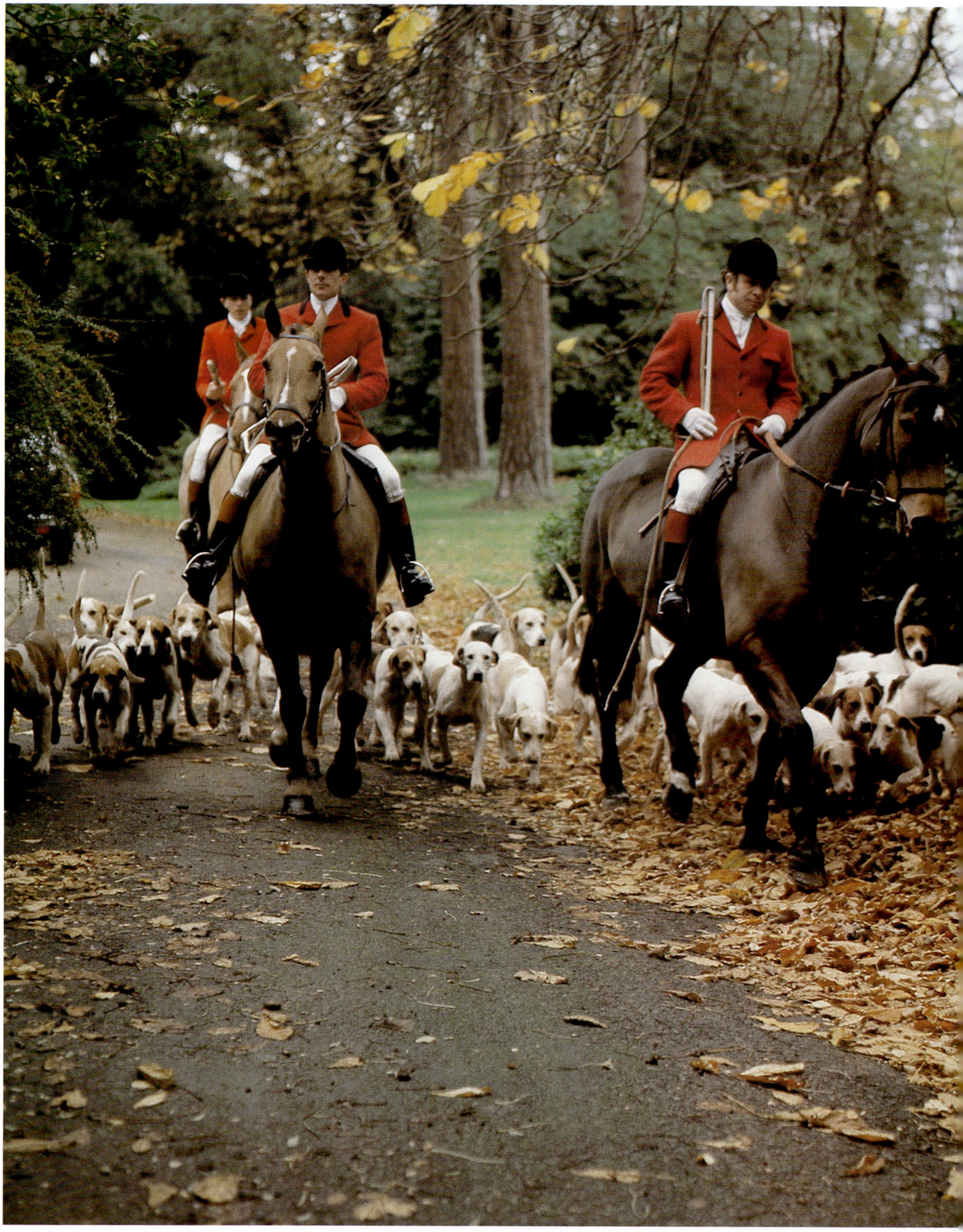

CHAPTER TEN

Riding Dress

Clothes Ancient and Modern
Whips and Spurs

Scarlet is the traditional colour of the hunting field, probably originating in livery dress. The cap, as opposed to other forms of headwear, was at one time the prerogative of the Master and his hunt servants, later being extended to farmers over whose land hounds hunted. Today the custom is 'more honoured in the breach than in observance...' and caps are worn generally by ladies and children and in frequent cases by men.

CHAPTER TEN · RIDING DRESS

Riding Dress · **Ancient and Modern**

The first surviving illustrations of men riding animals which can be positively identified as horses are generally accepted as being those found in the tomb of the Egyptian Pharaoh Horenhab (14th century BC). It is thus in this distant epoch that the development of riding clothes began.

Tunics and bare legs

The tomb paintings show Egyptians riding virtually naked. This is not exceptionally surprising considering the country's climate, the fact that during the early days of Egyptian civilization the lower orders went about entirely naked and that, even under later dynasties, man's clothing remained flimsy. The basic male garment was a simple loin cloth or a short skirt made of linen or cotton; members of the upper classes wore a long transparent garment over this. The riders' clothes reflected this general flimsiness of dress, while, since there was as yet no such thing as a saddle, there was no great need to protect the legs from chafing. Indeed, in a hot climate the skin would probably have given as good a grip as was possible.

As late as the time of the Greek general and historian Xenophon (c. 430–350 BC), whose treatise on horsemanship includes a description of clothes and equipment for the cavalryman, decorative vases and plates still depicted youths on horseback riding naked. However, except for one brief period of bare-legged horsemanship among some North American Indian tribes after the re-introduction of the horse into that continent during the 16th century AD, the trend down the ages has been for horsemen of all races and nations to cover themselves with a combination of protective and decorative clothing, using whatever materials were available and reflecting, to a great extent, the style of their local, everyday costume.

Among the earliest of the great horse peoples were the Assyrians, who lived in what is now the northern part of Iraq. Their riding outfit consisted simply of a long tunic, which covered the whole of the upper body and upper arms, was belted around the waist and finished just above the knees. Bas reliefs from the 9th and 8th centuries BC show that both mounted Assyrian civilians hunting wild animals and cavalry riding into battle wore this tunic. But whereas the civilians are usually shown bare-headed, the warriors often sport conical helmets and, in some cases, calf-length boots.

The demands of war

As soon as men began to ride horses into battle, they must have become aware of the need for some sort of protection. The mass of available pictorial evidence, ranging from coins and medals depicting kings on horseback to the greatest works of art—mosaics, statues, friezes, illuminated manuscripts, tapestries and paintings—bears witness to the number and variety of the various forms of armour which evolved in different regions.

Xenophon wisely emphasized the need for protection coupled with comfort and ease of movement, while at the same time taking into account man's love of ornamentation. He recommended that the cuirass, that part of the armour which covers the chest, abdomen and back, be made to fit the body, with: 'a covering rising out of the cuirass itself to fit the neck. This will at once be an ornament; and if it is made as it should be, it will cover the rider's face when he pleases as far as the nose.' This neck-protecting device was probably of eastern origin, observed by Xenophon during his period of service in his Persian campaign.

The head was protected by a helmet made, like the cuirass, of metal. This gave protection to both head and face. Flexible flaps of metal-covered felt or leather protected the groin and hips and also the right part of the body, which was exposed when

Right: An Assyrian, wearing a form of skirt, the coolest item of clothing in a hot climate, and also some form of protection on the legs.

CLOTHES ANCIENT AND MODERN

Left: The basic simplicity of the early horseman, who rides quite naked. Greek horsemen of Xenophon's time rode either entirely naked or with no more than minimal clothing. **Below:** Alexander the Great is skirted (possibly with cloth or even leather drawers underneath) and wears high ankle boots. **Far left:** This bronze of a warrior of 550BC shows some of the very earliest armour shorts. His legs, however, are bare, perhaps to give him a better grip on his horse.

the sword arm was raised. Greaves of metal-covered leather or felt were worn on the legs below the knee, while Xenophon also recommended the use of a similar device on the right arm. For the left or rein arm he favoured a piece of equipment known simply as 'the arm' to cover the shoulder, arm and elbow. Top-boots of **leather gave protection** to feet and shins.

Even in Xenophon's day, scale armour, made of small pieces of metal fixed to felt (which gave greater freedom of movement than plate armour) was not unknown. The Parthenon frieze, completed around 440 BC, depicts a rider wearing a combination of plate and scale armour.

As far as protection was concerned, the basic requirements of the mounted soldier scarcely varied down the centuries. The style of armour underwent many changes, however, reaching its zenith of complexity during the 15th and 16th centuries when knights were covered from head to foot in elaborately decorated metal suits—their horses also being armoured.

Clothes to suit the climate

When not engaged in combat, the Greek cavalryman wore a simple outfit and this was the accepted garb for the civilian riders of the day. This consisted of a short cloak known as a *chlamys*, which covered both the front and back of the body and was kept in place by means of a buckle fastened over one shoulder, high boots and a broad-brimmed hat.

Because of the mild climate of their country, the ancient Greeks, like the Egyptians before them, favoured loose garments of light cloth. In this respect, again like the Egyptians, riding clothes reflected ordinary everyday dress. Climate was a

241

CHAPTER TEN · RIDING DRESS

major influence in the development of riding clothes throughout the world, as evidenced by the clothes of the inhabitants of a country whose climate, terrain and lifestyle could scarcely be in greater contrast to those of the Mediterranean.

The ancient nomadic tribes of Siberia dressed to suit the cold weather of their northern homeland, whether on or off their horses. Although modern industrial man considers trousers the most suitable garment for the male form and the skirt for that of the female, in earlier times such matters were governed more by climate than by gender. The skirt was, and still is, the coolest thing to wear in hot climates—it is still traditional male dress in many eastern countries—while trousers were the best form of protection against the icy blasts of the far north.

Not surprisingly, therefore, excavations in the High Altai of Siberia have revealed that, while the Greeks wore skirts, the nomadic Siberian horseman of 2,500 years ago wore a loose tunic, belted at the waist, over baggy trousers tucked into short, pliable boots, which were strapped at the ankle. The outfit gave him overall protection against the extremes of the winter months. Climate and natural resources also governed which materials were available, so that garments of felt and woven hemp fibre were here the order of the day. Decoration was not neglected. It consisted of open-work applied designs in leather or felt, animals and birds being favourite motifs. The mounted nomads, their horses arrayed in decorative saddlery and exotic head-dresses, must have made an impressive sight.

Another notable race of horsemen were the Scythians, who lived much further south and prospered during the times of the Greek and Roman civilizations. They also adopted tunic and trousers as their basic riding clothes, as did the dreaded Huns of Central Asia and their great adversaries, the Chinese.

Breeches and boots
The Romans relied less on horses than the Greeks, the core of their armies being the courageous infantryman of their legions. It was not until quite late in the history of the Roman Empire that it proved necessary to increase the numbers of their cavalry significantly in order to repel attacks from their enemies—particularly those on the eastern frontiers, who had always been

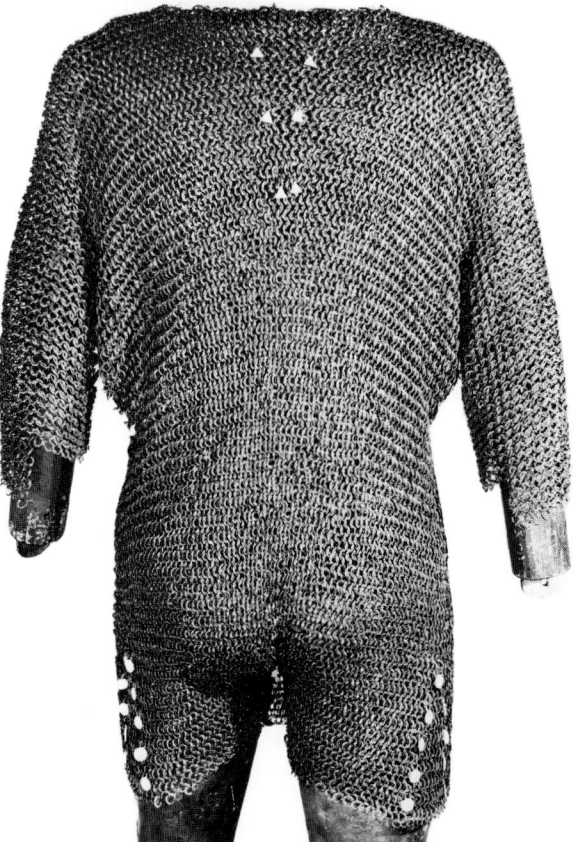

Above, left: A German engraving of the 16th century which shows the male and female costume of the period. The laced leather leggings of the man are of particular interest. **Left:** Armour formed a large part of equestrian military dress, often being worn over a shirt of chain mail, similar to the early example on the left. The suit of armour belonged to Henry VIII and can be seen in the Tower of London. **Below:** Chain mail stitched to leather jerkins was used by the Norman Knights of the Conquest. This particular example can be seen on the Bayeux tapestry.

Above: In this 15th-century picture of the hunt by Ucello the rough gartered trouser of previous years has given way to more elegant, tight-fitting nether garments made from wool or leather

great horsemen. Roman armour differed from that of the Greeks in its construction. The Greek cuirass comprised a back and a breast plate. Roman armour, however, was made of lames or strips of metal, which gave greater freedom of movement. A metal helmet, somewhat smaller than the Greek variety, was worn, with sandals or boots for the feet and legs. However, in the colder imperial provinces, Romans began to wear breeches. These, in their loose form with cross gartering, were to become the basis of European dress during the Dark Ages.

The Dark Ages themselves yield little material relating to the development of riding in Europe, but eastern art and literature are much more informative. They provide, amongst other things, fascinating information regarding the invention of the stirrup and its spread westwards. With saddles and stirrups in common use, it is safe to assume that the most comfortable form of male riding attire, even in hot countries, would have been some form of trousers and boots, the upper body being clothed in a garment suited to the climate.

The chief progression in armour at this time was the introduction of linked chain mail, a development of scale armour. With supple chain mail it was possible to make a single garment which gave protection to the body, neck, arms and thighs. Byzantine cavalrymen of around AD 500 are depicted wearing this type of shirt, together with breeches, boots and iron helmets.

Some 500 years later the Bayeux tapestry, depicting the Norman knights at the Battle of Hastings in 1066, shows that chain mail was still in favour. So, too, were conical helmets, not unlike those worn by Middle Eastern horsemen such as the Assyrians many centuries before. The great disadvantages of chain mail were its weight, which was supported mainly by the shoulders, and the constriction caused by creases forming when the arm was bent. Although it provided good protection against the weapons then in use, a heavy blow could drive it into the flesh, so it was necessary to wear thick, padded clothing under the mail to guard against this. Although it must have been extremely hot and uncomfortable to wear, mail was widely used until plate armour replaced it during the 15th and 16th centuries. At first, plate armour was used in conjunction with chain mail simply to give additional protection to knees, arms and shins, but its use gradually extended. By the middle of the 15th century—the golden age of armour—knights were covered in complete suits. These not only gave unyielding protection to the body but were so skilfully designed that they encouraged blows from an adversary's weapons to glance off, thus minimizing their effect. After this, chain mail was used only as a protection for the neck and to provide gussets at joints where the provision of plates was difficult.

Hunting and tournaments

As well as depicting cavalry, works of art of the period also provide a guide to the fashions adopted by horsemen and women when hunting or simply travelling from place to place. At the time of the Norman conquest male riding clothes, like everyday dress, consisted of a tunic worn over breeches. A woman either wore the normal long dress and sat sideways—alone, or pillion behind a man—or put on a divided skirt in which she could ride astride. Sitting astride was essential if she wished to ride at anything faster than a walk, since the true side-saddle, with a suitably positioned pommel over which the right leg could be hooked, was not invented until the early part of the 16th century. To sit sideways in a dress, a woman had to employ a man's saddle or a pad saddle, neither of which provided much security.

During the Middle Ages, the tournament became a popular pastime in many European countries, providing both a means of recreation and a good training for war. This provides an early example of the adaptation of general riding wear—at this time centring on military requirements—for a specific sporting purpose. Because the principal jousting weapon, the lance, was normally carried in the right hand and pointed across the horse's neck at the opponent's left side, specially designed tournament armour was devised. This was devised to give protection where it was most needed, being heavier and thicker on

CHAPTER TEN · RIDING DRESS

the left side than the right. It was also much more unwieldy than the armour used on the battlefield.

Flamboyance and fashion
From the time of the Crusades, the inhabitants of western Europe became aware of the silks and fine embroideries produced by the east and this soon had an impact on the riding clothes they wore. Although peasants and workmen continued to wear the simple, short tunic, great lords started to wear longer, richer clothes. Garments for both men and women began to be shaped to the body, with men generally wearing cloth or knitted woollen hose on the legs. Hoods gave way to hats, which at times became extremely large and elaborate, while the general increase in prosperity enjoyed by all classes of society was

Far left: Lady's driving habit of the late 18th century. **Left:** Military uniform of the late 17th century which has the high top boots of the period. **Below:** The 18th-century tapestry 'The March' from **The Art of War** shows clearly the type of boot which was in general use. The turned over tops could be pulled up for added protection in bad weather.

Left: The well-dressed equestrienne at the turn of the century, when the modern side-saddle apron had yet to be introduced. **Right:** Two French fashion prints dated 1914 showing respectively a male and female swell.

reflected in all types of clothing. The courts of France and Burgundy in the 15th century, for instance, vied with each other for supremacy in this field. Their fashions spread to other European countries and, in due course, blended with the somewhat less flamboyant styles of the Italian Renaissance.

From the mid-17th century onwards men began to wear coats and waistcoats with breeches, the first step towards male clothing as we know it today. This started in France and soon spread across Europe. The great European riding masters of the 17th and 18th centuries rode in knee-length breeches, high boots, long-skirted coats and tricorn hats. All of these were pre-eminently practical, though they still incorporated a good deal of ornamentation as well.

Hard-riding squires

While Continental riders tended to specialize in elegant high school work, Englishmen were taking up the much more vigorous pastime of riding to hounds. Dispensing with unnecessary frills and decoration, these hard-riding sportsmen laid the foundations of what is today the accepted dress for universally popular equestrian sports.

Coats, breeches, boots and hats were devised as essentially practical items of equipment, the velvets, silks and satins of France and Spain being abandoned in favour of more serviceable woollens and leather. The tops of high boots were turned down below the knee to give greater freedom of movement to the leg when riding across country, a fashion which led to the hunting boot as it exists today, with its tan top. Decoration was mostly confined to cuffs, collars and buttons, distinctions which some hunts still employ. During the reign of George III, the tricorn hat finally gave way to the velvet cap which is now worn by riders, both male and female, the world over. By this time, too, most women had elected to ride side-saddle, dressed in long, flowing habits of great elegance, their long hair piled high on their heads and topped with elaborate hats.

The Englishman's other great sporting interest, which took fire and spread across the world with the development of the Thoroughbred, was racing. Here the essential requirements of lightweight clothing and colours easily identifiable from a distance have remained constant down the centuries; today's jockey's outfit of light leather boots, tight breeches and silks in the colours of the horse's owner have changed little since the earliest days of racing.

As far as the military was concerned, the introduction and development of firearms during the 16th and 17th centuries signalled the end of plate armour. While the armourers did not find it difficult to produce bullet-proof protection, the result became so heavy as to be quite impracticable. By the 17th century, only the metal cuirass and helmet were retained and by the 18th century all but the ornamental gorget worn by officers had disappeared. From then until the horse himself became obsolete, cavalrymen wore variations on the theme of breeches and boots, or trousers, with coats of varying lengths, plus helmets of differing degrees of elaboration,

CHAPTER TEN · RIDING DRESS

which served as a useful means of identification on the battlefield.

Clothing for cowboys
In North America a whole new genre of clothing was produced as a result of the rise of the cattle-ranching industry. Cowboys needed clothes which were hard-wearing but comfortable, cool in summer but warm in winter. They copied and adapted the clothes of the Mexican *vaquero*. From the leg-protecting leather flaps which formed part of the Mexican saddle, the cowboy devised chaps, which were usually made of cowhide or sheepskin and took the form of a pair of seatless leggings, worn over trousers for warmth, grip and protection.

Below: Western dress is always practical and sometimes colourful as well. This rider wears a broad-brimmed stetson to give shade from the sun, tough leather chaps and blue jeans.

The world-famous stetson hat was designed and introduced by John Batterson Stetson to provide a better fit than the high-crowned sombrero of the Mexicans. The stetson's wide brim protected the wearer from the summer sun, while in winter it could be tied down to cover the ears. It was useful for scooping up water for drinking. Then Levi Strauss, a New York tailor who travelled west to search for gold, invented the ideal cloth for cowboy trousers—denim. His 'Levi's', made of toughly twilled cotton, with flat non-twisting seams, a low waist, narrow hips and tapered legs to fit easily inside boots, were comfortable and practical.

In addition, a cowboy usually wore a wool or flannel shirt with full sleeves to give maximum freedom of movement, and a sleeveless vest of heavy cloth or buckskin, sometimes lined with sheepskin. Around his neck he wore a cotton bandanna, which could be pressed into service when necessary as a bandage, a face mask or a filter for drinking water. Boots had to be extremely tough and, in addition to riding requirements, were fitted with high, forward-sloping heels which the cowboy could dig into the ground when holding onto a roped calf. Ornamentation tended to be restricted to hat bands and belts.

The clothes of today
Riding clothes for the millennium are a mixture of tradition, fashion and high-tech fabrics and design. Tradition is still important in the show ring and the hunting field. In Britain for instance, women exhibitors in show hack classes will wear black or navy blue jackets while those in hunter classes will wear tweed—although fabric technology means you can now buy Teflon-coated jackets which repel the rain. Side-saddle equitation is another sartorial minefield: the Side Saddle Association, which has members throughout the world, says the rider's apron should be level and about two inches above the seam of her left boot, while riders who do not have long enough hair to form a bun need to wear a false one!

Safety is important, and helmets and body protectors now give considerable protection against impact. Manufacturers are increasingly having to meet the challenge of combining safety with comfort. Helmet ventilation improves by the year, and body protectors are much more wearer-friendly.

Riding has also become more colourful. Thirty years ago, even weekend English-style riders would have worn beige jodhpurs and green, navy or brown jackets. Today, jodhpurs and breeches come in many different colours, and jackets are colourful and stylish enough to be high-fashion items. It is no coincidence that Puffa, the jacket manufacturer and a major supplier of equestrian clothing, chose top international fashion model Jodie Kidd – a former junior show-jumping rider – to show off its range.

This bright new look is safe as well as attractive, because a rider who can be seen more easily by drivers is much safer than one who wears countryside browns and greens and blends into the background. Colour has carried through into the eventing world: bright silks helmet covers and shirts have become as traditional on the cross-country course as tweed jackets in the show ring.

CLOTHES ANCIENT AND MODERN

Above: Correct dress for advanced or even three-day event dressage is silk hat, hunting tie, black tail coat, white breeches and black boots. The rider on the left is correctly dressed for novice level competition. **Top:** Formal hunting dress for a woman includes a black or tweed coat and either a bowler hat, cap or crash hat. Men who are members of the hunt wear black or tweed coats; only Masters and hunt officials wear red coats.

Right: Side-saddle equitation is the epitome of elegance. Side-saddle habits must be well-cut to flatter the rider but allow sufficient movement.

247

CHAPTER TEN · RIDING DRESS

Riding Dress · **Whips and Spurs**

In all probability, artificial aids have been used by riders ever since man first mounted a horse. Certainly it is known that there were accepted aids for training horses more than 2,000 years ago, since the Greek authority Xenophon described their application when teaching a horse to jump in his writings on horsemanship.

In their earliest form, whips would have been no more than switches cut from convenient bushes or trees—indeed one notable body of riders, the Spanish Riding School in Vienna, still employs this type of whip today. However, over the years man devised whips which were much longer-lasting, while whip-making itself became something of an art.

The structure of the whip
The main part of a conventional riding whip is the stock, which tapers from the hand-part to the lash end. Some whips are provided with a hand grip at the broad end and a plaited leather lash, or leather loop, known as a keeper, at the other, while others are left quite plain. Much depends on the use for which they are intended.

In former times, the centre, or stock, of a riding whip was made from whalebone, though in fact this was not bone at all, but rather a horny, elastic substance found in the upper jaws of certain whales. Carefully cut lengths of cane, known as splicings, were fixed round the whalebone with pitch. Then came the most skilful part of the whip-maker's art, which lay in the

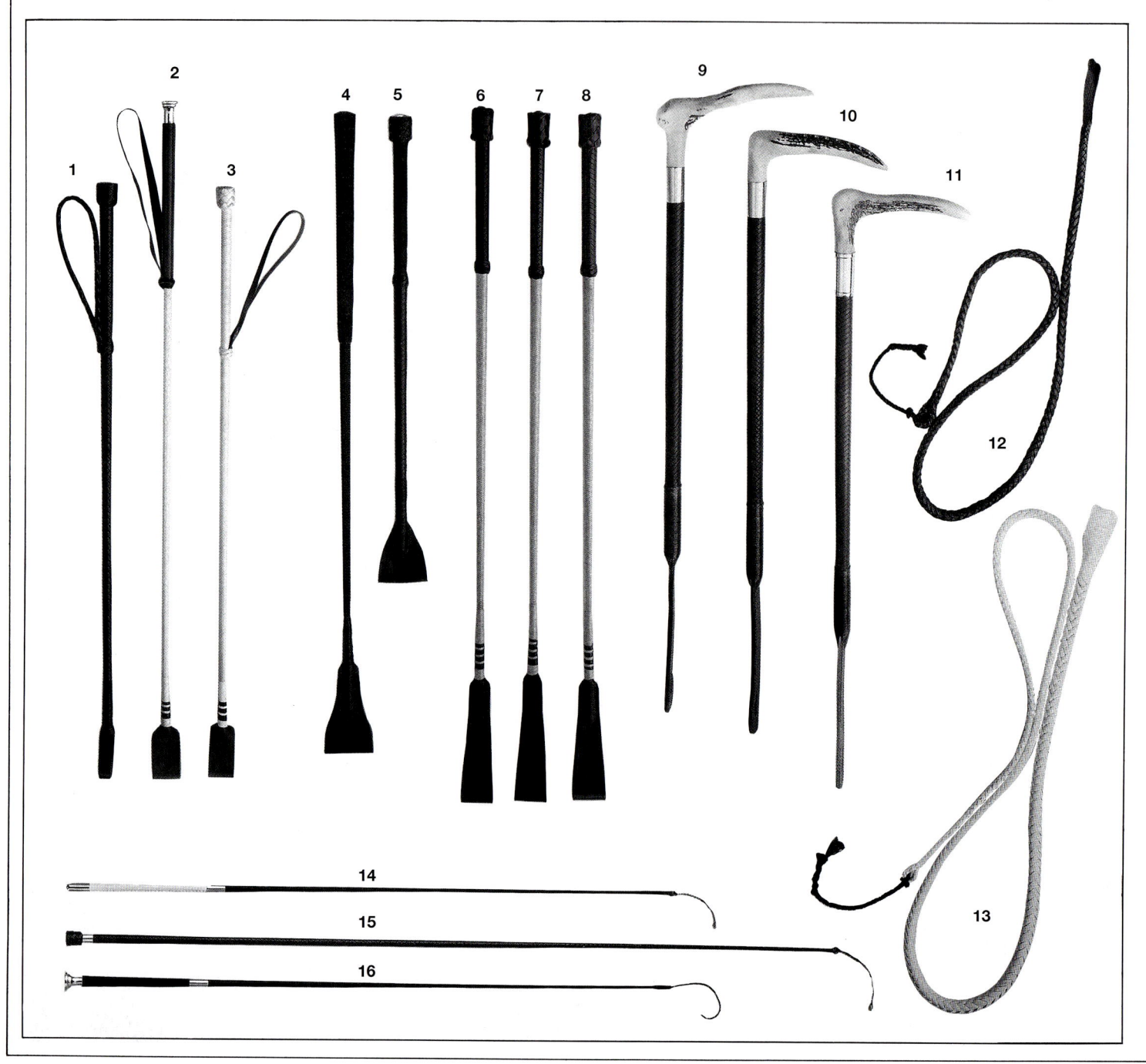

248

WHIPS AND SPURS

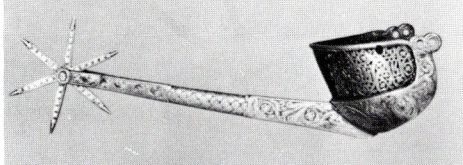

Top: A 16th-century German multi-rowelled spur of exquisite workmanship. **Above:** Three spurs from the Tower of London collection dating from the 15th–16th century. The spur was a mark of chivalry and originally the prerogative of those of gentle birth. When dubbed a knight, a gentleman also received his spurs. **Right:** Spur and bit patterns filed in the foundry of a British manufacturing company in the Midlands. **Opposite:** Modern jumping and schooling whips are generally lightweight. Wrist loops are not recommended—it is better to drop your whip in a fall than land across it and break your wrist! Hunting whips comprise a stock, lash and thong and are a specialized design. 1, 2 and 3. Riding whips; 4 and 5. Event whips; 6, 7 and 8. Race whips; 9, 10 and 11. Hunt crops; 12 and 13. Hunt thongs; 14, 15 and 16. Dressage whips.

planing down of this stock until it had just the right amount of play in it and until it bent equally well in all directions. Both these features are vital attributes of a good whip.

Fibreglass, which can be tapered fairly easily, now serves the same function as the old whalebone and cane combination. Steel is sometimes used in the manufacture of cheap whips, but it does not produce such a light, well-balanced product as does the more expensive fibreglass. The stock is given a protective covering either of plain leather or of braided rawhide, gut or thread.

Types of whip

Whips fall into two main types—those used by horsemen as an aid to riding and those used for specific jobs carried out on horseback. The latter include bull whips and stock whips, which are used by mounted herdsmen. Such whips consist of a short cane or wooden handle to which is

249

CHAPTER TEN · RIDING DRESS

attached a long plaited leather thong. Hunting whips are made in a similar fashion, having a plaited leather thong fitted with a silk or cord lash at one end and a horn handle at the other. The thong is used to control hounds, the handle for holding open gates.

A variety of riding whips has been developed for different purposes. Long schooling whips, which come in various lengths, can be used to activate the horse's hindlegs or to reinforce the action of the rider's leg without it being necessary for him to take his hand off the rein. Jumping and racing whips are a good deal shorter (under the rules of show jumping a whip may not be more than 2ft 6in long) and are used to encourage or correct a horse. There is also a wide range of canes, either plain or leather covered, which are generally used for showing purposes. In addition, the lungeing whip is used when training a horse by the dismounted trainer. Like driving whips, these need to be carefully balanced if they are to handle well; the best are normally of cane, steel being considered too heavy.

Spurs—design and use

The design of spurs has in a way come full circle since the aid was first devised. Early models consisted of a short metal goad strapped to the rider's boot, which is basically the same pattern as the one generally used in competitive equestrian sports today. Over the centuries, however, spurs underwent many modifications, at times becoming fearsome weapons. Generally speaking, the longer the rider's leg, the longer the spur must be if contact is to be made with the horse's side without undue movement of the rider's foot. For a long time horsemen rode with straight legs and this, coupled with the very restrictive leg armour used in combat and the rather common, cold-blooded type of horse much in evidence during the Middle Ages, led to the development of long-shanked spurs with enormous, sharp rowels.

Nowadays, spurs of this type are extremely limited in use. They can be seen on the heels of riders like the South American gauchos, who still use sharp rowels, and North American bronc riders, who favour blunted ones. They are also used on some ceremonial military occasions. The spurs in most common use are the short curve-necked pattern and the straight-necked pattern, which may either be blunt or fitted with a small rowel. The spikes of the latter are not unduly sharp and the longest neck does not, as a rule exceed about 1½in.

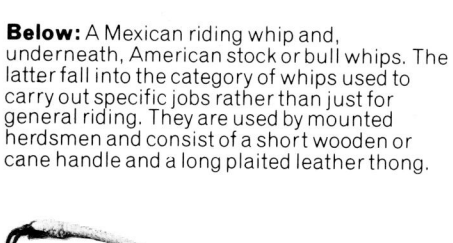

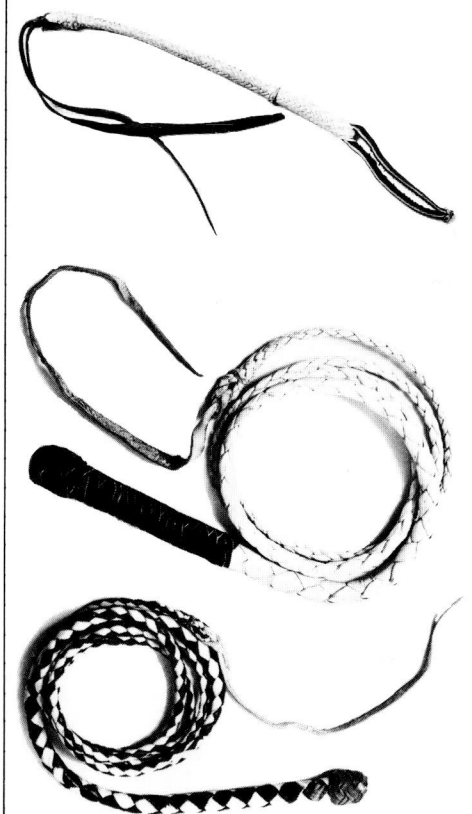

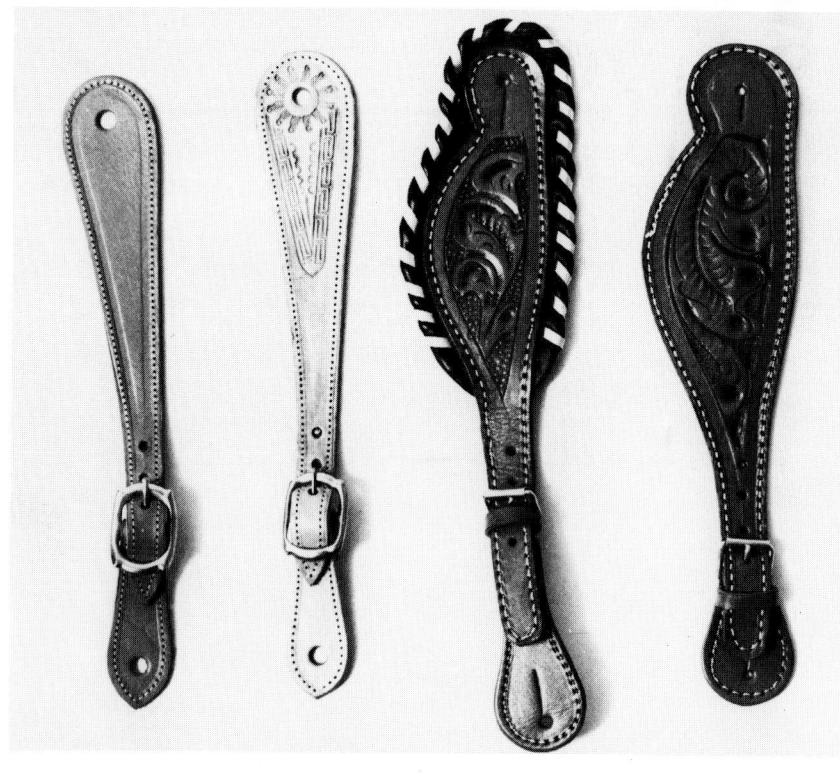

AMERICAN WHIPS AND SPURS

Below: A Mexican riding whip and, underneath, American stock or bull whips. The latter fall into the category of whips used to carry out specific jobs rather than just for general riding. They are used by mounted herdsmen and consist of a short wooden or cane handle and a long plaited leather thong.

Above: Patterned American spur straps. **Left:** Typical Western spurs, nowadays really the only type of spur found with such sharp, ferocious rowels, these having been superseded by the shorter, blunter and more humane varieties in general use.

USING WHIPS AND SPURS

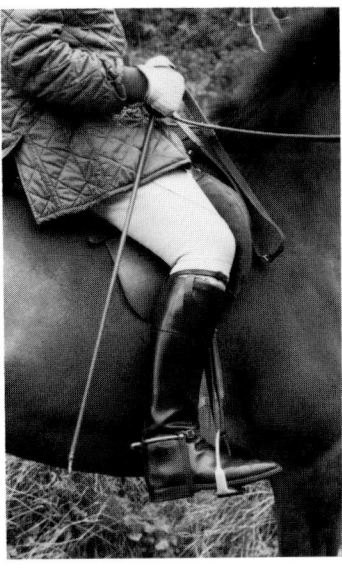

Top, left to right: The hunting whip held in the conventional manner with the thong and lash hanging down; a dressage or schooling whip which is used behind the leg to support the action of the latter. It is of fairly rigid construction so that a single tap only need be given; a longer, more flexible schooling whip which can be used to activate the hindleg.
Left: A plain, leather-covered showing or riding cane.

Right: The spur fitted correctly and resting on a small stop built into the back of the boot. **Far right:** The spur being brought into play by a movement of the leg.

Index

Page numbers in *italics* refer to illustrations

A

Abbot-Davies balancing rein *190*, 191
Alamo saddle *237*
Albion saddles 71–3, *72*, *73*
Alexander the Great 18, *241*
American barn system 198, *198*
American saddle seat 65
Arab saddles 22–4, *231*
armour 240–1, *241*, *242*, *243*, 245
    Assyrian *16*
    chain mail *242*, 243
    Greek 243
    horse *28*, 29, *29*
    of Knights *28*, 29, *29*
    Roman 243
Asia:
    bits *17*
    harness 13
Assyrians 15
    armour *16*
    bits *17*
    chariot harness *14*
    military accoutrements 226
    riding clothes 240, *240*
    saddle cloths 18
    warriors *14*
Attila the Hun 24
Australia, stockman's saddle 65–7, *66*

B

balance, point of 58, *59*
bandages 216, 219
    dressings 216
    exercise (working) 216, *217*
    stable 216, *216*, 219
    tail *209*, 215, 216, *216*
    travelling 216, *216*, 219
bareback riding 11
    in battle 18–19
    controlling horse 15, 16
    style 20
Barnsby collection, gentleman's saddle *8–9*
basket saddle 68
Bayeux tapestry 26, *26*, *27*, *242*, 243
bearing (check) reins 13, 14
    misuse 14
belly band 180
bitless bridle 116, *135*, 141, *144*, 145
bits and bitting systems 116–29
    see also curb bit; snaffle bit
    attaching cheekpieces and reins to 137
    attaching to bridle 53
    for breaking 34, 195
    Buxton pattern *158*
    cheekpiece design 122
    Chifney (anti-rearing) *207*, 215
    cleaning 201
    for driving 154, *155*, *158*
    fitting 139
    'flying trench' 33, 35
    for Great Horse 29–31, *29*
    for harness racing 167–8, *168*
    history and development 10–11, 15, 17–18, *17*, 37, 116, 117
    introducing to young horses 195
    kimblewick (Spanish jumping bit) *128*, 129
    Liverpool 154, *155*
    making 118–19, *120–1*
    materials 117
    military 230–1
    with mouthing keys 34, 195, *207*
    overcheck *172*, 173
    parts of head affected by 116
    patterns 118, *249*
    ring (Mameluke) 24, *29*
    Roman 21
    'rough' 17
    Segundo's interchangeable system 116, *117*
    for showing 17
    side-lining 168, *168*
    slip-mouth side-lining 168
    Speedway 173
    spiked 17
    stallion 208, *208*
    types 116
    Weymouth 122, *127*
blinkers 209
    on draught bridle 178–9
    on harness bridle 13–14, 154
    for harness racing 173
boots (horse) 217, 218–19, *219*–21, *220*, *221*, 244, 245
    brushing 218, *219*, 220
    coronet 220
    cowboy's 246
    elbow 173
    fastenings 220
    fetlock 218, *219*, 220
    for harness racing 173, *173*
    hock 217, *218*
    knee 173
    materials 220
    overreach (bell) 221, *221*
    problems with 220
    quarter 173
    ring 221
    sausage 221
    scalpers 173
    service 209, *209*
    skeleton knee *219*, 220–1
    tendon 217, *218*, 221, *221*
    types 219, 220–1
    Yorkshire 221
boots, riding:
    for battle 241, 243
    for hunting 245
bosal 34, 141, *142*, 143–5
bradoon 33, 35, 41, 122–3
breaking:
    aids for 34, 192–5
    for trotting 168
breast collar:
    development 12
    for driving 152
breast harness 167, 176–7
breastplates 15, 81–2
    Aintree pattern *81*, 82
    for hunting *81*, 82
    for polo 82
    for racing *81*, 82
    Western *97*, 98
breeching 13, 180
    attaching to shaft *152*
bridles:
    see also types, eg double bridle; snaffle
    attaching bits to 53
    cheek guards *135*
    cleaning 201
    draught 178–9
    driving, fitting 154
    fitting 137–9, *138–9*
    history and development 14, *14*, 15, *15*, 16–17, 18, 21, 36, 41
    lipstraps *135*, 137
    manufacture 53
    materials 137
    military 230–1
    parts 134, *134*, 137
    show 206–7, *207*
    stallion 208, *208*
    for trotting 167, 173
    types 134, *134*–5, 137
bridling aids *see* bits and bitting systems; martingales; nosebands
broncho busting *101*, 102
browbands 137, *137*, 139, 206
brushing boots 218, *219*, 220
Buffalo Bill Cody, saddle 90–1

C

Caprilli, Federico 38–40, 56, 58, 85, 105
carnivals, saddles for *100*
carriage driving *see* driving
cart harness 179, *179*, 181
    fitting 180, *180–1*
    removing horse 180–2
carts, Elamite 15
Castillo, Puerto Viesgo, cave paintings 10
Catherine de Medici 106
cattle *see* oxen
cattle ranching 92–6
cavalry:
    bareback 18–19
    ceremonial trappings 231–6
    early 18–19
    Household Cavalry *222–3*
    Hungarian 226, 229
    knights 26–31, *28*, *29*
    Persian 16
    riding style 24–5
    Scythian 21–2
    USA 233–6
    use of stirrups 24–5
    weaponry 24–5
cavesson, lunge 33, 140, 193, *193*
cavesson noseband 33, 132, *138*
    plain 33, *132*

ceremonial trappings 223–37
chambon *188*, 190–1
chamfron 29
chariots 11, *12–13*
    Egyptian 17
    harness *14*
    racing 14
check (bearing) reins 13, 14
    misuse 14
cheetah skins 232–3
Chifney (anti-rearing) bit *207*, 215
children:
    saddles for 67–8, *68*
    stirrup irons for 84, 85, *85*
chin strap 173
China:
    harness 13
    saddle 25
    tomb figure *25*
cinches 97
    see also girths
    centre-fire rigging 101
    double-rigging system 96
    in-skirt rigging 101
    single-rigging system 96, 101
    Spanish system 96, 101
    strengthening 96
    variable positions 101
classical riding 33–5
clothes *see* boots; riding dress
Cobber felt saddle 67
collar:
    design 178
    development 13, 177–8
    for draught work *176–7*, 177–8, *178*
    for harness racing 167
conquistadores 92
cowboys:
    clothes *93*, 246, *246*
    saddles 92–8, *93*, *94–5*, *96*, 100–2
Crosby saddles 75–7, *76*
cross hobbles 171
cross-country dress 246, *246*
cross-country saddles 60–1
    tree for 50
crupper 167
    fitting 153, *153*
curb bit 122–3, 140
    English 16th-century *29*
    German 16th-century *140*
    history and development 11, 17, 18, 20, 29–31, 35
    port 123
    slide-cheek 126
    Turkish design *141*
    Western *143*
    Weymouth *127*
curb chains *127*, 129
    action 123
    making *120*
curb rein 34, *35*
currying 46

D

dallying 98
Danloux, Colonel, jumping saddle *61*

252

INDEX

de Gogue *190*, 191
Distas Central Position saddle 56
dogs, as draught animals 10
domesticated animals 10
donkey two-seater saddle *67*
donkeys:
  controlling 10
  as draught and riding animals 10
  riding 15
double bridle 36, 41, *114–15*, 116, 122–3, 126
  action *126*
  parts 137
draught reins 158
draw reins 35, *189*, 190
dressage:
  bitting systems 117
  horses for 68–9
  saddles 61, 64
    Albion *73*, 75
    girths 81
    Klimke-Miller *77*, 77
    Lauriche classical *69*, 69
    tree for 50
driving 40
  saddles for *152*, 153
driving dress, women's 244
driving harness:
  furniture 148
  handling reins and whip 162–3, *162*, *163*
  historical accoutrements 148
  materials 148
  pair 158, *159*, 161, *161*
  present day 148–63
  putting on collar 150–1, *150*
  royal *234–5*
  for showing 148–50
  single harness 148–9, 150–4, *151*
  tandem 13, 154, *156*, 157–8, *157*, *158*
  team *160*, 161–2
  for trotting 167–73
  Unicorn *161*, 162
  whips 164–5, *164*, *165*
'dumb jockey' 192

E

Egypt:
  clothing 240, *241*
  nosebands 17
  yoked horses *11*
elbow boots 173
eventing, clothing 246, *246*, *247*

F

face masks 225
facsimile saddles 67
farm harness 176–85
  Bodkin fashion 185
  cart harness 179, *179*, *181*
    fitting 180, *180–1*
    removing horse 182
  history 176–8

plough harness 179, 182–3, *182*
trace harness 179, 185
types 179–83
unicorn method 183–5
variations 183–5
feed containers 198–9
fenders 94
fetlock boots *218*, *219*, 220
fiador 141
first-aid kits 203
'flying trench' 33, 35
foxhunting 35–6
France, riding dress 245

G

gag bridle *135*
gag snaffle 116, 129, *129*
gaited horses, saddlery 37–8, 64–5, *65*
gaiting pole 173
gaiting strap 173
general purpose saddle 60–1
gentleman's saddle, 17th century *8–9*
Germans:
  cavalry schools 38
  riding dress, 16th century *242*
  saddles 61, *61*, 75
Gidden saddles 73–5, *74*, *75*
girths 78–81, *78–9*
  see also cinches
  Aerborn 79
  Atherstone *78*, 79
  Balding *78*, 79
  buckles on *80*
  designs 78–9, 80–1
  for harness racing 167
  horsehair *78*, 79
  humane 79
  inserts on *79*, 80
  lampwick *78*, 79, 80
  Lonsdale (short 'belly') 81
  materials 79–80
  on show saddles 63, *78*
  synthetic 80
  three-fold leather *78*, 78
  web *78*, 79
Goths 22
Great Horse 26–33
Greeks:
  armour 243
  bits 17
  chariots *18–19*
  horsemen *18*
  riding dress 240, 241, *241*
  riding style 18, 20
  warriors 17
Grisone 33, 34, 35
grooming *203*
  equipment 202–3, *202–3*

H

hackamore 31, 34, *135*
  Blair's pattern 145
  European 145
  fitting 141–3, *142*

graduation to bit 143–5
origins 140–1
parts 141, *143*
two-rein bosal 143
Western 140–5, *141*
halters:
  control 192, *195*
  for showing 206
hames 178
Harbridge 191
harness:
  driving 148–63
  farm 176–85
  history and development 10–14
  in Roman times 12–13
  trotting 167–73
harness racing *see* trotting
haynet 199
hayrack 199
head pole 168, *169*
headcollar:
  doubling as noseband 230
  Dutch slip 209, *209*
  for stud 209, *209*
  as training aid 192, *192*
  for travelling 215
headgear:
  fashions 244
  helmets 240
  stetson 246, *246*
headstall, latigo 141, *143*
Hermès (English) saddles 63
hides *see* leather
High School movements 32
history and development 9–41
  Asiatic influence 13
  British tradition 35–7
  classical 35, 40
  early times 10–12
  Knights 26–33
  Middle Eastern developments 14–17
  military developments 18–20, 22–5, 26–31, 38–9
  of riding dress 240–7
  riding masters 33–5
  Roman times 12–13, 14
  Scythian influence 20–1
  stirrup invention 24–5
  tournaments and jousting 31–3
hobbles 169–71, *175*, 208–9, *209*
hock boots *217*, *218*
holsters 232
hoods *212*, 213
Horenhab, Pharaoh, tomb 15, 240
horse brasses 180, 224
horseboxes 204–5
  equipment for *204*
horses:
  American breeds 65, *65*
  armour for *28*, 29, *29*
  back problems 68, 72
  centre of balance 58, 59
  controlling without bridle 10
  controlling without saddle 15, 16
  domestication 10
  farm, decorating *176–7*

fat, fitting saddle 89
parts of head affected by bit and bridle *116*
size 11, 17
stable space required 198
strength 17
use of yoke on 11, *11*, *12–13*
horseshoes:
  invention 18, 20
  'sandals' 18, *19*
  use 20
Household Cavalry *222–3*
housen 179
housing 231–2
Humphreys Breaking-in Saddle 66
Hungarian 226, 229
Hungarians, cavalry 226, 229
hunting:
  in ancient Egypt *12–13*
  breastplates for *81*, 82
  bridles for 18
  developments attributed to 35–6
  riding side-saddle to 108–9
  saddles 24, 36, *38–9*, 41, 56, 60–1
    design deficiencies 59
  whips *248*
hunting dress *238–9*, 243, *243*, *247*
  boots 245
  for women 243, *247*

I

Iberian saddle *34*, 35, 66, *67*, *230*
India:
  harness 12
  religious festival 224
  saddle decorations 224
  toe stirrups 24
inflatable saddle 67
Italy:
  riding dress 245
  16th-century saddle *34*

J

jousting 31–3
jumping:
  point of balance 59
  saddles 41, *57*
    Pariani *57*
    Toptani 56–8, *58*, 59, *59*, 60–1, *60*
    tree for 50
  stirrup irons for 85
  whips *248*, 250

K

Kansu, frescoes 13
kimblewick (Spanish jumping bit) *128*, 129
  mouthpieces 129
Klimke-Miller dressage saddle 77, *77*

253

INDEX

knee boots 173
knee caps *218*
knights 26–33, *26–7, 28, 29, 30*

L

latigo headstall 141, *143*
latigo strap 96
Lauriche classical dressage saddle 69, *69*
leather:
  colours 48
  currying 46
  defects 44–5
  dyeing 46–8, *47*
  making 45–6
  parts 46
  polishing *47*
  preparing skins *44*, 45, *45*
  quality 44
  rounding hides 46
  scudding 45, *45*
  for seat covering 52
  slicking out (drying) 46, *46, 47*
  sources 44
  splitting 46, *46*
  storage 48
  tanning 45–6, *45*
length of rein 62
lever snaffle 129
lip cord 173
long reining (long lining) 4, 35, *186–7*, 192, 194–5, *194*
long-bow 27, *29*
looseboxes 198, *199*
lorinery 118–19, 120–1
lungeing 192–5, *193*
  reins 194, 195
  training aids for 188, *190*, 191
  whips *193*, 194, 250

M

McClellan saddle 98–100, 233–6, *236*
Mamelukes (ring bits) 24, *29*
mane covers 225
mangers 198–9
manufacture of saddles 43–53
  construction methods 48–53
  covering and padding 51–3, *52–3*
  economies 52–3
  leather for 44–5
    defects 44–5
    making *44*, 45–8, *45, 46–7*
  making trees 48, *50–1*
mare, stud equipment 208–9, *209*
Market Harborough 131, *131*
marriage, horse's decorations 224
martingale 130–1, *131*
  bib 131, *131*
  for eventing 130–1
  false 153, *159*
  forerunner of 11
  for hunting 130

Irish 131, *131*
Market Harborough 131, *131*
  for racing 131
  running 130–1, *130*
  for show jumping 130
  standing 130, *130*
mecate 34, 141, *142*
mercenaries 226–7
Mexico/Mexicans 16, 92
military saddlery 35, 36–40, 225–36, *228, 229*
  ancient 16–17, 24–5, 26–31, *26–7*
  ceremonial 231–6
Moffett, Heather, posture saddle 69–70, *70*
Mongolia/Mongolians 16, 24
  riding style 21
Mongols 224, 226
Moors 67, 140
mountings, saddle 78–85
mucking out tools 199, *199*
Murphy blind 169, *169*

N

Narrow Comfort saddle 72
neck covers 214
neckstrap:
  holding in place 14
  used with yoke 11
Neolithic age 10
Nobades 24
Nolan saddle 229, *229*
Normans 243
North American Indians:
  clothing 240
  Plains Indians 21
nose reins 191, *191*
nosebands 132–3, *132–3*, 137
  American cheeker 133
  Australian cheeker *133*
  cavesson 132, *132, 138*
  drop 17, *22*, 132, *132*, 193
  early development 16, 17
  fitting *138*, 139
  Flash 132, *132*, 133, *138*
  Grakle (figure 8) 132–3, *133*
  headcollar doubling as 230
  kineton (puckle) 133, *133*
  sheepskin 133, *133*
  with spiked nosepiece 16
Numidians 10
numnahs (saddle pads) 71, 86–7, *86–7*
  advantages and disadvantages 86
  materials 86
  modern 87
  Scythian 20
  Siberian 225
  traditional 86

O

onagers:
  controlling 10
  as draught and riding animals 10, 11
  riding 15

overcheck bits *172*, 173
overcheck (check) rein *171*, 173
overreach (bell) boots 221, *221*
oxen:
  attaching to vehicle 176
  controlling 10
  draught work 10, 76, 178
  yoked 10, *10*, 176

P

pacers 169, *175*
pack saddle 229–30
Paleolithic age 10
Pariani saddles 40, 56, *57*, 58
Parthenon, Athens, frieze *18*, 20
Pazyryk tombs, finds from *22, 23*, 224–5, *225, 226*
pedigree horses 14
pelham 34, 116, 126, 129, *135*, 230, 231
  Hanoverian 126
  jointed 129
  mouthpieces 126, 129
  mullen-mouth 126, *128*
  parts 137
  in position *128*
  reins on 126
  Rugby 126
  Scamperdale 126, *128*
  SM 126, *128*
Persians 16–17, 20, 27
Pignatelli 33, 34
pillion riding 106, *107*
PJ nose reins 191, *191*
plough harness 179, 182–3, *182, 183*
point straps 167
point-to-point, riding side-saddle 39
police saddle *229*
Polish saddle *232*
pollguard *211*, 215
polo 38
  breastplates for 82
  saddles:
    development 36
    Gidden 74
ponies:
  fat, fitting saddle 89
  pulling chariot 12
posture saddle 69–70, *70*
Przewalskii horses 16

Q

quadriga 11–12
quarter boots 173

R

racing:
  blinkers 14
  breastplates for *81*, 82
  clothing for 245
  riding position 105, *105*
  stirrup irons for 85
  stirrup leathers for 82–4

racing saddles 104–5
  exercise *104*, 105
  exercise pad 105
  flexible *104*
  fitting 105
  for flat racing 104, 105
  for point-to-point 105
  for steeplechasing 104, 105
  trees for 50, 104–5, *104*
  weight 104
    increasing 105
  weight cloth *104*, 105
Rarey, John, training aids 195
Raymond overcheck *172*, 173
Reactorpanel saddle 70–1, *71*
rein, length of 62
rein terret 21
reindeer, as draught and riding animals 10
reins:
  Abbot-Davies balancing *190*, 191
  attaching to bits 137
  attaching to bridles 137
  check (bearing) 13, 14
  curb 34, *35*
  draught 158
  draw 35, *189*, 190
  driving:
    fitting 153, *154*
    handling 162–3, *162, 163*
  for farm work 183
  lunge 194, 195
  materials 137
  misuse 14
  overcheck (check) *171*, 173
  PJ nose 191, *191*
  running 35, 190
  for schooling 188–90, 191
  Schoolmasta 191
  side 188–90, *188*, 195
  types *136*
Renaissance 33
riding dress 239–51
  see also boots, riding; spurs; whips
  Assyrian 240, *240*
  cowboys' *93*, *246*
  cross-country *246*
  for dressage *247*
  for driving 244
  Egyptian 240, 241
  18th-century *244*, 245–6
  English 245–6
  European 244–5
  for eventing 246, *246, 247*
  German 16th century *242*
  Greek 240, 241, *241*
  history 240–9
  hunting *238–9*, 243, *243, 247*
  modern 246
  of nobility 244–5
  protective 246
  for racing 245
  Roman 242–3
  Scythian 242
  17th-century *244*, 245
  Siberian 242
  for side-saddles 243, 245, *245, 246, 247*
  suited to climate 241–2
  for tournaments 243–4

INDEX

20th-century, early *245*
  women's *243*, *244*, 245, *245*, *246*, *247*
riding halls 33
riding masters 33–5
riding styles *18*, 20, 21, 24–5, 33–5
ring bits (Mameluke) 24, *29*
rodeos:
  broncho-busting saddles 102
  parade saddles *100*
rollers 195
Romans 12–13, 14
  armour *243*
  riding dress 242–3
rugs 210–15
  cooler *212*, 213, *213*
  exercise sheets *210*, 214
  fastenings 210–11, 214–15
  fitting 211
  materials 210, 212
  New Zealand *210*, *211*, 212
  outdoor 211–12, *214*
  stable 212–14, *215*
  summer sheet 213
  thermal 212–13
  types 211–14
  vintage American *212*
running reins 35, 190
Russians, saddles *227*

S

saddle blankets *87*, 94, *96*, *97*
saddle mountings
  see mountings, saddle
saddle trees:
  cut-back *51*
  cut-back spring *50*
  development 37
  driving 153
  fibreglass 48, *50*, 105
  fitting 88
  head types *50*
  manufacture 48, *50–1*
  military *229*
  racing 104–5, *104*
  rigid 48, *50*
  sizes 50
  spring 48, *50*, 52, *57*
  Toptani 56–8
  types 48
  Western *92*
  wooden *104*
saddlebags *233*
saddlecloths 86–7
  early *18*, 20
  from Pazyrk tombs *22*, *226*
saddles:
  see also types eg hunting; jumping; side-saddles
  adjusting for long reining 195
  built on 'tree' 21–2
  cart (cart pad) 179–80
  for children 67–8
  cleaning *200–1*
  development 18, 20–1, 34–5, 36–7, 40–1
  fitness for purpose 56–61
  fitting 21, 88–9, *88–9*
  German influence 61, *61*

for harness racing 167
with high cantle 21–2
horn on 66–7, 94–6, *94*, 101
inflatable 67
Italian 16th century *34*
for jousting 31–3
making *see* manufacture of saddles
military 226, 227–30
ornamentation 225, *225*
parts *49*
protecting horse's back 94
Rugby panels 36
Selle Royale *33*, *34*, 35
specialist 91–113
standing on 21
synthetic 77, *77*
trees *see* saddle trees
20th-century 55–89
  variations 62–77
Western 92–103
Santini saddles 58
Sarmatians 21–2
  belt buckle *22*
scalpers 173
Scandinavia, draught horses 177–8
schooling:
  bits for trotting 168
  training aids 188–91
  whips *248*, 250, *251*
Schoolmasta 191
Scythians 20–1, 22
  riding dress 242
seat covers 86
seat-savers, sheepskin *75*
Segundo, Don Juan 230
  interchangeable bitting system 116, *117*
Selecta saddle 71–2, *72*
Selle Royale *33*, *34*, 35
service boots 209, *209*
shabraque 225, 231, 232–3
shadow rolls 169–71, *170*
shaft thimbles 167
shafts 13
show jumping:
  horses for 68–9
  saddles 41
show saddles 62–4, *62*, *63*, 207
  Albion *73*, 75
  Gidden *74*
  girth straps 63
  Hermès (English) 63
  Owen 63
  stirrup bar 62
  straight-cut *61*
  trees for 50, 62, *62*
show tack 206–7, *206*, *207*
  breed differences 206
  stallion *207*
  Western *206*
showing:
  categories 206
  driving harness for 148–50
  in-hand (halter) 206
  ridden 206–7
Siberia:
  clothes 242
  Pazyryk tomb finds *22*, *23*, 224–5, *225*, *226*
side reins 188–90, *188*, 195

side-saddles 106–13, *106*, *108*, *110–11*, *112*, *113*, 243
  balance strap 108, *110*
  changes dictated by fashion 108–9
  clothing to wear on 243, 245, *245*, *246*, *247*
  cut-back head 106, 109, *111*
  early 106
  falling from 109
  fitting 112–13, *113*
  Gidden *74*
  for hunting 108–9
  leaping head pommel 108
  linings 113
  marques 109, 112
  measuring 112
  Mexican *93*
  19th-century 106, *106*
  origins 106
  Owen models *112*
  parts *110*
  pommels 106, 108
    position 112
  20th-century 109, 112, *112*
  Walsall model *112*
snaffle bit:
  see also gag snaffle; lever snaffle
  action 122, *122*
  designs 117, 122, *124–5*
  double-jointed 117
  early use 11, 15, 26–7
  eggbutt 122, *123*
  jointed mouthpiece 17
  mullen mouthpiece 117
  riding style with 20
  rollers on 117
  single-jointed 117
  straight-bar 117, *123*
  three-ring 129
  Wilson 4-ring 155
snaffle bridle *138*
  early use 18, 21
South America 16
Spaniards 92, 141
Spanish Riding School 35, 134, *192*, 195, 248
Spanish saddlery 16, *34*, 35
Speedway bit 173
spurs:
  American 250, *250*
  design 250
  patterns *249*
  Roman *20*
  16th-century *249*
  using 250, *251*
stable equipment 197–221
  at stud 208–9, *208*, *209*
  bandages and boots 216, 219–21
  grooming 202–3, *202–3*
  in horsebox 204–5
  rugs and travelling dress 210–15
  show tack 206–7, *206*, *207*
  tack cleaning 200, *200–1*
  tools and fittings 198–9
stables:
  American barn system 198, *198*
  design 198

doors 198, *198*
space required by horse 198
stallions:
  show tackle *207*
  stud equipment 208, *208*
stirrup bars:
  inset *57*, 58, *59*
  positioning 68
stirrup covers 94, *100*
stirrup irons 83, 84–5, *84*, *85*
  Australian Simplex 84, *85*
  Kournakoff *84*, 85
  Moorish influence *230*
  Peacock 84, 85, *85*
stirrup leathers 82, *82*, *83*
  attaching to racing saddles 105
  'hook-up' *82*, 84
stirrup tread 84
stirrups:
  invention 24–5
  'safety', for side-saddles 109, *109*
  standing in 71
  toe 24
  Western 94, *97*
stockman's saddle 65–7, *66*
Stübchen saddles *61*, 75
stud equipment 208–9, *208*, *209*
surcingle 232, 233
swingle tree 13, 182–3, *184*, 185
synthetic materials 77, *77*, 80

T

tack cleaning 200, *200–1*
tail bandages *209*, 215, 216, *216*
tail casing *34*, 225
tailguard *213*, 215
tandem harness 13, 154, *156*, 157–8, *157*, *158*
tanning 45–6, *45*
taps *see* stirrup covers
tendon boots 217, *218*, 221, *221*
terrets 21
  from royal driving harness *234*, *235*
tools, for stable 198–9
Toptani saddle 41, *54–5*, 56–8, *58*, *59*, *60*
  aiding point of balance 59
  disadvantages 60
  general purpose 60–1
  inset saddle bar *57*, 58, *59*
tournaments 31–3, *31*
  clothing for 243–4
trace harness 179
traces 152–3, 167
  connecting to vehicle 152, *152*
  trace ends *158*
trail riding *40–1*, 100
training aids 187–95
  breaking 192–5
  schooling 188–91
travelling dress 210, *211*, *213*, 215

255

boots and bandages 216, *216, 217, 218*
trees *see* saddle trees
trekking saddles 67, 100
trotting *166–7*
   coping with pulling 171–3, *171, 172*
   equipment 166–73
      bits 167–8, *168*
      breast harness 167
      bridle 167
      girth 167
      saddle 167
      traces 167
   fitting harness *174–5*
   keeping straight course 168–9, *169, 172*
twitches 208

U

Universal Pattern Saddle 229, *229*
Universal Purpose Pack Saddle 229–30

USA:
   see also Western saddles
   cavalry 233–6
   saddlery developments 37–8

W

warriors 14, *14*
water containers 198
weights:
   adding to saddle 105
   for feet 35
Western blankets *87*
Western hackamore *see* hackamore
Western saddles 38, 65, *90–1*, 92–103
   bareback rig 102
   bronc saddle 102
   broncho-busting 102
   Californian 96–8, *102*
   cowboys' 92–8, *93*, 100–2
   deep-seat cutting *103*
   exercise *101*
   Grand Parade *100*
   horn on 94–6, *94*, 101
   McClellan 98–100
   Mexican-style *94*
   modern changes 100–2
   parts *92*
   pleasure saddles *98*, 100–1
   racing-type *99*
   skirts of *94*
Weymouth bits 122, *127*
Weymouth bridle 122, *134*
wheel, invention and development 11
whipple-trees (swingle tree) 13, 182–3, *184*, 185
whips:
   American *250*
   Coach (bow-top) 164, 165
   Dealer's (dropthong) 164–5, *165*
   driving 164–5, *165*
      handling 162, *162*, 163, *163*
   signals with 164
   specialist 165
   types 164–5
   Victorian *164*

woods used for 165
lunge *193*, 194, 250
maintenance 165
riding 248–50
structure 248–9
types *248*, 249–50
using *251*
Wintec endurance saddle *77*
wither pads *79*, 86
wrap straps 167
WS bitless pelham 145, *145*

X

X Group 22
Xenophon 11, 17–18, 33, 116, 240, 241, 248

Y

yak tails, as insignia 224
yokes 10, *10*, 11, *12–13*, 176
   use on horses 11, 12–13, 176
Yorkshire boots 221

Credits

Quarto would like to thank and acknowledge the following for providing pictures used in this book. While every effort has been made to acknowledge copyright holders, we would like to apologize should there have been any omissions.

Key: t=top; b=bottom; c=centre; l=left; r=right

Aerborn 79
Albion 72, 73
Ashmolean Museum 243
Beebee & Co 62l
British Driving Trails Association 151t
British Library 26t, 30
British Museum 14, 17tr&br, 19, 20tl, 20r, 21r, 240, 241
Cooper Bridgeman 12, 13, 18
Mike Davis 66t
Charles de Kunffy 7
Frank Dolman 113t&br
Mary Evans 15, 26b, 32, 35, 39, 68l, 203b, 242tl&br, 245
A J Foster 69
Michael Freeman 222
W&H Gidden 40tc, 74, 75, 86, 136, 139, 165, 209br, 210t, 218c, 219tr&br, 220l, 221l, 247bl, 248
Elwyn Hartley Edwards 34
John Henderson 186-7
Kit Houghton 7, 41b
Howell Book House 205
Hulton Picture Library 28, 29tl, 31, 34t, 39, 83br, 249t
Terry Keegan 224
Leslie Lane 235b

Bob Langrish 5, 40b, 65r, 70r, 130r, 139l, 141l, 177, 183, 188t, 189, 190, 192, 193t, 193b, 194, 206, 207, 208, 209, 210b, 213t, 217b, 238, 246, 247t, 247br
Janet Macdonald 112, 113bl
David Miller 6
Millers Harness 76, 77, 130l, 138br, 191, 192cr&br, 214, 215, 218cl&cr, 221r
Heather Moffett 70
National Gallery 27
Gillian O'Donnell 71
Photosources 22, 24, 25, 225, 226
QED 19, 49, 189bl&r, 199, 233
Quarto/John Henderson 198bl, 200, 201, 202, 204b
Walter Rawlings 236t
Peter Roberts 33, 198r
Ronald Sheridon 10, 11, 17l, 20l, 21l
Shire Horse Centre, Devon 181b, 183, 185t
Tate Gallery 39
Diane R Tuke 48, 50cr&b, 53b
US Travel 40-1
Victoria and Albert Museum 244
Harry Weber 176
The photographs on pages 29t&br&l, 242tr&bl and 249c are Crown Copyright
The photographs on pages 164l, 227, 228, 230, 231 and 234 were taken at the Royal Mews, London, and are reproduced by kind permission of Her Majesty the Queen
All other photographs are the copyright of Quarto
All other illustrations by Edwina Keene
Index by Dorothy Frame